A Monument to the Memory of George Eliot

Edith J. Simcox's
Autobiography of a Shirtmaker

LITERATURE AND SOCIETY IN VICTORIAN BRITAIN
VOLUME 4
GARLAND REFERENCE LIBRARY OF THE HUMANITIES
VOLUME 2054

Literature and Society in Victorian Britain

Sally Mitchell, *Series Editor*

A Monument
to the Memory
of George Eliot

Edith J. Simcox's
Autobiography of a Shirtmaker

Edited by
Constance M. Fulmer
Margaret E. Barfield

Garland Publishing, Inc.
a member of the Taylor & Francis Group
New York and London
1998

Library of Congress Cataloging-in-Publication Data

Simcox, E. J. (Edith Jemima)
  [Autobiography of a shirtmaker]
  A monument to the memory of George Eliot : Edith J. Simcox's Auto-
biography of a shirtmaker / [transcribed] by Constance M. Fulmer and
Margaret E. Barfield.
      p.   cm. — (Garland reference library of the humanities ; v. 2054.
Literature and society in Victorian Britain ; v. 4)
      Complete transcription of Simcox's journal from the handwritten manu-
script housed in the Bodleian Library (MS. Eng. misc. d. 494), including the
letters and notes inserted therein.
      ISBN 0-8153-2782-X (alk. paper)
      1. Simcox, E. J. (Edith Jemima)—Diaries.   2. Women authors, English—
19th century—Diaries.   3. Women social reformers—Great Britain—Diaries.
4. Eliot, George, 1819–1880—Friends and associates.   5. Shirt industry—
England—History—19th century.   I. Fulmer, Constance Marie.   II. Barfield,
Margaret E.   III. Title.   IV. Series: Garland reference library of the humanities ; vol. 2054.   V. Series: Garland reference library of the humanities. Literature and society in Victorian Britain ; v. 4.
PR5452.S27Z47   1998
828'.803—dc21
[B]   97-38310
                                                                                                    CIP

Printed on acid-free, 250-year-life paper

Manufactured in the United States of America

CONTENTS

PREFACE

This complete transcription of the *Autobiography of a Shirtmaker* by Edith J. Simcox (1844-1901) is a significant addition to women's studies, women's history, economic and social history, literary studies, and gender studies. Never before printed in its entirety, the *Autobiography of a Shirtmaker* is a personal journal—not intended for publication—in which Simcox made entries more or less regularly from May 1876 to January 1900.

The diary describes both the day-to-day activities and the private reflections of Edith Jemima Simcox, an independent Victorian woman who succeeded in several arenas usually reserved for men. Interspersed among the details of her public life as businesswoman, social reformer, scholar, and journalist are intimate passages which reveal her reactions to her associates and to her accomplishments, her disappointments, and her observations on gender. She describes herself functioning as a shirtmaker, an activist for economic reform and improved working conditions for women, an elected member of the London School Board, a representative to the Trade Union Congress on at least eight occasions, the author of three published books, and a regular contributor to the leading periodicals. Simcox also makes insightful comments on her extensive reading and writing and on her relationships with many of the leading literary and political men and women of her day including the novelist George Eliot (1819-1880). She wanted everything she accomplished to serve as a tribute to Eliot.

The *Autobiography of a Shirtmaker*, MS. Eng. misc. d. 494, is housed at the Bodleian Library, University of Oxford. Margaret Barfield and I gratefully acknowledge the fact that Mary Clapinson, the Keeper of Western Manuscripts, has given us permission to publish this transcription of the entire journal and the letters and notes inserted therein.

The original journal is about an inch thick, is bound in dark green morocco, has brass hinges and a broken brass lock, and is written in blue ink now faded almost purple. It is a quarto volume of 183 pages; the written portion extends up to page 175 on the right-hand pages only. We have included as an entry for March 28, 1880, a letter to George Eliot; this letter is the only part of the Simcox-Eliot correspondence which has been preserved. It was inserted between the pages of the manuscript along with two short notes written by Simcox and three letters written in 1951 by a Mrs. Annie Gill of Leeds which provide one phase of the rather unusual history of the manuscript; the Gill letters and the short notes by Simcox are included in the Appendix.

In our transcription of Simcox's handwritten journal we have made changes for consistency in punctuation and spelling; for example, we have added apostrophes omitted from several "one's," used double quotes, written "&" as "and," and have written "á propos" in a uniform way. Everything else—including notes written in the margins and on the blank left-hand pages and her "unique" spelling of words such as *waggon* and *befel*—we have presented, as much as possible, as written by Simcox.

This journal is the only surviving Simcox manuscript even though Edith Jemima and her two brothers George Augustus and William Henry were all prolific writers. Edith Simcox was born August 21, 1844, died September 15, 1901, and left all of her effects to her older brother Augustus Simcox, who was a fellow of Queen's College Oxford from 1863 until his death in May 1905. All of the Simcox family papers and manuscripts which Augustus held were left in the keeping of the executor of his will, J. R. Magrath, Provost of Queen's College. Subsequently, according to John M. Kaye, now Keeper of the Archives at Queen's College, the Simcox family papers were disposed of by Magrath's executors after he died in 1930.

In 1930 or 1931, the *Autobiography of a Shirtmaker* came into the possession of the son of Annie Gill. In the first of her three letters, which are included in the Appendix, she explained that her son died while he was an undergraduate at Oxford. She found the manuscript among his effects but did not know "whether he picked it up secondhand or had it lent." Annie Gill had no idea of the journal's significance, but using a magnifying glass, she read enough of it to recognize George Eliot's name. Twenty years later, when Gill heard a BBC broadcast on George Eliot in the "Woman's Hour Series" presented by Gerald Bullett, author of *George Eliot: Her Life and Books* (Collins, 1947), she wrote and asked Bullett if he would like to see the journal. He replied promptly in the affirmative; she sent the book to him, and although he never published any part of it, he kept the journal among his papers which were bequeathed to the Bodleian Library and were added to the collection in May 1958.

Keith A. McKenzie, on study leave from the University of New England in Australia, was at Oxford University in 1958; he discovered the *Autobiography of a Shirtmaker* among the Bullett papers. His book-length study *Edith Simcox and George Eliot* (Oxford, 1961) is based on his reading of the *Autobiography of A Shirtmaker*.[1] McKenzie gave a copy of his transcription of the manuscript to Yale professor Gordon S. Haight, a leading Eliot scholar, who wrote the Introduction to McKenzie's *Edith Simcox and George Eliot*.

---

[1] In the footnotes throughout this volume, references to McKenzie's volume have been abbreviated so that (McK, 54, n. 7) means Keith A. McKenzie, *George Eliot and Edith Simcox* (Oxford University Press, 1961), page 54, note 7.

Haight subsequently used information from the *Autobiography of a Shirtmaker* in writing *George Eliot: A Biography* (Oxford, 1968).[2] And in Volume IX of the *George Eliot Letters* (Yale, 1974),[3] he quoted extensive excerpts from the passages about George Eliot using McKenzie's transcription of the *Autobiography of a Shirtmaker*. More than half of Simcox's journal, however, has never been published in any form.

The time has come for Edith Simcox to be recognized for her own accomplishments and to have her story read as she told it. Reading Simcox's private reflections about George Eliot within the context of the entire *Autobiography* places them—for the first time—in the proper perspective and provides a broader framework for understanding Eliot as well as Simcox. In addition to and totally apart from Edith Simcox's relationship with Eliot, the *Autobiography of a Shirtmaker* provides source material for those interested in gender and/or women's issues and in other aspects of literature and society in Victorian England.

Margaret Barfield and I appreciate the generous support in released time and travel money given us by Pepperdine University. I am especially grateful to James Smythe and David Baird, chairs of the Humanities Division at Seaver College; Margaret expresses appreciation to Dean Cynthia Greer of the Law School. We are both thankful to William B. Phillips, Dean of International Programs, for allowing us to stay at Pepperdine's London campus while doing much of our research; to Dan Kelo, Manager of Computer Services at Pepperdine University School of Law; and to Craig Bowman, Manager of Academic Project Design at Pepperdine University, for providing invaluable assistance in the technical aspects of preparing the transcript of the manuscript. We also acknowledge the gracious assistance of numerous librarians at the Bodleian; the British Museum, particularly those in the Map Room and at the Newspaper Library; the Trade Union Congress Library and the Offices of Public Records in London; the National Library of Scotland; the UCLA Research Library; and the Pepperdine libraries. We remember with pleasure the friendly assistance provided by the inhabitants of Aspley Guise near Bedford, where Edith Simcox and her mother are buried. Margaret Harris, Professor of English at the University of Sydney, has been supportive of us in each phase of our work. We

---

[2] In the footnotes throughout this volume, references to Haight's Biography have been abbreviated so that (H, Biography, 5) means Gordon S. Haight, *George Eliot: A Biography* (Oxford University Press, 1968), page 5.

[3] In the footnotes throughout this volume, references to Haight's Letters have been abbreviated so that (H, IX, 64) means Gordon S. Haight, *The George Eliot Letters* (Yale University Press, I-III, 1954; VI-VIII, 1955; VIII-IX, 1978); volume IX, page 64.

also appreciate the help provided by Sally Mitchell, Professor of English at Temple University, series editor, and Phyllis Korper, senior editor at Garland Publishing.

Although I assume responsibility for the translations, I gratefully acknowledge the assistance provided by Annette Smith, Professor of French Literature at California Technical Institute in Pasadena, and David Dowdy, Professor of German at Pepperdine University in Malibu, California.

Constance M. Fulmer
Professor of English
Pepperdine University

INTRODUCTION

Edith Jemima Simcox was born August 21, 1844, and died September 15, 1901. She was involved in the co-operative movement and the establishment of trade unions, served as a representative to the International Trade Union Congress, worked to promote women's suffrage, was elected to the London School Board, and lectured for the Socialists and numerous other groups; she was not only well acquainted with the leaders of these movements but with many other outstanding intellectual, political, and literary figures. She was an admirer of the novelist, essayist, and poet George Eliot and was herself a regular contributor to the major periodicals and the author of three books.

From 1876 until the beginning of 1900, Edith Jemima Simcox recorded details from her public and private lives in a journal which she entitled *Autobiography of a Shirtmaker*. This text, a complete transcription of her personal diary, thus provides a record of the thoughts and experiences of a Victorian woman who was successfully filling public roles usually reserved for men, working out her own personal system of ethics, doing research, writing and publishing, handling domestic responsibilities, and dealing with personal pain, rejection, and grief. The detailed accounts of her efforts to improve the circumstances of women's lives, to better working conditions for men and women, and to enhance educational opportunities for all British children make the text a valuable resource for anyone who is interested in Victorian society, economic history, politics, ethics, literature, women's studies, gender issues, autobiography, or writing as catharsis.

Simcox was literally a shirtmaker. In July 1875 she and her friend Mary Hamilton started the shirtmaking co-operative, Hamilton and Company, located in London's Soho district, to employ women and to offer them decent working conditions. Simcox managed the daily operation of the enterprise but frequently expressed the wish that she could devote more time to her writing. She sold her shares on January 25, 1884, when she was confident that the co-operative was stable financially and could continue without her.[1] She reported her experiences in a *Nineteenth Century* article entitled "Eight Years of Co-Operative Shirtmaking."[2] Being a successful shirtmaker and employer provided evidence that a woman could succeed in business and thus added credibility to her other reform efforts.

---

[1] January 27, 1884

[2] "Eight Years of Co-Operative Shirtmaking," *Nineteenth Century* 15 (June 1884): 1037-1054.

Along with Emma Smith Paterson (1848-1886), who began organizing women to improve their working conditions when she established the Women's Protective and Provident League in 1874, Simcox worked tirelessly to promote the establishment of trade unions and supported not only shirtmakers but tailoresses and tailors, nailmakers, bookmakers, miners and metallurgists, tenants and lodgers, and hammermen. She worked with Annie Besant, Harriet Law, Charles Bradlaugh, William Morris, and other leading reformers as she delivered orations to public gatherings of all types of workers and visited numerous shops asking questions, comparing wages and prices, looking at the finished products, and taking notes to substantiate her arguments. In 1875 Edith Simcox and Emma Paterson went to Glasgow as the first women delegates to the Trade Union Congress. On at least eight occasions Simcox served as an elected delegate and even delivered an extemporaneous address in French in Paris;[3] she made daily reports on the 1889 Congress to the *Manchester Guardian*.

In the *Autobiography* Simcox mentioned "writing wholesome moralities" for the *Co-Operative News*[4] as well as reporting to the *Labour Tribune* and the *Women's Union Journal*. She frequently described her involvement with various groups dedicated to reform: drawing up constitutions, preparing statistics for the Industrial Remuneration Conference, nursing the Women's Trades Council into "larger life," writing a paper for the Fabian Society, lecturing for the Socialists, supporting a deputation of Pimlico factory women, publishing an article "on the wrong side of any issue," and posting circulars. On June 19, 1884, she mentioned delivering a lecture on behalf of women's suffrage at St. James's Hall. Whatever her role, she worked diligently for any good cause—particularly if women might benefit from her efforts.

In November 1879 Simcox was elected to represent the Radicals in the Westminster district on the London School Board and served until October 15, 1882. Women had been eligible for membership on School Boards since their creation under the Education Act of 1870, and in 1880 primary education was made compulsory for all British children. Among the forty-five members of the London School Board, Simcox worked most closely with Dr. Elizabeth Garrett Anderson, Eliza Orme and her law partner Miss Richardson, Emma Paterson, Benjamin Lucraft, and the Honorable E. Lyulph Stanley. She alluded to "going fiercely from school to school" to make visits, looking at examinations, listening to geometry lessons, receiving kisses from pupils, and encouraging members of Parliament to enforce compulsory education for all British children. On July 23, 1881, she told of being part of a delegation to represent the Board which was sent to William Harcourt, the Home Secretary.

---

[3] November 11, 1883

[4] July 28, 1878

Edith Simcox's numerous contributions to periodicals reflect her enthusiasm for women's issues, her support of economic reform, and the breadth and depth of her knowledge of ethics, science, art, and languages. At the age of twenty-five, eight years before she began to make entries in the *Autobiography of a Shirtmaker*, Simcox regularly contributed reviews to the *Academy*, beginning with its first issue on October 9, 1869, and using the pseudonym H. Lawrenny. She often wrote the "Critical Notices" for the *Fortnightly* as well as longer articles such as "Mr. Morris's Hopes and Fears for Art" which appeared in 1882.[5] Simcox continued her periodical writing until a few months before her own death; in the last entry of the *Autobiography of a Shirtmaker* on January 29, 1900, she mentioned having written an article for *Nineteenth Century* entitled "The Native Australian Family."[6]

In addition to her book reviews and articles related to intellectual issues, Simcox was continually writing articles which supported women's causes. She advocated establishing trade unions for women in "Women's Work, Women's Wages," which appeared in *Longman's Magazine*.[7] Three articles in *Fraser's Magazine* argued for economic reform which would benefit women: "Organization of Unremunerative Industry," "Industrial Employment of Women," and "Turning Point in History of Co-Operation."[8] In an article entitled "The Capacity of Women," she addressed all of the traditional stereotypes which judge women to be inferior to men and demonstrated the need for women to have equal rights in every aspect of existence.[9]

Her books were *Natural Law: An Essay in Ethics*, 1877; *Episodes in the Lives of Men, Women, and Lovers*, 1882; and *Primitive Civilizations, or Outline of the History of Ownership in Archaic Communities* in two volumes,

---

[5] "Mr. Morris's Hopes and Fears for Art," *Fortnightly Review* (June 1882): 771-779.

[6] "The Native Australian Family," *Nineteenth Century* 46 (July, 1899): 51-64.

[7] "Women's Work, Women's Wages," *Longman's Magazine* 10 (July 1887): 252-267; reprinted in *Prose by Victorian Women: An Anthology*, ed. Andrea Broomfield and Sally Mitchell, (Garland, 1996), 556-582.

[8] "Organization of Unremunerative Industry," *Fraser's* 18 (November 1878): 609-621; "Industrial Employment of Women," *Fraser's* 19 (February 1879): 246-255; "Turning Point in History of Co-Operation," *Fraser's* 22 (August 1882): 222-235.

[9] "The Capacity of Women," *Nineteenth Century* 22 (September 1887): 252-267; reprinted in *Prose by Victorian Women: An Anthology*, ed. Andrea Broomfield and Sally Mitchell, (Garland, 1996), 583-597.

1894. In *Natural Law*, written before the journal entries began, Simcox formulated her own system of ethics. *Episodes in the Lives of Men, Women, and Lovers* is a series of twelve fictional vignettes, five of which were originally published in *Fraser's Magazine* in 1881. Her major work was the history of the appropriation of property in ancient civilizations in which she demonstrated the principle that any civilization in which women were permitted to own property was also intellectually superior in other ways. Beginning in 1878 the journal entries indicate that for a decade and a half, Simcox spent an enormous amount of time reading about the acquisition of property in Assyria, Egypt, China, and Babylon, organizing her notes, and writing her magnum opus.

Although Edith Simcox never married, she certainly was not free from family responsibilities. She managed the Simcox household and described herself paying the bills, recording the finances, seeing that frozen pipes were repaired, finding suitable houses, arranging the moves, hiring and firing servants, and taking care of all of the day-to-day needs of the family. She was aware of the technological advances of her day and mentioned her own delight at finding electric lights in the reading room at the British Museum, riding a bicycle, purchasing a typewriter, and using the telephone and telegraph.

She tirelessly cared for her mother, Jemima Haslope Simcox (1816-1897), during her many years of growing weakness and sickness and did everything possible to keep her comfortable and happy. She read aloud to her, provided her with a horse and a dog, saw that she could attend church regularly, took her on trips for her health—to the French Riviera, to Switzerland, and to the Bavarian Alps. Mrs. Simcox died December 18, 1897, only four years before Edith, and the two women are buried together in the graveyard at Aspley Guise near Bedford.

Edith Jemima Simcox's parents, George Price Simcox and Jemima Haslope, must have been of the upper middle class since she mentioned that her mother's marriage settlement was £5000;[10] apparently her father had died before 1876 since he is never mentioned while her mother played a significant part throughout the journal. Although Edith Simcox had some schooling as a child, she was largely self-educated. She read German, French, Italian, and Latin and mentioned teaching herself to read Greek, Dutch, and Flemish. She was accomplished in mathematics and accounting, conversant with topics related to art and scientific advances, widely read, and well prepared to write with authority on a wide variety of topics.

Two older brothers were both educated at Oxford and are mentioned frequently in the *Autobiography*. George Augustus (1841-1905) was a classical scholar, edited Greek and Latin texts, and from 1863 until his death was a fellow of Queen's College Oxford. William Henry (1843-1889) was a clergyman, first

---

[10] March 2, 1891

at Weyhill and then at Harlaxton. He married Annie Ludlam in 1875; her death and William's are described by Simcox in her journal. Both brothers were recognized as distinguished writers and scholars; neither left heirs.

Edith Simcox began her journal soon after her thirty-third birthday, which she commemorated by quoting Byron's lines: "Through life's dull road so dim and dirty, I have dragged to three and thirty."[11] This quote is typical of her self-effacing irony; in reality she raced vigorously through an exciting and profitable life. She walked across London at all hours in all kinds of weather and never complained at crossing Hyde Park alone at night, being drenched with sleet and rain, or at having to walk because she had not so much as a sou to pay her fare. On one occasion she drove the dog-cart from one end of England to the other, staying alone at country inns.[12] At times she walked twenty miles or more from one village to another. Through all of her experiences Edith Simcox's emotional stamina was even more amazing than her physical vigor.

On April, 16, 1882, in taking stock of her life, which she often did, Simcox said that during the past ten years she had learned to make shirts and manage schools, had written two books, and had lived through the love-passion of her life.

The love-passion of her life was for the novelist George Eliot (1819-1880). On one occasion Simcox actually wrote that her autobiography was not that of a shirtmaker but of a love.[13] Edith Simcox adored and admired George Eliot, who was twenty-five years older than she, from the time they met in 1872 when Simcox was preparing her review of Eliot's novel, *Middlemarch*.[14] For the next seven years, Simcox frequently was among the literary elite who gathered on Sunday afternoons at the home of George Eliot and George Henry Lewes. The journal entries for 1877 and 1878 provide detailed accounts of the conversations on these occasions.

Edith Simcox was completely aware that her affection and admiration for Eliot were not reciprocated, made it absolutely clear that she knew it was her

---

[11] August 20, 1883

[12] June 2, 1885

[13] May 26, 1878

[14] Review of *Middlemarch*, *Academy* 4 (January 1, 1873): 1-4; reprinted in *A Century of George Eliot Criticism*, ed. Gordon S. Haight, (Houghton Mifflin, 1965); *George Eliot and Her Readers*, ed. John Holmstrom and Laurence Lerner, (Barnes & Noble, 1966); and *George Eliot: The Critical Heritage*, ed. David Carroll, (Barnes & Noble, 1971).

mission to love rather than to be loved,[15] and repeatedly determined to make her life and work a tribute to the memory of George Eliot. In addition to her excruciatingly honest assessment of Eliot's lack of encouragement to her, Simcox was aware of the ambiguity of her own relationship to Eliot's beloved "husband," George Henry Lewes (1817-1878). She felt a genuine camaraderie with him in his love for Eliot and frequently commented that he was kinder to her than George Eliot was. After George Henry Lewes died, Simcox grieved for what his loss meant to her as well as to Eliot, regularly visited his grave at Highgate, and even planted and tended ivy on his grave. And with the painful insight that only a rival in love could experience, Simcox all along sensed something more than friendship between John Walter Cross (1840-1924) and George Eliot and was perhaps the only person who was not surprised when they were married on May 6, 1880, only eighteen months after the death of Lewes. Cross did not have much time to share with Eliot because she died seven months after their marriage. After Eliot's death, Simcox and Cross saw each other occasionally and discussed their mutual grief as well as the biography of Eliot which Cross wrote;[16] he asked Simcox to write the article on Eliot which appeared in the *Nineteenth Century*.[17] And Simcox expressed her amusement on October 30, 1881, upon hearing gossip of an "engagement" between her and Cross; she commented, "I don't know any other woman who wears spectacles and doesn't frequent 'society' whose name is made free with in that way.—I only know that it is more than unprovoked."

Immediately after Eliot's death, Simcox described going to Nuneaton and Coventry to visit the places of Eliot's pre-London life and to talk with those who remembered her as Mary Anne Evans.[18] Simcox cultivated lasting friendships with several of George Eliot's dearest friends such as Barbara Bodichon, Elma Stuart, and Maria Congreve. Barbara Bodichon shared her letters from George Eliot with Simcox; before Simcox returned these letters, she received permission to copy long passages from them into her journal.[19]

Simcox frequently stated that she preferred the friendship of women to that of men and that women had always responded to her more positively than men had. She thoroughly enjoyed her own androgyny. She referred to having

---

[15] August 30, 1878

[16] *George Eliot's Life as Related in Her Letters and Journals*, 3 vols. (Edinburgh and London: W. Blackwood and Sons, 1885).

[17] "George Eliot," *Nineteenth Century* 9 (May 1881): 778-801; reprinted *Littell's Living Age* 149 (1881): 791-805.

[18] January 2, 4, 6, 8, 11, 13, 1881

[19] These copies are made as part of the entry for December 25, 1881.

always thought of herself as "half a man,"[20] commented that she liked boating in her "young Manhood," and laughed at having signed her name E. J. Simcox on purpose to get "mistered"[21] and, as a result, having been called Mr. Simcox in the *Times*.

On October 17, 1887, an entire lengthy section of the *Autobiography* is devoted to gender issues. Simcox began the section: "I confess I should like to hear a few more frank autobiographical details as to women's intimate natural feelings about men than the sex has yet indulged in." Then she proceeded to share her own opinions on marriage and confessed that even as a small child (under twelve) it was a mild domestic joke to enquire after her and her two brothers as "the three boys." She goes on to explain: "The base of the preference was a want of sympathy with girls' games and talk—I did not care for dolls or dress or any sort of needlework."[22] But she definitely cared for work which was directed toward any useful movement and devoted much of her time and effort toward making the world better for other women, men, and children.

On February 22, 1884, Simcox recorded in her journal, "Have been to Oxford on a quaint errand—to 'read a paper' on Women's Work, at an assemblage of town and gown in a room at Balliol." The *Autobiography of a Shirtmaker* provides an excellent example of one woman's work, reveals a glimpse of her heart and mind, and records her truly monumental accomplishments which serve as an appropriate tribute to herself as well as to George Eliot.

Her own autobiography is successful when measured by the standard Edith Simcox set forth in one of the earliest articles on the craft of autobiographical writing in which she said, "Every autobiography depends for its value and interest upon the measure of common human passion and experience concentrated in its pages, or on the degree of vividness with which they depict common human situations and sentiments."[23]

This text is a repository of facts and feelings for anyone who is interested in Victorian literature and/or society. It provides the mental history from 1876 to 1900 of a remarkable Victorian woman.

---

[20] October 1, 1877

[21] January 13, 1878

[22] October 17, 1887

[23] "Autobiographies," *North British Review* 51 (January 1870): 383-414; *Prose by Victorian Women: An Anthology*, ed. Andrea Broomfield and Sally Mitchell, (Garland, 1996), 527-563.

A Monument to the Memory of George Eliot

Edith J. Simcox's *Autobiography of a Shirtmaker*

May 10, 1876

> "Since nothing all my love avails;
>   Since all my life seemed meant for fails;
>   Since this was written and needs must be"—[1]

behooves one to realize and accept the fact, with everything involved in it.

October 1, 1877

I have been looking over my journal[2]—acta diurna amoris[3]—and counting the days till I may hope to see her[4] again. I do not hope for anything else. I don't see how I can possibly be mistaken as to the interpretation of her letter; my uneasy instinct has not misled me all along; there is some radical discrepancy—if I have the ghost of a hope it is that she may let fall something that may help me to guess whereabouts it lies. In the rest I have written *finis* on my tombstone and in sanquine moments force myself to mutter "Sat est vixisse"[5]—I *have* lived for a few seconds now and then. I love her just as much as ever and a touch would bring me back to unconsciousness of everything but the love. But I have no hope or not enough I think even to pay toll in the "City of Dreadful Night"[6]—I should hardly venture even to hope that this month may come to an end in time—were it not that wages are due every Saturday and monthly bills on the 1st proximo![7] The struggle for existence is an infernal process.

---

[1] Robert Browning (1812-1889), "The Last Ride Together," in *Men and Women* (London: Chapman and Hall, 1855), lines 3-5.

[2] This journal has not been located.

[3] "daily accounting of love"

[4] For "she" and "her" the antecedent is always GE; see May 26, 1878, and "there" is where GE is; see November 3, 1878.

[5] The title of the last of the *Episodes in the Lives of Men, Women, and Lovers* (London: Trübner, 1882).

[6] James Thompson (1834-1882) wrote a lengthy poem "The City of Dreadful Night," which was published serially in the *National Reformer*, March 22 - May 17, 1874. He sent GE a copy (H, VI, 53).

[7] EJS paid the wages and kept all of the accounts for Hamilton and Company, the shirtmaking co-operative, which she and Mary Hamilton started to provide decent working conditions for women. The successful enterprise began at 68 Dean Street, Soho, in 1875 and moved to larger premises at 27 Mortimer Street in 1878. EJS describes her connection with the business in detail in her *Nineteenth Century* article, "Eight Years of Co-Operative Shirtmaking," 15 (June 1884): 1037-1054.

November 7, 1877

My whole soul is a longing question. I am going to see her. It rained this morning; now the sun is coming out. I feel as if that were a bad omen. She will be pre-engaged.

November 9, 1877

I was ushered in without hesitation. They[8] were together sitting reading; he was at the second day of a headache. I tried to say something easy—that it was her fate not to get rid of me. She—that it seemed rather hard on me on Sunday,—and—was she afraid of my poisoning Johnny's shirts? [Mr. Lewes had invited me to come early on Sunday, before other people; but I only contrived to get a few minutes short of J.C.][9] which she seemed inclined to parry by saying many other people came. They had tried battledore and shuttlecock as a substitute for the exercise of lawn tennis which had done her so much good. He had had a letter from a young Cambridge man,[10] who had dreamt so vividly and repeatedly that she was ill that he couldn't help writing to ask—enclosing a directed card for reply "only a dream" or something of the sort to prove that he was not in quest of an autograph. She said perhaps that would make me more charitable to men-folk. I protested I wasn't otherwise, and she said she had always owed me a grudge for not being grateful enough to the Italian officer who was kind to me when the train was snowed up beyond Foggia.[11] She said unlike most people, she believed I should have thought more of the adventure if a woman had been kind to me. I said I might have if I had had the opportunity of being kind to a woman: But that I had no prejudice whatever against men. He and she said as they have before, that among chance acquaintances men are more appreciative and courteous to her than women. I said that I had found women kinder than men, which she was "glad to hear," as showing they could be kind to each other—and I didn't explain either that I had always taken their kindness as a sign that I was half a man—and they knew it; or that I thought it rather hard she should visit, as a fault, my constitutional want of charm for men. I did not stay long and she only said—Are you going so soon. I spent an hour afterwards in

---

[8] George Eliot (1819-1880) was the pseudonym of Mary Anne Evans, novelist, critic, and poet. She lived with the journalist, critic, philosopher, and scientist George Henry Lewes (1817-1878) from 1854 until his death.

[9] Johnny is John Walter Cross (1840-1924), EJS's "rival" for GE's affections. He was a banker and author of *George Eliot's Life as Related in Her Letters and Journals* (Edinburgh and London: W. Blackwood and Sons, 1885). He married GE on May 6, 1880.

[10] Haight identifies him as Leonard A. Montefiore and says he was not a Cambridge man (H, VI, 413, n. 8 and H, IX, 200, n. 4).

[11] In Italy

hunting for a book[12] she wanted in the Holborn bookstalls, then attended the Shirtmaker's Committee and walked home—crossing Hyde Park for the first time in the dark. I have been very wretched since, and even more perplexed. Clearly she has nothing to say to me about the book; and it is hardly for me to open the subject now. I have seldom been more entirely at a loss what to do. I know they would be annoyed if I simply asked Trübner[13] to withdraw the book[14] when it had covered his expenses, and yet I daren't, and to tell the truth hardly feel a wish to dare—to ask her counsel again. It is not pride, because if I could ask, it would be more humbly than ever. I shall wait, dragging out useless days as heretofore till some irresistible impulse declares itself.

November 17, 1877
When I am happy I am not in a hurry to say so. Last Sunday—the 11th—it rained with such preternatural violence and constancy that very slowly and diffidently I came around to the conclusion—that I had better go to the Priory![15] I arrived at a quarter to 3. My only terror was lest they should have had

---

[12] William Cobbett (1762-1835), *Rural Rides* (London: J. M. Dent, 1830). New Edition with notes by J.P. Cobbell (1853) (H, IX, 200, n. 5). EJS delivers the book on November 17, her next visit.

[13] Nikolaus Trübner (1817-1884) was one of the leading publishers of his day. His story and that of his firm is in Frank A. Mumby, *The House of Routledge, 1854-1934, with a History of Kegan Paul, Trench, Trübner, and Other Associated Firms* (with portraits) (London: G. Routledge, 1934).

[14] *Natural Law: An Essay in Ethics* (London: Trübner, 1877). Spurred by GE's inspiration, EJS wrote *Natural Law* to demonstrate her devotion. On the half-title page of the copy she gave to GE, EJS wrote: "Marian Evans Lewes/June 21, 1877—." The final sentence of the book reads: "Heaven and hell are names or visions; the earth is ours—here a hell of sensuality and hardened cruelty, there a heaven of love and wisdom, with a tender smile upon her gracious lips, and yearning prophecy in the melting depths of her unfathomable eyes." Whether GE failed to notice the addition or was embarrassed by it, she never mentioned the dedication to EJS. On the opposite page EJS wrote: "Schwarzer schatten ist über dem Staube/Der Geliebten Gefährte;/ Ich machte mich zum Staube/ Aber der Schatten ging über mich hin" (Goethe, *West-östlicher Divan, Goethes Werke*, Weimar, VI, 286) (H, IX, 203, n. 1). See August 28, 1895.

[15] The Priory, 21 North Bank, Regent's Park, on the Regent's Canal was purchased by GE August, 1863, at £2000 with a forty-nine year lease (H, Biography, 371). It was the scene of the famous Sunday afternoon gatherings and was called the "Priory" by GHL because the worshipers came to pay homage to the Madonna. GE and GHL lived there until his death. It is described in detail by Lucy Clifford in her "Remembrance of George Eliot," *Nineteenth Century*, 74 (1913): 109-118.

people to luncheon by invitation. My spirits rose when I saw the hall innocent of hats and cloaks, and when I found them alone together, the world began to smile again. I laid the blame deprecatingly on the rain—thought if I didn't come there would be nobody to ask after Mr. Lewes's headache; and they said, well, I should have the afternoon to myself and—we had better sit down; which I proceeded to do on the rug at her feet, which I kissed; while observing that Lady Paget[16] had adopted the same seat, she intimated a preference for my taking another, which of course I also did. She gave me a book of Miss Phelps's to read "Avis,"[17] which the writer had sent her, seeming to think that her promise to read the book when she could might be supplemented by any charitable judgment I could give more promptly. She said Miss Phelps would know my name from Trübner's series[18] being published in America. Before that, á propos of bonnets, she said her recollection of people's clothes was a part of her general mental image of them, and that she suffered much when worthy men were unfortunate in their choice of

---

[16] Lady Paget is not listed among GE's "spiritual daughters" by Haight (H, Biography, 452). His footnote says "A few weeks after GE's death Lady Paget wrote to her son: 'The more one thinks of her and her deep affection for your father, the more one feels how she stood alone, amid the many friends he has won. I never can think of her without a strange feeling of jealousy over her, a kind of regard and admiration I can't describe. She was so gentle, so generous, so affectionate, so charitable in her spirit towards others" (Stephen Paget, ed., *Memoirs and Letters of Sir James Paget*, 1901, 402) (H, IX, 202, n. 6).

[17] *The Story of Avis* (Boston: Osgood, 1877). "Miss Phelps's partly autobiographical novel of a strong-minded woman" (H, VI, 417, n. 5; GE's Letter to her, VI, 417-418). *The Feminist Companion to Literature in English* tells more; she was Elizabeth Stuart Phelps (later Ward) (1844-1911), who wrote her novels as "Mary Gray." She was the daughter of a novelist Elizabeth Wooster Stuart Phelps. *Avis* is based on her mother's life and shows the devastating effect of marriage on a woman's artistic potential. Reviewers expressed concern about the effect this novel would have on young women. Her novel *The Gates Ajar* (Boston: Osgood, 1868) examines notions of heaven, feminizes religion, and demonstrates women's right to self-fulfillment and the need of female support in gaining such fulfillment; *Hedged In* (Boston: Fields Osgood, 1870) is about factory women; and *A Singular Life* (Boston: Houghton, Mifflin, 1895) explores temperance issues. She also wrote articles advocating women's rights, suffrage, and dress reform and protesting domestic confinement. Her autobiography was published in 1896 and a memoir of her father in 1891 (849).

[18] Trübner's English and Foreign Philosophical Library, vol. 4 (H, IX, 202, n. 8).

trouserings,—Herbert Spencer[19] had improved on that particular—but improvement had been needed. This led to the mention of his having been one of the visitors the Sunday before; his companion was an American admirer.[20] Everyone, Mr. Lewes observed, had *one* American admirer. I suggested there might be a few books that didn't get even so far as across the Atlantic; to which he replied with the story of two books both of which were puffed in 4 or 5 leading papers, of which one did not sell a single copy and the other only 50 copies taken on speculation by the trade. I can't recal in what context it was that Mr. Lewes spoke of the unreasonableness of people who ask of one advice when the last thing they would think of would be to take it if it didn't fall in with their intention. Then I said, I should have asked his advice, if I hadn't known it could not fall in with my intention—about Trübner. She said, of course, what business had I to have the book printed if I didn't mean it to sell and to be read, that anyway the edition had to take its chance, that there would be no second edition unless it were all sold off pretty quickly, and he suggested that the only thing to be done if one were dissatisfied with a written book was to write a better. I intimated that that was not exactly my difficulty, I don't know what I succeeded in saying at last,—I kissed her hand—I guard my own—I implied that her approval or blame ended everything for me. I think she said, Why should I have supposed she—not disapproved—that was too arrogant a word, but failed to sympathize! Then as by an effort of recollection: "I think I never told you what I thought of the book after the first chapters!"—I could not say, that was just why I despaired. I did say that these were stern judgments she had pronounced, which I had been loth to think deserved—though of course she must know best—that I had reason to despair if the book gave her no reason to modify those. Of course she has never known how every word of hers enters into my flesh, but this much at least she said to me now: That there had been nothing that jarred on her in reading the book—if there had she should have remembered it, of course she did not always agree, but the general impression was of sympathy; there were no passages that struck her as cynical—she had been somewhat uneasily on the lookout for them; she thought what I said of religion was good,—barring the somewhat too impersonal, unconcerned or hypothetical way of saying it;—it rather confirmed what she had thought before that I might write a history of religious thought, or a natural history of Christianity. I said I had been glad the book gave no scandal: She, that it could not, its tone was perfectly reverent. I told her that I had had the fear—or rather the love, of her before my eyes and had struck out any of the little malicious tails to a sentence I thought she might not

---

[19] Herbert Spencer (1820-1903) was a dear friend of GE; Haight frequently uses him to illustrate one of the men GE "needed to lean on." Also see Nancy L. Paxton, *George Eliot and Herbert Spencer: Feminism, Evolutionism, and the Reconstruction of Gender* (Princeton, 1991).

[20] Haight identifies the American admirer as Edward Livingston Youmans (1821-1887) (H, XI, 202, n. 9).

like, but explained that theology had always been so uninteresting and meaningless to me that I should not care to have to get up its history. She said that Charles Lewes[21] had read some of the book with interest, and appealed to Mr. Lewes if he himself had not sympathized with its spirit—to which he in a somewhat uninviting tone—Oh yes, what I read of it.—In my desperation I had just utterly ignored his presence, which is, perhaps hardly the way to a man's tender mercies. She used the words "sound and wholesome" and thought it would be useful. I did not deserve to be told this, but she had had serious thoughts of recommending the book to a lady who had "difficulties"—one who would be flattered by the argumentative apparatus and the rigidly meager assumptions of the first page. She had not done so on the whole because the said lady would have known I was a friend of hers and so—might either I suppose have identified us too much, or have attached less weight to the supposed echo. In all she said there was nothing to flatter any author's vanity—rather the constancy in tone and implication—so I have the more respect for my spiritual sincerity seeing that I can write that the clouds of misery and despair lifted themselves from my heart. I walked back through the pelting rain with inward sunshine, and I have been soberly glad and happily loving ever since. I had a note from her yesterday, referring to the remainder of the conversation. I had been more than an hour alone with them when Locker and his daughter[22] came, and afterwards Myers;[23] the former was talking to them about some unpublished poems of Tennyson[24]—whose dramas, by the way, they admire. On Thursday I was fortunately able to get her a copy of Cobbett's "Rural Rides" which she had expressed a wish for; the same evening I went to Queen Street to see what a proposal made to revive the International[25] would come to. A Committee was

---

[21] Charles Lewes (1842-1891) was the oldest child of GHL and his wife Agnes; he was like a son to GE and was supportive and particularly helpful after the death of GHL.

[22] Frederick Locker (1821-1895) is mentioned numerous times in the GE Letters; his daughter Eleanor married Lionel Tennyson. He wrote verse about social trivia of everyday experience in upper-class London. He added Lampson as a second surname in 1885.

[23] Frederic William Henry Myers (1843-1901) is frequently a visitor at the Priory; he wrote an article on George Eliot for the *Century Magazine*, 23 (November 1881): 60.

[24] Alfred, Lord Tennyson (1809-1892) is not generally known for his verse dramas.

[25] This was the International Working Men's Association, or the "First International," formed in London in 1864. Odger and other London trade union

appointed to report, Mrs. Paterson[26] was nominated and declined to serve—on which Mr. Headlam[27] proposed me, and I made no objection, feeling since Sunday equal to inventing a dozen Constitutions, if anyone would have them. Still I should have repented if the number of votes given to my unknown name had not been, as it turned out, as numerous as those of the most "undesirable" representatives. The meeting was all of men—barring 4 women unionists in the background, so I took it for a sign that if I were nominated for the Parliamentary Committee, the election would not be at all impossible.[28]

November 18, 1877

      This morning I have been writing a long defense of the economical attitude of H & Co[29] to Mr. Verney[30] and am meditating a constitution for the International. I am happier in my mind than I have been for years—I think than I

---

leaders were associated with it, but Karl Marx soon assumed the leadership. See G.D.H. Cole, *A Short History of the British Working Class Movement, 1789-1947* (London: G. Allen and Unwin, 1948) (McK, 41, n. 3).

[26] Emma Smith Paterson, the pioneer of women's trade unions, in July 1874 founded and organized the Women's Protective and Provident League, whose members were largely men and women of the upper middle class and whose object was to help women form trade unions. She was honorary secretary of the League until her death in 1886 and also edited the *Women's Union Journal*. She was actively involved in the formation of many unions including the Shirt and Collar Makers' Union in 1875. Along with EJS, she was one of the first women to be admitted as delegates to the Trade Union Congress (McK, 36). EJS uses her as an example of the good which one woman can accomplish in her article "Women's Work, Women's Wages," *Longman's Magazine* 10 (July 1887): 252-267; *Prose by Victorian Women: An Anthology*, ed. Andrea Broomfield and Sally Mitchell (Garland, 1996), 565-582.

[27] Stewart D. Headlam (1847-1924) was a Christian socialist, assistant curate of St. Matthew's, and loyal supporter of Charles Bradlaugh in the trade union movement.

[28] McKenzie comments: "Evidently Miss Simcox would have liked to be a member of the Parliamentary Committee of the Trade Union Congress. Mrs. Paterson was on it for a year, 1872-3, but was not re-elected. The members tended to be the same from year to year" (McK, 42, n. 1).

[29] See October 1, 1877.

[30] Frederick Verney was a friend of working men and women and along with S. D. Headlam was a patron of the Working Men's Club and Institute Union, founded in 1861.

have ever been: it is good for me that I have been afflicted. I think; I hope, that all the trouble once egotism has been "brayed out of me." I don't feel as if I had got to curses creative because there is nothing very great or glorious or delightful predestined for my accomplishment. Through this sad summer I have been conscious of the first dawning feelings of what I call middle-aged content,—the physical absence of conscious unsatisfied craving; a state of mind, or body, which makes the day's life tolerable—as a fact—without reference to some future good that it may seem to tend toward. I thought thus that if she were reconciled and I had something to do, I might live off counting the days to the end. Now that she has spoken, I am not afraid but what something possibly feasible will turn up, and meanwhile I am more than content to love her, and to feel that there is no need for me to vex her any more. The past distress has not been altogether anybody's fault, not even mine. It is naturally difficult for the inmost soul to speak out to anyone, and who can interpret the unspoken riddles! But now all is peace.

November 19, 1877

Nay more: I have got out this book only to write again that I love my darling and am not ill-content. All my woes and grievances seem to have melted, there is not—as so often before—a faint concealed sense of self-denial, of being content under difficulties. I know there are many good things which I might wish for, which I could have enjoyed, which are, over and for ever, not for me, but I do not feel toward any of them as toward the very bread of life, without which existence is a slow painful death by inanition. Of course I had reason enough for my misery, there are so many things she would like that I am left so many that I am which she cannot like—but what does that signify? it is enough if we are of one mind at bottom,—and she will love me well enough—oh immeasurably better than I deserve—when she finds that—when I have got what I wanted I know how to be therewith content.[31] My darling! I shall see you next Sunday.

November 26, 1877

One day last week I was walking along Knightsbridge and as a matter of course thinking of her. All at once I heard a stable man or groom say behind me; "The ladies seem pleased this morning, they're a'laughing," which recalled me to a sense of earth, and a kind of gratitude that on the many occasions when I had walked along the streets very much the reverse of pleased, it didn't occur to anyone to observe that the ladies were crying! The end of the week the barometer fell—decidedly. I felt hopeless and alone—was it any use—trying to mix oneself up effectively with the desires of the people, when after all one could do nothing, except, if possible, not lose one's temper over these less inspired moments. All the obvious reasons against doing anything were present to me, and I was saddened, but I was not overcome, one was to live, and love her *grand mère*[32] everything beside her love was pain and grief. Yesterday I went to the

---

[31] An echo of the apostle Paul's statement in Phil. 4:11

[32] "with a grand passion"

Priory,—Johnny and I met at the gate—nothing particular passed; she was beautiful as ever, said that Trübner had thanked Mr. Lewes for recommending him to print my book in his series; it did the latter good to have an original work. I came away after an hour feeling only inwardly jealous. I like people to love her, I like best those who love her most devotedly, still—among all who have their reward, I envy those whose reward is larger than mine. But things must be as they are fated—and I too have my share. Ja, ich kann wohl sagen, daß ich allein durch ihn empfunden habe, daß das Herz gerührt und erhoben, daß auf der Welt Freude, Liebe und ein Gefühl sein kann, *das über alles Bedürfnis hinaus befriedight.*[33]

December 1, 1877

At the second meeting of the Committee appointed to construct a constitution for the International, somewhat to my confusion, I was appointed with Jung (a watchmaker who has impressed me favorably) to draw up the report for the general meeting due next Thursday. Alsops Hill made the proposition and two or three of the members seconded and supported it off hand, so again it wasn't my business to demur; we arranged to meet at Jung's house, in Clerkenwell, and I was glad of an opportunity of seeing him in his *intérieur.* On Wednesday saw Trübner, who hadn't much to say: about 170 copies of the book appeared to have been sold in England. I went through some unprofitably strong emotions about a thing he told me. He has got leave to reprint her translation of Feuerbach,[34] and he was so ill-advised as to suggest to Mr. Lewes that some *raison d'être* for a second edition would be advisable and to propose that I should write an introduction on the life and writings of Feuerbach. I was annoyed at my name having been used so without my knowledge, because of course *I* knew beforehand how unhesitatingly Mr. Lewes would negative such a proposition on her account. But the thrill that went through me while Trübner was telling his story gave me a rather sad intimation of all the happiness that might be possible—where such relations were possible. Tonight I have been crying again, with the old physical heartache, but my mind is at rest. I seem to have outlived the "thirst" denounced by Buddhism; I have felt almost of late as if I had actually attained Nirvana; without choice or will of my own, my whole being seems to have become passive; my "karma" is too feeble to do any harm to posterity.

---

[33] "Yes, I can indeed say that through her alone I have felt that my heart was stirred and elevated, that there can be joy, love and a certain feeling in the world, a feeling that goes beyond all desire."

[34] *The Essence of Christianity* (London: J. Chapman, 1854), was reissued in Trübner's English and Foreign Philosophical Library (1881) (H, IX, 205, n. 3). GE translated *Das Wesen des Christenthums* by Ludwig Feuerbach (1804-1872) for John Chapman's Quarterly Series; he paid her two shillings a page, "a little more than £30—surely not exorbitant wages for such skilled and arduous work" (H, Biography, 137). This is the only work on which her name appears as Marian Evans; she is identified as the translator on the title page.

December 2, 1877

I have been reading Wilhelm Meister[35] through again—after 15 years: it struck me as curious to come again *in situ* on the passages that had struck me as mottoes in days when I wasn't apt to over estimate the values of what was given. Also—it would be a hard case if one learned nothing in 15 years—there seems to me more reality than of old in the division between the two pasts. My understanding seemed to leap, with visible power· for apprenticeship, to the Hebraic of renunciation but—one thing was wanting, without which who could tell whether my faith was living?—I had nothing to renounce: I did not understand what it felt like to care very much about anything—and I thought that very ignorance was the renunciation of unwise care. Now I know. The book impresses me still; fresh sentences stand out clearly, the embodiment of a wide wisdom, not least those in which Goethe confronts the claims of the many or chooses between them the mottoes—"the best for all" "the desired for many" *vielen das Erwünschte*[36]—the limit of my own small efforts. But even in these passages, the writer is a student, a poet, one who does not live in the common world, and I have still the same feeling as when I read it first, if we were to play at living, we couldn't have a better picture of how to play. Alas that no one has ever given us such wise counsel fitted to the more difficult task of a real life. I began an article the other day and wrote 3 pages; next day I tried to read them and couldn't so gave it up. I am tired, but it is a pleasure to feel only tired after one has been in sharp pain.

December 8, 1877

If things are less pleasant today I can scarcely blame myself. It is nothing—a trifle—but then the wise agree that trifles are much. It is a card from Lewes, asking me if I was coming today not to arrive early as they had some business matters to discuss. As it happens today was the anniversary of the day—5 years ago—when I first saw her handwriting[37]—of the day three years ago when I dined with them and she read her "Symposium"[38] to me. What a

---

[35] Johann Wolfgang von Goethe (1749-1832) wrote this "apprenticeship novel," (1794) which relates the process through which a young person is educated for living.

[36] "that which is wished for or desired"

[37] "A note inviting her to call 13, December, 1872" (H, IX, 206, n. 4). McKenzie, 88, gives December 8 as the day EJS first saw GE's handwriting and December 9 as the day of their first meeting. His note on 84 refers to EJS's entry for July 21, 1880 when she "was reading *Middlemarch* and as yet knew her not."

[38] GE's "Symposium" is the early version of her poem "A College Breakfast-Party." It grew from her impression of her talks with the young Trinity men during her first visit to Cambridge (H, Biography, 507). It was published in

singularly complete ass I must be to remain even more of a stranger to her now than three years ago. But I have renounced. I will not "thirst" again. I hardly do. My heart has ached, a few tears have come, but the pain is passive.

December 9, 1877

At first I took for granted that I should write today to say I had not meant to come because I was afraid to visit, on so sacred a day, the likelihood of not being able as much as to kiss her hand; then it occurred to me that I need not write at all, but might take my chance of her guessing whence the flowers came, and of being able next Sunday to say why I hadn't meant to come. But I was after all most afraid of her thinking I was hurt or huffed, and also of really failing to give any fit expression to the love which has a right to keep holy days.

December 12, 1877

After all I did write—briefly and affectionately. At 5 o'clock next day i.e. the Monday 5 years of her first letter, a note came asking me to go and see her one day this week. Of course I went yesterday. She kissed me at length. Lewes also was kind. I forget what was spoken of first—no I don't—it was the state of the shop, trade in general, French politics and the fall of Plevna.[39] Then I said Mary Hamilton was gone to Scotland and that her mother was getting tired of not going up the Nile, and mentioned casually that she was unhappy at her daughter's not marrying. Mr. Lewes seemed to think there was no hurry, and I said at 27 there was not much time to lose. She said marriages had seemed to be getting later and later and she was—of course—rather wroth with me for expressing a prejudice against late marriages; she thought that people who go on developing may have a much better chance of happiness in marrying after thirty than at 20; she was so beautiful and I was so fond of her that I wasn't angry when she proceeded to affirm that I had never been so fit to marry as now—I answered "that wasn't saying much"—to which with a sweet laugh and a still sweeter gesticulation—that brought her hand within reach of my lips—that she didn't pretend that her speeches amounted to much—it was enough if they came to a little. At which I laughed resignedly. Then she asked what I had been doing, and I said nothing—: I had been reading Wilhelm Meister; she was curious to know how it impressed me: she had much disliked Lothario, his special objection was the *bedeutende Märiana* and the Macaria business:[40] she thought it strange that

---

Macmillan's Magazine, 38 (July 1878): 161-179, and reprinted in the *Jubal* volume. The British Museum MS is dated 1874 (H, VI, 388, n. 5).

[39] "Plevna fell to the Russians in 1877 after being defended by the Bulgarians for three months" (H, IX, 206, n. 7).

[40] Wilhelm Meister's first love, the protesting but unfaithful actress Mariana. The mysterious Baron Lothario, head of a secret society into which Wilhelm is initiated, marries Theresa after discovering that she is not, as was thought, the daughter of his old lover. To eke out a second volume Goethe got Eckermann to patch together a group of isolated tales found in Makaria's house. See GHL's

with such perfectly finished dramatic passages, all Goethe's prose works should be so unequal and without finished unity; was grateful to me for quoting the phrase *vielen das Erwünschte*. Then I made the confession I wished—that I had shaken hands with Bradlaugh[41] and Mrs. Besant.[42] Of course she asked how that might be—and of course, on the whole, all things well weighed, she wished me not to have my name printed in the same list with theirs or Mrs. Harriet Law's.[43] She gave full weight to the dread of Pharisaism, and said incidentally some

---

Life and Works of Goethe (London: D. Nutt, 1855), II, 410-413 (H, IX, 206, n. 8).

[41] Charles Bradlaugh (1833-1891) and Mrs. Annie Besant (1847-1933), joint editors of the *National Reformer*, were active in the movement to revive the International Working Men's Asociation (H, IX, 206, n. 7). McKenzie describes Bradlaugh as "freethinker and Radical, elected to the House of Commons in 1880" (McK, 42, n. 2). See also David Tribe, *President Charles Bradlaugh, M.P.* (London: Elek, 1971).

[42] McKenzie says of Annie Besant (1847-1933), "She lectured and wrote many pamphlets. Her increasing tendency towards revolutionary socialism led to a break with Bradlaugh, a break completed by her adhesion to the Theosophical Society. She became a pupil of Mme Blavatsky, and her subsequent career was largely associated with India" (McK, 42, n. 2). The *Feminist Companion* introduces her as reformer, orator, theosophist, journalist, and editor. After a religious crisis she left her husband in 1873, taking her daughter. In 1874 she met Charles Bradlaugh, the crusading atheist and under his influence started lecturing and writing for the National Secular Society, publishing *The Gospel of Atheism* (1877); the same year they were prosecuted for publishing Knowlton's pamphlet on contraception. She joined the Fabian Society, was known as "the greatest woman public speaker of her time," led the first strike of match girls (1888), formed their union, and was elected to the London School Board. She made India her home, founded several schools there, launched the journals *Commonweal* and *New India*, formed a Home Rule for India League in 1916, and became President of India's National Congress in 1917 (89). A picture of Annie Besant is in Tribe, 166. See also Gertrude Marvin Williams, *The Passionate Pilgrim: a Life of Annie Besant* (New York: Coward-McCann, 1931) and Anne Taylor, *Annie Besant: A Biography* (New York: Oxford, 1992).

[43] According to Gertrude Marvin Williams, *The Passionate Pilgrim: a Life of Annie Besant* (New York: Coward-McCann, 1931), 72-73, Mrs. Harriet Law (1832-1897) was "a stout, loud-voiced person, a daughter of thunder. For thirty years she had travelled up and down the land, crude, earnest, the only woman Atheist speaker, one of the very few women speakers in England. Until 1875 she frequently spoke at the Hall of Science" (McK, 43, n. 1). Haight simply calls her "a notorious champion of atheism" (H, IX, 207, n. 1).

kindly sounding things of my qualifications for useful influence, suggested that I should lecture to these friends and brothers. I disclaimed any such arrogant pretensions, said my only *locus standi*[44] was as one of themselves, to which, she, did I leave my grammar behind me, and if not there might be other qualifications as inalienable. I haven't said that this was all because last Thursday when the new International formed itself, a Council was appointed to which I was nominated, then Mrs. Besant, then Mrs. Harriet Law and Mr. Bradlaugh in between. I had grave doubts what to do, feeling it to be rather mean to desert a sound principle because an undeniable person gives in their atheism too. On the other hand I don't at all like being brought into any kind of relation with that type of woman. And on the whole I have no real doubt that it is best to be guided by her advice; though I confess it riles me a little to retreat—as if I wasn't a match for any number of Besants. She was most kind all the time, and when I was leaving asked me to come at that time when I had anything to say, not early on Sunday, for they were going to have people to luncheon after, and besides even if there weren't one never had any interesting talk ("like this" implied), if I liked to come later when other people were there,—and make myself agreeable, by all means to come—but in point of fact when any one else was there I was always "as mute as a fish"—which nobody can deny! She was so sweet and beautiful. I went back to Dean Street and when there I settled to come home instead of going on to the International.

December 16, 1877

 Since this I have been busy taking stock, and keeping in the physical state of weariness, nay rather, of unpainful lassitude, which, when overshadowed by the broad sense of love for her refreshes my nirvana. I am tired. When I go to her next, I shall try to talk as freely as last time, and tell her that I don't quite like to go on stupefying and brutalizing myself like this, while leaving her under the impression that I am virtuously engaged in disinterested work.

December 17, 1877

 Another card from "mine fraternally" the secretary of the International announcing meeting tomorrow night. I don't exactly know how I am to get out of it, and after all hardly have a fond resolution to do so unless the new elements seem sufficiently prominent to give a real motive.

December 24, 1877

 I went on Tuesday to the meeting in question, at the office of Alsops Hill's Labor boss. I found that Jung persisted in without moving and the only acting—or at least speaking—members were Bradlaugh and Hales;[45] I let things

---

[44] "standing"

[45] John Hales along with Marx was one of the leading figures within the International according to David Tribe, *President Charles Bradlaugh, M.P.* (London: Elek, 1971), 129.

15

go on and spoke and voted as if still concerned and have now written to resign without giving any reason. I signed the letter "yours fraternally" by way of a parting protest against the English of the friends of woman—I am alone here, and now have 3 days leisure before me.—Either to write my article on the Utility of Competition,[46] or that on "The Patriarch and the Chief" or the new one "Reuben"[47] or all three! Yesterday was divided between unwholesome reveries and the reading of Victor Hugo on the Coup d'Etat.[48] His narrative simply explains the success of the *Coup*—not one of the Assembly, Left or Right showed the flash of any political gumption. To tell the truth, the Council of the International reminded me a little of them. Today I have been to the shop and wrote letters thence, came in about 4 since when I have read through a History of "Lloyds."[49]

December 25, 1877

Today was down late, tried writing a little, gave it up and took to reveries and Kaye's Sepoy war.[50] Felt cross and have just been reading the self-gratuitousness of the last few pages. What has helped to muddle me is that the last time I saw her she hesitated about dissuading me from going on with the International supposing I had "a strong inclination" to do so—or rather made the wisdom of the cause conditional on any such an inclination. This touched on old wound: I have *no* inclination—except always to dwell on the objections of any possible course, and in view of them abstain; am I therefore right to abstain? I have no overmastering feeling—except one of distaste for every kind of contact with my fellow creatures—and thus she says "these relations must be renounced if they are not easy."

---

[46] "Organization of Unremunerative Industry," *Fraser's Magazine* 18 (November 1878): 609-621.

[47] Reuben appears in the "Vignette" first published as "At Anchor," *Fraser's Magazine* 21 (November, 1881): 624-629 and as one of the *Episodes In The Lives of Men, Women, and Lovers* (London: Trübner, 1882).

[48] Victor Hugo (1802-1885), *Histoire d'un crime*; English translation subtitled "The Testimony of an Eye-Witness" (London: G. Routledge, 1877).

[49] Frederick Martin (1830-1883). *The History of Lloyd's and of Marine Insurance in Great Britain* (London: Macmillan, 1876).

[50] Sir John William Kaye (1814-1876), *History of the Sepoy War in India, 1857-1858*, 3 vols. (London: Longmans, Green, 1864-76).

December 28, 1877

Yesterday went to Mudie's[51] and got a volume of Daniel Stern's "Esquisses,"[52] then to the Grosvenor Gallery and went seriation[53] through the old masters. Lionardo[54] was perhaps the most unexpectedly well represented: some caricatures and exquisitely finished folio of sketches reminded me of an old scheme, to "get up" Lionardo and find all the wisdom of the moderns hid in his Mss. Home to tea and at 5 heard the postman's knock, went presently to see if it was—something—though I honestly expected nothing. But it was—enough to make me placidly happy since, with the pure pleasure of loving. Today back at the shop—I am thoroughly idle and in a most useless state of mind (and body), but once again I have that sense of delight in her being "das über alles Bedürfriss hinaus befriedight."[55]

December 30, 1877

Very idle and unprofitable,—i.e. reveries and Kaye's Sepoy war instead of Reuben, or shirtmakers' accounts: I am easily stirred to wish to do something profitable—a Times leader on the depression of trade, a magazine article on the wrong side of any question—and most sides are wrong!—but half an hour of projecting entirely my feeble resolution, my mind becomes a blank and then what answer is there to the question, why should it be for me? Love for her is always a motive in reserve for doing *something*, but it does not help me in the least in the choice of what to do—though my conscience certainly inclines to the belief that any or all of the others that flit across my mind could be better in her eyes than this nothingness. On the other hand it seems too much lost time— what I have been kicking at all these years—none the less certainly true in the abstract because it is a sentence of death for myself, that no particular good thing will be done by anyone who has not a personal selfish desire prompting him to do just that. I am not in a hurry to see her and I think dimly of January 9 which would be after 4 weeks, and I am shy of letting any hope build upon the thousand chances of an interview; but it does seem to me, sometimes, as if it *might* be possible to lay the case before her in a spirit that should not wholly repel her

---

[51] Charles Edward Mudie (1818-1890) founded Mudie's Lending Library. His establishment was at 28 Upper King Street (now Southampton Row, Bloomsbury).

[52] Daniel Stern (1805-1876), *Esquisses Morales: Pensées, Réflexions et Maximes* (Paris: J. Techener, 1856).

[53] "in an orderly fashion"

[54] Leonardo da Vinci (1452-1519) was an Italian painter, sculptor, architect, and scientist.

[55] "satisfied far beyond all need"

sympathies. I have wasted the strength of my life in always trying to do some unprofitably distasteful thing. All my days have been spent in doing or trying to resolve to do what I disliked, and it seemed horribly hard that the verdict should be given in favor of him which, by comparison, in my jealousy, I should call self-indulgent. And yet of course it is plain enough—where is the merit of a martyrdom that serves no creed? Again if circumstances had favored even I might have done something—perhaps much, and that again was what I hated to admit—that one's fate was in the hands of chance.

January 6, 1878

I have forced myself into the acceptance of truths repugnant to my inmost nature—the effort of submission took all my strength and I have none left to live with afterward. Last night again—if my mother were a husband and lover how tragical it would seem—I lay in bed strangled with the sobs I could not stop and feared to have overheard. It is painful to me to feel that my love for her is to bear no fruit but the occasional momments of selfish pleasure, when the thought of her sometimes makes me glad. And yet I cannot blame myself—at least for not much more than weakness: after my soul passes out of my own keeping; it was she, not I, who had power to dispose of its future.

January 7, 1878

Went today to see her—after looking again at certain of her letters last night. Arrived about 5, stooped and only kissed her hand. Lewes stooped to kiss me, and I said I wasn't to kiss any one because I had kissed Mary who thought she was going to have the mumps. He said they weren't catching and she that it was an awful complaint but she must risk it. She asked what news? if my people[56] had come back? said they had expected to come and wish them a happy new year—in a sceptical way—; she had lost her cold; he had had a headache, but both were in a tolerable state of perservation. She said, á propos of the shop that she kept hearing fresh people say in a matter of course way that they were going to "Hamiltons," and mentioned somebody who was coming to us in the wake of a certain Hennell, of whom I knew nothing but wondered if he might be a relative of Sara.[57] Mention of Oxford men who wear shirts brought up the Pattisons;[58] they said he was so interesting in conversation if he once got

---

[56] "Her mother Mrs. George Price Simcox and her brother George Augustus Simcox lived with Edith at 1 Douro Place, Victoria Road" (H, IX, 211, n. 6). Her mother was Jemima Haslope Simcox (1816-1896).

[57] Sara Sophia Hennell (1812-1899) was one of Mary Ann's close friends in the Coventry days after she spent six week at Rosehill in the summer of 1842. She "became an important correspondent for many years to come" (H, Biography, 46-47).

[58] Mark and Emilia Francis Strong Pattison lived in Oxford at Lincoln College. A visit with them in May of 1870 was GE's first trip to Oxford (H, Biography, 425-426).

launched; and Mrs. Lewes thought she had been getting up her book ever since she had known her.[59] All this took but a few minutes and I had hardly begun to despair of reaching more interesting topics when the fatal Johnny came in, he had missed his train yesterday and had a book to return by way of pretext. Mrs. Cross[60] was mending; á propos of a sister going to see a married sister,[61] something was said concerning the comparative wickedness of husbands and wives to each other. They thought there were extenuating circumstances for Dickens[62] because his sister-in-law did everything for the family and for him, and his wife did nothing. From such conjugal trials it was a step to an absurdly circumstantial dream of Lewes's,—that the archangel was in love with a humpbacked nobleman in holy orders—which he persisted was a most plausible combination of her three weak points! He was exercised how to make her realize the extent of her delinquencies against him, and thought of going away for a night—again in reference to her real dread of such an event, but he decided that would be so great a punishment to him that he would try the effect of a reproachful scene instead—at which point he woke. This she capped with a rather ludicrous dream of Stanley's[63]—who thought he was elected Pope; then they talked of FitzJames Stephen[64] on Bright[65] about Indian irrigation—I not

---

[59] Mrs. Mark Pattison, *The Renaissance of Art in France* (London: C. Kegan Paul, 1879) (H, IX, 212, n. 7). She was the daughter of an Oxford bank manager and came to London in 1859 to study art. In 1861 she married Mark Pattison, the Rector of Lincoln College, who was twenty-seven years her senior. They were frequent guests at the Priory (McK, 14-15).

[60] Anna Chalmers Wood Cross (1813-1878) was JWC's mother; she died ten days after GHL.

[61] JWC had five sisters; Mary (1843-1902), Florence (1857-1915), and Eleanor (1847-1895) were unmarried; Elizabeth (1836-1869) was married to W. H. Bullock and Emily (1848-1907) to Francis Otter; in this case the married sister was Emily.

[62] Charles Dickens (1812-1870) was unhappy with his wife; her sister lived with them throughout their marriage.

[63] Edward Lyulph Stanley, 4th Baron of Alderley, was a frequent caller at the Priory. He was a leader of the progressives and was associated with EJS in her work with the London School Board.

[64] Sir James FitzJames Stephen (1829-1894) was Sir Leslie's older brother, a High Court Judge, and the author of *A Digest of the Criminal Law* (London: Macmillan, 1883). He is mentioned in a letter from GHL to JWC, May 26, 1873, as being one of the guests (along with EJS and her brother), on an occasion at which there was "the best of talk!" and at which "the Crosses *ought* to have been present" (H, V, 414). In a letter from GE to Frederic Harrison on June 20, 1873,

remembering till I was on my way home the objections to the former's answer which had occurred to me. I stayed about half an hour, all told and left the field for Johnny. Was not very dismal as I came away, for after all I really had no definite hope. I do rather want her to understand that everything is at an end for me, but that is a kind of news that will keep, and as I don't expect anything from her to alter that,—well, it doesn't much matter how or when the truth leaks out. Found my mother poorly, and nervous—I am slow to imagine that it can be with any reason. Still I think her age and state of health is a reason against taking any more external, uncongenial labors on myself.

January 13, 1878

—Since which Dr. Andrew Clark[66] has advised Mary to go abroad for the rest of the winter. It is nothing serious and she is glad enough to go, barring some dutiful remorse at the thought of leaving me alone. It is not much disturbance to me as I have been preparing to part from her, though it is a little awkward the thing coming without notice, and with the question of our moving still undecided.[67] Mrs. Johnson[68] has been here today, a sort of farewell before she goes to Chile. I have been answering Sir E. Beckett's answer to my letter to the Times about his.[69] I had signed E. J. Simcox on purpose to get "mistered" of course with success. Reuben 1878 is written, but not well. I have decidedly grown stupid. The worst is that I don't care—about that or anything else—: it is possible to me to stay away from her; I am not actively unhappy; I laugh off my

---

she comments at length on Stephen's book and on Harrison's *Fortnightly* review of it (H, V, 421-422).

[65] John Bright (1811-1889) was a friend of the Lewess; "We read aloud Bright's 4th speech on India" (H, V, 6), and GE and GHL had dinner with him in July, 1877 at Witley (H, VI, 394).

[66] Sir Andrew Clark (1826-1893) was GE's personal physician; he diagnosed her kidney stone on February 3, 1874 (H, Biography, 477) and was present when she passed into her final unconsciousness on December 22, 1880 (H, Biography, 548).

[67] Hamilton and Company moved from 68 Dean Street to 27 Mortimer Street in 1878.

[68] Mrs. Johnson was a friend of Mary Hamilton.

[69] Sir Edmund Beckett had blamed strikes and trade unionism for the current severe trade depression. EJS replied with a defence of the workers and of the hope that lay in the international organization of labour. Beckett did refer to her as Mr. Simcox in his reply. The letters appeared in *The Times* on 8, 12, and 13, January (McK, 36-37).

mother's protestations of concern; the days kill themselves somehow. It is in cold blood and with a kind of unconcern that I despise and condemn myself.

January 16, 1878

After hesitating "to go or not to go" Monday and yesterday, a kind providence took me N. W. today. Mr. Lewes had gone to see a man with an artificial larynx[70] "could anything be more delightful?"—and she was alone. *Could* anything be more delightful? First she took me to task again about Cobbett and said she wanted me to get her another book and wouldn't tell me what unless I confessed the price of the Rural Rides. So I had to own to 10/6 and then it appeared she wanted our old friend: "The Child's Own Book."[71] That I was delightedly able to promise anyway to lend her. She said they had laughed at the fatality of my crossing with Johnny last week: I said I knew I should poison his shirts some day, and she hoped I would not, he saved them a great deal of trouble about money affairs, besides being the best of sons and brothers—I said of course, that was just why; I was jealous. Then I told her of Mary's departure, and tried to explain why I thought I might do more work in consequence. I talked of a German dictionary—she was not enthusiastic, but said Sander's German one (like Littre's)[72] would be a good foundation; but it would be useless unless one were employed by a publisher. I also mentioned as possible themes folk lore and a history of property.[73] She wanted a book made out of all the nice stories of ancient and modern history—the stories that all modern writers leave out to make room for characters &c quite as mythical as the stories and much less entertaining. She also wished I could get one of the new primers, like Macmillan's, to do. Otherwise she encouraged the folk lore—she was much interested in the subject—the history of property likewise, though with rather more latent doubt as to my making the most of it. She thought it was a failing of mine to want to make my work impracticably complete—instancing "Natural Law" as well as what I said now of the unsatisfactoriness of the folk lore investigation unless one could reach a satisfactory theory. She also urged me to

---

[70] GHL writes to Madame Bodichon on January 31, 1878, "What will science do next?" (H, VII, 13); n. 3 records that Sir James Paget and Huxley were also present; the physician who was responsible was from Glasgow. See November 28, 1878.

[71] EJS had brought GE *Rural Rides* on November 17, 1877. Haight (IX, 213, n. 2) identifies *The Child's Own Book* as the 13th edition, 1869. It is a collection of illustrated tales, published by Tegg.

[72] Emile Littre (1801-1881) published a French dictionary in 1875.

[73] EJS published her history of property as *Primitive Civilizations, or Outline of the History of Ownership in Archaic Communities*, 2 vols. (London: Swan Sonnenschein, 1894).

say and make people feel what she, as an author had a scruple about saying critically, that authorship should not be regarded in the same light as other professions, that every writer was *ipso facto*[74] a teacher,—an educational influence—on his readers—and the lightest poetaster could not escape the weight of attendant responsibility. She wished me to write because she thought the root of the matter was in me—concerning the moral relations of life—and whatever one wrote about, the work would be "informed" with one's fundamental views. She wished people would think more of the real matter of life—even the word "right" had come to have a dangerous metaphysical use—people would say you ought to do a thing, not for the real present reason, but because it is "right" to do it. I stayed nearly two hours, and talked round and round, sometimes getting out something that I wanted to say, sometimes feeling helpless, as when she laughed at me again for being like Mr. Sidgwick[75]—talking as if what "bad people" might do was out of the question; (I had said that I had hit on the rule of never doing anything I could help, that of course I didn't mean one was to do any harm, or leave undone any obvious duty); or when she said I was the most curious reasoner, for a subtle person,—that in moral matters, if anything was to be done or felt I said Oh of course but that was nothing—and so on. At one moment I felt very despairing as if I was to go away as I came only worse; then she went on speaking of our fundamental agreement and of the extent to which one's character was in one's own hands; this *á propos* of my reference to the old difficulty. I said, did she not believe that it depended on the strength of a man's own inborn inclination whether he ever did anything to count in the world; she first said I was perverting her doctrine, and then agreed to my statement of it and quoted a definition of genius "God's gift, a man's own exertion, and circumstances to suit." But she added what was true, that it is suicidal to stop one's life in the middle by the application of a formula—that might cease to apply if from then onward one gave one's mind to making the application cease. She insisted on calling the co-operative scheme "admirable" and on being glad that I had taken up some practical work besides authorship. I said after all the root of the evil was idleness. I spoke of the creeping inroads of middle-aged content—or resignation—which I refused to call a progress when the evils were unaltered, only grown tolerable by use. I said, and she agreed that it was evil when people can do no more than—as in Mary Cross's story[76]—"find life

---

[74] "by the very fact"

[75] "Henry Sidgwick in *The Methods of Ethics*, 1874, argued that egoistic hedonism determines volition, 'since to conscientious persons the pleasure in conduct is more or less dependent on its righteousness.' In 1877 he published a supplement to the first edition in which ch. 1 and the first section of ch. 2 were almost entirely rewritten, and the view on hedonism was retracted in ch. 4" (H, IX, 214, n. 3).

[76] "Mary Cross, 'Marie of Villefranche,'" *Macmillan's*, 24 (August 1871), 297-303. Heinrich, billeted in Marie's house after the German occupation, loved her,

possible and even bearable without any happiness in particular." She said no one could take a sadder view of life than she did—sometimes not on account of her own experience, that had been, but she had gone beyond it,—she lay back in her chair, and I said caressingly, it would be ungrateful if she did not like to live when she made so many people happy—I kissed her again and again and wondered meditatively how it was that one should be so glad just because somebody else was what she was. She wondered why I was so fond of her and I did not know unless it was because she was herself and not somebody else, whereto she, that was no merit of hers, and I—no I gave providence the glory. On the whole I was very happy, and came away consoled and resigned—to not being resigned just yet to final, fatal failure. She said once that I was wiser than I used to be—I talked less discontent—I hinted one might think the more. She admitted that there might be cases—though infrequently—of people to whom opportunities do not come, and said in answer to my charge that she believed in providence that she had never risked her influence more than by breaking out to a young woman who was sobbing to her—"I know it must be all for my good"— "it" being a trial proceeding from somebody's wrong doing—"Nay, but a great many things happen to people that are not at all good for them." Altogether she is a darling, and I shall proceed to write—at the office on the Utility of Competition, the Patriarch and the Chief, and send them and the Basques[77] to the 3 leading monthlies; also it has just occurred to me that if Macmillan is going to have a Mythology Primer, I could do that very well, and that I might offer Hodgson Pratt[78] a lecture—on Lakes and Parks and popular rights[79]—or anything else. Could one carry docility further?

January 20, 1878

And today though it is Sunday (I have not been since November 26) I will take "The Child's Own Book"[80] with me and just see her and make wild attempts to talk to somebody the few minutes I stay—then come back and go on, if I can with my scribbling.

---

but goes away when her husband, long thought dead, returns with one leg" (H, IX, 214, n. 4).

[77] This could be a review of Wentworth Webster (1829-1887), *Basque Legends* (London: Griffith and Farren, 1877 and 1878).

[78] Hodgson Pratt wrote pamphlets on India and served as chairman of the meetings of the Westminster Democratic Club (April 20, 1879).

[79] Bradlaugh, Besant, and the other radicals argued "away with parks and ornamental lakes." They thought land must be cultivated or it should be confiscated by the state. The Game Laws were to be repealed.

[80] GE had asked EJS to get it on January 16, 1878.

January 22, 1878

There were few visitors, so if I had not been stupidly modest I might have had "good times." Lewes was affectionate. I took her the book and talked mostly—for 20 minutes to him and W. Cross.[81] He said Herbert Spencer was preparing autobiographical materials[82]—it will be entertainingly wooden and arrogant. Yesterday got a July list of Macmillan's primers and wrote in the evening to propose one on Mythology. Civil note from Macmillan today saying some one else is going to do it. I suppose it *is* civil, though one can never feel flattered by a "declined with thanks." I had wriggled through the day in Dean Street, sorting papers and so forth till late, came on to tea about 6 and received the note at 9; whether because I wrote the offer to please her or because I was physically tired, I felt more than proportionately knocked down, though I had expected a refusal less unexceptionably outlined. Well, she cannot blame me—and unluckily abstention is always the basest task for me. I will still try to have the 3 articles rejected and then I *must* get some penny a lining to do.[83]

January 27, 1878

Today I have written to her, in lightly loving strain—after burning two sheets of more earnest matter. Read Holyoake's Co-Operation.[84] If I lived with people, and had access to all the news, concerned about the social questions that I care for, no doubt I should be drawn on to take a more active part in this discussion.

February 2, 1878

Nothing has happened since. I have reigned alone for a fortnight at the office and begin to suspect that if we are moderately busy through the season, I shall find it only too possible to keep a page of writing on hand for weeks together at the shop untouched. On the other hand when I come home at 1/2 past 6 to dinner, the evening is too long to be certainly killed over trashy library

---

[81] William (Willie) Cross (1838-1916) was the older brother of JWC.

[82] Spencer began his autobiography in May 1875 (H, VI, 310-311, n. 1). By October 1889 he had printed six copies of both volumes to share with his friends if they agreed to keep them "under lock and key." It was not published until 1904, after his death on December 8, 1903.

[83] Editorial work was "cheap" labor.

[84] George Jacob Holyoake (1817-1906), *A History of Co-Operation in England*, 2 vols. (London: Trübner, 1875-79). He was a radical journalist, editor of the first aetheist journal *The Oracle of Reason*, and a well-known Chartist and Owenite Socialist. In 1842 he served six months for blasphemy after he suggested that the Deity be put on half-pay while the people were so distressed at their taxes.

books. The alternative is some out of door nightly opiation, penny a lining that I can take up when I come home, however tired, or—which is impossible, freedom and energy of mind enough to take up original work or useful reading. By the way it is Max Müller[85] who has been "spoken to" about the mythology primer . . .

I have idled away the morning without even writing to her. It occurs to me to record that I have never met with the slightest objective encouragement in any course except that of suicide.

February 6, 1878

Yesterday I went to see her, and have been in a calm glow of happiness since:—for no special reason, only that to have been near her happens to have that effect on me. She had had headaches and was in a somewhat despondent mood, so I did nothing but make reckless love to her. I told her about the International[86] (how I withheld my name from the Council and then in remorse offered to lend Dean Street for a Council chamber!) and she seemed to think me well out of it. I brought her two of the least spoilt of my Valentines, which she humanely forbore to read in my presence. She said it was a pity my letters could not be kept some 5 centuries to show a more sober posterity what hyperbole had once been possible. I asked if she took so gloomy a view of the future as to think 5 centuries hence there would be no one as adorable as herself:—of that, said Lewes, you may be sure. I agreed and she professed to be silenced in confusion. I had told her of my ambition to be allowed to lie silently at her feet as she pursued her occupations, and that made her refer to my last letter. She also said—as she once wrote—that I "knew all the craft of fyne loving,"[87]—as she also tells her husband; he and I pelted her with a little loving chaff about her own unamiableness, and when he affected to agree with her I said it was a mean attempt to curry favour with divinity—I would be no party to such hypocrisy—unless I had as much as he to gain! I tore myself away with difficulty, choked with tears in the passages—and so came away. Today I tired myself for 5 hours putting up circulars (value 1/6!), wrote letters and saw customers; shirtmakers' committee in the evening: the half-week quickly gone!

---

[85] Frederick Max Müller (1823-1900) delivered three lectures on the Science of Language and Science of Religion and its place in general education at the Oxford Extension Meeting, 1899, and wrote *Essays on the Science of Religion* (London: Longmans Green, 1901).

[86] EJS represented the Shirt and Collar Makers at the Trade Union Congress in Glasgow in October 1875 and at Newcastle-upon-Tyne in September 1876 and was interested in the efforts to revive the International (McK, 36-51), (H, IX, 216, n. 6).

[87] Chaucer's Alceste "taught al the craft of fyn lovinge" (*Legend of Good Women*, Prologue, l. 544) (H, IX, 216, n. 8).

February 13, 1878

By Sunday was in a somewhat dismal mood and wrote—and burnt—a letter to her in that vein, and wrote another leaving out everything but love and went to bed resigned, I thought partly because I had also written some pages of the "Utility of Competition." Next day at Dean Street, I attempted to go on with the same and found my mind a blank and what I had written incoherent. In the evening read over all her letters and was desperately miserable. Next day took up the Ms again and found it less hopeless; earned 3/ in the evenings by directing envelopes! Heard from Trübner that a second edition of "Natural Law" would be wanted soon. Today wrote a little "Competition" and—just before 3—a visitor was announced!—Came forward and lo! in the middle of the room was my goddess! I threw my arms round her—she had on a spotted net veil that could have grieved me but for the angelic way in which she took it off at my prayer. A propos of the second edition we got on to high problems of ethics. I said I was in doubt whether to give any explanation about Utilitarianism; she thought the misunderstandings of reviewers hardly amounted to a presumption that one was wrong. She thought the weak point of Utilitarianism, in Sidgwick and others, lay not in their taking human welfare as the *standard* of right but in their trying to find in it the moral *motive*. We agreed I think in substance there, and they assented to my objection to Huxley's last article evening Darwin's Origin of Species[88] with Harvey's circulation of the blood.[89] I proposed to add a paragraph in the sense of what she had said to me, of the dangerousness of making "right" into a metaphysical abstraction, severed from the intuitions which constitute its nature, and said that I felt myself that that might be a snare. She was rather slow to believe that it could be a snare to me to take anything for granted, and I said she didn't know, I was always very much of my own opinion. Then (there had been some professional transactions[90] first of all) they arose to go; I should say that for the last few minutes I had been kneeling by her, looking up into her face with my cheek resting against a bit of fur round her wrist,—we went down stairs and at the door Maria was admitting a man, he advanced to the foot of the stairs and lo! The Rector of Lincoln[91]—tableau! They turned back and there was more

---

[88] Charles Darwin (1809-1882), *The Origin of Species* (London: J. Murray, 1859).

[89] For the tercentenary of William Harvey's birth, Thomas Henry Huxley (1825-1895) gave a lecture at the Royal Institution, January 25, 1878, published in the *Fortnightly*, 23 (February 1878): 167-190. He comments on the fact that Darwin's concept of evolution was generally accepted within two decades while it took much longer for Harvey's discovery to be accepted (H, IX, 217, n. 1).

[90] GE had come to order cuffs (H, IX, 217, n. 2).

[91] Mark Pattison (1813-1884) (H, 217, IX, n. 3), see January 7, 1878.

conversation, concerning Jevons on Mill[92] and the rising school in Oxford which follows Green[93] and Caird[94] to think English philosophy nowhere, Kant and Hegel on the right track, but they themselves in some unexplained way, many leagues in advance even of them—She thought there was a dangerous tendency among second and third rate thinkers to go on inventing something that shall catch disciples without any strong preliminary conviction. She instanced Schopenhauer[95] and a man for whom she had a great respect—I guessed Herbert Spencer. The Rector thought professional jealousies were not offically to blame for this, but quoted Pusey[96] on the other side. Then they really went, but I got yet another kiss and am considerably consoled.

February 16, 1878
    For as long as it lasts.

February 26, 1878
    Unluckily one is a miserable sinner and it does not last long. When the last entry was made I had been working over "Natural Law" and was rather disgusted with it—at least it failed to interest me and I seemed to understand that she could not care for it. On the next Tuesday I went to the Priory to take her the cuffs she had ordered at the office and to tell her I didn't want to have a second edition. However he had a headache and she, I thought was tired with her drive,

---

[92] William Stanley Jevons (1835-1882) published in the *Contemporary Review* for December 1877 the first of three attacks entitled "John Stuart Mill's Philosophy Tested." Robertson replied in *Mind*, 3 (January 1878): 141-144 (H, IX, 211, n. 4).

[93] Thomas Hill Green (1836-1882), Fellow of Balliol College and Professor of Moral Philosopher at Oxford (H, IX, 227, n. 8), is mentioned in a letter from Benjamin Jowett to GE on May 7, 1878, who says he "can never go along with" his friend Professor Green and others in "attempting to bring back the antiquated philosophies of Germany. But about human motive there is a great deal which might be taught mankind and has never been taught them, to their great loss. It is the natural way of supplying the religious want which is so deeply felt just now" (H, IX, 227).

[94] Edward Caird (1835-1908) was a student of Jowett, became a fellow of Merton College, was a professor of moral philosophy at Glasgow, and then succeeded Jowett as master of Balliol in 1893.

[95] Arthur Schopenhauer (1788-1860) was a German philosopher who was frequently alluded to by nineteenth century British writers.

[96] Edward Bouverie Pusey (1800-1882) was, along with John Keble and John Henry Newman, a leader of the Oxford movement within the Anglican church.

so I said nothing. I forget what we spoke of, besides the Rector of Lincoln and Pierre Leroux[97]—they were gratified at my remembering his "Il ne s'agit que d'y arriver"[98] (quoted by Lewes who forgot having done so). Stayed only a short time—returned to the shop and tailoresses. Two days after saw Trübner, and felt it would not be possible to withdraw the book as it was in his series. He rather wanted me to translate Hartmann,[99] talked about £100, half on delivery. After leaving her on the Tuesday I wrote something to say I was idle and my shirtmaking was only a kind of suicide; on Wednesday, when I came in at night, there was a note from her—inviting me to write and to make use of her while she is alive—. Strange to say I was in no hurry to profit by this permission. I did not want to vex or estrange her again and yet all the "internal discords" were from feelings that I could not bring into harmony with her spoken counsels. I knew not whether to write or not—I wrote 3 letters in succession and burnt them all, and then in a kind of despair, wrote on Saturday afternoon from the shop—a letter no more to my mind than its predecessors. But I posted it in a kind of despair of being able to say what I wanted. Since then I have half-repented and half been glad that I had got rid of the ungracious complaints. Sunday I revised Natural Law and wrote about shirts for the Co-Operative Congress.

March 3, 1878
On that day wrote again—half-explaining half-apologizing for what I had written and not written.

March 17, 1878
On the 11th—after 3 weeks all but a day, ventured again. She had been poorly, with a cold "thought I was never coming again." She was alone when I got there, but all is gone from me of what passed except that I found myself being scolded by both of them at once for unresponsive, cold and apparently supercilious manners.—Oh yes! ~~Lewes~~ I asked about the Lifted Veil.[100] Lewes

---

[97] Pierre Leroux (1797-1871) had been one of the visitors at 142 Strand; GE "had long conversations in which he expounded his unique plan for a new society uniting 'the love of self with the love of one's neighbour'" (H, Biography, 99).

[98] "the only thing is to succeed" (Success is the only option.)

[99] Eduard von Hartmann (1842-1906) *Philosophie des Unbewaßten* (Berlin: C. Duncker, Verlag, 1873); *Philosophy of the Unconscious*, (London: Trübner, trans. William Chatterton Coupland, 1884).

[100] "The Lifted Veil" is a short story by GE. It appeared in *Blackwood's* 86 (July 1859): 24-48. It was chosen by Sandra M. Gilbert and Susan Gubar for *The Norton Anthology of Literature by Women* (New York: W. W. Norton, 1985) and has received considerable attention from feminist critics.

said it came out in Blackwood without name soon after Adam Bede.[101] He asked what I thought of it. I was embarrassed and said—as he did—that it was not at all like her other writings, wherefrom she differed; she said it was "schauderhaft"[102] wasn't it and I yes; but I was put out by things that I didn't quite know what to do with—it was a shame to give such things a moral, but—: He Oh, but the moral is plain enough—it is only an exaggeration of what happens—the one-sided knowing of things in relation to the self—not whole knowledge because "tout comprehendre est tout pardonner."[103] She said he wasn't in the habit of asking people before her what they thought of her books—which was rather hard on the people—I it was at least unneccessary then since she must know. She said she did not at all, and she had never felt with me as she had with many people what it was in her books that worked on me; she had never felt that I had been influenced either by what she wrote or what she said. I looked protests and then they both went on. Lewes said that it was months before I so much as looked at, let alone spoke to him: his amour propre[104] was not hurt, but he observed it. She said—if he was not sensitive in that way, she was. I hardly said anything in self-defence. I quoted George Sand "On n'aime pas ceux qui ne s'aiment pas eux—mêmes et qui par consequent ne tâchent pas de plaire."[105] She said but I had wanted to please her—and the sentence finished itself "and you see you did not succeed"—in the same breath she said—"I don't mean that"—But it was something to know that all my tears and agony had not been for nothing. I was as miserable as ever I had believed.

March 18, 1878

I went today again as I had meant—All the more tho' for a letter that came this morning—she had been cheered by a letter I wrote last Thursday (about the effect of her books on me) after an abortive attempt to see her, baffled by the sight of a pony carriage at the door. Today Lewes was unhappy about a friend, a self-taught correspondent for whom he had got a clerk-ship, who is threatened with blindness.[106] I stayed a long hour, yet have not much to record. I got out most of what I meant to say about my general social demeanour. Lewes laid it down as a principle that a man would much rather forgive you for boring him

---

[101] *Adam Bede* (1859)

[102] "horrible"

[103] "to understand all is to forgive all"

[104] "self-esteem"

[105] "If one does not love others, he does not love himself and consequently does not try to please."

[106] Robert Ripley (H, IX, 221, n. 5)

than for letting him imagine he bored you. He said he was not speaking for himself, for there was nothing he was so impatient of as being bored. When reviewers were spoken of I said I hoped they sometimes spoke the truth by mistake and quoted the Athenaeum;[107] she seemed interested but surprised and said "No doubt he had a nasty meaning"—which Lewes said was hard on both him and me. She is a darling. I told her I was going to do Hartmann and she wanted me to make notes of my dissent as I went along and publish an independent criticism. Lewes would not hear of the idea of a dissident preface. She is a darling—I feel as if I was going to be good for a long time on end.

March 26, 1878

She said, when I referred to my former desperate attempts at sociability, that she thought I had sufficient relations with people through "the business" and that I need not trouble myself about "society." She added "Elma[108] is coming to live at Putney and you must be kind to her." I hesitated a little and confessed I did not know whether she had dropped the correspondence. In the evening under the influence of the beloved, I wrote her a few lines of affectionate apology for all my sins known and unknown, and yesterday had a short grateful answer from the midst of thorns—i.e. pains.

April 1, 1878

Last Wednesday I went again; stayed only a few minutes as she was reading the Ms of his book,[109] but I got a kiss or two, and the chance of bemoaning myself at the coming summer; I said I wished her house[110] ready

---

[107] "Reviewing *Natural Law* in the *Athenaeum*, 13 October 1877, pp. 460-461, (Henderson) wrote: 'The author, however, to whom we should say Miss Simcox has been most deeply indebted, and from whom she has learned most, is George Eliot. There is the same stoicism, tinged occasionally by the same hues of tragic sadness, which are prominent in our greatest living novelist.' GE is mentioned only once in the book with three lines quoted from 'Armgart' (p. 138). GHL is also referred to: 'And just as we find Mr. Lewes speaking of the world and the system of things which constitutes what we call reality as being still the same, though all our theories about them are nought, so is Miss Simcox contented to accept things as they are . . . '" (H, IX, 221, n. 6).

[108] Elma Stuart met GE October 3, 1873, at Blackbrook near Bickley, Kent; she had sent GE a bookslide which she carved for her in January, 1872. She considered herself to be GE's "spiritual daughter," called her Mother, and is buried next to her in Highgate Cemetery (H, Biography, 451-52, 467).

[109] *Problems of Life and Mind* (London: Trübner, 1879) (H, IX, 223, n. 1).

[110] The Heights, Witley, was the country retreat of GE and GHL. JWC located it for GE to buy in November 1875.

betimes and so on for her sake but *not* for my own. She said she liked people to be a little unhappy when she went—did not care for a too disinterested affection. I had a commission which will give me an excuse for going again this week, and today I have written to her—what I hope will not be displeasing—oh! I love her dearly dearly. Today—or rather tonight—have been promoting the formation of a Co-Operative Store for the women. My own sweet darling! I wonder whether I have ever passed a whole month before without mental caviling? I am quite content now—all that has been said was well said. I am unspeakably thankful for her love, my own, my beautiful darling!

April 6, 1878

Last Wednesday, though I had done my best to hurry them, her things were not ready for me to take, so I resigned myself to waiting till Monday. Yesterday I had a few lines bidding me come on Wednesday at 3:30 for an hour to "hear and say more that can be written."—I am anxious and yet content, I feel that nothing that she can say will fail to touch me. There was no effort in the submissiveness with which I have written of late—and oh! how sweet to sit by her alone, to be folded in her arms—to say a little of the gratitude one has only written. My darling, my darling!—But alas, there are still 4 times 24 hours first.

April 14, 1878

The hours crept more and more slowly till at last it was Wednesday. To help to kill the time I had come home to dinner, but started early again in order to call at a shop in the Edgware road—which failed to find. Arrived to the moment. Began with little talk about cuffs and handkerchiefs. Elizabeth[111] brought tea. Presently she said: she knew so well the state of mind in which I had written, when there seemed no inducements to choose one kind of work rather than another. She had nothing to suggest as to ways of determining oneself, only thought it a pity to feel bound to produce; I tried to explain that production—or the inclination thereto—came of itself if I took up any subject—but I was blankly idle now. She could not understand the want of natural interest without ulterior purpose, but said Mr. Lewes also, unlike her, only cared for lines of enquiry etc. in view of a particular end, she sometimes wished he had more hobbies.—Could I not take up a language or a science? I had referred to an old taste for teaching, she thought it was a pity I should not have pupils. She said once, more as an assertion than a question that I was sincere in wishing to do and would take any opportunity that came even if it was rather hard. She called the shirtmaking an excellent bit of work, only had hoped that the idea might have spread more rapidly. Mr. Lewes was dining out and I prayed to be allowed to stay without talking till he came in. She said she couldn't read with me there. I complained a little at such evidence that one did not belong to her and she spoke of her complete dependence on his society and unreasonable anxiety when he was away. This was all on the 10th.

---

[111] GE's maid

May 26, 1878

On Easter Sunday (April 21) went to Manchester.—This is *not* the autobiography of a shirtmaker but a love so I need not speak of the Co-Operative Congress. I feel as if I had "lost a month" because I cannot from memory recal which day it was (Monday 29th) after my return that I started to go there: ("there" is always one place as "she" is always one person). At the West of Dean Street I met the carriage and caught Lewes's eye; they were just going to the shop with shirts of his. I kissed her glove on the street and betrayed that I was going to them. Lewes asked me to come with them to a furniture shop, she negatived· it would be too tiring and ran over the coming evenings; something was due for each so I was to go at my leisure and wait for them.

June 2, 1878

So I went back to the shop with Lewes's parcel, then up Baker Street to Watts' to order a dress for a customer and still arrived before them. She was tired and I did not stay long. Spoke briefly of the Congress,—as less practical and real than the Trade Congress. Heard their plans and left—with a melancholy sense of impending farewell—last May I had hardly seen her at all. Wrote self-denyingly to say all that on Saturday. Still self-denyingly sent the parcel of mended shirts by a girl. On the next Tuesday (14th) he was ushered upstairs bringing another parcel, and when I heard she was in the carriage I rushed down rather uncivilly; stood on the pavement kissing her hand and was made happy by being asked to get her patterns of soft slim silk for summer wear. Wrote next day to send items and called on Friday for the answer, which got both on paper and by word of mouth. Again did not stay long, got leave to send a cream white silk nightgown to let her see if she could wear a morning dress of the same. On Monday next (20th) Mary came back from Egypt and just as she was leaving with her mother, the carriage drove up. I was in the doorway with Mrs. Hamilton and their cab had just drawn up so that the Lewes's carriage stopped further down the street. I rushed down the muddy pavement to greet them and then beckoned *Mary*, who was kindly welcomed—then Mrs. Hamilton came and begged to introduce herself. Then they (the Lewess) drove off. We spoke for a few moments about silks, then the vision was lost. On Friday I went with fresh patterns of silk; Johnny was there and she—asked me to come some other day, Sunday or Monday or Tuesday. Returning home through Kensington Gardens, if the truth must be told I sat down under a spreading tree and cried. By the next day I was ashamed and on Sunday, rather than write to her, I resolved to go.— Arrived just after 5, found Miss Helps[112] and a lady, Lord Acton,[113] (I think)

---

[112] Alice Helps was one of GE's "spiritual daughters"; she was the daughter of GHL's old friend Sir Arthur Helps (1813-1875) (H, Biography, 452). She visited GE the widow at the Heights, as EJS did not (H, Biography, 505), and she put her arm in EJS's at GE's funeral. See December 29, 1880.

[113] John Dalberg-Acton, 1st Baron (1834-1902), was a long-time friend of GE and wrote "George Eliot's Life," *Nineteenth Century* 17 (March 1885): 464-485.

Pauli the historian, another German,[114] Mark Pattison,—later Kegan Paul[115] and his wife. Talk was of Shakespeare's generic superiority to other dramatists. After the first set had left (I was going but she bade me stay) talk was of translations, ignorance in print and the unprincipledness of even good people like Mrs. Oliphant[116] who write of that whereof they know nothing. I asked Lewes if the poem announced in Macmillan was the "Symposium"[117] as I supposed and he said yes. I am keeping back the sheets of Natural Law so as to get a motto therein. A note concerning silks was posted on Sunday, which got at the shop on the 28th. I in answering half-apologized for my appearance on Sunday—a living refutation of the charge of misanthropy she brought in Johnny's presence. On Wednesday was in doubt whether to take or send another variety of silk—at last resolved to take it and leave the parcel at the door if need were. The servant made me come in; she was very tired, but as I kissed her, her cheek pressed caressingly against mine. She threw the folds of the silk round Lewes to see the effect in a mass, and as her hand passed near him, he seized it, even as I do, and left a kiss thereon; one of the things for which I am thankful through every jealous pain is the perfectness of the love binding those two together. For myself, the last six months have been purely wasted; I am thinking seriously at the end of the three years of turning over the shop to the work people, and trying again to live the life of a rational being. One day when I went to the Priory, she said I was looking thin—I mustn't vanish away because I was useful when I got patterns of silk: In my secret heart I was a little pleased, because my face is growing very old and worn, and I might not have liked for strangers to notice the

---

[114] The lady was Henrietta Rintoul and the other German her friend Paul Friedmann (H, IX, 228, n. 9).

[115] Charles Kegan Paul (1828-1902) was an Oxford graduate, who after some years as a chaplain at Eton and a co-worker with F. D. Maurice (1805-1872) in London, left the church altogether to become a publisher (H, Biography, 407).

[116] Margaret Oliphant (1828-1897) was a novelist, biographer, historical writer, and critic. She published almost 100 novels, and although she was not an overt supporter of female equality, her novels shrewdly record the stresses and compromises of women's lives. She also wrote stories and over 200 articles for magazines such as *Blackwood's* and *The Cornhill.* She edited the prestigious Blackwoods Foreign Classics series (*The Feminist Companion to Literature in English*, 812-813).

[117] This was published as "The College Breakfast-Party," *Macmillan's* 38 (July 1878): 161-179. Frederic Chapman came May 10 and offered £250 for permission to print the poem. GHL told him that "Macmillan must have the first refusal." Lewes adds "He lunched with us. Then went to Macmillan, who is 'to consider,' and wrote the next day 'to accept with delight'" (GHL Diary) (H, IX, 228, n. 1).

fact if she did not care to see it. I am habitually tired. The one thing I want to know is whether she would think me wrong for trying not to care.—This is elliptical—I mean I am tired into a dull despondency—is it lawful not to care that "all one's life seemed meant for fails."[118] I shall I suppose see her once more before she goes and then the long *blank*! "Oh my love! My love!"

June 16, 1878

I told her (on the 29th) that my idea of happiness was to buy her slop-pails for her—whereto she—"They are all bought now"—I wrote in sending the desired bill for the silks,[119] that that completed the definition in a tragic fashion, and rashly committed myself by a promise to leave her alone for a space. The next week I took holiday from the shop and for the last fortnight have been trying the experiment of living like other people—gardening, visiting, shopping, reading, sewing, carpentering and so on: I have not minded it for a change—but the fortnight has not been short. Last Sunday—only 10 long days after my rash promise, I wrote to her again—partly about Daniel Deronda that I had read through in the first days of my holiday. After luncheon on Wednesday I went to take some syringa, not knowing whether she would be back from Oxford. They were out driving. Last night came one of those sweet envelopes—bidding me come tomorrow for the dreaded farewell: after which life becomes a blank for alas! nearly 5 months.

June 22, 1878

I went on Monday "towards 6 o'clock." She was alone and very beautiful. The travelling book case was in the hall and general signs of discomfort; they were going down on Wednesday. Elizabeth is going to be married. I just remember exchanging a few words about these things and then—I cannot in the very least recal the transition, she said it was a shame to find fault with me the last day but she wanted to give me a parting exhortation.—The old story: she said I was uncivil to Johnny the other day—my unlucky "only Mr. Cross" I suppose; that my manner really was supercilious and indifferent, that she herself even now had a difficulty sometimes in realizing that I was not feeling superciliously toward her. She said perhaps one reason was that I "did not like men"—against which I protested as usual—perhaps as usual in vain, and then by way of diversion I related my last attempts at sociability. At half past six Lewes came in and asked me if I had prayed for him for his goodness in staying away:— as usual I was unready with the answer. Then I had to go; they left the room with me. She said to him she had been finding fault with me—I think, but am not sure, adding it was good if I did not mind, anyway adding that she did not like people to find fault with her.

---

[118] Line quoted in first entry of *Autobiography*: see May 10, 1876.

[119] GHL's account for June shows Hamilton and Company: £6.12.6 (H, IX, 232, n. 2).

June 23, 1878

Last night I wrote to her, in the mood which has been almost uninterrupted since—of frank penitence for every unintentional offense and willing determination to amend all that one can. My own darling—I do love her more and better every day and week and year.

. . . . Have read all her letters through once more: and—with shame mastered by delight—I see now that I have been always unreasonable, peevish and exacting and she all generous forbearance and tenderness. I am so glad. It is an absurd thing to say; but now that I see I have been wrong—am I not right for the first time at last! It is impossible that I should ever again have a rebellious feeling toward her—all my longing is to let her see the fruit of her hands and be content. My own darling! I feel as if I couldn't have been always quite horrid, or she would never have put up with anything so horrid as I was sometimes. She *is* a darling.

June 30, 1878

As I have written again today to tell her—having kept pretty straight in the interval by means of Hartmann to translate, short attendances at the shop, people to dinner and decent Mudie books to read. On Friday I secured the new Macmillan, and today let the printer have the proofs he has been waiting for so long. There were 3 or 4 mottoes I might have taken: I did not take the one that I had been waiting for:—after the lapse of years it struck me as too desponding.

July 6, 1878

Last week has been tolerably representative of the way in which the summer will spend itself. Every day I have got up at 6 or soon after, translated two or three pages of Hartmann before breakfast: Monday went to the shop, left a little after 5 with my mother, asked Mr. Headlam to dine next day, stayed at home, translated little in the morning; afternoon muddled over the shirtmakers' accounts, evening with Mr. Headlam to their meeting: scanty attendance; a member proposed a vote of thanks (which I was pleased to think sincere) for my services as Secretary; Mr. Paterson[120] enforced the same and I returned thanks—with real feeling. Wednesday, at home, not too industrious over translations: Thursday ditto, but less idle. Mary and Miss Othé[121] to dinner. Read in evenings &c Hüffer's Troubadors[122]and a volume of Landor's Conversations.[123] Friday to

---

[120] Emma Paterson's husband was Secretary of the Working Men's Club and Institute Union and supported the trade union movement.

[121] Miss Othé is mentioned frequently with Mary Hamilton.

[122] *The Troubadours: their Loves and their Lyrics. With Remarks on their Influence, Social and Literary* by John Rutherford (London: Smith, Elder, 1873) had been reviewed by EJS in the *Fortnightly*, 78 (1873): 141-142.

the shop—but little Hartmann. Today ditto, ditto, only when I came in at 3 had a bath and read Cornhill, then wrote to her before dinner, that tomorrow may be quite clear for translating. Am perfectly at peace in my mind as regards her: but a mood, no doubt physically conditioned, which is upon me now conduces to waste of time. Wrote the other day to Mrs. Menzies[124] to ask after Elma. Appleton[125] has sent a confidential circular to supporters about the Academy—proposing to double the price and halve the pay. Of course if either or both of these are done its days are numbered—I wonder whether anything that happens will be likely to make any opening for my "Iago" plan.[126]

July 14, 1878

Today have written but think I will not post the letter; the week has gone in much the same fashion as last. Yesterday I half-suspected in myself a rudimentary tendency toward trite reflections—I was unhappy because she had never been to see me here—and so forth, but it is possible (now) to turn from these distressing thoughts. Nothing is changed, and I do not see why I should pass from pain to gladness when all of the causes of pain are unchanged, but if one ceases to look for gladness or to complain of pain, there is rest once more within the soul.

July 16, 1878

I had thought myself so good, and reasonable and patient—content to write to her and expecting nothing in return: and so today when I catch myself with the first real heart ache, the blank sense of longing and unsatisfied hunger,—I find all at once—that the ages of deprivation have lasted—a bare month. So I will force myself—hardly to think of her less, but to suppress all the letters that begin to compose themselves in my mind the moment the last one is posted—say for a fortnight, for three weeks if I could, but I doubt it. I first make a note of why her hopeful suggestions give me such pain,—if she can only make the present bearable by the prospect of a future that will never be, that is a confession that the present is unbearable—not a help to bearing it. I am not going to dwell on these things, but the history of the years that I have known her might be told in two words—Love and Pain—endless, intense. Now I will do Hartmann.

---

[123] Walter Savage Landor (1775-1864), *Imaginary Conversations of Literary Men and Statesmen* (London: Taylor and Hessy, 1824-28).

[124] Catharine Tharlow Fraser Menzies was a friend of Elma Stuart (1837-1903).

[125] Charles Edward Appleton (1841-1879) founded the *Academy* in 1869; EJS was a regular contributor from the first issue.

[126] EJS's Iago plan is mentioned several times, but apparently she never published it.

July 21, 1878

—And the endless intense joy that comes from the love, that is akin to pain. On Tuesday I saw Trübner who asked if I had heard of the Lewess lately—which I, not since they left town—I was leaving, but compelled myself to ask had he! and heard that Mr. Lewes has written 10 days before when they were well and enjoying the country:—in the strength of which news I have felt better. Though I must promise for the rest of the summer to be able to do more than force my mind away from triste subjects of reflection when they occur. I am not writing to her today.

July 28, 1878

Today I have written—only love, an unexpressed interlude of tears, and then—of its own accord, a formal profession that "I am content because of her love." Of course I am always liable to wish, painfully, that I were nearer to her, or had been able to come so, but the dominant feeling is gratitude for her goodness and content in my own utter devotion. Last Tuesday Trübner wrote to ask me to push Hartmann on one side till he had heard from the author, was inclined to feel put out, as I had been depending on the very mechanical occupation it gave to every spare moment; however, I remembered that it had put the Greek grammar out of the way, which was as good a morning mouthful while any whole days I have to spare may be spent in writing wholesome moralities for the *Co-Operative News*. Trübner also forwarded a review of "Natural Law" by the "one American admirer" Mr. Lewes promised me;—a Unitarian minister, Gilman by name;—I was pleased till I saw the letter to Trübner, which was very American. Altogether I felt like a public character this week, as somebody else wrote to Trübner to ask for biographical information not to be found in "men of mark" and Lord Houghton[127] invited me to an "at Home"—to which I am happy to say I did not go. The end of the week I was at the shop and had the Artizan reports of the Paris /67 exhibition to read, so have not done much work else, also the hot weather, combined with much Hartmann had rather tired me. I am wishing seriously to free myself from the shop at Xmas. I find I cannot get started into real original work again with that uncertain demand on me to idle many days away waiting for customers in Dean Street. I can't do anything more there, and the degree of success which—to my complete surprise—the book has met with, encourages me to think that I shall do most by following my own bent, which is now towards a "History of Appropriation," or of "La Propriété"—which might be of any size and later in anything I wanted to say about anything. It is a subject that has not inexhaustable ramifications, so that my passion for an exhaustive beginning might have a chance, and when one was well into subject, one would have no inducement to get out, because each step would repay thorough investigation. My ambition would be satisfied by a place in libraries

---

[127] Richard Monckton Milnes Houghton (1809-1885), 1st Baron, was a frequent social companion of GE and GHL.

with Hobbes,[128] Gibbon[129] and Adam Smith[130]—It is *not* satisfied with a place by Lubbock,[131] Tylor,[132] or Sidgwick.

August 9, 1878
 The letter last referred to crossed one of hers asking for news of Elma, which I got on the Monday morning. Of course, wrote at once—trying in vain to write briefly. Last Saturday went down to Wimbledon, at Mr. Lawrence's[133] respected request, drove in Richmond Park in the evening, next day to Harrow, to lunch with his sister, Mrs. Hart; back by train to Grosvenor gallery: remarkable that the women thought nothing that was there odd—not even Whistler.[134] On Monday wrote to her to say I had still no news of Elma—On Wednesday morning, a letter with a familiar scrawl thrilled me. It was from him; I go there at last I may say tomorrow! I am more than commonly rejoiced. It does one good to be happy before one has quite worn out one's powers that way by privation.

---

[128] Thomas Hobbes (1588-1679), social philosopher, wrote *Leviathan* (London: Andrew Crooke, 1651).

[129] Edward Gibbon (1737-1794), historian and philosopher, wrote *The History of the Decline and Fall of the Roman Empire* (London: W. Strahan and T. Cadell, 1776-1788).

[130] Adam Smith (1723-1790), political economist, wrote *The Wealth of Nations* (London: J. M. Dent, 1776).

[131] Sir John Lubbock (1834-1913), 1st Baron Avebury, wrote *Pre-Historic Times* (London: Williams and Norgate, 1865) and *The Origin of Civilisation and the Primitive Condition of Man* (London: Longmans, Green, 1870).

[132] Edward Burnett Tylor (1832-1917) wrote *Researches into the Early History of Mankind and the Development of Civilisation* (London: J. Murray, 1865) and *Primitive Culture: Researches into the Development of Mythology, Philosophy Religion, Language, Art, and Custom*, 2 vols. (London: J. Murray, 1871).

[133] The Lawrences are friends or members of the Simcox family. See September 6, 1879.

[134] James Abbott McNeill Whistler (1834-1903) was an American painter and etcher who was well known in Victorian England; John Ruskin (1819-1900) had harshly criticized his contributions to the Grosvenor Gallery exhibition of 1877.

August 11, 1878

    —A wet morning; took Beccaria "Des délits et des peines"[135] to read in the train—which was moderately punctual at first. I knew the line as far as Woking, it seemed long between that and Guildford; then by some mental confusion I began to expect Witley as the next station—we reached that at last and lo! it was Godalming—a very pretty place, pine woods beyond, a pretty line but the very longest 4 1/2 miles I ever went by rail. Witley at last! I have hardly time to look and leap out when I see Mr. Lewes, dear fellow, they have sent the carriage; as we drive round to the house he tells me I am their first visitor; and they have heard from Elma. The only drawback is that he is unwell; his face made me rather unhappy by the look of ill-health without a shade of ill-temper which beautifies it in a melancholy kind of way. I flew across the drawing room into her arms; then Elizabeth's successor took me upstairs to take off my things and then we sat in the drawing room till luncheon. She read me part of Elma's letter and said—which I was heartily delighted to hear—that on some old man's death she would have £20,000. They scolded me for bringing rain, and I said there could not be two suns in one firmament; he said that was his name for her, and began seriously enumerating the points of resemblance; but he identifies the two and calls the sun "Polly"—which was an ingenious way of meeting any metaphysical difficulty of two suns at once for him. After luncheon we walked round the garden, which is quite perfect, then drove round and about between fir woods and healthy commons and shady lanes with quaint tiled cottages, and I thought the country too was very worthy of its happiness in harbouring her. She told me about Browning and his wife's Portuguese sonnets,[136] and she said once more that she wished my letters could be printed in the same veiled way—"the Newest Heloise."[137] After dinner I talked about retiring from the shirts and she was strongly against complete retirement and the loss of such humanizing influence as we might be supposed to exercise, but agreed that such supervision as one could exercise by coming in once a week was enough. I was particularly touched by the little commonplaces of hospitality, coming from them,—when I was going she came up with me to the bedroom, and he insisted on walking with me to the station, and in driving, though with much remonstrance I was allowed to sit opposite them at starting, he made me change afterwards that I might see

---

[135] Cesare Bonesano, Marchese di Beccaria (1735-94) published *Dei Delitti e delle pene*, his famous essay on crimes and punishments, in 1764. EJS was reading a French translation by Faustin Helie (Paris: Guillaumin, 1856) (H, IX, 235, n. 6).

[136] Elizabeth Barrett Browning (1806-1861), *Sonnets from the Portuguese* included in *Poems* (London: F. Warne, 1850).

[137] Pierre Abelard (1079-1142) was a French philosopher and teacher whose letters to Heloise are preserved as a tribute to their love.

the view better. The return journey was as marvellously short as the outward one was long. I thought of her and the happy hours all the way,—and laughed at myself for the thousand sensible things I had meant to say not one of which I had remembered. I am quite happy about her, contented to live, to strive, and if one's ambitions are to fail, still to strive for duty rather than success, to aim at the good—and not be selfishly pained when one does not reach up—Only, for her sake, I should like to do somewhat that she might be glad to have inspired.

August 18, 1878

Since yesterday morning when I found a letter from Elma at Dean Street I have done little but read it, and cry over it and over the recollection of it, and write my admiration to her, and forward the letter itself to our lady. I showed it to my mother, who read it twice; the first time saying only—"it is a very nice letter." The second time only speaking of the will;—the feeling of the letter was clearly a thing to be as little spoken of as religion—afterward she said "She is very much to be admired." It was a great pleasure to me to be able to admire her as intensely and unreservedly as even she could wish. Du reste[138]—let that bide.

August 20, 1878

Yesterday Appleton said to Augustus—So I was translating Hartmann?—Instantaneously and with a feeling of relief I saw that in this case I will not translate it. I only consented if it were anonymous,—if it cannot be so, and perhaps I was impractical in supposing it could.—Then decidedly I won't. As I said to Augustus when he could not see why I objected—one may sell one's conscience for £100, but not one's character.—And even the money is less temptation with the winter date at which one has a chance of receiving it. On the whole I feel it a deliverance on the eve of one's 34th—or rather 35th—birthday, one may say one has no time to waste, and this would be wasted: it would be an excuse for putting off for 6 months the real work I want to begin. It is nonsense waiting for encouragement, or supposing that the thing which comes is the thing good to receive. My fault has been too little energy rather than too much self-will; or rather, since I really *can't* take up heartily and efficiently the uncongenial task; I ought not to let it block the way to what I really could do.

Since the interruption of the translation I have gone on with Greek rudiments—and for longer than I have ever done before, and though I give up "paradigms" in despair, I am now reading the Symposium[139] with moderate success,—taking out every other word and referring to Jowett[140] (who is conveniently paraphrastic) whenever I can't see the drift of a sentence. If I go on

---

[138]   "furthermore" or "moreover"

[139]   Plato (c.428-c.348 B.C.), dialogues on love

[140]   Benjamin Jowett (1817-1893) was Regius Professor of Greek at Balliol College; his translation of Plato (1871) was a standard work.

with this for three months, I shall see daylight. I mean to do this, both because I must be able to use Greek quotations at first hand for the book that is planning itself, and because it is something tangible to go on with, as a help to restoring the habit of work. I am a good deal happier since I have felt able to give up the translation, and have visions of divisions and topics in a quite wholesome manner. As I have only just begun to think about the matter really, I may as well write down the first notions that occur. To begin: should like an introduction on the psychological base of acquisitiveness. Then, I think, a general survey of the different kinds of property, which might be written after the work for one volume was finished. Thus much of introductory generalization would be wanted to give the key to the spirit of the narrative, and to give a meaning to the bold un-ethical details. Then one would begin with savage appropriation and go over the ground of the abortive "Natural History," from savagery, pastoral tribes up to "primitive property"—so called, of the communal type, where one is on beaten ground. The original thing would be to include the really primitive and the archaic-civilized states in one treatment. I see room for a digression on mythological thieving.

August 25, 1878

On Wednesday had a note from Lewes, returning Elma's letter and telling one of "la pluie et beau temps."[141] I wrote to her this morning and have just been looking at some of her letters since—enough to make me feel that I had not written half-lovingly enough. She was wonderfully good to me!—and I am thoroughly happy and contented now because of it. I am thinking about the "History of Appropriation" though I shan't begin to do much till October, as I go to Bristol on the 9th and the week after take Miss Mitchener's[142] place in "the room." I think it is a good subject, and am pleased because I can speak of it with some approach to enthusiasm to her.

August 30, 1878

Discovered yesterday that it was 4 years today since Elma came to see me here for the first time. Read over all her early letters, and thought myself rather a monster—for though I did try hard to be kind and loving there wasn't much to show after all the efforts. Have written her a volume and told her—as I caught myself saying the other day to myself—(with perfect contentment and no recollection of the extreme unlikeness of this sentiment to the former me), that I was happy in having discovered that my mission was not to be loved, but to love.—And not a bad mission it is. For the last few days I have been idle—i.e. not read much Plato (the Symposium) but time is not wasted that goes in dwelling on the thought of love.

---

[141] "the rain and the fair weather" (to chat of this and that)

[142] The forewoman at Hamilton and Company, see September 24, 1878.

September 3, 1878

The idleness continued, but I have read Romola[143] through—and been angry with myself for the slow growth which prevented my being moved by that as I was later by Middlemarch.[144] On Sunday I wrote for a change a volume to Mr. Lewes, but my letters are getting tiresome, and must stop or slacken shortly. I wonder whether my brain is quite spoilt yet—I am always tired and dull.

September 6, 1878

Four whole weeks today since I saw her,—they have been much shorter than the others and I record with amazement that I have not cried for her once! This sentence in Romola delighted me much. "Unscrupulousness gets rid of much, but not of tooth-ache, or wounded vanity or the sense of loneliness, against which, as the world at present stands, there is no security but a thoroughly healthy jaw, and a just, loving soul."—'Tis not much use trying to write, that dash stands for an hour of happy loving meditation. It is marvelous the revolution that has affected itself—as it seems to me, at last and forever; it is deliverance—to feel that one asks nothing—only to feel tenderly towards all men, whether they accept the affection or not, and anyway to be *ready*—always eagerly ready to give out whenever one may. This is her doing and truly it is marvellous in our eyes. By the way I think I have made my peace with Mr. Lewes. I did not guess 5 years ago that it would add to my happiness that he should sign himself "your loving."

September 16, 1878

All last week was at Bristol for the Trades Congress; the Sunday before was alone here and spent absolutely the whole day in writing lovingly to her. Yesterday was similarly alone and wrote at length about a strike we had brought to an end and the divisions of our brothers at Clevedon. Have told the same story more or less briefly to so many people that I don't feel equal to writing it here.

September 17, 1878

"Was never true love loved in vain, For truest love is highest gain" —I have begun to say my prayers again. I think it is rather heathenish to throw oneself on the bed at night, to tumble into the world in the morning without a form in which to render homage to the higher, holier spiritual powers of life. What is the use of an ingenious turn if one cannot invent tricks for charming one's own evil propensities. It seems to me that I *must* forbear to end or begin the day amiss when the first and last thing is always to kneel in thought of her;— not only that everything wrongly done or wrongly left undone would have to be thought of then in relation to her, but also do you not see that there is a bribe to make one go to bed and get up when it is fitting, because then failing any sins to

---

[143] *Romola* (1863)

[144] *Middlemarch* (1872)

confess—there is the delight of meditating on her sweet loveliness, and one will learn to hoard up this delight and instead of stealing (as I have been doing now!) moments from the day's work to dwell in tender thoughts of her, one will turn away sternly, and keep the exceeding great reward of a faithful love for the evening's "Benediction."—I want to have got started in my new work before she comes back to town. If only I have not wasted my powers of doing anything strong, I think myself rather a happy creature. I am afraid I cannot veraciously affirm that my happiness is *quite* independent of the fact that I may begin to count by weeks instead of months to the moment when I may hope to see her again.

September 24, 1878

The history of each Sunday is—wrote—or did not write to her. Last Sunday I did not. Have finished off a paper on organization of employment &c for Fraser[145] which Augustus pronounced "not inspiring," wrote to Elma again at length, have seen a new aspirant for the honours of a partnership with H & Co and wasted some time in house hunting. Next week have to play forewoman and after that shall really be ready to prepare for the History.

September 28, 1878

After some idling and daydreaming—and omitting to say my prayers— (it pleases me to attribute transgressions to that cause), was lamed today with a headache and vile melancholy—was fool enough to dwell painfully on a dream. I thought there was a letter from Mr. Lewes, with two enclosures, one from her, one I know not what.—I read (in my dream) not her letter but his, and found in it a sentence to the effect that it was possible to have too much of a good thing— even so good a one as my letters! I woke myself with a blush, as if I had not said the same to myself very often!—and so, even in my sleep, I did not get any word from her. And this afternoon that came over me with pain, I felt desolate, useless, loveless. I have been expecting such a time, and wondering how my new found resignation would stand the test. In my gloom I thought, the resignation is unconditioned, while the mood lasts it is well enough, but why should it last if I have objectively nothing to content me? And I remembered what I had said to myself and her and something within me asked, letting the fact be so, What is the use of your loving if no one counts your love? and it seemed to me again that life was all endurance. And then I remembered the sentence in Romola—the only security against "wounded vanity and the sense of loneliness"—and now I am at rest again. As she wrote to me last year to be in a cheerful mood about oneself is not necessary "to loving resolute life"—when the sadness comes I will not listen to it but work. Who knows better than I that we do not love for the pleasure of loving, but because of the tenderness within us and god helping me, I will let no selfish sadness rob me of that. My darling, my own!—and I will say my prayers more dutifully!

---

[145] "Industrial Employment of Women," *Fraser's Magazine* 19 (February 1879): 246-255.

October 6, 1878

The other day I wrote to her from the shop and to Elma also in answer to another letter. I have been reading Boeckh's Public Economy of Athens[146]—the treat of a book that is well done! and lots of other things partly bearing on "property." I have a dim vision of the monumental chapter on "Rent" that would delight me if somebody had written it. This week we begin to try the new régime of a late déjeuner.[147] I have proposed it, partly in the interest of work, partly health, as I want in future to get a stretch of work at Greek before going out, a stretch of reading at the museum without getting a headache, and an hour at the shop without putting my brains out of condition for the day. We shall see how it works: if the shop goes on well, and the book gets started,—and she comes back to town—I shall be tolerably well provided for!

October 13, 1878

Nothing is the matter only the strain of absence is telling. I have written letters and torn them up and then sobbed heartbreakingly that I should need to think whether what I want to say will be wearisome for her to hear. And then when the sad doubt has come in, one has no heart or strength to write at all. And so I haven't—I am horribly afraid as well as hungrily eager for her return. The horrible thing is that I do not feel as if I were any nearer a solid footing in her life than I was 4 years ago, and therefore—much worse than the question may I write or no, is the doubt how and when I may venture to go to her when she is in town. My heart smiles even at the thought of the first sight of her—for all these last years that has been—not a disappointment, but a sad setting things as they are—and oh, that's not as I wish for them. And, making every allowance for the fit of sadness that is on me now, I see ever fresh reason to fear whether I shall ever be seriously nearer her—whether my saner more virtuous moods will touch her any more spontaneously than my rebellion! Well, I had better read Herodotus[148] and forget as if I can which of the Arab's "two comforts" is my chosen saviour.

October 16, 1878

After tearing up the letters that could aid in a lachrymose wail and being very miserable I took to saying my prayers and felt better! Also I found a

---

[146] August Boeckh (1785-1867), *Public Economy of Athens* to which is added a Dissertation on the Silver Mines of Laurion, 2 vols. (London: J. Murray, 1828). Trans. from German. The work deals with economic conditions of Greece to 146 B.C.

[147] breakfast or lunch

[148] *History of Herodotus*, new English version with notes by George Rawlinson (London: Murray, 1862).

nice devotion in Bishop Andrewes,[149] and I felt better. Wrote to her yesterday and feel less miserable. Am dimly encouraged perhaps by the thought of encouraging one girl and making the acquaintance of another who wants to be encouraged in good work; also by the prompt printing of a paper sent to Fraser,[150] which suggests the acceptance of another on the industrial employment of women.[151]

October 20, 1878

My daily devotions take the form of simple addition and subtraction sums. I believe she will be in town for the 3rd, but this is mere guess. I let my hopes build on it and if I am disappointed there cannot be more than one week more to endure. Endurance has become very hard, and as usual when I am most miserable I cannot help asking myself whether in any other case than this when so little would make so much difference, she would refrain from giving the little. However, I know and accept with all my mind all the time what is my sufficient though rather grisly comfort:—that the fault is in me for failing so hopelessly to hook myself on in any way to her natural life. Oh, I hope for the sake of my fellow sinners that not all faults are visited with such remorseless severity. Auf! I meant to do nothing today but read Herodotus to keep myself out of mischief. I am only dismal for want of her: all that I wrote earlier in the summer stands fast.

October 30, 1878

On that Sunday I wrote long *triste*[152] letters which I was happily too much taken care of to send, and, with difficulty, I wrote myself out of the worst dismalness. Now I am divided between passionate longing, unhealthy dreams, impatience, resignation, the counting of endless days, heart-aching love, and patient gratefulness—to say nothing of Herodotus and Fraser. Oh when, when, when! I am hungry! Oh the howl that is in my mind there are no words to spell, but it echoes wolfishly.

November 1, 1878

No word of or from her, and though I made up my mind not to begin hoping for any till tomorrow, in spite of myself my heart is in my ears at every possible—and impossible post-time.—I dreamt a postcard from him the other

---

[149] Lancelot Andrewes, Bishop of Winchester (1555-1626), *The Devotions of Bishop Andrewes* (Oxford: J. H. Parker, 1824-44; 1861).

[150] "Organization of Unrenumerative Industry," *Fraser's Magazine* 18 (November 1878): 609-621.

[151] "Industrial Employment of Women," *Fraser's Magazine* 19 (February 1879): 246-255.

[152] "sad"

night which I seized with eager hope and found to bear only the information that my *"casuistic"*(sic) letters were rather oppressive to her tender spirit. I am not specially unhappy—only savagely restless and impatient—all day long there is an undercurrent—of that feeling which comes between Dorothea and the geography of Asia Minor.[153]—This shall be the last year: with leave or without, I will go and see her oftener:—it is killing—and life is short and it is horrible to waste it in counting the days of pain.—I have not heard from Elma for over a month—a fact of which I was reminded yesterday by a sentence of Allingham's[154]—it is so true that I make sure of it by quotation: "I could name several people (and I too) to whom I used to talk in frank and friendly manner, my very best and most intimate talk, trusting in their comprehension and sympathy: but this puzzled and vexed them—I was queer, *gauche*, troublesome. Very well: I saw my mistake after a while; and now, when we are thrown together, I no longer attempt real conversation, but exchange civil nothings and we agree capitally."

I am hungry. If there is no letter tomorrow morning (and I have no earthly reason to expect it) I foresee that I shall drift around to the Priory in the afternoon and watch if wheels have turned at the door and if blinds are drawn up within, and be too modest to ask the housekeeper when she is expected, and cry along the streets as I come away as wise as I went—which is saying much, for it is hard to achieve quite so large a negative quantity. But there is one thing that I never hesitate to acknowledge—in word and feeling—if a glance at the professions of happier days or anything else calls me back to it. Namely, that if I am unhappy and the world blank and desolate, it is my unloving and desolate soul that finds it so, not any fault of others that makes it so.

November 2, 1878

This afternoon I passed her house. It was a cold, snowy looking sky with bits of pale blue here and there and the premature 3 o'clock sunset of winter. I walked on the other side of the road and saw from a distance windows at the side of the house shut up: on coming nearer it was still so; no wheels had drawn up to the house, and the sitting room windows had shutters up though the bedroom blinds were not down. I was glad to know it to know that I had nothing more to hope for tonight. And I would rather she were not in town than that she would be there without telling me. Since I came in I have been reading a story of Black's: "MacLeod of Dare."[155] It has touched me in a way such books seldom

---

[153] *Middlemarch*, bk. 8, ch. 83

[154] William Allingham (1824-1889) was a native of Ballyshannon, Ireland; in addition to writing poetry he was subeditor of *Fraser's Magazine* under Froude and then editor-in-chief and associated with Tennyson, Carlyle, and the Pre-Raphaelites.

[155] William Black (1841-1898), *MacLeod of Dare*, 3 vols. (London: Macmillan, 1879).

do, for there is a lover with just such restless heartache as mine—and there is the same kind of forcible and yet not visibly necessary barrier between him and his happiness. The picture did me thus bits of good however,—it suggested her kind of comments—other people suffer something in the same way, and we all have to carry it silently and make it as little the worse as may be for each other. It is difficult to know what one must do—one cannot dethrone the passion, though it were all sadness and renunciation, it should still be chief and ruler, and it is hard to see how the rest of one's life is to be cheerfulness and kindliness when one's own part of it is pain. And yet, as one writes, it seems as if that should be possible, it is not the worst pain, because one has something; it is hard—to take gladly and gratefully as much as is given—and bear uncomplainingly one's selfish grief that no more is given—and passing by this pain and longing, proceed to give, with diligent love, whatever one may. It is hard my darling; and yet—is not your cross something like that? I live in hopes of being able to talk to her more freely this year. There is no doubt in spite of the natural sadness that is upon me now,—that the work of self-conquest has begun; it is I that triumph now (in the power of the thought of her) over the thoughts which used to be myself vainly resisted by deliberate endeavor or resolve. My darling, my darling,—it will not be long now, and surely there will be a choicer happiness in seeing you when one is not only trying to be good but happily agreed with you as to the kind of goodness to be sought. I can imagine myself confessing to her something about the selfish greediness that makes one feel as if one could not do anything one ought when one is so thoroughly soul-sick and faint—and I might ask her how one was to resist the temptation. My sweet darling!—and then I have great fright, as if the coming happiness would be dashed from my life—Oh God not that!—I will write—as I have come to it now, but may wander from it hereafter as heretofore—that even if it pleases her to be seen not altogether in private—I will be content and grateful and wait my time for the chance of pouring out all this love that is burning in my soul. My own love—my sweet!—

November 3, 1878
This morning had Miss Orme[156] and Miss Williams[157] to breakfast, who were both very happy in life's "discourse." 'Twas not bad of its kind, but on the whole I am not sorry to have outgrown that appetite too, so that it will soon not be as a *pisaller*[158] but from complete choice that I live my hermit's life. Tomorrow or next day methinks I must wander round there again—now the time is so near I cannot wait patiently to be summoned—I was a fool not to ask their

---

[156] Eliza Orme was a member of the Royal Commission on Labour to Report on the Employment of Women in 1893. She was one of several Lady Assistant Commissioners. She had a law degree, and Miss Richardson was a partner in her law firm. See January 5, 1879, and January 28, 1879.

[157] Miss Williams seems to have loved EJS "lover-wise."

[158] "last resort"

plans when I was there. "There" it seems means only the place where she is. I am vexed with myself for being so idle, but I doubt whether I physically can help it.

November 5, 1878

At last! The dear fellow has sent a card (and I hope it was she who corrected its reading)—within 13 days from now I shall be happy. I was disappointed at first to find that they were coming so late, but I guess they only arrive the end of the week before, and I am glad not to be asked to come on Sunday. Must read Stubbs[159] and haunt the museum to kill the time: and perhaps before the end of it I may have some translating to do, which Max Müller has sent me, having, I think rather to the disgrace of the University, no one else to recommend.

November 8, 1878

The time goes slowly; can't fix my mind on serious reading. Read the Idylls of the King[160] yesterday and am trying Rossetti[161] today. Partly owing to this idleness, partly from external worry, I am dispirited—inclined to complain of the dull loneliness of the world, want of hope in one's well-meant endeavors—and I suppose general want of faith in all the spiritual objects of one's worship—then when one translates all these negations into the promise of sad and weary years today—that is no one's fault but one's own, does not make the prospect less uncheerful.—One asks oneself then again—Is life to be all endurance? And along side of this misgiving there is a half-sad, half-contented recognition of the fact that—one no longer wants the things one wanted once and could not have: a half-sad, half-pleased self-questioning—Is there anything that one wishes for now?—except of course always to see her again. I have no hopeful or consoling answer to make to any of these misgivings; but this is what she has done for me. I don't feel justified in or desirous of dwelling on them; granting that there is no hope or comfort and that the prospect is dim and cheerless, well, one has to endure just that and not make it worse by groaning—amidst which one may forget to love. But though I have all faith in the virtue of that last prescription, I do not see that it is of universally easy application; and this by the way is my crowning cross—that it *is* so hard to mold in any way the daily

---

[159] Charles William Stubbs (1845-1912), Regius Professor of History at Oxford, 1866-84, wrote *Village Politics: Addresses and Sermons on the Labor Question* (London: Macmillan, 1878).

[160] Alfred, Lord Tennyson (1809-1892) began his *Idylls of the King* in 1859 with four verse poems on the Arthurian legends; he added and revised the series until 1888 when it included twelve poems.

[161] Dante Gabriel Rossetti (1828-1882) had published a number of individual poems and the volume *Dante and His Circle* (London: Ellis and White, 1874).

relations of one's necessary outside life upon that soul-satisfying spiritual intercourse—which the more precious it becomes only seems to leave the common world the further behind. But I know that is my fault too, or part fault, part misfortune and she is coming back to me, oh joy!

November 12, 1878

Yesterday packed my mother off for Cornwall, am attending to the shop, writing letters and translating for Max Müller. The Charity Organization— foul fare them! have asked me to preach on the text of my Fraser article on December 9—the day on which I fondly hoped of getting at last one more happy anniversary. 'Tis like my fate—but I will bemoan it to her. And I will lie on the rug and kiss her feet—whether she likes it or not. Less than a week!

Unmöglich scheint immer die Rose.
Unbegreiflich der Nachtigall.[162]

November 16, 1878

The time draws near—I cannot express the passion of glad longing that possesses me. There is only Sunday and Monday! I mean to be so good and make the time fly by translating furiously. I dream of all sorts of new ways of wooing her—if I could feel that she was learning to know and love me more!— after all I have never given myself a chance with her.

November 22, 1878

Monday came at last, but hardly the greeting I had dreamt of: the first thing I saw was Lewes stretched upon the sofa, and in concern for him I lost something of the sight of her. He was affectionate and when I said I wanted to kiss her feet he said he would let me do it as much as I liked—or—correcting himself—as much as she liked. He could enter into the desire though she couldn't. I did in spite of her protests lie down before the fire and for one short moment gave the passionate kisses that filled my eyes with tears;—and for the rest of the evening her feet avoided the footstool where I had found them then.— Still though I would rather have had the kisses ungrudged—I would rather have the memory of them thus than not at all. She was unhappy about him, I cried all the way back—at the intense pain of her anxiety—which I was tempted to share. I was sorry for myself too: all one's gladness turned to pain; and the hopes lost of pleasing her for a moment with loving sense and nonsense. At first I felt hopeless, what could one do but shut oneself up with one's grief? but I knew she would not think that right, so I have rather more than less socialized—going to a vicarage, with well-brought up children—*à propos* of a unionist meeting in the schoolroom—where I hemmed 1/2 a yard of flannel and felt like a wolf in lamb's clothes all the while, and again to supper, violin cello and Luca della Robbia's

---

[162] "The rose always appears to be impossible. Inconceivable the nightingale."

photographs[163] with a couple living a very pretty, innocently happy life. Here too I was disguised—being too polite to explain how utter was my unsocial incapacity: and really I enjoyed the moaning of the strings as I felt the passion of the figurines on the frieze. The maid said on Wednesday he was better.

November 26, 1878

On Monday the doctors were there and he was very ill. Today I went in the morning and the answer was the same. In the afternoon I went again; trying to hope she would let me be with him in the night. I sent up a written line with the prayer. It came down I think unread in the servant's hand—she could not attend to anything, "Mr. Charles" would write to me! I could not expect anything else, and yet her intense excitement and distress—the servant said she could do nothing but cry and fret—make it cruelly unfit for her to be alone. God forgive me! I feel as if I would give my mother's life for his!—There is nothing left but tears—and duty; I feel no impulse to blaspheme, only deadly grief; it seems that he must die—and then her life is one blank agony and—if that mattered—mine too—only that for me duty is left and for her scarcely.

November 28, 1878

This morning Sir James Paget[164] thought him a shade better. All day yesterday the rain fell—I remembered such days at Bude—somehow I did not dare to go and ask and came to the house this morning with a deadly fear.— Perhaps he will recover? I dare not hope, I only know that if he dies the world will have nothing left for her: he has been all the world to her and the world is punished by being nothing. She will hate, she has a right to hate, all love that is not his. I suppose it is because I know and love her so well that I do not dream of a future in which she might find comfort in the love that is left—if she could ever in any, it would be a strange, new, shallow loving that called up no memory of the old. It is something to be thankful for that this trouble has not come upon me—one has to be thankful for small mercies, since it comes now—when my mind was troubled with the feeling of conflicts with her. I wonder at my own slow stupidity in not grasping the difficulty more firmly at the time, but my understanding was bewildered with the new fact of selfish passion. I had said— in my tears—it is wise and right to renounce—and not to set one's heart on pleasure, it is a small thing as well as unattainable, strength and virtue lies in being able to live without it. And so I lived, *enduring* firmly asking nothing and not complaining when I got it: but this philosophy did not teach me what to do; and while I told myself and believed it is as right to be able to do without

---

[163] Luca della Robbia (1400?-1482), Tuscan portrait painter and sculptor, who is discussed by Walter Pater (1839-1894), in *Studies in the History of the Renaissance* (London: Macmillan, 1873).

[164] Sir James Paget (1814-1899), Serjeant-surgeon-extraordinary to Queen Victoria, was one of the foremost medical men of the time (H, Biography, 417). He was the Lewes family physician.

pleasure, I did not think or feel it right—or possible—to be content without action; and to her I spoke my discontent at a life of powerless inaction. She said—love and feel—and I felt a passionate love for her and—oh letters!—I wrote a book. Then it appeared to me from her criticism of this book that she thought, not indeed that pleasure and virtue were one, but that virtuous action was the natural fruit of untaught, involuntary happiness, and that no good thing came from any other root. And I remembered what was written in his Ms of *Adam Bede*, I thought how even my own poor offspring had been born and bred under a glad vision of her imagined approval: it seemed she meant this and I could not believe but what she was right.—And I understood how people have called Calvinism a damnable creed, for by that, as by this, we are shown people as if alive, but a doom not of their own making holds them back from living rightly. That this was horrible I knew gave no assurance why it shouldn't be true, but if true it was a damnable, a damning truth. It seemed to be a light thing to give up happiness, but I did not care to give up conscience too—had only those fortunate a right to be good and must one renounce one's earliest lessons and wait upon Providence for luck that should inspire one with virtuous power?' I knew she did not say this, but it seemed to follow from what she did say. This lasted on, for I had found no work, to prove that one could work well without luck, and I was more deeply luckless than ever; then thence came the deliverance of despair: I saw myself with nothing to hope for, nothing to have and—thanks to her—I saw then moral motives left alone in the void. And since I owe her that I have not cared to argue further only in the face of utter calamity, real, unescapable, I feel again that I could not live without the faith that the best life does not become impossible though for her, and therefore for me, the springs of gladness may dry up forever. It seems to me a part of the very human strength that people complain of as decaying, to be able to look an irreparable calamity in the face, and say and know there is no help, and have courage to bear both the knowledge and the fact and live none the worse, it may even be the better, for the shock which has killed all one's power of selfish asking. It may be necessary to understanding and sympathy, that one should know what the face of happiness is like to look on, but love and truth and endurance—happiness may be the petted child of these she visits as her fancy pleases—but the divine eternal parents never leave the faithful worshipper, and it is they, not she that is the parent of fruitful deeds. Only let me be ever faithful to the secret truth to which the soul clings the closer the more bitter the hour of searching trial! Let me never ask from love ought but a loving heart, from truth the glory rather than the duty of finding it, from endurance escape from pain rather than strength for serviceable work. And oh! May the blessing of her teaching to others be with her in this time of agony.

November 30, 1878

Yesterday the answer was "just the same"—Charles Lewes and Johnny Cross were with him. She had written to the latter—whom he wished to see— and who came from his mother's death bed. Today I reached the house about half past three, a private cab was driving up and down slowly before it, I waited till that was gone and then rang at the gate. Brett with a white face and dark eyes answered me: "He is very ill—" then "there are no hopes"—I stood stupefied, without word or sign, without feeling, and so turned away. It was as if something quite different from my fears had come. I could not leave the place and walked up and down, and almost immediately a carriage like a doctor's drove up fast and two men got out. I hastened after them and they entered the gate; the other carriages followed and the two, with their 4 sleek horses stood a few paces back. The coachmen talked and laughed, cabs and coal carts and men and women on foot passed by as I stood behind the carriages, watching the gate down the fog-bound road. Then—in about 20 minutes, the 2 figures came in sight. I strode towards them and as they stood speaking together, I asked was there no hope. A tall man—probably Sir James Paget answered kindly; None: he is dying—dying quickly. Then again I could not speak, but the tears rushed up—shading my face with a hand I cried hard with this worst of griefs. She cannot bear it: there have been unendurable sorrows, but I do not see how any can equal hers—who can feel as she does, who could have so much to love?—I am dimly thankful that I parted from him with a kiss—I feel the touch of his hand as I held it at Witley—but oh! what does anything matter—would God the grief might kill her even now. But whether she lives or dies—there is no comfort for her left on earth but this, to know that their love and life have not been in vain for others, that the happiness which is dead and the sorrow that endures bind us for evermore to love and service of the sorrowing and the glad.—But oh! to think of that sweet frame shaken with the unconsolable anguish!

December 1, 1878

He died at a quarter to six—an hour and a half after I left the house. She sees no one, is in hysteric agonies. I can only think of her with dread. I shrink from ever going near the house again—to the gateway where through that dread hour outside—worse anguish was being endured within. It seems to me intolerable—what must it to her? To think of seeing her again without him.

December 2, 1878

All day and night I think of him with love and tender sorrow—of her with blank dread beyond grief. Charles Lewes says she is sustained by the effort to carry out his wishes. One says God help her! because there is no help in man. One knows it is too hard, she will try, but it is too hard to find any comfort in such pious thoughts as mine—which are good for endurable griefs. I have given thanks for their love, I have worshipped the meet holiness of mutual devoted service. What has been and cannot die—it is ours "to pass her gift to others who may use it for delight." I never had—apart from her—any vision of delight for myself and now, in the shadow of her infinite grief, it is impossible for me even to remember that I have lost a selfish pleasure. I feel strong—not to resist but to bear—I feel it is right to live for a few days of mourning, alone with the thought of what is gone, nay rather, with the thought of what is left, all that is left of him is the memory of his pure goodness and I feel as if it was not selfish to wish to be alone with the thought—how may one live in loyalty to that. The feigned immortalities seem to be more unreal than ever—what folly to mock such grief with promises of a grotesque resurrection. The only life to come—how can any life to come make her grief less than infinite? and yet she will not sorrow as those quite without hope,[165] for she will try to believe, what my lesser sorrow comforts itself with already, that their love and the goodness born of faithful love will make, had made themselves a temple within the lives of those who are left, that his memory is a consecration making duty precious and service dear, that the thought, nay the worship of his unselfish, generous kindliness will be cherished as a religion, as a god, preserving tenderness and sanctifying work. It is well to write this while one's whole soul is possessed with its truth. Weakness and temptation may come, but what has been seen—as in the valley of the shadow of death[166]—"asserts itself and will not let us see as we saw in the days of our ignorance." God—the god of their goodness—grant me such faithfulness that if it is her doom to live—she may be cheered some day by finding his love again in her child's life. I daren't call her sweet names or think of the utter desolation. I wonder whether I shall ever again wish to see her.

December 3, 1878

"Comfort her, comfort her all things good!" Waking in the night, waking at dawn, I thought what it must be for her to wake and know herself alone. The sun is shining today—if it were not for the rest of the world I should wish it would not. It may sound like folly but I have just pushed the half-closed shutter further and the twilight seems more bearable. My heart is sore for her. I shrink as from the sharp edge of a sword from the night of that "dark door"—and I feel that life for her must be all such edges and no heart can come between her and them. But for me there is a strange sad comfort in the thought—not of change or loss, but as of a silent, secret espousal of the unchangeable. God forbid that I should love her less in her anguish, but all the glad lover-like indiscretion—that was more welcome to him than to her, that is over, like her lost happiness, a memory of what has lived. That lover's love belonged—oh I see it now—to his loved and loving wife and all my pure gladness came from nothing of my own, but from joy in her love-filled life; and now her life is empty of all but memory and I—who am young enough to have more years before me than they knew of happiness together—I who have "a life to fill with love"— I will fill all these years of life with love—of their lost blessedness. I will answer the claims that come to me but I can make none—I have asked once and this has been given to me—it is not a small thing; that and my constant soul, bound together like lovers in a fresh embrace, will live through the years unflinchingly, and we shall die: undivided. It is not good for the soul to live alone and yet mine has always rebelled against the thought of taking happiness to itself—not from any rare unselfishness, but because it was not given me to imagine happiness as my gift to another—and if I tried to think of it as a gift that might be brought to me, I felt myself shrinking back in imagination and making way for this one or that who might have a better claim. But this soul's bridal to a sacred memory fills all the aching needs of a jealous heart, that no living love would bear still.

---

[165] An echo of I Thes. 4:13

[166] Ps. 23:4

The memory is not cruel in taking no service at my hands, what service could I bring it but the echo of a service done for its sake to others. And so I am fain to hope that what is left of my love—of the selfish love that put her first, alone,—will be less likely to jar upon her lasting grief, and will cease for ever from tearing my soul with selfish cravings to be something more or nearer to her. I feel no such hunger now—she is a part of the world upon whose bidding I would wait in meek obedience. It is strange, surely though my instinct serves me well and this is what must be least displeasing to her tear-worn eyes. Oh it is sad! I see her dear hair whitening beneath the burden. I know that while he lived I only loved him as one may those that heart and mind are free to judge, but his love was so bound up with the life I worshipped idolatrously that I cannot sever them now; all of her that I loved so has died with him and they shall not be divided in the temple the sanctuary of my vows. Since I have loved her I have sometimes idly wished that there was a religious order, a cloister where one might spend one's days in worship and commemoration; and now it seems that the world is not too wide for a devout enclosure and that it is there one's vows have to be paid. I am afraid of writing what I would vow—how could I bear to break faith with the sacred memory? and I distrust my power of doing anything worthy of a solemn pledge, but at least I can pledge the will, and God knows it is not with any personal vanity that I fear whether I may ever be seen to redeem it duly. This is what I would undertake, and it is the answer to the long drawn cry after a place, a function in the world.

December 4, 1878

What is called practical philanthropy, the manipulating of Committees and subscription lists, the prominent place in all good works and the gift of moving eloquence are not for me. I cannot identify myself—to me it would be a backward step—with the machinery of any useful cause; I see so many who can do that only too completely and easily and it seems more necessary to try to direct and harmonize their unthinking zeal, and if it may be let the waste of honest force be brought to a minimum by friendly wisdom. This is not the work for one, but one may help and enlist others for the same kind of mediation. Again I am a radical and have won a place from which I have a chance of being heard by those who do not readily trust *a voice* from the place which, nevertheless, I have not lost. Here too there may be modest service done in accordance with my strongest tastes and instincts—the saying which may be truly said on both sides. This is the literary side of the more directly social work, but I accept the conclusion that my own work must be mainly literary if the best of me is to go most easily into it, only this work will always have a social bearing; I cannot interest myself in any writing where such bearing is remote or forced, but I believe, if I have not already worn out my powers by the (morally) riotous living of the last 6 years, that the work I have dimly in view will shape itself wholesomely and manageably as I go on and however mediocre it may turn out as a literary achievement, in substance and temper I hope it may be such as I can dedicate, at least silently, to the memory of friendship.

December 5, 1878

Yesterday went to see Elma; she grieves as much as I—and yet—she is able to go to shops, to visit strangers, rail at things and people and even half jest—I wonder as of old whether the strong feeling is *as* strong there where it does not always rule. Today I went to Highgate—I learnt incidentally from her that he was buried there yesterday. It was hard to have to ask where the grave was—of cheerful officials who look it out in a book like house agents—No. 84 "in the dissenters' portion." I asked a gardener—with half-a-crown—to find it for me and he got a relenting clerk to come—then at last I was close by the desolate new mound. Two white wreaths were on the grave and I laid mine of heather between them. Then I lay on the grass just beyond, and after a while the spot did not seem so hideous; it is there, not to the ghostly portal of buried hope and joy that I must go now to pray. Oh it is strange to see the crowded streets—I asked the man how many graves they made each day—he said 5 or 6, sometimes 2 sometimes 10—I thought that was hardly enough to make them care so little; a funeral came while I was there—with nodding horse-plumes; the clergyman went away jovially before me—tapes were hanging down from the sleeves of his surplice. As I was lying on the grass a grave-digger came to me. He said he had put forked sticks to keep the white wreaths from the wet; he had been told the lady was coming to see it this afternoon and he had tried to make it "look nice": I gave him a shilling and hoped—perhaps in vain—that the next comer might be spared his talk. He promised soothingly to turf it over soon—I asked when and he didn't know—"You see the ground may sink a little, we have some more earth at the side to put on if it does"—then he went and I think I cried, till looking up I saw two dark figures I thought were Elma and her friend; I rushed back—behind the shelter of an evergreen clump—a withered azalea bloom still hung on one branch. Then I sobbed bitterly and when I rose after a while no one was there, visitors are many, it was probably not they. Then I walked across to Hampstead and passed hesitatingly their son's gate; as I turned back some one in black (? "Octavia")[167] was going in—I had hardly meant to go today, but somehow the aspect of the house was not forbidding and I thought I might dare to go tomorrow. When I came in I wrote letters to Rhodes[168] about technical education, prefatory note for Noiré,[169] read some Fortnightly review—you may

---

[167] Octavia Hill (1838-1912) was the sister of Gertrude Hill, wife of Charles Lewes. She was involved in many reform efforts, particularly housing reform, and in 1869 helped found the Charity Organization Society; the papers of this organization were published as *District Visiting* (1876, 1877). Her two books of essays were *Homes of the London Poor* (London: Macmillan, 1875) and *Our Common Land* (London: Macmillan, 1877).

[168] Cecil John Rhodes (1853-1902), South African statesman

[169] Ludwig Noiré (1829-1889), *Max Müller and the Philosophy of Language* (London: Longmans, Green, 1879).

say then I should not wonder at Elma, but *I* am not there, not in anything but an agonized consciousness of her agony, a consuming sense of hopeless personal misery which makes all the lesser acts or duties of life one no harder than the other. It is a cruel thing to say of so good a mother, but if she only *had* children of her own to comfort her now—perhaps Johnny does, but one feels now without selfishness what one used to grudge at wickedly that none of the gladness from another's being, which is still my note of love, that none of that—or not enough to count—ever came to her from us.

December 8, 1878

I saw Elma yesterday and heard that she was not as well after coming downstairs for the first time. Elma wished Mrs. Charles Lewes were less "hard" and more appreciated the privileges and rights of a daughter; she herself while feeling I do not doubt all the silent horrors of despairing sympathy for our desolate beloved, had tears too for the loss of her own bright visions of the home to which she might welcome them:—I neither said—she had never visited me— nor that the overwhelming shock of her loss had paralyzed at once all my private dreams of happiness to come through them. The fact is I have felt the depths of her despair, her endless grief so thoroughly that it is even possible I have underrated her strength to endure, and it is certain that no kind of mental occupation is more entirely restful and passionless—to those whose bent is that way—than such speculation as she has to give her mind to for his sake. It is a strange feeling that haunts me through the night—of old if I have been awake it seemed uncomfortable and against nature, one tried to go to sleep again as soon as possible; now I wake many times in the night and always with a clear consciousness of "looking into the eyes of sorrow,"—of that being a task of which one cannot weary, something one has to live to do. Truly I think my longing is to comfort her, ever so little, without thought of comfort to myself.—It is deliverance, a deliverance worth all the sad years, the passionate despair it has cost one, to feel at last that unselfish love and unambitious work are enough to live for—enough to fill the life in which appetite has died in the face of one boundless love, one boundless sorrow. God help me to keep ever in this mind, for this is my own and all the others are shortlived and unreal.

December 12, 1878

Yesterday I saw Charles Lewes. He is good to her and I never liked him so well,—he has no thought of sparing himself in caring for her. For her my instinct has not been wrong. She proposes to live on as she is,—he says, she is able to live alone, and cannot bear to have, even a niece she is fond of with her. She has but the one thought to make his wishes her law; the rest of the world she would have think of her "as a dead friend." It is not strange, knowing her and loving and worshipping as I did, it is not strange that my instinct should have divined this; Elma said—That is hard for her friends—I have hardly ventured to think so more than if she were dead indeed. I said she had no duties left. He said, after a long time perhaps she might make a new life with new interests, she was so full of sympathy she could hardly fail to do so, but her feeling now is that no one can give her any comfort and she has a right to avoid the agitation which might hinder her work. Charles said, she can speak of nothing but him, and she can only speak of him to me. Mrs. Cross died on Monday. I sat up writing a few lines of sympathy to Johnny—uneasily though with complete sincerity—through blinding tears. I have not said how hard it was to go to the house for the first time after that evening of death—and yet it was a common duty to go and ask how she was. At last I went—without wish, as a duty. I took a cab; I could not bear to traverse the so well known track. The maid said she was better than she had been yet, "seemed more cheerful"—God help her! If anything could be harder it was to enter the house, to wait in the dining room—Charles was out and had left word for one to wait: I had never been in the dining room but with him, and usually it was for some kind purpose that he called me there. There he showed me all her manuscripts. There he gave me "The Spanish Gipsy,"[170] there he has come to answer my questions about her. Is it disloyal to say—He was kinder to me while I thought of him as a stranger than she when I had given all my love. I waited half an hour, standing on the rug looking at her portrait and finding more sweetness in it than before. Lying on the chimney piece under my eyes was an open bill—1 widow's cap—7.6—and something else—that is how I see her—with a set, worn, white face.—My poor darling—it is too hard—I think of meeting her—it seems years hence, with a mere hand clasp and a sad, silent look.

December 13, 1878

Today I went to ask Mme Bodichon[171] if she would go and see Elma, left the message in charge of Miss Marks as Mme was tired and had a visitor coming; she sent word she had been reading the paper in Fraser with much interest. I have said nothing—why should I?—of the discussion on Monday that I had hoped to please them with. The thought of Mme Bodichon always raises a regret that I had not sought or found her just half my life—17 years ago, and through her Mrs. Lewes. The difference it would have made! Yet—such is one's cowardice, I cannot help thinking that if that had been, I should be left now with more to regret—is it not harder to lose a happiness one had than to have lost only a chance of the happiness one has not had? I hardly care even to think which

---

[170] "The Spanish Gipsy" was GE's verse drama set in Bedmár in Andalusia Spain about 1487. Fedalma, the Gypsy, renounces her happiness to answer the call of duty to save her race. The first edition was published by William Blackwood in 1868.

[171] Barbara Leigh Smith Bodichon (1827-1891), the daughter of a Unitarian abolitionist, met GE in June, 1852. She was one of the founders of Girton College (H, Biography, 105, 396-397); She was independent financially but argued for the necessity of paid work for women in *Women and Work* (1857). She helped Bessie Rayner Parkes set up the *English Women's Journal* (1858). She was also an accomplished artist, advocate of women's suffrage, women's property rights, and the abolition of slaves (FC, 109-10). She takes EJS to vacation at her estate called Scalands.

answer one would give to the question in the abstract. It seems a strange and cruel thing to give up one's friend because of the irretrievableness of her misfortune, and yet if one divines that this is what she wants? It seems to me that I have given her up—not as one renounces a joy or a hope, reluctantly, letting one's eye seek for chances of escape—but calmly with a sense of present necessity—the cup prepared for one, shall I not drink it, uncomplainingly to the dregs. Six years all but 10 days, that is the sum of my own life—anything that is left may belong to the outside world—even she, henceforward, will be outside. God knows I would never see her again—would endure the sight of her daily grief—just whichever one for her peace if only either could lighten her burden by the weight of a hair.

December 14, 1878

Today saw Elma, who praying for absolute silence about what she said, spoke the misgiving I have silenced—Is it right and good for her to bury herself alone with grief—and servants? I enquired at the house and after what Elma had said was jarred upon a little by the maid's hope that "we shall get her round in time." She said "It was hard" I said I had known and felt it all from the first and she—that if it must be, she would not complain—"He doeth all things well"—but meanwhile, it was hard to flesh and blood.—I don't know whether we are both improved or only I, but we have no disagreement now. It is a comfort to me to have her to be kind to.

December 15, 1878

I think the half-critical impulse is wrong. I trust her wholly. She will do all that is now possible and right. Her strength is small; we could not wish that she should force herself scrupulously to action against her bent. I put myself in her place and should feel and do as she has. If one is first and the rest nowhere, there is—not disloyalty but yet a kind of lightness in turning for comfort to the second best. Work and solitude are enough for a hopelessly saddened love: when the light of her favor has seemed withdrawn from me, I have found it physically impossible to seek or encounter my fellowmen. Even now I have no impulse to seek, only a set purpose to respond. I could almost reproach myself with it as if it were a cruelty, that in her bereavement my old passion seems to have deserted her—as if it had been her happiness I loved. And yet—it was never the selfish passion that she cared for, and the disinterested tenderness is stronger than ever.

December 17, 1878

One forgets what has been said and what only thought. Mrs. Cross died on the 9th: Charlie told me—Johnny had written to him and to Mrs. Lewes. I would have given a great deal to know that she had seen or written to Johnny, but I judge it to be impossible from his answer—thank heaven a kind one—to my note of sympathy; I wish she would see him, for his sake and for hers, I wish it more than anything for myself. I have no selfish inclination in the matter at all, but I do not know what is best and kindest, that I might choose that. For instance, I had thought of making it a daily task to call and ask how she fared, but the servant would weary of answering me and I hardly like to assume that she is to be treated as an invalid from henceforward. Besides the daily visitation might grow troublesome to her as a silent claim. And yet to go rarely looks careless, to go never undutiful—I am in a straight.

December 21, 1878

Yesterday I heard from Johnny, with sad and touching submission to her withdrawal from the life that is left. It was very good of him to write after seeing Charles Lewes. I am anxious to see him and hear him speak of her. I left the letter with Elma this afternoon. She had had a card from Brett. I felt I could not endure that. I must go rather to Mrs. Charles Lewes. I thought about Christmas I would write a few lines to her and enclose them to Charles to give to her or not. Johnny like Elma speaks of the "void everywhere" and seems to have the feeling of his own loss. From the moment when with tearless astonishment I heard he was to die I have had no hope or wish left; it is not that one is hopeless or despairing—only the craving of desire has died. I marked a passage in a strange book the other day, strange I mean to find one's own deep feeling in. "The love that survives has strangled craving; it lives because it lives to nourish and succor like the heavens. But to strangle craving is indeed to go through a death before you reach your immortality."

(In the Ms this note is on the page opposite near the last part of the entry for December 21.)

The passage (in Harry Richmond III. 262)[172] begins: "You may learn to know yourself through love, as you do after years of life, whether you are fit to lift them that are about you, or whether you are but a cheat, and a load on the backs of your fellows. The impure perishes, the inefficient languishes, the moderate comes to its autumn of decay—these are of the kind which aim at satisfaction to die of it soon or late." then "The love that survives" &c

December 28, 1878

On Christmas day with great hesitation I wrote a few lines to her,—of his divine presence—which I enclosed in an open envelope to Charles Lewes asking him to give it to her or not as he thought best. He returns it, with a note that tells me nothing new, only makes the silence, which seems heartless, a plain necessity. Am I nearer or not than Johnny and Elma, since I *cannot* wish to see her again—if she offered to see me, it would be a pain to endure—like the first revisiting of the dark doorway only harder.

---

[172] George Meredith (1828-1909), *The Adventures of Harry Richmond*, 3 vols. (London: Smith, Elder, 1871).

December 29, 1878

In a letter of Sydney Dobell's[173] I find a good saying, or rather perception concerning the "wonderful divineness and glory of marriage"—"that it makes total self-abstention (the imperative condition of all high beauty—and virtue) consistent with that temporal good and personal welfare, without which (as we see in the great mistakes of monasticism &c) the body becomes too arid a desert to nourish the best flowers of the soul."—"There is possible therefore to the dual being a combination impracticable to any unit—*blessedness and happiness*, earth and heaven at once." This is putting well the view—nay I will say the truth—which it has cost me so much to make a place for in my practical "scheme of salvation." Yesterday I was jarred and irritated by a trifle—a shirtmaker who asked for extra pay for some common work—on the top of an agitating letter, and all night I was trying to escape from both into a solution of the problem—how can one keep the affection ever tender and responsive, so strong and ready as to give their love to the character if the self-abandonment of complete, fortunate love is impossible, if one has always to check the feeling that becomes exacting, selfish in wanting the answer which does not come: the perfect love gives everything and receives everything without thought or effort, almost without consciousness of desire. I suppose there is still too much self, too little love while one has the feeling of such check. In regard to Her I have never felt that. She had all one's love and that was blessedness, as one knelt in sight of the happiness it would be to have hers. And therein I have my answer, if one loved others with as pure a tenderness, there would never be the sense of chill or check. But then—how about the "personal welfare, the temporal good" without which the best flowers of the soul do not open according to our poor married poet! "The supreme and sufficing love" which I would have lived a thousand lives to preserve for her! The love that has "strangled craving" that is stronger than death or any other distance—can live without happiness, but can love prosper a whole lifetime widowed of perfect joy. I answer without haste and after listening to every doubtful pause—It can. Married love and passionate friendship are the first open gates; the way of salvation leads plainly through them, and the flames that dart across the portal and fasten consumingly upon the selfish lusts of those who would pass through have not much terror for the happy elect who enter hand in hand. But there is another gate, narrow, obscure, to which each one draws near alone and the path to it is through the valley of the shadow of death: we tread barefoot and the stones are sharp, we fall, the ground is a flame, the air is a suffocating smoke, invisible demons ply their scourges: there is one strange pleasure in the agony—to feel sharp flames consuming what was left in us of selfish lust, there is one pain passing all the rest, to feel the same flame fasten upon our every wound, within, without, and consume the very pain as if that too was sin. The path is long: who knows if we shall live to reach the end, where is

---

[173] Sydney Dobell (1824-1874), *The Life and Letters of Sydney Dobell*, 2 vols. (London: Smith, Elder, 1878).

the gate of religious love—and few there be that find it.[174] But that fierce trial can teach as much as the sacramental mysteries of double love. And it is lawful for each of those who have followed the divine teaching to the end to feel that no other lesson could have been so full of instruction for themselves. God forbid I should blaspheme the sacredness of such love as has been her life because the gladness of it is now turned to a spreading desolation. Only to me this death is not the end of life, rather the beginning of a lifelong worship and this too is a way of salvation. The gladness of the religious life, for this too shall bring forth sweet and tender blossoms, this gladness does not spring once for all of itself from the one irrepressible source of nature. It is fed by devotion to this present memory of the love that once was glad, by unselfish love that finds its bliss in giving, and—this is the one bit of personal life that saves one from the unhealthy barrenness of pure asceticism—besides the love that flows for one's own sake and that which answers to a claim—because of the strength of both these—one may trust oneself to live too in the pure, painless impersonal world of truth and beauty, in a word,—one is wedded to the last God and Love, to her children who remain to be comforted, and to the chaste, cold, fair She who had one's first young love—true Philosophy—whose consolations are not wanting to Her also. When discouraged over one's small attempts to act directly for good and thrown back on the intuition that one has not force enough to effect much without a distinct opportunity or "leading," it is an unspeakable relief to think of the world of pure thought and disinterested study, where one may take refuge and where I at least have never known inward disquiet. In something like another fortnight I hope to be free to begin a saner life of continuous but not unbroken study. Charles Lewes said in his letter that she would never be able to endure any caress—I knew that—and so was not specially hurt by his saying it—though I cried behind my veil all the way across the Park yesterday.—But there is an inexhaustible tragedy in the thought of that last visit and the last stolen passionate kisses—it is pain to think that it may be one more hurt to her, as well as a fresh stone on the barrier between us, yet in my inmost heart I cannot repent—even if I had not stolen, the barrier would be impassible now. Let us take what good is left—Charles will gain from her dependence and the close intercourse with the higher nature. It is better to feel that than to say that Johnny would have been more worthy of the son's privileges. My jealous rebellion is silenced absolutely in the face of the greater loss to those whose deserts are far above mine. Though I wish from my soul that they were so, my flesh escapes a trial in not seeing them preferred before me. I write all this fully that it may bear witness for me, or against, when time has shown the worth of the inner resolution.

January 5, 1879

The week has passed away without much thought. Mary came back in another tribulation—some lovers' quarrel between Rhoda[175] and Miss

---

[174] An echo of Matt. 7:14

[175] Rhoda Broughton (1840-1920) was a novelist. EJS reviewed her work in the *Academy*, January 24, 1874. See November 30, 1882.

Richardson[176] and herself. Elma is in a state of mind about Roland's[177] wanting to join the army—what she opposes in an excitable rather than a practical way—in a tone which rather courts defeat. Workmen have still been about at Charles Street, and 5 or 6 hours were wasted on a dentist. Longmans' proof drops in and I wrote a longish letter to Miss Orme about Harrison's paper on jurisprudence, which she was afraid of not appreciating as he is an examiner: have also written three notes to or about Mr. O'Donell, a friend of Elma's who wants reviewing to do, and in the evenings have read—some of Seeley's Heine,[178] which I think badly done—Bagehot's literary reprints[179]—good but rather youthful in style—also some Chaucer. So one endures time without much self-reproach. Yesterday—I can hardly believe it was a whole fortnight since I had been, but so it was; I had lived on the news in Charles Lewes's letter and in Mrs. Stuart's reports of the answer to her enquiries—yesterday I was going to the house to ask when I met the two Crosses (the girls) coming away, unhappy and excited at what Brett had told them. They wanted to ask Mrs. Charles if Dr. Andrew would go and see her of his own accord. They thought Charlie meant well and was very good, but he had no authority, and that if she would only see Johnny, he would know how to make her live more wholesomely. I spoke to them as I do to Elma—it is impossible any way, is it not likely that she knows best? One of them seemed to think that you could, the other that you could not, judge for her as for other people. I hardly know. Knowing her intense pride and sensitiveness one is afraid of her being hurt—as a reminder that he is not there to think for her—if anyone else ventured to try—as if they were so far intruding, trying to take his place? Of course it is not so, but might she not feel as if it were? Would she see Dr. Clark even if he went? Would she refuse to see Johnny if he asked for her? I see how Elma's want of energy to plan a future for her son comes from the want of such fresh life as over and over again the sight of her, even the hope of a word from her, has brought to me. I am vexed with myself for not having yet learnt the art of responding graciously to the words of strangers,—or for the matter of that—friends, if the required manner is at all doubtful or hard to find.

---

[176] Miss Richardson was a member of the London School Board and a partner in Eliza Orme's law firm. See November 3, 1878.

[177] The son of Elma Stuart (1837-1903) who edited GE's letters to his mother, *Letters from George Eliot to Elma Stuart, 1872-1880* (London: Simpkin, Marshall, Hamilton, Kent, 1909).

[178] Sir John Robert Seeley (1834-1895), *Heine* (Oxford: Clarendon Series, 1856, 1882).

[179] Walter Bagehot (1826-1877), *Literary Studies*, ed. R.H. Hutton, 2 vols. (London: Longmans, Green, 1879).

January 6, 1879

After luncheon I went up there: I had rung the bell and was looking vacantly eastward when I saw a tall reddish bearded man coming up, I stared without moving and when he had come within two or three paces he made some sign of recognition and I knew it was Johnny. I had thought we should never meet so again. It was an intensely painful moment; there is nothing much more pathetic than a look of set gravity on a habitually cheerful face. We went in together and I asked him to question Brett. She had been out that morning in the garden for a little and felt the better. Johnny said "Give her our love." I listened and came away without speaking but was faintly pleased at the strange chance which brought us there together, because I thought, servant-like, Brett would tell her of the fact and I hoped it would please her to think of our meeting as friends. On leaving the house we adjusted our directions so as to cross Regent's Park together. The anxiety was less after Brett's report—he only felt that the life of isolation could not last, that it might be the only possibility for her at first, but that it would be fatal if prolonged too far. He comforted himself that perhaps she felt if she saw one person, there would be so many who would be just a little hurt if she did not see them too. But clearly he looked forward to a time when she would receive again a few constant visitors. His sober, earthly sense cheered me a little, and though I cried most of the way it was with the quiet sadness that can break no peaceful slumber. Today after going to see Elma, who sent Roland to tell me she was in bed with gout, I went on to the Priory to get my own account from Brett, who said she was very ill on Saturday but better yesterday and better still today, "she varies so"—how should it be otherwise? after a few days' comparative calm a paroxysm comes over one, and it seems to begin afresh as if the pain had but just begun. Surely it is all that can be asked that she should be alive and grieving—it was but seven weeks ago on Saturday—a kind of anniversary, a week of weeks enough to set her mourning the desolation afresh. She has not been able to drive out because the coachman has been ill, and will not be able to go out for another fortnight. I asked Brett how she herself was and she professed to be quite well. I said I had seen the Miss Crosses, who were "such nice young ladies," I asked her to give my love, and she said oh yes, Mrs. Lewes always asked after me and liked to hear when I had been.—God knows I think there was no selfishness in the flood of gratitude with which those words filled my whole soul and frame. I hastened to explain that when I did not come it was in order not to be troublesome and because I heard of her through other people who asked. But I vowed not to trust too much to that method in future lest I should lose any other such blessed hints. This comforted me unspeakably— it shows she is not—I knew she never could be—indifferent to the old love of years, and more than that—it gave me a vision of the future; the second best love that is left can never be enough to give her pleasure, but the loss of it or the apparent withdrawal of silence might give her pain. I have half felt as a possible issue that some loves might leave her in bereavement as the Graf does Armgart[180]

---

[180] "Armgart, a poem," appeared in *Macmillan's Magazine*, July 1871; later in *The Legend of Jubal and Other Poems* (Edinburgh: William Blackwood and Sons, 1874). Graf Dornberg does not marry Armgart after she is no longer

and it is a blessed thing to have the assurance that she will never wish one to love her like that. I want, but hardly dare, to warn Elma not to despair and rush impatiently into any life that takes for granted a separation from her. By and bye, as time goes on, if she lives, she *must* want love and service—it is not now for one's own pleasure, but only of pure tenderness for her that one longs to be ready then. The image came to me of years hence, when her steps are feeble and perhaps some of those who were proud of an entreé to the Sunday afternoons are tired of the unchanging sorrow, then it may be she will turn and be content to lean on one's arm, and oh! to let her feel then that she has indeed been the salvation alike of father, husband, and and loving child. I am patient—I could intercede without jealousy for Johnny, though months or years had to pass instead of weeks, I should not weary of waiting her good pleasure; I should always have "my mother's business"[181] to be about, and his perfect loveableness to feed the memory.

January 11, 1879

Two or three days later I went in the morning, wishing to suggest that she should take indoor constitutionals—with open windows and out of door clothes—during the bitter cold. Brett was probably with her and I saw the cook, who does not see her everyday. She confided to me that their pipes had burst with the frost, and made a merit of not troubling the poor darling about that. I made my suggestion which she promised to pass on to Brett, but said "She tells me not to ask her to do things" and another phrase or two that brought back the picture of her aching loneliness.—It is unutterably sad. When one thinks of her desolation, it is impossible to feel any stirrings of self-pity. Yesterday about 1/4 past eight came a letter from Elma saying her gout had been maddeningly painful the night before in her head and neck. I was alarmed and went to her at once— preferring to risk a refusal of some extent to the chance of leaving her alone in pain and danger. She was better and of course declined my company. Of course I was physically hurt, but I controlled my spirit, and I think was quite gentle and patient. It is something to ask one's instinctive stoicism on the side of charity in one's "struggles with unconquered self." Truly I am not alone—she is always with me, to control and guide and strengthen.

January 13, 1879

Yesterday afternoon I went again to enquire. Brett said again that She was always pleased to hear when I had called. Afterwards I met Miss Othé who said Mrs. Trübner gave "such a sad account of her"—I asked from what source and it appeared only the servants. Miss Othé said or quoted something of her

---

successful as a singer. She thinks her life has ended but learns to "bury her dead joy" and live for others.

[181] As a boy Jesus was lost from his parents, and when after three days they found him in the temple talking with the doctors of the law, he told them, "Wist ye not that I must be about my Father's business?" (Luke 2:49).

self-control breaking down entirely—her screams heard through the house.—My poor darling—I had often thought with dread of hysterical weakness and the horrible moments of exhaustion and loneliness afterwards, but these are not things to be spoken of and I made up my mind today to give a hint to Brett to give the other servants a hint not to be too communicative. I hope it did no harm—I think she quite understood. She said she was expecting Charles Lewes any minute. I walked away and then turned back on the faint chance of meeting him—which I did. She knows best. She not only must be left to choose her own way and her own time of struggling back to life—her choice will be the only possible and wise one. But oh! it is hard. The sense of her anquish is like a scourge, if it were only one's own pain one might try to bear it, to harden one's senses against the feeling, but her pain! God forbid one should shrink from one pang that she must feel or turn away from the cup of sorrow that she must drain.—Not that anything can lighten her grief,—sympathy is good for lesser natures in a finite grief—nothing can avail to help or comfort her, and yet love will not be denied a share in the pain. Surely as one's flesh quivers under the thought of the merciless thoughts that make life one long agony for her—one is learning to be tender and helpful to her children, to all who can be helped, to all without exception, for all may be loved. Charles seemed uneasy about her. He said She could do if she worked on and once or twice in the day her feelings found vent or relief in tears, otherwise at night then came terrible hysterical fits. She said to him the other day that it was still as hard to bear as ever—How should it be otherwise? I feel most strongly that the time is short, that the six weeks or so is but as a moment when one thinks of the height and breadth and depth of the calamity into the face of which she has to look. I have no thought of impatience—my feeling is one with hers. His idea is that by and bye she will all at once resolve and begin the new maimed life afresh—with what passion of submissive tenderness one will wait upon her wishes. Oh Mother! "after death as well as before" most fondly loved most reverently worshipped!

January 16, 1879

Yesterday about noon found a letter to say Maria Sharwood was dying, took it home at once and went with my mother to Waterloo, then to see Mrs. Verney, to the Priory to enquire:—I rang the bell and it was not answered for 5 minutes—I did not like to ring again, thinking Brett might be engaged with her and so went away—then to Mrs. Stuart for a few moments, who had been in the morning to enquire, and had had "a kind note" from Johnny, proposing to call: She also said Mrs. Charles Lewes was coming back in a day or two and would probably call then. There was a petulant note from her in the evening which I burnt and I thought answered quite disarmingly. Then read Tasso.[182] I remembered, I found, a good many passages concerning *Bildung*[183] and the like,

---

[182] Torquato Tasso (1544-1595), *Gerusalemme Liberata;* Goethe wrote *Torquato Tasso: ein Schauspiel von Goethe* (Leipzig: G. J. Goschen, 1790).

[183] "education" or "culture"

but the refinements of sensitive and jealous friendship touched me little when I read it long ago. It is well that I did not read it 2 or 3 years ago when I might have taken too much of Tasso's role for myself; now it touched me with interest rather than distress to find a good deal of Elma and myself each partly in the poet, partly in Antonio. Today I went to the Priory early; saw the cook's daughter who said she seemed better "more cheerful." Another note from Elma thinking I thought—something or other. Thanks to my vow, my God, it is not hard to me now to look away from the momentary small susceptibilities, half vain, half jealous, and go on loving with true love that paid no effort in patience. I am doing no work myself, but oh—God—my God grant that I am able to make the work of life less hard by and bye for some.

January 19, 1879

Yesterday Eleanor Cross came here. She is a good girl, and I was fed by her mention of her last visit to the Heights with Johnny: they went over for a call one day in October when they were able to leave their mother for a few hours, and were made to stay to luncheon and dinner. In the afternoon they went on long lovely drive; they had never had a happier day and she quoted from Dante (a passage she asked me to find) that they would never see the dawn of such a day again. "The dear little man" as she calls him, laid himself out for their amusement, sang to them in the evening, was if possible more actively kind than usual.—When he was dying he told them to give his cigars to Willy Cross—who is a great smoker. Poor Elma (whom I have just been to see) is not so well again: I am afraid the visit from Johnny and Miss Othé was too much for her. I went on to the Priory and saw the cook's daughter, who said She seemed still mending a little. She rarely comes downstairs, is very weak. And—oh! how one's heart is wrung with every word that shadows forth her hopeless grief. The Crosses had just seen Charles Lewes: he also spoke of her as better—she reads the Times and takes pleasure in her work—it is a fit monument of the unequalled love for surely no thinker before ever dared to leave the expression of his thoughts to another. But She says to him that it grows no easier to bear, and I think with dread that she has not yet tasted all the hardship. The grief will have a fresh beginning whenever at last she resolves to try once more to live in the empty world. Who can wonder that now and for as long as it can be, she shinks from the encounter with the changed outside. As long as she can live in her study only—the day is one prolonged morning of uncheered work; the grief breaks out only because the interruption of his brightness makes itself missed—for ever: harder than this, oh! impossibly hard will be the first attempt to enter alone upon the life that was shared, to its least vibration, with him. It is strange how the vision of him has taken her place as the object of grateful love and clinging tenderness; it is of him one thinks with the involuntary smile of loving pleasure—of Her one thinks with utter, unselfish sorrow, nothing is left of one's craving, but a sad thankfulness that one knows how to grieve with her: I am glad to know that my sorrow is as unchangeable as hers. I found a motto for him in Dante the other day—

"Come anima gentil, che non fa scusa,
ma fa sua voglia della voglia altrui."[184]

The secret of his lovableness was that he was happy in being kind. Some other lines say what I wish someone could convey to her for me.

"E io ch'al fine di tutt'i disii
m'appropinquara, si com'io dovea,
L'ardor del desiderio in me finii.
——a sign and smile bid one look up
                    ——ma io era
già per me stesso tal qual ei volea;
Chè la mia vista, venendo sincera,
e più e più intrava per lo raggio
dell'alta luce che da sè è vera."[185]

January 26, 1879

It was not till Thursday that I could go again to ask. Brett said she had been pretty well through the week, though not able to get out because of the snow and East wind. Yesterday I went again, much the same report. Elma had heard from Mrs. Charles Lewes that she has begun to look at her letters:—of course hundreds had come and she reads two or three as she feels able or inclined.—I am glad there is none of mine among the number. By and bye I will write to her—I wonder when "mothering Sunday" falls, if one could wait for that—: I would write of small bits of work one might have on hand, of other people's troubles, and dimly of the blessedness of having seen and loved perfectly generous, loving goodness, which leaves the world through which its steps have passed, evermore a sacred place, a temple where one dwells thankfully and wherein one may only dare to dwell if one's soul is subdued to thankful humility and eager devotion. Miss Helps[186] came to Charles Street on Thursday. She has not been to the house herself—says everyone speaks well of Charles' goodness to Her—wonders how she looks—said her father had so many stories of Mr. Lewes's kindness and generosity to young writers. Elma was much depressed yesterday:—she is a difficult person to get on with. I am sure it would not be good for her to settle abroad as she talks of doing; it would intensify the scrappy way of living which makes it so difficult now for me to sympathize with her life;—I mean the depending on short relationships or abrupt tragedies for bringing her in contact with her kind. It is this that fosters the rather arrogant

---

[184] "As a gentle soul which makes not excuse, but makes its own will of another's will" (*Divine Comedy*, "Purgatory," XXX, 131-2).

[185] "And I, who to the end of all desires was approaching, even as I ought, ended within myself the ardor of my longing. . . . a sigh and smile bid me look up—but I was already, of myself, such as she wished; for my sight becoming pure, was entering more and more through the radiance of the lofty Light which in Itself is true" (*Divine Comedy*, "Paradise," XXX, 46-54).

[186] See June 2, 1878, and December 29, 1880.

way of looking at people as the recipients of kindness, persons "to be helped," as if that were so easy and no one were worth knowing for their own sake or because *they* might help. There is a certain love that people get from living always with inferiors, which unfits them for fuller, more complete association.

January 28, 1879

I wish I could help feeling this constant half-irritation—anyway I oughtn't to allow myself to strengthen it by expression. Have had to hold myself in in order not to be put out by Mary's proposal to escape with Miss Richardson to Mentana at a moment's notice. It comes the very day I was proposing to settle down to Greek and Appropriation, after a quiet week with Mr. Lewes's book.— After all my only *serious* objection is the misgiving that nothing will ever pay so long as I have to do with it. God forbid that the small personal annoyance should for a moment overcloud—it has not for a moment overclouded—the blessed feeling of communion with Him as well as her. My poor darling—one's heart yearns over her—Oh! how does she bear the long, dark days?—The thought, the love of them is indeed a God, a Saviour to my soul; I am too thankful for the blessing to reproach myself for not having hasted sooner, when one's sympathy and assent might have been glad at the answering love, but I have a shame faced consciousness that if I had been quite good to her, had been taken closer to his dear heart—I could not have borne to be cut off from her now and I would rather have rebelled in the days of her happiness than now.

January 30, 1879

Yesterday I stayed at home—a day was more than enough to clear off all trace of mental annoyance.—Went to the Priory to enquire: just the same. Then walked on to Hampstead, with some trepidation, meaning and fearing to call on Mrs. Charles Lewes.—Rang and the door was some time in being answered, was ushered in and waited some time in the pretty little cottage drawing room; then Mrs. Charles came in with her things on and explained her children were spending the afternoon with friends and she had to fetch them home before dark, would I walk with her—I assented gladly and soon began my enquiries. She said there seemed little to tell; her health was fairly good—for her; the hysterical fits recur, but she says though she is weaker after them, they relieve the brain—there are times when she cannot shed a tear and then the physical oppression is terrible. I asked a little how she occupied herself and learnt that besides reading and looking over manuscript for his book, she is also reading through old letters and journals of his, going back to quite early years. It was strange to find her daughter-in-law complaining, with even a little jealous bitterness, of never having been taken into the "familiarity" of intercourse—to use the word pedantically. She said He was glad—it added to his happiness that she should exist, but she had never been able to feel it was so with Her. I hardly ventured to suggest qualifying consolations—it would only make matters worse if I knew better than she if she was dear to her husband's mother. She said she thought even Charlie was only valued because he was his father's son. She took credit to herself for having proposed that he should go and stay there, feeling that all *she* could do was to give up her claims to him. It is not like me to find pleasure in the woes of others, and yet I cannot quite help feeling relieved when others make such complaints, and I feel how I indeed have not—have never had any ground for complaining—I have been exacting, troublesome, and she patient and generous. I wonder whether they will come—I have asked Elma, Miss Helps and Johnny and Miss Cross to luncheon on Sunday—shall we succeed if so in making the meeting a service of commemoration? Dear one—will it comfort you bye and by to know what comfort you have given—how, for me, your teaching has made all the world anew. A little cheque for a review came in today—I am promising myself to take some flowers to Highgate on Saturday.

February 4, 1879

Instead I waited to see Mary off en route for Italy and had only time to go round to the Priory to enquire. She had had to go to bed with a headache. Miss Helps and Mrs. Menzies came to luncheon on Sunday. Elma being not so well. When they were gone, I went to the Priory again; Sir James Paget has been seeing her. One fears what that may mean. I asked Brett if she still had the same hysterical attacks—she said not so often. In spite of the ever present comfort of the truths that she has brought home to one's heart; in spite of the loving memory of his sweet goodness—the weight of life presses hardly,—oh God! how can she endure it from hour to hour? Most evenings, when every one is gone to bed I let myself dwell upon what has been and what is, and the tears flow in pure sorrow now, without a trace of bitterness.—But I cannot comfort Elma. I wish I could be sure there was no bitterness in her grief, I am afraid to try even to win her confidence, lest she should resent the indiscretion.

February 9, 1879

Yesterday She went out for a drive, for the first time. I thought of her the moment I woke for the sky was blue, a sight so long unfamiliar as to take me by surprise, and I wondered if she would be well enough. Brett said she had not complained of pain for two days. Today she was also pretty well—not the worse. Went to Elma in the morning. She is fretting about Roland:—not quite reasonably, but I think what I said did not leave her more unhappy. For myself, I am a little afraid whether, if I am hindered too long from setting about the "History of Appropriation" my mind will get out of tune, otherwise, I am tolerably at peace: even the other night, dog tired, discouraged and walking in boots that let in the wind, still I held to the truth which is my deliverance—and while that holds to me, how can I call myself alone? One gets sad and weary but that is *common*—one is not perplexed. I have read through his first volume of "Problems" again: the ground is well cleared in that, but I am uneasy as to how far he may have prepared the positive construction to be raised upon it.—And it is horrible to think of her prostrated with pain and unable to work—and he, whose voice was never able to continue audible in reading aloud save when she was ill and needed it!—When one thinks of her in pain alone, one might almost be tempted to ask what difference it has all made—as if she were wicked and we did not love.—And yet not so.

February 12, 1879

Yesterday Eleanor Cross came to see me, and I asked about the beginnings of their intimacy. They knew him for about a year before her. The first acquaintance was mainly with the elder sister before her marriage; then in 1869 they were at Rome when Johnny, his mother and Mary were there at the same time as Mr. Bullock and his wife. She was interested in them and in his devotion to his wife, but the sister never became really at her ease with them. After her death, Johnny as well as "Henry" was drawn to Her by the strange likeness I have heard of before, but for a long time they were jealous because they thought she didn't do justice to Johnny and cared so much more for Henry. I told her that the first time I saw her welcome the latter—without knowing who he was—I wished I was that man. I did not tell her—what I have just remembered—that I felt as if I could have married that man if he had asked me! Mrs. Bullock's book of extracts was shown to Mrs. Lewes and many passages were the same as She herself had copied out. Today I went to the Priory about 3—she had been out for a drive again yesterday and today; Sir James Paget had not been since Saturday.—Oh one other thing Eleanor said: they had a note from her—only a few lines, and it was about oatmeal—but still it was a comfort—a sign of life. I had a struggle with my self on Sunday, whether I should write to her at once,—having heard of her driving out, or whether I should keep to my plan of not writing till "Mothering Sunday"—some six weeks off. I would not wait too long and yet—long enough.

February 17, 1879

She was not as well all last week—and on Friday after a violent hysterical attack Dr. Charles was sent for: yesterday he and Sir James Paget were to see her. She had been in the garden for a little in the morning. One fears that it is this way—as soon as she is physically better and as it were ready to come back to life, the sense of the infinite loss comes over her afresh and it has all to be lived through from the beginning.—And then she will despair of completing her work with this failing strength—oh Mother! Mother! Now, how is one to comfort her—it grows harder and harder—one feels that one must try to comfort her and then as one feels the utter hopelessness—how can there be any comfort left?—one dares not try and one longs all the more.—If not before I must write to her next Sunday 4 weeks.

February 23, 1879

The doctors according to Brett said, "with care" "in a few months' time"—she would be herself again.—Three months have passed already—one can hardly believe it—and then one begins to ask oneself after all this time, after the time that is still to pass, how will it be possible for her to arrange any plan of life in which we can have any part—except as superfluous visitors. One can only wait with patient love—I am ready for whatever she may choose. My life is rather a strange one: rather more of the "business" than usual, for a sort of material necessity is upon me to make it pay—as a step to being able ever to do any thing else. Meanwhile I have got to lecture to workmen's clubs, attend clergy conference, and read such odds and ends as I am up to in the evenings, while the circuit to the Priory to enquire 3 or 4 times a week completes the fullness of as many days; last week Elma has not been well enough to see me; one is deeply sorry for her, but somehow she has never grown to be a selfish pleasure to me, so that one should feel the loss, except for her sake. As a matter of ethical judgment I find myself on the point of admiring Mrs. Menzies most. It is strange that so much childish pleasure-seeking should have survived the hardships of her life—I suppose she must have clung in earlier days to this power of being amused as an escape from fiercer passions, and she does not see how, in altered circumstances, it looks like common wilfullness or self-indulgence.

February 27, 1879

On Tuesday I got to the Priory late, saw Brett who said Mrs. Lewes wanted her to order 6 shirts made—like Mrs. Stuart's; when could I come and see about them. She was better and had been out for an hour and a half. Brett looked more like herself and I too was comforted. Yesterday morning I called about 11 and was taken into the drawing room.—While Brett left me I looked round—wondering with tears how she was able to live at all:—the room looked bright and pretty—the only change long white curtains to the front windows, like a veil making it impossible for people to see in: the sofa was not against the wall, but out in front of the fire as it was the last time I had been in the room, when he was lying there. Brett said she was already down in the dining room,—much stronger, "quite cheerful this morning." It was almost as hard as seeing her to pass outside the room with but a door between us. Cards from Herbert Spencer, Trübner and George Smith were lying on the table. She has offered to see Mrs. Charles Lewes and the children on Saturday. The latter wrote kindly to tell me this:—I open every letter from Hampstead, Weybridge or anyone to whom I have laid my heart open for the sake of her love, with a kind of physical dread—she has spoken of that "feeling of repulsed tenderness which is almost more of a sensation than an emotion," and I cannot doubt that what seems half to disappoint some of her lovers now,—the feeling that she accepts love for their sake rather than her own comes from the often repeated experience of such checks which has ended in her learning to give, asking for nothing again, to all but the one, with whom giving and receiving were the same.—And there is a sweetness of its own in the chastened love that asks nothing but power to bestow.

March 2, 1879

One more step was taken yesterday—Oh God,—it is hard to bear—and yet it is just pure grief, with anger or reluctance, and who should know better than I that this is not the worst. God forbid I should complain for myself—only—good and brave as she is—one's heart smiles with the sense that her burden is heavier than she can bear, and alas, none can help or comfort. The Sunday morning alone in quiet is sacred to her and grief—it is all I save for myself now, and I could hardly do without it—it is the one bit of one's real life; but then—I have not said yet what it is that has agitated me but I can only think with dread and shrinking of the first interview when it comes; I understand her dread, because I feel the same, and yet it must be. Yesterday I think she drove to Hampstead to see Mrs. Charles Lewes and the children, and Brett says in driving when she comes to a dry place she gets out and walks a little—oh cruel!—Can it be *alone!*—and yet—as easily alone as with any one else.—One must prepare oneself for that—it will be very, very little, very seldom even if there is a little ever that she may be able to accept at our hands—and one must leave it to her to choose what she will take, when every act and word must be pain, God forbid one should give her the pain of saying No. I have been troubled to know how I shall write to her. She has often signed her letters "M." and with my wonted stupidity, I have been shy to conclude whether it stood for her name or "Mother"—though she has often signed that too. She left a note for me—about the shirts—my heart stood still when I saw the envelope—She was out driving, and Brett took me into the dining room,—her portrait always looks at me now with a sad appealingness, the drawing room door was open too—I hated myself for being in the house—what right has anyone to fill the space that is all bitter emptiness for her? I laid the note down—I could not bear to open it before Brett and went on speaking to her—then she referred to the note—I read it, just the matter of fact message and thanks and apologies as of yore. I walked back to Charles Street with dim eyes and then as I went on to St. Paul's, sitting veiled in the corner of an omnibus, I read the words again and again and again was choked with a hopeless passion of sorrow for her desolation; she has written to condemn the petty pride which takes refuge in isolation, but how can such grief as hers be shared,—she has spoken too of the living griefs as to which "even sympathy may wound"—may one at least be kept back from wounding her. Fortunately, it was not till I was alone at home that I dared to look with all my eyes to see to whom she wrote. It was not a pain to know, I had accepted that even before Charles wrote first, even before all hope was gone. The withdrawn endearment grieves me only as a measure of her utter desolation—how utter is the loss which forbids to feel that anything precious can be left. My loss is little by the side of Hers, and yet—it is not enough to fill one's life and leave no space for petty mournings. One should try, but oh—it is sad. Today is bright and sunny, I welcome it for her sake—for my own the long chill darkness seemed fitter.

March 5, 1879

Better news from Brett yesterday, confirmed by Mrs. Charles, whom I shall see tomorrow; shall have to bury my news of her by throwing all my mind into something else. I am just the least bit what people might call busy now — having Elma to see as often as I can, and when I don't go, I make a conscience of writing, to amuse her a little—Mrs. Lewes to enquire after 3 or 4 times a week, the shop always, today the father of a would-be partner to interview, Saturday the adjourned meeting of trade unionists and clergy and a paper to arrange for one of the latter to read, same evening a lecture to a club in Bermondsey which has to be invented and written, Sunday another lecture to read and for next Saturday another paper to write and now Mrs. Charles Lewes wanting to enlist me for the Commons preservation. However I can't go far wrong in consenting to write or speak on the side of any useful movement when I have a distinct personal sense of the utility. I am a good deal pained by the consequential tone of Octavia Hill's

"Letter to My Fellowworkers";[187] have been thanking heaven all this evening I am not one of the godly—but I am sincerely grieved at the mistakenness, which must do harm, and I *do* pray heaven—nay—there is no need to pray for what one has and can never lose, but if it had not been given me already I would pray to see myself always in the light of her goodness, and in that light self is not to be seen at all unless it has transgressed and is called up for condemnation. One's efforts are dedicated to her—the result of them is of no worth, only it is the symbol of the undivided love of Her and Righteousness.

March 9, 1879

It served me right for going to Miss Hill's meeting for the sake of something else than its object that Charles Lewes and his wife were both much too full of the cares of organization for me to be able even to ask what news they had of Her. My own news had been good, so I was not very much cut up. On Friday Eleanor Cross came to the shop and said they too had better news. She had written to Johnny on business; they hoped she would see them soon: and Saturday—that is yesterday, she was to see Mrs. Charles and the children. There has been nearly a week of sunshine—they say she is stronger—more cheerful—but oh! it is impossible!—I think of this time last year of the happy days when my love poured itself out by the side of his—nothing can make all that less dear or precious, but it is miserably sad—she was not less to me—I dare to say it—than he to Her, but the love was longing, instead of possession and my loss is as much less as my past happiness. It helps me to measure hers—and oh the cruel desolation! A selfish shudder of dread came over me just now, I thought I had given up all hopes and wishes, except to become, if it might ever be, of a little use to her, but all at once I thought—when she is gone to him, when there is nothing left but a memory, when tenderness can no longer wait upon the hope of service—how shall I be able to live then—in loneliness more complete even than hers.—That too will have to be endured, and without moan or feebleness. I will not own that that then can be desolation—as I have said, the world shall be sacred to their worship—only I am an unworthy servant of the sanctuary. It is not easy for instance, to try when one is no longer young to learn to do for the sake of others what, long ago one might have done easily, for one's pleasure:—I always have some case of conscience on hand, and I ask myself now how much labour it is right to spend in trying to do what is so far from coming easy to me that no trying can end in its being really well done. However, I am so lazy that it will be safe to begin by trying—this is á propos of my Second Workman's Club Lecture. Yesterday I read fast and awkwardly what was meant for a popular subject. Before night was writing to prepare a better delivery for a duller subject.

March 10, 1879

The lecture was no doubt "instructive," as those things go and the people were perhaps not more bored than they settle down to being under the circumstances, though they were only quite "here" with the little bits of

---

[187] See December 5, 1878.

extempore application I gave now and again. They ended with "hoping to see me again," and I felt that on any subject about which my mind was full, I could talk to them with moderate success—only moderate but then what would one have? Today I went by the Priory and took Brett's orders—and Manchester Street where saw Elma, to the shop where saw Miss Williams. In the afternoon Eleanor Cross came to mend drapery, and she told me Mrs. Lewes saw Johnny for a little while on Saturday on business:—and was to see Henry Sidgwick yesterday also on business—she thought about some endowment at Cambridge which Mr. Lewes had wished for. He thought her as well as could be expected or hoped—much changed but that might be partly the Ms,—not more changed that he expected. And she spoke of delighting in her work, being completely interested in it—for which one cannot be too thankful. She also said to him that Brett and Sir James Paget kept urging her to see people—"they don't know that there are many worse things than solitude." It was all welcome news to me—I always felt Johnny had a right to be the first admitted, it will be far less painful to her to see people with some sort of business than a mere visitor—I cannot even envy them—my dread of seeing her grows with time that only seems to bring more home to me the sense of her desolateness—the awful change that stands between Her and love.—All that is left of my jealous hunger is the feeling that I could not have borne it had they seen her and I not heard of it. I came back across Hyde Park after Sunset, and seemed to commune with her. I felt that she would be thinking of me if at all as one to whom she was a loss—not as one who might be of any service to her and in imagination I answered her questions from the calm of my set, unhesitating view of her life in front:—a vision of labour, not much lit up by hope—rather cheered by the unexpectedness of the thin rays that one does not rest even upon,—of solitude, because one has strength enough to renounce the sweet longing to lean upon another's strengths and yet solitude without desolation because now and again a hand rests on one's own for support,—of sadness, no doubt, because there is nothing but sadness for her, but yet, through all the sadness, the solitude, the unhopeful labour the vision is still—of peace and blessedness; it is a good gift when in later years we find what we have longed for during a youth granted us and know it for the same and welcome it with unchanged desire. So I felt after the spirit of a religion that was no more: and now, when the burden of life is heaviest there is a haven of rest—whither one flies to worship, a spiritual world within the other—and then he is ever kind and loving and there is a memory of the pearly sky at eve—the "touch of a vanished hand"—the glance of ineffable love that—oh I know it!—She would never have cast on me if his love had not warmed and gladdened her tender soul!—At least the aching of my heart answers the idle question—Is life worth living?—Yea verily as long as one's heart can ache so sorely for grief without a touch of gall.

March 12, 1879

Like an answer to what I say of this "good gift" I find a saying of Goethe: "Das ist der glücklichste Mensch, der das Ende seines Lebens mit dem

Anfang in Verbindung setzen kann."[188] It is a sign how much I have lived through in the last six years what very different passages from of old touch me in Goethe's writings, and yet Hamilton and Co is in close connection with the 2nd part of Faust. She drove out for 2 1/2 hours this afternoon: the accounts of her continued cheering—and yet—oh, how can she endure it?—One can do nothing for her but oh! the pity of it! Eleanor spoke as if she was going to keep on Witley as a summer dwelling place.—Of course she has nothing to stay in London for but somehow whichever way one looks at it the sense of her utter desolateness comes over one afresh and the sad feeling that there is no one whose being is a cause of loving gladness to her now. It seems to me that one needs all one's old wisdom, as well as all the new, to bear unshaken the vision of such a fate for the beloved—how could I live if I did not love them? This morning I thought it sad—Mrs. Menzies said of Elma, as a kind of reason why she might as well live abroad "there is no one she cares much about except me and Roly"—it is strange as a commentary on our first letters that this should be true and I reflecting on it think only "Poor thing,"—She would deny it, but what I have always missed is the genuine lasting affection that comes to be felt without blessedness.

March 16, 1879

The accounts are still that she is better and stronger. It is even possible that after a time she may be stronger—the nervous strain of thoughtful care for him being removed, and making place for the uneventful calm, the death like peace of those who "have lived." I wonder whether it will be kind or not to write next Sunday—I shrink from it as from seeing her—any way I should write but once. Am looking forward to renewing acquaintance this summer with my old schoolmistress—what one hears of her makes me think she would be cheered by a little kindness from her old and most troublesome pupil. Time goes on and I have not been able to do anything in the way of work—only rambling papers which won't do much for one's reputation and which on conscientious grounds one ought to try to improve.

March 19, 1879

This afternoon Eleanor Cross came again. Johnny saw her on Tuesday and thought her better, but I grieve to hear she is dissatisfied about her work—if that anxiety begins I fear neither peace nor health can be looked for.—If one could only help and comfort her in that—but no possible changes in the past could have made that less impossible than now. She was going to see Mrs. Congreve[189] yesterday.—She told Johnny she shrank from seeing people—also

---

[188] "The person who connects the end of his life with the beginning of his life is the happiest person."

[189] Maria Bury Congreve (d. 1915) was the daughter of the Coventry surgeon who attended GE's father during his last illness. The wife of Positivist Richard Congreve (1818-1899), she was a dear friend of GE's from February, 1859, at Holly Lodge, Wandsworth, until her death. Maria was seventeen years younger

that she was going to see Mrs. Stuart.—I think that must be my doing—on Monday at the end of the short note acknowledging hers about the shirts, I said Elma was better, going to leave town in 2 or 3 weeks, and "as she talked of wintering in a warm climate it might be a year before she was in England again."—I feared whether this was saying too much—seeming to make a suggestion, and yet I feared for Elma's soul if she had to leave England without a word. My dread of seeing Her grows more and more intense and yet—if one only might, there are so many ways in which I could serve her more easily and gladly than perhaps anyone else—if she could feel it possible. Johnny said she seemed better. Yet whatever happens there is always in my ears as it were her voice silencing every half-rising murmur "Am I then upon a bed of roses?" Dearest—I would be content to live forever outside your love if my endurance could spare you but a moment of the scorching pain.

March 23, 1879

On Friday as I was going there, I met Charles coming away and turned and went with him to the station. She has sent to the printer the first "Problem" about 200 pages, and is going to publish them in that way singly, not in large volumes. He rather negatived her being discouraged, but said it was well that it should be out of her hands, otherwise she only read it through and through, wondering if it was yet complete. He said she was always much exhausted after seeing anyone and he never went himself the day anyone else did: also that she had been much interested in arranging for a memorial endowment at Cambridge, about which she had been seeing two or three people,—Sidgwick, Foster,[190] &c, besides Johnny about changing investments—it was such a comfort being able to trust that to him as both a friend and so excellent a man of business. She is going to try living at Witley this summer, and let it if she cannot bear it—I fear whether she will, since the only idea of breaking her loneliness is that "Gertrude and the children should stay there for a week at a time." Elma is still a difficulty to me— to know how to help a mind so ingenious in remembering things its own way.

March 30, 1879

It is 4 months since. My grief is just the same as ever—how should Hers grow less. I used to count my life by the days she lighted up—there is nearly a whole year dead. God knows I have no wish but hers—it shall be as she pleases whether hereafter—Oh I don't complain—I have had my life, I will set about the book even yet! So long as one can live and work harmlessly what does any other failure hurt? What a tough life would have been had her loss found me happy without her?

---

than GE and is included by Haight among the women who loved her "passionately" (H, I, xlix and 68).

[190] Dr. Michael Foster was helping GE to correct the proofs for GHL's book (H, IX, 274, n. 2).

April 5, 1879

Day after day as I walk about London my eyes fill with tears and I have to fly and hide myself from the daylight in other thoughts. I am not pining for her—sometimes it is pure love and sorrow for him who is gone, sometimes the cruel sense of her loneliness and grief, sometimes perhaps the sad helplessness of love that cannot help the loved one—but I have no craving to see her, no jealousy of other friends, only a dire dread of the sad meeting—when we shall touch hands in silence across the awful gulf. At the beginning of the week I was occupied with the thought of saving the life of the Women's Printing Company by bringing out Iago. But on enquiry I was afraid there was not enterprise enough among the founders for it to be safe for me to undertake so much fresh work. I think on the whole I must go on with Hamilton and Co till it pays and try and keep my mind fresh for work after that result sets me free. Tuesday, Thursday and today I went to ask after her—saw the cook on Tuesday; Thursday she was better after 2 days' headache. Today Brett looked more cheerful and said she was better—less depression when she was able to go out every day—she was out driving then, and I had some dim hope that the difficult meeting might be got over by accident if I met her alighting as I was leaving the house—but chance is seldom kind. I dined with Elma last night—she is just in the same mood about Roland—I can't feel that it would be any kindness to join her in blaming him, and yet I have hardly any power to influence her to take a happier view.

April 11, 1879

Tuesday morning I went to bid her good-bye. Today I have written to her—I hardly know whether it can do any good, and I would as soon have left it alone, but I was afraid of its being one of the "leavings undone that make a great difference to other lives."

April 12, 1879

There are days when one seems taken care of from above.—I was kept at the shop till after 4 writing letters &c; sleet and rain were falling heavily—I was in two minds whether to carry out my purpose of going round by the Priory—but I had not been since Wednesday and I did not like letting so many days pass, besides, I had almost made up my mind to write to her on Easterday, but I couldn't risk doing so unless I knew how she was—so I went. Brett exclaimed at my being out such a day and said—Would I come in for a little? I said—Oh no! and then she; perhaps I was too wet to stop now, but Mrs. Lewes had said she would like to see me the next time I came. Fortunately I had on a long jacket and had fastened up my dress, so that when one was off and the other down I was not apparently drenched, and she went to ask Mrs. Lewes if I should come in, presently the answer came, she would be glad to see me.—I came in with my veil down—she received me almost as usual and but for the veil which she made me take off would have received me with a kiss of welcome.—I spoke with effort of the long cold, and the danger of inclement holiday times. She said the coffee palaces seemed the only resource—had I seen much of them? I spoke of my lecturing for the working men's clubs.—She had in her hands some of his Ms and proof and said she would leave me for a moment to put it in a place of safety. I tried to force back the tears, and stooped as she came back to move the footstool out of her way. She called me a thoughtful child and presently as another easy subject I spoke of Mrs. Stuart. She was sorry for her without blaming the boy, and said she had begun to defend him a little, when Mrs. Stuart was overcome and apparently they spoke of other things. She said she had seen no one but men about the Studentship, Mrs. Congreve and Elma. She spoke about the foundation and the volume she was bringing out and when she found I knew of both, she touched my cheek almost playfully and asked me how I came to know so much.—Before this I had risen to go, fearing to weary her, but instead, she made me sit down on her footstool, and she took my hand in hers. I told her how I had met Charlie and that Eleanor Cross had been to see me and given me news of her from Johnny. She said the latter told her he had seen me— and he praised me for unselfishness—said I never seemed to think of myself. She spoke, to my delight, freely and often of her husband, and said at first she had an intense repulsion from everyone—it seemed wicked—but she could hardly bear even Charlie—who was as good as a son could be, but—so different. She said the Studentship had made it easier to her to see people—she was going tomorrow to see Mr. and Mrs. Harrison who had been so kind; but other people she could not attempt. She spoke of the servants: of the comfort of human kindness without companionship when any nearer sympathy would be intolerable.— Nothing could be further from morbid sensibility than her whole manner and words.

April 13, 1879

She said she did not know how she could have lived if she had not had his Ms and the Studentship to think about,—she could read nothing else and went over that again and again till her brain went round; but she was comforted in reading the proofs after an interval. She had always identified herself with his Ms so that he said she found more fault with them than she would if they had belonged to anyone else, and now she had a dread of any light words that might be said in forgetfulness of the unfinished state of the work:—which was foolish, since he would not have cared,—he was the only man who really delighted in adverse criticism—in a fair spirit as a means of reaching truth. Her pleasure in the endowment is that he would delight to live in a series of lives—he had always looked to the younger students and been patient of the unreceptiveness of others—who if they accepted his views did not own to doing so,—which was the rarer merit since he delighted so much in any sympathy that came:—only the week after their return from Brighton he had been pleased by receiving from some young men's reading club at Liverpool notice that the book they were going to discuss this winter was his. I was inexpressibly thankful to find that one might speak freely of the dear one. It had seemed to me cruel to be shut out from that, and yet I had the intense feeling of gratitude for an unexpected, unmerited boon when I found myself received as near to her as ever—the delight of receiving as a gift what one had made up one's mind not to claim.—She is so good she will find comfort yet in the blessedness she sheds on her children.

Elma is really very good: she sends me double thanks for my letter, she will not answer but will *think* about it. This is very generous. I said something to Mrs. Lewes about her having an unhappy nature—setting her heart on things and being cast down from a height when they failed her—which She translated better—she does things under an impulse and then feels they give her a claim. I said I had told her when she spoke of Roland as ungrateful that by asking for gratitude one ceased to deserve it. Mrs. Lewes said "How did she take it?"—and all that I wrote on Friday must have been to the full as hard—tho' doubtless she was helped by having seen Mrs. Lewes, and perhaps, such is human nature—by the thought that she had seen her and I had not! One smiles at those little jealous promptings, and yet I cannot but own to a selfish joy at finding that she places me only after Johnny and one of her oldest friends—for I feel no jealousy of the Cambridge men or Elma, who owed something to my intercession:—"such is human nature"—I mean such as to prompt that last clause. I am unspeakably thankful for her goodness—for the future hope that she will accept a daughter's duty at one's hands. The African daughter-in-law has sailed to England with her children and as soon as they arrive she will go down to Witley. I hope Mrs. Congreve will be in the neighborhood still; otherwise one fears as her strength increases the complete solitude will have its risks, in letting her labour too exclusively at the Ms.

April 14, 1879
    Dearest, will it be painful to you to hear how completely the blessing of your goodness possesses my soul, how the still sweet power overshadows one—one has the sense of being folded in the Everlasting Arms:—the inner life is fulfilled, love and reverence leave nothing more to ask and the outer life springs unfettered.—It is strange, I never wanted or sought a religion and it has come to me of itself as the supreme blessing of one's life.

April 20, 1879
    On Monday I went to ask—excusing myself to Brett by anxiety lest she should have been wearied on Saturday. Brett's version is that it "cheers her up" to see anyone—one never knows whether she or Charley is the best judge—it is a little hard to have to depend on them. Thursday I went again—with a little of the old anxious hesitation—but this I will not indulge. I wrote to her on Tuesday—craving her leave for such constant calls:—I shall go this afternoon too—it is raining fast, but I will not expect to see her.—When I do, however, I shall be able to talk to her about the women at the Army Clothing Works. The women affected by the reduction had been invited to a meeting at the Westminster Democratic Club, lent by the men for that purpose. I got down there about 7 expecting the usual meager congregation, but as I looked up at the bills posted in the Club windows a man accosted me, was I looking for the meeting?—it had been adjourned to Portcullis Hall just across the road, their room wasn't large enough. That sounded encouraging and I crossed over to be accosted by another man, was I one of the friends expected? I asked for Mrs. Paterson and was shown into a small room through the door of which one heard a Babel of voices; the Hall was already packed as full as it would hold, ground and gallery, sitting and standing. A subterranean way led us to the Platform and when I saw the crowd of faces, I wished for the moment I was an orator—had a sense of lost

opportunity in remembering that I had no speech prepared. The first episode was a cry from the hall of "A spy, a spy" with hisses and suggestions "Turn him out." Mr. Hodgson Pratt, who was chairman and had no sinecure—immediately called on all the men in the hall to take their seats on the platform; the hisses continued till two men disappeared—they were the obnoxious manager whose salary has been raised, they say, £250 a year and his son. Then after a little explanation of the objects of the meeting Mr. Hodgson Pratt asked for facts and without the least hesitation a succession of women—a dozen or twenty—climbed up on the platform and gave their depositions. The upshot of it is that many of them have been in the habit of working a day and a half—one woman told me by taking work home and working very hard in the stores besides she could never earn over 17/ or 18/ and that if people earned 30/—they never did it all themselves. Say however a woman earned as much as a pound at the old prices, she loses now certainly a quarter of her work by not being allowed to take it home which brings her earnings to 15/ old style, which at new prices would only give 12/—they would have put up with either change alone but the two together are too much for them. The woman who has had 20/ gets 12/, the one who has had 15/ gets 9/— Mrs. Paterson suggested a demonstration—those turned off to go to Westminster and send a deputation to the house, which was done next day; and yesterday still at the Democratic Club we began receiving names and subscriptions for a Pimlico branch of the Tailoresses Society. 140 joined off hand and I thought my darling would be pleased if she heard the women one after another expressing their gratitude to me for coming there and to the meeting. Their speeches were often quaint with a deliberately chosen point—I don't know whether the large proportion of Irish recruits had anything to do with that—One woman expressed her readiness to declare solemnly before God and anyone else!—Another who seemed to wish to make a whole speech said they weren't to steal, and they weren't to beg—begging was worse than stealing—and even if you commit suicide, they give you 7 days, so what *were* they to do? It is very very mysterious the way all my mental energies are stimulated by a touch from her. On Sunday I began—and have nearly finished—going through his 3 volumes in a kind of half comment, half analysis, which will be of use if I find it possible to get a notice of his new volume printed in some quarterly. Otherwise I am thinking of writing to Longman to propose a small volume on the lines of the two articles in Fraser.— There might be an appendix on the discovery of "the intelligent working woman" by the League and Hamilton and Co.

April 25, 1879

Last Sunday I went through the rain, with which after that wet Saturday I am more in love than ever. The answer was short—much the same. Wednesday went again and exchanged a few friendly remarks with Brett—the widow and children from Natal had not yet arrived. Thursday for reasons I did not wish to be at the shop all day so seized the opportunity to go as I had long wished to Highgate. I walked to Charles Street first, then to Gower Street, Covent Garden, Trafalgar Square and then started north. Where the trainway and Hampstead and Highgate roads fork off I turned by mistake to the left and found myself landed at the Church above Haverstock Hill; made straight across the hill towards Highgate by a faint muddy pathway, at the centre of which 2 parties of birdcatchers were at work at their unsatisfactory trade—an hour or two before I had been pitying the caged larks in St. Martins Lane. At last I reached the cemetery; men were at work again; I doubt if the grave had been visited since I was there: the white wreath was withered to a brown skeleton; the fir twigs of mine were still just green and in the centre of it I laid a bunch of fresh primroses:—then I fled from the workmen with their well-meaning assurances the slab would look better when it was cleaned up a bit; it was a flat marble slab with his name and the date of birth and death. I roamed about and then turned to the Church of England portion, where the slope of the hill is steeper, the trees shadier and the whole aspect less like that of new built suburb. Then I came back and passed near the workmen again—then, a little before 3 I turned to leave; as I was walking down the lane below the cemetery, I saw a carriage half open—and a well known face—set and sad she was looking straight before her and did not see me and my first impulse was to look away as an intruder; my heart was wrung for her and I walked up and down long, but it was some time before I began to feel what I have felt with bitter regret ever since,—that I might have turned and tried to overtake her—have met her at the gate and let her lean on me as she walked and perhaps come between her and the workmen. I lost this chance and had only the comfort of hoping that she would be glad to find the fresh flowers as a sign he was not quite forgotten. I have regretted my cowardice ever since, all the more because I think if I had thought first of her only my impulse must have been to fly to her side—and yet one hardly knows—could she have borne for any one to be near? Since then I have longed to write to her, but all words seem a profanation—I shall try to call tomorrow after attending to the tailoresses; it is horrible to find oneself craving selfishly for the privilege of seeing her once more—Her book is announced, as well as his.—Oh it is a cruel pain—one complains of nothing for oneself but sometimes the thought of her pain is more even more than one can bear.—For myself I hardly feel pain, only now intense difficulty.

April 29, 1879

On Saturday I saw Brett, who said she had just returned from her drive. I was resolute in not expecting anything more, but on Sunday, with much hesitation I wrote to her—saying what had happened, and then speaking of his book. Today I called as usual; Brett was out and "Mary" answered my questions. Mrs. Herbert Lewes and the children had arrived, on Saturday, and had been to see Mrs. Lewes, and she had just driven them back and was still out. Mary was full of the beauty of the children. Sometimes one is forced to believe in a Providence. I was hardly outside the gate when I saw the carriage driving up—this time there could be no hesitation and I dashed up to open the door for her and give my hand; she asked me to turn back and come in with her. There is something infinitely touching to me in what one sees as a resolve to throw off the overmastering sense of grief and "live for others in a living world." She spoke of the loveliness of the children and said, though it wasn't right or reasonable, she could never care for a plain child, though with dogs or any other kind of creature ugliness appealed to all her sympathies. She was tired with the children, who were full of life and restlessness and said she was glad she had not even attempted to have them with her. She smiled compassionately at the good friends who think these children will be a comfort and interest to her—of course she is glad to be able to provide for them, but they cannot enter into her life. And yet she said, if the girl had been alone in the world, it would have been a temptation to her; but it was best as it was; she always became a slave to the child or whatever else she lived with. Her sister had a little girl, since dead, who used to stay with her, and notwithstanding the biting things she has written since about maternal follies, she used every night long before bedtime to undress this child and rock her to sleep in her arms, feeling a sort of rapture in the mere presence, even though she might want the time for reading. She spoke half in self-reproach of the people who live in so many relations that their life must be always full, whereas she always sent the strength of her feeling in the channel which absorbed it all. It had been so with her father. And then she said something that I cannot quite repeat,—a reference to the step they had taken, which, without injuring, perhaps favoring the work they could do best for other people, forced them to live for each other and in such complete independence of the outer world that the world could be nothing for them. She said it seemed a sort of dual egoism: but then again that it must surely be best to make the nearest relation perfect: it was sad to see husbands and wives running away from each other after philanthropic works while the one life was left unblessed. I asked about her nephew Vivian who is to be married at Christmas. I tried to say I had been interested in that love story because he spoke of it to me, but I broke down, swallowed the last of my tea and said I must go. She said she was tired, and that I must not cry: she could not bear it: she was obliged to turn herself by force from the passion of grief. That she had the comfort of knowing his life was perfect to the last, that mind and character suffered no falling off, and she—here she broke down into sobs, that she must live while she could—as he would have wished for her.—I knelt and kissed her, reproaching myself inwardly for having brought on the painful outbreak, but she recovered herself again. Said she was anxious to be at Witley and free from disturbance.—That what she missed most was the moral support— that she ended once—she was glad now to think she had—a summary of a year's journal by saying his presence was a check on all that was evil, an encouragement to all that was good in her: her feeling was of rest and freedom from all difficulty, because her pleasure was to do what he wished and he never wished anything but the right. Her one pleasure now was to read appreciation of him. She mentioned a letter from Peter Bayne[191]—a man she had only seen once but who had written her a letter of such just estimate of what was most characteristic of his criticism that she had been truly grateful. He mentioned his reluctance to give pain and she quoted as a fresh and precious memory how some three and twenty years before when she was, for a short time, writing reviews, she had referred to some inadequate translation with a strong and appropriate adjective— and he asked her to leave out the adjective—why should she make a poor man

---

[191] Peter Bayne (1830-1896) called at the Priory December 9, 1877. His letter (H, VII, 282) is at Yale (H, IX, 266, n. 9).

miserable unnecessarily? She spoke of having the perfect life to look back on—which might have been a hell: death would be welcome when it came—the path that he had trod.—At least, she said, she had more duties, she could do hard things now—he had kept all difficulties far from her. I said her duty would be to let other people do all they could for her, but she clung to the scourge and called herself self-indulgent. Then she referred to the time when they were poor and how then and since they laughed at all their troubles and how he exaggerated hers—which would have been quite intolerable to her—who had had a very luxurious life—but for the happy love,—which reconciled her to having nothing but a very hard chair covered with moreen to sit on when her head ached badly. I said I had read all that between the lines about Lydgate and Rosamond.[192] At 6, after 3/4 of an hour, I left—gathering up her things, and she came with me to the door and I put my arms around her for a last kiss. Nearly the first thing she said was that morbid time of repulsion was over for ever—that it was a strange and horrible experience to her to feel the springs of affection dried up, but it was over, and love and tenderness were as precious—or more precious—than ever. She said she had written to me and this evening the sweet lines came. If the mere thought of her pain seemed to me to make discontent at one's own small ills impossible, how much more the thought of the pain not merely suffered but endured as she endures with upright loving courage?

May 1, 1879

The thought of her loving resignation, of tender patience, of loyalty and gratitude—of the presence which cannot be lost or lessened—this is the ever present background to the life without, in which one makes clothes, alters the house, reads about Egypt and talks and writes to friends or philanthropists. I am jealous for those I love and I could not love her as I do if I did not know that all the world is as little to her now as it has been to me apart from her. God forbid that her grief should be such as love or worship of mine could lessen. Our souls are at one, and therefore it seems to me that I shall not lack all the love that I can wish her to be free to give. The rest of the world is pretty grey and blank, but I cannot care—more, than just as much as one ought—for any thing except that love and the hope that it will make one or two moments a shade less grey and blank for her.—She wants companionship "not for her own sake but for that of the companion."

May 3, 1879

On Tuesday I noticed some bowls full of primroses, violets and other fresh spring flowers which she said had been sent—some by friends who left no name—she thought that was unkind—she liked to know to whom to be grateful. She said she had seen no cowslips—they seemed neglected nowadays and their fragrance was as exquisite as the little orange pencilling inside. Yesterday I meant to go and ask after her and contrived to pass Covent Garden where, to my delight I was able to fill a basket with cowslips—left them with my love—she

---

[192] In *Middlemarch*

was not very well. In spite of the sorrow with which one thinks always of the sorrow to which she is wedded, there is, for me then there must be always a strange deep sweetness in the mere thought of her being, in the memory of her presence—dear one, forgive me, the happiness of loving you lives still—through the pain of knowing that your happiness is dead forever. I shall see her once before she leaves and then I will try to speak freely—of love, submission, and the dutiful hoping to come as near to her as one may. The constant blessing of her influence is not only, as she said of His—a check on all one's evil, an encouragement to all the good—the thought of her is peace and strength whenever the inevitable feeling of weariness and discouragement comes over one, when one is just tired and ready to justify one's weary moaning by pointing to the little fruit to be seen from all the labours. What is one's weariness by the side of hers? And if its labour is vain, it is because one's efforts have been too feeble—let us forget the weariness in fiercer struggles.

May 8, 1879

Amen! Amen! but the difficulty remains—can one do the best without encouragement? how far is one right to be indifferent to the absence of an outer call—to thrust oneself forward, a volunteer unsummoned and reluctant! Alas! I can always answer my own difficulties, and the fact is one should not be reluctant when there is even a chance of possible service. But with the best will it is hard to be sure—and one's will I suppose is seldom more than second best. This evening I went—which I didn't want to do, to a talk at St. Paul's Chapter House on Co-Operation; but I didn't speak, because I don't like doing that unless I'm obliged, and I think I ought to have spoken.—The real difficulty is—how far one can, how far one should try to do without the stimulus of contact with her.—Her work waited "for the happiness which his love brought into her life"—is it for me to be stronger than she was?—I am tired and depressed—but one's face is always set the same way. I suppose it will always come over me at times—the pitiful feeling of one's own loneliness—Dearest, dearest one would endure worse than this rather than wander into thoughts that might end in ought less than grateful loyalty. Let me grieve for your grief rather than my own.

May 10, 1879

Yesterday I had a sweet line from her at the shop, sending a cheque and the promise of a goodbye before she left. Today after the shop and a brief visit to Westminster, I hesitated whether to go to the Priory or no—was a little selfishly afraid of going and failing to get any clue as to when she would like to see me, but decided since the hesitation was only selfish, to go and enquire as of old and take my chance. Brett asked if I could wait—Mrs. Lewes had said she would like to see me if I came. She is anxious to get to Witley—there are so many people she feels she must see, lest they should be hurt, and one tells another—they do not all understand—She spoke of there being perhaps 150 people to whom she owed some debt of gratitude. Mrs. Ritchie, Mrs. Burne-Jones, Herbert Spencer and Leslie Stephen happened to be mentioned as people whom she had seen. She asked what I was doing—if I did not mind being asked—she did. I said no—I wished she would ask that I might be ashamed of saying "Nothing." I talked a little about the Westminster Women, Workmen's Clubs &c, and she accused herself of having spoken ill of philanthropists when she said some went far afield after mechanical work in the name of benevolence leaving the nearest need unsupplied: I said I had not misunderstood her. I asked about the children—she had been to buy them toys—the first time she had been into London—to the din of Oxford Street. I asked about the Scholarship and she said there was some delay, a difference of opinion among the trustees—there was no real hurry, but she was impatient, always wanted things settled and had written to ask Mr. Sidgwick about it. I had not said anything that I wanted when Mr. Pigott was announced. I offered to go at once, but she said, sit down, and so I exerted myself to make conversation with him, wondering all the while whether he came on business or as an old friend,—he referred to a former visit. Then he turned his back to look at some flowers and I rose with a questioning look; she assented, and said hurriedly as she kissed me—"Go into the dining room, there is something you will like to see."—An enlarged photograph of him, framed and put over the chimney piece where her portrait used to be.

May 11, 1879

She is so unutterably good—it was always almost painful that anyone should be so perfectly good and now it is too pathetic, when one knows she has lost the help and happiness which made the self-devotion sweet.

May 14, 1879

I wrote to her on Sunday, of him, and I spoke of the instinctive understanding by which desire died when He was gone: and on Monday night came a most precious answer—when she gives so much, how can one wish to ask that she should add the selfish unreasoning fondness which may be the best gift of less rich natures. Her love, her tenderness, her generous recognition of all the little one is worth, all these are more than enough to make life sweet. No word in her note but was grateful to my soul and though I am incapable—it is for that she is grateful—of the stupidity of proffering love is in every wise a consolation for her irremediable grief, still I know that her loving soul must be comforted as the days go by with the recurring proof of words and deeds which show how her love has indeed brought peace and light into a lonely life.

May 17, 1879

Yesterday came another sweet card, bidding me to see her tomorrow. On Thursday I had called to ask after her and left a big handful of forget-me-nots—She is unspeakably good to me. I cannot help being gladdened by such tokens of her tender thoughtfulness, though it seems almost cruel to rejoice in the love that can never more bring joy to her: and yet I know she would not have one reject the blessing of that sweet feeling of thankfulness and delight.

May 22, 1879

I went on Sunday: she looked ill and answered my anxious question by saying she was very ill, I must not stay long.—Her face was like Watts' Paolo[193] with a deathlike expression of overpast pain. She had exhausted her powers of endurance in the attempt to do too much for—I imagined—the daughters-in-law: they weary her and she does not like to say so—she said to me—"One cannot enjoy vicariously."—and then she checked herself and said she ought not to grumble. She leant back in her chair exhausted but told me to wait while she tried to remember what she had to say to me.—It was to ask about the plan of shareholders for H & Co.—I answered very shortly and took my leave; before—through all the grief for her grief and pain, selfish comfort came to me because she was able to bear my nearness; her hand rested in mine and when I kissed her in farewell, the dear cheek pressed itself caressingly on my lips. It is so sweet of her to endure to be loved. On Monday I went to ask and was told she was better, had been for a drive in the morning. Wednesday I wanted much to go but was hindered, I had settled mentally she would leave town on Thursday and thought to find out when or dreamt of lurking at Waterloo to meet her carriage by each possible train and press her hand once more—risking the dread that she would as soon be alone. But it was not to be.—She had left. This morning, an hour or so before I called. I tried in vain to find a secret place in Regent's Park where to lie on the grass and sob out one's first bitter grief. It was a warm shady May day and strollers and children were everywhere—also my moans were choked by the awful thought—her desolation is even more complete than this. Eleanor Cross came to the shop today and asked me to go to them on the 6th—I shall hear of her then no doubt, which is something to look forward to—and then there is her book, and his.—And I have got Gardner Wilkinson's Egypt[194] and mean to plunge into "Appropriation"—surely a harmless opium for the gnawing grief. It is dangerous to listen to one's own heartache if one indulges in such listening it will go on all night. How I rebelled once at her saying—"Why do you do it if it isn't an indulgence?"—"it" being the old habit of mournful cavilling.

May 25, 1879

Have read his Psychology[195] with pleasure—a sad pleasure, for the book is full of life and cheerful confidence—there is one note, inexpressibly sad now, where he quotes a suggestion of hers. I read the book yesterday afternoon—the first day warm enough to try the hammock—I needed to be out of sight of observant eyes, for my own were constantly full of tears.

---

[193] George Frederick Watts (1817-1904) was an illustrator and portrait painter; Paolo and Francesca are from Dante's *Inferno*.

[194] Sir John Gardner Wilkinson (1797-1875), *Manners and Customs of Ancient Egyptians* (London: J. Murray, 1837).

[195] GHL, *Problems of Life and Mind* (London: Trübner, 1879).

May 29, 1879

I wrote to her on Sunday about his book and am now counting the moments till I see hers. Elma is ill again, Mrs. O'Donell has lost her husband,[196] Wilks wants to be paid £120, Professor Bain spoke yesterday of the "very sad story" of Mr. Lewes's first marriage.—The difference she has made to me is that "All the troubles of all the people in the world" move me now to a compassionate sharing in their calamity rather than as formerly to the sense of self-justification in pouring out one's own complaints.

June 1, 1879

"The disloyal attempt to be independent of the common lot and live without a sharing of pain"—this is the sentence out of her book that always stays with me. This feeling of community can hardly be described or inculcated. I think it must have its origin in the growth of deep feelings twined round the being of others; and then, though the joy and the desire may have failed, the fellowship subsists, as a disposition within even if there be no relation of intercourse without. It just occurs to me as one of the things I might ask her— does she count the inner feeling as enough? How would she meet the difficulty that occasions of intimacy are rare.

June 2, 1879

(Whit. Monday). Wasted time and worried in the morning over the firm and Mary's withdrawal, and so having done nothing to Egypt, soothe myself by re-reading Theophrastus. The close compactness of the writing makes much of it gain on a second view. When the book was announced I felt there was a danger lest the valued epigram should have sometimes too cumbrous a setting and this is perhaps the case sometimes, to take a merely literary view—but—and this is very cheering as to her future work, which will hardly be fiction—there is nothing cumbrous or pedantic in her serious writing when launched on *a train* of thought or feeling. There is nothing laboured, e.g. in her charge against Sir Gavial Mantrap[197] or her *plaidoyer*[198] for the restoration of the Jews.

I haven't got fairly started into the History yet and feel depressed when for want of a leading book or from sheer preoccupation I find my mind passive and empty. Then I wonder whether it is after all worth while, whether the fact

---

[196] See January 5, 1879.

[197] In *Impressions of Theophrastus Such* (Edinburgh: William Blackwood and Sons, 1879), GE's narrator Theophrastus is a middle-aged bachelor who records his observations of life in a series of character sketches. In Sec. 16, "Moral Swindlers," Sir Gavial Mantrap is a swindler who is excused and pitied by some because of his good moral character.

[198] "plea"

that her influence has always acted discouragingly is not the real "leading," and the lingering impulse of ambition a snare to be avoided.

June 9, 1879

Last Thursday Mrs. Charles Lewes came to the shop and I was sustained by hearing that she was better: in the evening to my delight and surprise came a few kind, sweet lines, accepting what I had said of him and asking me to see that the ivy was growing at Highgate. Every word was unutterably sweet to me. I went there the next morning and was thankful to have a right to pull away the withered leaves, the few dead shoots that had perished in the raining. On Saturday I was to go to Weybridge and wrote to her in the morning. The visit was pleasant, the girls and the Halls affectionate—Johnny it seems does not like many people much. Walked with Eleanor in the morning of Sunday, drove with the Halls in the afternoon, watched lawn tennis, dined and in the evening Johnny read Browning and Tennyson—"Ulysses"[199] is his favorite of the latter's. Evaded the invitation to write in their book of "Likes and Dislikes"—Mr. Lewes's was dated 1867. His favorite reminiscence was 1854. Came up to town this morning, by 8:45 train with Eleanor, reached the museum by 10, read Dr. Rongé[200] in the intervals of rather sad feeling—how can one taste the sweetness of kindly intercourse and own human fellowship to be the best of goods without suffering a sick sense of deprivation when the momentary glimpse is over and one finds oneself alone again. If one is to tell the whole truth, I think too, that I was hurt that Johnny—whom I have been scolded for not valuing enough—should as it seems to me make always the minimum of response to my civilities. The feeling is in no way personal, only I always feel as if she might have told me to believe it was right or wrong, wise or foolish, to try to reason oneself into endurance of the patent and trivial fact that one's existence is not a boon to one's fellowmen. I cried a little behind my spectacles over a notebook and my heart ached sorely, but that was not for long—to love her and do what work one can—that is my "formulé de la vie"[201]—I can no other. Then the lingering ache was dispelled (till I let myself remember it now) by the whirl of people of all sorts at Charles Street, Mrs. Green,[202] Miss Steavson and Company,

---

[199] Alfred, Lord Tennyson (1809-1892), "Ulysses" (1833).

[200] Johannes Rongé (1813-1887) wrote on education and theology; *A Practical Guide to the English Kindergarten, An Exposition of Froebel's System* (London: Hodson, 1855).

[201] "philosophy to live by"

[202] Perhaps Mrs. Green is the wife of Mr. Green whose death is mentioned March 13, 1883.

Mrs. Bodley, Heywood[203] &c &c. Have been reading Mallock[204] now for prompt review.—It is so painful when good people will persist in admiring one's doings.—One can't be cross—one can't explain that they aren't admirable—one can't accept it in silence. Poor Mary Cross came upstairs with me on Saturday— she is so good and thoughtful a hostess—and I asked about Mrs. Lewes, whom she and Johnny had been to see at Witley—She was better, and was to have Mme Bodichon to stay with her, and Mary added—she spoke about me—said how she admired me "as of course you know!" Good God! Poor Mary little knows, and yet it is sweet to know that she speaks of me—how could she speak but kindly and tenderly. Dearest! dearest—no one who knows the anguish of love can doubt—Is life worth living?

June 10, 1879

Dearest, dearest—I hardly know that I have anything else to say, only the sense of cleaving to you is always precious. It is a weary world—dearest keep me faithful.

June 15, 1879

I have just written to her. Have been taking Winifred[205] sightseeing. Yesterday had a parliament of the "ladies." I shall try before July to ask her one thing—or rather to mention—the doubt which has so often passed my mind, as to whether she thinks it is worth while that one should make time for oneself to write.

June 22, 1879

On Tuesday had a precious letter from her—with only too sad news of her having been in pain: answered it next night and wrote again today—forcing myself for her sake not to speak too much of love and sorrow.

June 29, 1879

Last Friday took the morning for myself and went to Highgate. A strange still compassion almost swallows up one's sorrow. It was as if I were less desolate because she was more so—I longed to give up to her that hour of silence and tears. I knelt at the railing and gathered one by one each yellow or faded leaf. I wondered whether he would have felt it to be natural that out of all the warm friendships of his life, only mine should follow him thus after the end.

---

[203] Ezra Heywood (1829-1893) supported abolition, labour reform, anarchy, and free love.

[204] William Hurrell Mallock (1849-1923), *The New Paul and Virginia, or Positivism on An Island* (London: Chatto and Windus, 1878).

[205] Winifred Simcox was a cousin of EJS; she is remembered in EJS's will when she was living at 12 Calthorpe Road, Edgbaston.

There was a high wind, not cold, the trees and grass bent before it and it played with comfort on my burning eyes: a gorgeous tuft of buttercups bloomed just below. I sat on the step of a large stone grave and looked down on the flat slab— where all my desires lie buried. Last night the evening was clear and bright and long after sunset I stood on the bank gazing westward as the evening star grew brighter and the lime trees blacker against the sky, and as my tears fell it was no longer, as in so many of the summers that are gone, with the pain of hunger—the fierce longing for a word, a look, a thought—it was just the fearless sorrow in the face of fact, submission to the inexorable—a submission which is felt to be absolute if we own the need at all—and there is no reasoning away with death. One other involuntary change too I must note. It used to pain me beyond anything else when she spoke or thought in deprecation of my speech as if life for me began and ended with the relation to her: it seemed an inconsistent cruelty that she should seem to wish to send me to live outside with others, and even to please her I could not make believe any possibility of content in such exile of the heart. Yet now when my life is sadder than before by all the boundless weight of her sorrow, now without insincerity the impossible effort seeks to make itself and just because there is nothing else one feels one *must* give her the cold comfort of a not too desperate solitude and—

July 6, 1879

I wrote last Sunday a letter I repented of when sent—speaking of the summer—seven years ago when I wished to know her. On Friday night a fresh impulse made me write—to beg her not to think it matter of disappointment, if serious notices of his book delayed: and then I spoke—more kindly than usual— of myself and my hesitation about claiming for myself time enough to enter for the only prize that has ever tempted my curious appetite—a place as writer of one of the books "no gentleman's library should be without." I daresay, if well enough, (that is my haunting fear) she will answer this part of the letter, and though I am resolved not to depend on her for a determination, it will make decision much easier if she lets me read her own feeling. I have, I trust, wholly ceased to claim from her any selfish interest—every natural feeling of my own forbids the thought that she can really, selfishly care for anything I leave undone or do: I do not ask or wish for this,—but I am as little able as ever to submit to her caring *for my sake* about what I only care for—in that same secondary way. The faintest, slender shade of a half preference or mental inclination on her part would be everything—the other is that worse than nothing—a something which one does not want.

July 9, 1879

I don't like to own to myself how anxious I am, lest she should be ill, or bothered: I have not heard since the 17th of last month and then she was only better for the moment. Tomorrow I shall go to the Priory or Hampstead. I begin my month's holiday by writing some letters, and I am reading through Augustus's Ms. Till I know how she is I have little heart for the History of Property in Egypt.

July 13, 1879

After all I did not *go*. I have not been. Partly I shrink from the step—partly from having to say I take it, and then again commonsense suggests, silence need no more prove illness this week than at any other time, but I think I shall be able to ask at the Priory tomorrow and if she is as usual, my mind will be at rest, I would much rather feel free to write with the dread of her feeling as if what I wrote asked for reply. The craving and the delight have passed into silence. I confess I am enjoying my rest; it is pleasant to sit at my desk again with big volumes open around and small prim generalizations recording themselves happily in my notebook. If only H & Co is solvent enough to let me go on keeping my whole mornings for such relaxation, I should not mind the future. If I had £500 and could give £5 a year to each member of the council for learning to do the financial business, I should be easy enough. By the way I'm not at all sure that the History of Appropriation will be an immortal work. Hitherto I feel no touch of inspiration, but it gives one a purpose and an interest. I wonder whether she would be angry or grieved if she knew that with the return of spiritual peace there comes back to me momentary feelings of real content to be alone—because that is so much the easiest—the least troublesome.

July 18, 1879

Friday. By the time a full week was completed I had grown weary and mistrustful. Day by day I put off going to the Priory—just an idle cowardice—but it was too strong for me. On Wednesday—by an artifice—I went without needing to say to anyone I was going.—A woman with 3 children came to the door; at first I thought she was going to disclaim all knowledge then she said Mr. Lewes had been there Friday before and she asked him and he said Mrs. Lewes had been very poorly all the time since she left town up to that week when she was really better. I was cheered by this and in the evening read the Odyssey in prose with calm content. Next day I wrote to her, but feel now no expectation of reply.—If I have no word of her for another fortnight—which will bring us to August, about the time of his summons last year—I shall ask how she is at the Priory and then steal down uninvited for just the usual afternoon's call, after a day with his memory among the heather.—The night cometh.

July 20, 1879

That is the ineffably sad part of it. The only end to one's self-denial will be the end that strangles self-indulgence too—the power before which all wills are bowed.—And yet I hate myself for feeling my own solitude—in the face of hers. I don't complain or flinch. I keep my mind fixed on the dim possibility that the History of Appropriation may become something—a standing object or occupation—an aim if not an interest and it as much for the sake of this chance as from laziness that on the whole I think it perhaps best not to listen to the stray possibilities that present themselves, so that I don't write on the Industrial Employment of Women, or on the Federation of Trade Unions or even on

Herbert Spencer's Data of Ethics.[206]   To do either of these, it seems I want encouragement: but to write a big book which there is likely to be a difficulty in getting published—that is a trifle that may go of itself if one just lets it. Otherwise I am discouraged and out of spirits. I feel the want I don't allow myself to acknowledge—at least in owning how I want her help I don't allow myself to wish that she should give it—and when one is down, smaller things have double power to annoy.—I should have done much more work today if I hadn't been put out by a lazy turn of Mary's—which would have been nothing at any other time but just now jarred on me—egotistically as a disturbance of my peace, and more lawfully but not less painfully as a sign of inconsiderateness.

July 21, 1879

As evening came round I drifted back to the more wholesome view in which one's mind is set towards the positive side of things—I have nothing to wait for; the years to come are in my hand. Yet I have spent a couple of hours in representation to her about one sentence in Theophrastus. It is the only one that struck me as cynical, and perhaps some day I may vindicate my claim to her praise of honesty by telling her how it has affected me. Theophrastus speaks of the renewed experience that people appeal to his sympathy for themselves and uniformly cool at the first hint of reciprocity. Her experience of the world is such as to allow that to be written. Well, if any personal life, any history of the inner consciousness could be absolutely and entirely interesting—both in itself and because of deep sympathy: the listener—it would be hers; yet she could write this. At first I felt puzzled—as *if* for want of a corresponding experience: I have never (I thought) put my fellow creatures to the dangerous test, being sufficiently preoccupied with my own private cross, that no one cared enough about me even to claim *my* sympathy for themselves. Thus then there flashed across my mind the unhappy thought of the one exception—was not my experience with Elma the very same as that described by Theophrastus? was not my one real allusion met with that very "your own fault my dear fellow?"—And if one half the world spends its time in claiming a sympathy it will not give while the other half stands offering such as none will take—how one asks sadly is the world to be saved by the great power of loving sympathy. I can hardly describe the feeling of distressed surprise—one is stunned as if by a blow in the face from a friend—and to me the disappointment is almost the keener for being disinterested. I should never have thought of claiming the sympathy for myself, because any time for the last 20 years I could have seen that my case was objectively uninteresting—I never thought it was interesting because it was mine: and I have never even been tempted to resent a want of interest in others as a fault of theirs, being preoccupied with the intention to be free myself from the fault of unreasonableness in demanding. One sees now easily enough how this half sympathy with her favorite counsels led to results not wholly in her mind. It is

---

[206] Herbert Spencer (1820-1903), *Data of Ethics*, published June 17, 1879, became the first part of *The Principles of Ethics* (London: Williams and Norgate, 1892-93).

true I never felt the need to blame my neighbour, but I failed to become his debtor for love and gratitude, and just when I am prepared to take all the blame for this upon myself,—lo, this is her account of the results of a confiding appeal. Must one choose between the two experiences? We both take for granted that we who speak are to give unreserved sympathy upon each claim—there is no doubt or disagreement about the duty of the individual, but in giving an account to ourselves of the general result, how sad a conclusion have we got to face? Of course I don't really make too much of the expression of a single mood—and I know that there is ample warrant for the remark as a criticism of external selfishness,—but I feel as if it would do me good to get just for myself, a postscript qualifying this application—after all the sentence only hurts me because it is hers.

July 23, 1879

Yesterday the longed for letter came at last, with the expected dreaded news, of her continuous ill health. I had not the heart to write; besides I feel she would have opened the letter with just a little dread of a despairing outcry, so I sent a card with 2 lines in German: now one knows it seems easier to bury oneself in books; what was wearing me out was the double anxiety—lest she should be more ill than one knew or lest one should in any way unwittingly have jarred upon her in anything said or left unsaid.

July 26, 1879

Yesterday went to Hampstead: walked up the heath with Mrs. Charles Lewes who was good in telling me of her: the nerves are very anxious, the internal irritation having set up inflammation: the doctors trust to the strength and soundness of her constitution, but Mrs. Charles said she was fearfully thin, and I doubt her having much power now to throw off any serious illness. I remember what he told me: and there remains the possibility behind of terrible pain and perhaps an operation—one can only live from week to week. She was downstairs with Charles on Sunday, but had a very bad night and they dreaded another relapse, but since then she has written to say she is better and to urge them to make no change in their summer plans on her account and to start without any haunting fears of a telegram.

July 29, 1879

On Sunday read (*inter Alia*)[207] Newman's Sermon on Personal Influence—with rare pleasure. It is very comforting to me to come across a bit of religious writing that one can annex almost whole without violent translation of the author's meaning. This sermon is perfectly—exquisitely true—without the slightest reference to any theological belief. It is a bathos after the picture of such in life or character to speak as if there could be any other "reward" needed than the fact that it has been through life the only reward of such well doing is the growing power of doing and being better, a growing stringency in the

---

[207] "between times"

compulsion to pursue a more and more exalted ideal. I should like if it were possible once to see and speak with the good Cardinal of those more subtle shades of duty and discipline which he understands so well. Imagine myself telling him that my religion is the same as his, minus the church and heaven: he would be less inclined than most to say I had left out the essentials. But it is hardly likely to be.

August 4, 1879

I wrote to her on Saturday begging for the return of a colored envelope by way of bulletin. Yesterday I walked round Paddington, Hampstead, and Highgate. I must go to Highgate again the first day I can, some of the ivy is dead, and I know it will be a disappointment to her if it is not all fresh and thick when she comes back. Since it needed care, I was very thankful to have a right to speak. My last week of quiet has begun—I daresay it is as well—if it were not for the money worries I should not so much dread the return to "business." For the rest one is always more or less "down" except now and then by chance for a day or two, but one's mind is clear—and settled—as it used to be, when I was young. Then Herbert Spencer is quite right about the clear gain of altruistic pleasures—I was pleased by a happy letter from Mr. Lawrence. On Saturday I heard from Roland that his mother was better. I am easy too in my own mind about her—i.e.—about my duty to her—I do not think I am to blame for the cooling of her regard, she cannot be quite happy with a friend who only admires after judging and one's judgment of so strangely mixed a character cannot be always favorable.

August 7, 1879

On Monday I was pained and shaken—though hardly surprised: I was obliged to turn my mind away—I hardly think of it. At the same time I was a little jarred by Mary's want of considerateness—it makes one glad of the old habit of not depending on any one. I think on the whole one must say that it is dangerous rather than right to cultivate the habit. Yesterday afternoon I went to Highgate to speak about the ivy. On the way and in the evening read Newman's Apologia.[208] Was struck in reading by a simple passage he quotes from a sermon on Divine Calls—"to feel that the one thing which lies before us is to please God! What gain is it to please the world, to please the great, nay, *even to please those whom we love*, compared with this? What gain is it to be applauded, admired, courted, followed,—compared with this one aim, of not being disobedient to a heavenly vision?" Now it is not to "please God" that I would obey the heavenly vision—my God is a human being, and the reason that this passage soothes me like a revelation is because the pleasing God seems a matter open to the chance of circumstances—there is no providence to ordain that the fullest obedience will be visible or acceptable personally to her. So with regard to Herbert Spencer's

---

[208] John Henry Newman (1801-1890), *Apologia Pro Vita Sua* was originally published in seven parts issued weekly in 1864; revised editions were published by G. Routledge in 1865, 1869, and 1873.

distinction—the worship of the absolutely right, the absolutely nearest approach to its efficient promoting—seems the only certain, permanent and sufficient goal. Even in the days when pleasing God and pleasing those whom we love seemed one and the same happiness, it always haunted me like a mean desertion of the many—what is to become of the millions who are less happy than I? I want a faith that I can share with them, which is independent of good fortune. It always comes back to that—surely not by any force of mine but by the natural cogency of mental association—which is based upon fact. No doubt the personal relation—if it so fall out—presents the strongest motive to feeling, as one's worship of the God is but the expression of what remains unqualified after the doomed proportion of one's impulses have suffered check and disappointment. But the worship of the God at any given moment may have no apparent bearing on the action of personal motives, present or absent. This is the place for what I am inclined to value as the most deeply wise passage in her writings—the one in *Adam Bede* when she speaks of the sense that our lives have visible and invisible relations beyond the sphere of our own consciousness present or to come "grows like a muscle one has to lean upon"—She could say and perhaps it is true, it must be true as a rule, that sooner or later in the course of a faithful life, moments of sensible contact come when it is felt that the faithfulness has not been in vain, but God forbid that one should live for the sake of this or any other reward. What says Newman again in scornful reply to a charge of Kingsley's?[209] Some day one may borrow this for a motto, answering Spencer:—or rather, happy thought! Why not write an article on Spencer for the sake of being able to say that "for its own sake" does enter (and rightly) into the idea—both with Kingsley and Newman: because just as an unconscious generalization of the organism allows pleasurable feeling to crystallize round action wholesome for the individual life, so an unconscious generalization of thought and feeling erects an ideal, which is cherished in a way as special to itself as the natural desire which belongs to pleasure. The right is that which ministers both to growth and to enjoyment and it is valued for its own sake, not for the sake of its elements, which though simply good and desirable, are newer and greater combined:—it is a chemical, not a mechanical combination.

(In the Ms this note is on page opposite near the last part of the entry for August 7.)

> Pray, what kind of a virtue is that, which is *not* done for its own sake? So this, after all, is this writer's idea of virtue! A something that is done for the sake of something *else*; a sort of expediency! He is honest, it seems, simply *because* honesty is "the best policy," and in

---

[209] Newman wrote his *Apologia Pro Vita Sua* in answer to remarks made by Charles Kingsley (1819-1875) such as the one in *Macmillan's Magazine*, 1863: "Truth for its own sake had never been a virtue with the Roman clergy. Father Newman informs us that it need not be, and on the whole ought not to be."

that sense it is that he thinks himself virtuous. Why, "for its own sake" enters into the very idea or definition of a virtue. Defend me from such virtuous men ever as this writer would inflict upon us!

August 17, 1879

Friday morning (the 8th) brought a considerate after thought. I was perhaps glad—though I had done without it. When I am surprised at my own calmness it comes back like something remembered "Surely the bitterness of death is past?" It seems that I do even without trying, think of her as a "dead friend"—there is the irretrievable change between the past in which I hoped and the present, when I cannot even wish. I have no longing to visit her, such as last year had grown well nigh unbearable before I was rejoiced by the summons to them. One's heart yearns over the thought of her loneliness and suffering, but who knows better than I do that for the deepest grief there can be *no* comfort, *no* help, that sympathy is pain and even forbearance an intrusion. This does not grieve me as a selfish hurt: how could I wish that she were different and I too, to love a slighter nature: but oh! it *is* hard—for her to endure without any comfort!—It does not matter for me: I shall die in time and I can bear anything but to crave something and or she refused. *Could* I have borne—the idle wonder comes in an hour of dreary sadness—could I have borne to have all my longing and then to feel ought but death parting us?—but it is Death. I do not murmur—only for you, my sweet Darling, my own beautiful Love, whose smile was sunshine and whose tenderness the joys of heaven—for you, Mother, Dearest, Dearest—it is too hard.

August 24, 1879

I have thought of her much through the week, but have not been much conscious of my own life. Trade is bad and the women's earnings low—it is dead against my nature to live in hand to mouth anxieties; read a volume of Rawlinson[210] in the evenings and am hoping to have time next week for the museum. On my birthday Augustus got me the Cabinet Edition of Adam Bede. In the evening when they were gone to bed I read some of it turning first to the passage I referred to lately. Then I had a living sense of the immaterial, impersonal Divine—an object of love and desire which is as far from a human love or human happiness as man is from God. I wondered whether she would think this hard and unreal. But may not God have mercy when man has none? I was a little saddened today by looking up from Appleton's letters—all about Academy affairs but all so good tempered as to make one feel self-reproach at having always thought him a bit of a goose and a bore; then too—though of course he never knew that I had borne him some malice for being the innocent cause of the *canard* which led her to be "glad" on hearing it. The letters reminded me too of a lost chance—or something like it, of editorial work, I might have certainly reigned in Mr. Dobell's place—and I shrewdly suspect that this

---

[210] Sir Henry Creswicke Rawlinson (1810-1895) wrote extensively on Egyptian and Assyrian antiquities.

would have been the worse had my life been that much the easier. I have been rather glad this week of one thing, viz. that twice 35 is 70.

August 28, 1879

This morning my mother saw "Vivian's" marriage in the Times[211]—by the way he was married on my birthday—on the strength of that I have written to her—there has been an interval of nearly three weeks, and now that I am stronger able to hide from myself in Egypt and Babylonia, I shall put off as long as I can the recurring impulse to remind her that she has a "loving child" out here. I wonder when she will come back to London. I must force myself to make no attempts at uninvited approach. Poor Darling! I am so thankful I did not send the letter in which I asked her in play if *she* would not find the summers too long if he were away. I cannot say the time is short, but one marks its course less painfully when it no longer stands between the grey present and a longed for moment of delight; I cannot but be glad when she comes back, but a year will come—I know it—when she does not come back, and I am left without even the pale comfort of a last farewell.—But then too her pain will be over and after that what will anything matter to me? It is only now that one's heart aches to bring her comfort. I fear the worst both as to her health and my chances of being near her, but if she is able to bear the winter much as usual at the Priory, I could meet her more easily than of old in the sense that we both had the same effort to make.

September 6, 1879

Have been looking back a year: the pity of it! Oh—it was very cruel! and yet—as I begin to think of the bitter loss to me, that turns into a measure by which I sound her infinite grief and I cannot cry out: and yet it was sad. On that Saturday when we came in from driving, she was still taking off her things, I was in the drawing room, when he came in and sat down, tired and looking ill; he put out his hand and asked by actions for the kiss I was still too shy to give unasked, and mixed with thankfulness for his asking is the memory of regret that the caress which was in my mind passed ungiven. I remember too with tears—half for myself and half for him—how on that day I held his hand longer than needed with something like the first appealingness of a silent child—and he was always too kind to repel, too sincere to respond. It is a horrible thought but a true one, that any comfort there can be for her in her loneliness, must come from others, for I can give her none. I cannot set my heart on anything that is left: I can keep silence and endure, but I cannot live. Mr. and Mrs. Lawrence have been staying here for a week, and she still appeals to me as an oracle and would like an equal confidence on my part, but I have nothing to say, nothing to ask?—from any one but her, and with her it is as if the last parting were over already,—has death more bitterness than this?

---

[211] Vivian Byam Lewes was married on August 21, 1879, to Constance, daughter of Thomas R. Abraham (*Pall Mall Budget*, September 5, 1879, 898) (H, IX, 266, n. 7).

September 10, 1879

Sunday got back to Egypt, looking over notes and yesterday spent 3 or 4 hours at the museum. I don't know that it will come to much but it amuses me better than anything for the present: it is humanizing too, for I find myself still almost capable of wishing to go to Egypt. I settled on Sunday the route by which the founders of the people reached the Nile valley!

September 14, 1879

I have not written to her again, I do not feel the impulse; there is something silencing in the contrast. It is now seven years since the years began to count for me as a single moment—with 6 months of hope before, six months of something less than fruition, after. The restless passionate longing, the uncontrollable hunger, the almost delirious intoxication of past Octobers—that is no more, but as it is not I that change, only the outer world, I have no feeling in the place of that which has been, there is only a void space, to be passed by in reverent silence. I cannot speak to her of this. He was dear and kind, and I have grieved for him—more truly and constantly than many nearer, but while I share her sorrow, she can have no part in mine. Life parted us before: death parts us now. I know not which was hardest to bear, but one is silent under the irrevocable. The terms of the Memorial Studentship have been published. Heaven send a hopeful candidate this year—that will be a fresh interest for her— young lives that come to her through him, if they can cheer her a little, I shall be too grateful for jealousy. As a matter of duty I wrote a while back to Elma, who has not written to me for months. Of old it used to make me unhappy to imagine that Elma was a disciple more advanced than I, better skilled in the teaching of our Lord. Now it saddens me to see that after all I am in the main the better scholar; how can one who has learnt from her fall away? or was it true that part of what I had from myself—not from her and which I was wont to chafe at because it was not from her, and Elma pleased her as well without it—could it be true that this too was needed—that I had known best even then and that giving pleasure is not the whole duty of man?

September 21, 1879

Egypt is rather going back under interruptions and the dearth of books nearer than the museum, or perhaps it is only that one has entered upon the less interesting phase of an enquiry, when instead of learning something fresh one is turning over books to make sure that one is not omitting something that might be learnt. Was pleased this week by a sentence in Theophrastus, (p. 51) which I had not noted before, and which promises some indulgence on her part to the instinct of religious *recueillement*[212]—which has inspired a few pages elsewhere. I don't know whether it comes from the withdrawal of her personal influence, or only from an inevitable instinct of self-preservation, but it is at once easy and necessary to me now to give up the wearing attempts at a kind of social intercourse which I am not born to achieve or to enjoy. All the feeling that

---

[212] "collectedness, mental repose"

devotional writers have expressed towards God as a refuge from the sorrows and evil of the world answers to my own sense of inward deliverance as the affections cease to be covetous without ceasing to be responsive. I think it is right even to cease from coveting the call that may not come. Meanwhile one's own life is not narrowed by the absence of personal ambition; we may not be called to a wide immortality, but I contend that the life which is spent in the service of ideas, upon a rational plan, though it gives no visible unity to the individual career,— such a life is no more scrappy and patchy than those to which births, marriages and deaths give a dramatic air of personal unity of action. It depends upon the comparative strength of the objective and subjective elements in the single consciousness, whether the bent of one's mind is to rest satisfied with the orderly succession of personal experiences or whether it is necessary to one's peace to be engaged in promoting the invisible outer order and to seek in the approach to that the meaning and justification of one's own existence—my feeling is still with the hymn I was fondest of at 13—"Is this a time to plant and build, add house to house and field to field?"—I feel more and more impelled to withdraw into myself—without regret or self-reproach and to devote the rescued years to the solitary calling of divine truth.

September 24, 1879

Was revived yesterday by the assurance from Mrs. Charles Lewes that she was really better, better than before her illness—wrote to her a little objective chat in the evening and could not help feeling happy all day though Hamilton and Co was *minus* £5 as to its banking account and an odd cheque not presented and everybody who owed a big bill with some excellent casual reason for not paying it. I don't know about the *haec slim*,[213] but meanwhile I fly to the museum and am solaced by Chabas's renderings of the Bolopre papyri.[214]

September 26, 1879

I had a letter from her yesterday—crossing mine, and written (this is my inference)—blessings on her thoughtful kindness—because *I* had not written on the Sunday before. She *is* better in health and that leaves one's mind free to realize the utter sadness of her solitude. I know so well the length and breadth and height of such desolation—it is past comfort, past sympathy,—and yet she is always good and tender: and oh! how unspeakably dear. She is coming to London the beginning of November. There is something soberingly painful in the thought of how glad one will be to see her, even now when she and gladness have become strangers for ever.

---

[213] "hereafter"

[214] Francois Joseph Chabas (1817-1882), *Notices sommaires des papyras hiératiques egyptian: Deux Papyrus hiératiques du musée de Turin* (1868); *Egyptologie* (1874).

September 28, 1879

Have been moderately industrious today, digesting notes upon Egypt. It adds a good deal to the labour when one reads books by chance as one can get them so that the notes are in no way sorted, but it is only a few days' employment to copy out the fragments in sets; I want to begin writing while I am alone, indeed the Egypt chapter ought to be written in such a way as only to want general revision. There won't be so much of Assyria and Babylonia, and before one has done with that, she will be back and I will save up the Jews to talk to her about. It is just possible if I get a little time at Xmas that the old world portion might be finished in the year.—My own sweet mother!

October 4, 1879

The impatience of past Octobers is no more. God knows I do not love her less but how could one link the thought of her with eager gladness; I grudge myself even the quiet sweetness of the thought that one will be near her once more—I cannot bear to rejoice without her. And to me too grey peace is deliverance from a rending pain—to her the endurance is of a darkness that may be felt. My poor dear one! The days to you are a slow pain—keener than the sharpest pangs that ever seemed more than I could bear. Dearest, dearest, it is for you that my tears fall now and yet and yet—I thought that was true as I wrote it and yet—it is like a flood of terror over my soul to think what my life would be if I had not you to mourn for. God forbid one should mean to live alone with one's own grief—the year has changed me much—I think I shall see her now without being devoured by selfish longings. I think of writing to her, not tomorrow but the next Sunday—it is better to nurse one's patience while it is still young.

October 10, 1879

All this week the thought of her has been constantly present without covetous impatience. I have felt intensely how dear she is, all the sweetness of loving her and an infinite tenderness for her grief. I have been reading Romola through slowly; that and Middlemarch are the two books which give me the most continuous feeling of spiritual oneness; and as it is written "unto him that hath shall be given," I am always finding fresh sentences which supply just what I used to crave for when my own bent towards an impersonal, semi-ascetic religion seemed condemned by her constant reference to internal claims and relations as something that ought to be, even if it wasn't. She speaks of the "intensity of life which seems to transcend both grief and joy—in which the mind seems to itself akin to *older forces that wrought out existence before the birth of pleasure and pain.*" No doubt—I may say to her some day—I needed to be reminded of the sacredness and force of internal relations which—I complained—were too accidental to be the cornerstone of life, but also, I fretted myself needlessly over the fear that she looked upon all aloneness as a sin, had no mercy for the trials which had been fashioned by forces behind and around them into such an amalgam of impulses and feelings as no ordinary chance could provide with the desirable food or opportunities in the reasonably to be anticipated life.

October 14, 1879

It is curious how much more slowly the days go when one has them to oneself and aims more at doing what one likes. I have done nothing to Egypt, except re-read Lady Duff Gordon's letters[215] and go through Mariette's Catalogue of the Boulak Museum[216] which Mr. Loften lent me. I wrote to her yesterday and find myself still capable of feeling the 3 weeks that are left to be intolerably long, unless I take pains to be "good."

October 19, 1879

It is ungrateful to contrast her prompt response to any practical question with the silence that used to meet my speculative "cases." On Friday had a letter with 50 or 60 signatures requesting me to stand for the school board in Westminster, and under the first impulse of the appeal, I wrote to tell her of it and ask, or at least wonder how if I had the power of choice, she would wish me to choose. Yesterday afternoon I had to decide on the spur of the moment, Mr. Nettleton, the secretary of the club coming to fetch my answer. I had no choice and said no, not without reluctance when it appeared that there was a considerable chance of one's return. I don't think there was any vanity in the pleasure I certainly felt in hearing how the dear fellows had been making up their minds to work "heart and soul" in the cause. She writes kindly about this and gives me very welcome news about herself: but oh! the sadness of her "Ebenezer."[217] I am anxious in laying my affairs before her never to think more of my own wants than of the degree to which she will be able to interest herself in the matter without effort and indeed with relief. She speaks now of returning to town the end of this month. God knows the sight of the dear face will be more than welcome.—It makes no difference and yet I am glad that she comes back within the year. I could not bear to meet her on a day that recalled the last meeting with him—or the awful days to come.

October 26, 1879

Yesterday on my way back from the cemetery, called at North Bank to ask which day she was expected and heard Friday. I am not restless now and the week will go on at its normal pace; if only the old covetousness will not spring up again it will be good to have her here:—but oh! how hard for her to return alone—to the memory of the last return. I have just been reading through—living again through those winter months. I shrink from opening any of the letters that came then—I am loth to look even at hers—some of the old dread of

---

[215] Lady Lucie Duff Gordon (1821-1869), *Letters from Egypt, (1863-1865)* (London: Macmillan, 1865).

[216] Auguste Mariette (1821-1881) wrote about ancient Egypt and antiquities.

[217] "stone of the help": In I Sam. 4:7 Samuel set up a stone after the defeat of the Philistines as a memorial of help received.

seeing her again comes back to me. But I know all this is morbid—the simple fact is still that I cannot live too long on memory alone, that the colours of the image which lives in one's affection turn from the soft luminous grey of sorrowing love to the dull lead of self-reproaching loneliness. I wonder whether to write to her today about the "New Quarterly" and the ivy—which still grows but slowly:—on the whole I think not: I cannot say anything so unquestionably welcome to her as to show that I did not write to please myself: and I am disinclined. Am still idle about Egypt. When I was rereading my notes it struck me that there was perhaps just a popular article with an anti-Khadivial moral which I might extract for immediate publication and leave the background till I had finished getting up the ethnology and generalities of the other part. I had meant to ask Augustus's opinion but his nonreturn and my discovery of one and another still unread "sources" put off the question till it seems natural to leave it as a subject to talk to her about. A note came from Trübner yesterday—in answer to a formal enquiry of mine—to the effect that the sale of the 2nd edition up to June was 45 copies and the loss upon the 2 editions so far £80—which I confess doesn't trouble me as the good man told me himself that a sale of 300 copies would pay the expenses of the first edition. I confess my first thought was a modest surprise that 45 people should really and truly and unprovokedly buy the book in the course of a year or less—(I can't in the least remember or find any note to show when the 2nd edition was published), but second thoughts explained the mystery: some people buying vols 3 and 5 of Trübner's library buy vol IV for symmetry—this hypothesis is more credible than that of a new reader a week!

(In the Ms these two notes are together at the bottom of the page opposite. She indicates that they are to be inserted on the 26th.)
> November 19, 1880
>> He reports sale of 112 copies having nominal loss of £74 odd.
> November 19, 1881
>> "We bound 100 (?200) copies of the second impression of which about 20 still remain. The balance after the book is now about £65."

October 29, 1879

I have been reading Daniel Deronda through. It is strange that with all the intensity of my love for her, I never cease to feel as if the physical part of our conscious nature was more than remote—opposite. Somehow it is a more depressing book to me than her others, perhaps because it is a faithful transcript of the coexistence of unreconciled tendencies. I am more struck by the pathos of Gwendolen's rejection than by the healing power of Daniel's virtuous conduct and counsel. As in the passage of Theophrastus which hurt me one is reminded at once of the solitude of eminence "the impossibility of reciprocating confidences with one who looks up to us" and the double solitude when the confidence we wish to make is suppressed, or one we wish to receive is withheld. She speaks of the skepticism which people call "Knowledge of the world and which is really disappointment in you and me."—Is not the world made of yous and mes and if it falls into these two classes with a minority in whom are answering needs—to bestow and to receive—is the Knowledge of the world a hopeful science? I know with me faith, hope and charity remain unhurt because I live outside the world, which is of a nature to make those virtues difficult.

November 9, 1879

The day after that last entry another appeal from Mr. Paterson on behalf of the Westminster men sent me back into uncertainty as to whether I ought not to try for the chance of risking the 3 graces in the mêlée after all. I wrote at length to Augustus putting the case in its entirety and as I expected, he said "stand." Since then I have been seeing and hearing a great deal of the world's wickedness—Helen Taylor lies and George Potter is for sale—&c &c but also my own experience of the goodness and kindness of friends and acquaintances far exceeds anything I could have dreamt of expecting. It is pleasant to be made ashamed in this way of one's scanty deserts. Certainly if I am returned it will be more "by good luck than good guidance" except in the choice of friends. The boys have been very useful in securing safe-sounding names, Miss Orme single-handed converted James Beals the Liberal agent into a sense of my overwhelming merits and power. Mrs. Paterson I imagine "sat on" the Westminster Club and Nettleton, of Nutbody, has been enthusiasm personified, while MacClymont has identified himself absolutely with the affair as a matter of course, without so much as offering to help. I wrote to Her a report of the election proceedings up to Friday and last night had a word of thanks to say it had amused her. I saw her on Tuesday having settled to leave Sunday and Monday for rest. She was looking much better and said the constant care of the local doctor had been much in her favour. She had not seen or heard much in detail about Dr. Roy yet. She had been to the Cemetery that day and was disappointed with the ivy and the place of the grave. She had been vexed, as I feared at the well-meant blundering way of the article in the New Quarterly—which she said was written by a clever man and a friend.[218] "Don Garcia in England"[219] had been sent her with an inscription, she thought because of one sentence about him. She spoke of the difficulty, after living an ideal life—thinking of things and people as they might be—to come back into the real world and exercise the virtues one had been dreaming about; and she assented without demur to my remark as above, that one's charity was warmest when least tried. But I must try not to let her worry herself with the thought she ought to do more than she likes or can. I shall go again—if possible on Wednesday straight after the nomination if there is any contest.

---

[218] James Sully (H, IX, 277, n. 7)

[219] Don Garcia was a stock character in Spanish drama; one of the characters in *The Noble Heart*, a play which GHL had written; it was performed in London, New York, and Boston.

November 23, 1879

These three weeks of electioneering have gone slowly and wearisomely, so that it is a comfort to think there is less than one whole one left. I was not able to get to her till this Saturday afternoon and then Lady Paget was there, so I only left my love. On the 19th I saw her, for about half an hour; she protested against the time and mental force spent in writing to her—another long report.—Spoke to the wearisomeness of business and letters—a man called sending in an impertinent note—"My dear George Eliot" which she answered by a message, she was not able to receive strangers: said he used to tease her for not being content with dispatching a letter unless it was a composition—his own notes were scribbled off with ease and he comforted himself that no one would ever wish to print them. She added life wasn't long enough to read up old productions of the penny post, then looked at me to make an exception and when I said "those least of all" she denied—thought if my letters could be printed anonymously, they would make a very pretty complete romance. Then she went on to say how horrid it was to hear indirectly that some letters, even of sympathy, were only dictated by the hope of an autograph. On the other hand some perfectly beautiful letters came unsigned—she had one such from a gentleman in New Zealand lately, and they were the most precious tribute: Johnny came in and I could have kissed him for he kissed her hand when he came in. I can't be bothered to write here about the election.

December 10, 1879

On Wednesday (26th) I went to the Priory, she was engaged. Wrote to her to ask what I should do about the offer of divers people to subscribe to the election expenses. She answered accept, and so I ceased to refuse. Then came the election and on Sunday, the 30th I forgot everything except that day last year, and the sadness of her maimed life and the grief that one may share but cannot lessen. I could not bring myself to write to her though I had her note of counsel to acknowledge. The next day brought me a card of affectionate congratulations, and then I went to see her on Wednesday—after writing what I could. I was shown in at once, Leslie Stephen was there, Mr. and Mrs. Beesly[220] came. The talk was of Pope, Gladstone, James Payn[221] on educating authors, Afghanistan and Secocoeni.[222] My heart ached for her—it was like the Sunday afternoons, without the one who could always shield her from fatigue and come to the rescue in endless ways. I talked, not badly, but I did not see her alone. Last Friday I had

---

[220] Edward Spencer Beesly (1831-1915) was Professor of History at University College, London, a leading Comtist, trade union adviser, socialist and author.

[221] James Payn (1830-1898) published more than fifty novels, some of them serialized in *Chamber's Edinburgh Journal*, which he edited (H, IX, 280, n. 2).

[222] Secocoeni or Sikukini was a powerful native chief on whom the Dutch settlers of the Transvaal made war in 1876 (H, IX, 280, n. 3).

one of her remorseful afterthoughts by post, she was afraid she had spoken with needless severity of Overton's[223] literary shortcomings, and this gave me the opportunity of delivering *my* remorseful afterthought. There are so many for her to see—is it kind to make one more? if only one could have any natural reason—besides one's own longing—some material excuse that brought one without the haunting suspicion one might just as well have stayed away. That doesn't hurt me now as it used, but for her sake I feel the fear as much as I used for my own.

December 21, 1879

Last Thursday between a day at the shop and an evening at the Craven school, I made up my mind to seek her. She was alone and we were uninterrupted. She was looking and feeling well in health—surprisingly so to herself—she was sweet and dear, showed me bits of letters about him—one from a German who said how few writers either German or English understood equally his philosophy—or even the philosophical languages of the two countries as he did. I asked about Mrs. Stuart, she had not heard from her since she went south, but thought she was at Alássio. She had thought her much changed by her illness—I suggested that she had only seen her before in a happy mood. I stayed an hour and hardly know what we spoke of—School Board, Delboeuf[224] on double consciousness in dreams, Cabul[225] and Ireland, Dr. Roy[226] who is full of delightful young enthusiasm about the heart and pulse, and has sent her his published Memoirs and a letter from Leipzig where he was studying to say Ludwig[227] knew all about the Studentship, thought the arrangements admirable and hoped it would tend to raise the *status* of physiological research in England. I mentioned what had struck me as curious in walking there—a waggon came close behind me as I was crossing a side road up which the waggon was turning out of the main road. I had a dim vision of it out of the corners of my eyes as dangerously near and had to control the first irrational impulse to start *back* right

---

[223] John Henry Overton (1835-1903) published *The English Church in the Eighteenth Century*, 2 vols. (London: Longmans, Green, 1878) (H, IX, 280, n. 4).

[224] GHL read Joseph R. L. Delboeuf (1831-1896), *Essai de logique scientifiques*, and cited it in his *Problems of Life and Mind* (H, V, 160, n. 5).

[225] Cabul or Kabul was the capital of Afghanistan, captured by the British and held for a time in the second Afghan War (H, IX, 281, n. 5).

[226] Charles Smart Roy was nominated by GHL as the first recipient of the George Henry Lewes studentship. He was educated at Edinburgh, worked with the well-known scientists of the day, including Cohnheim in Leipzig, and was Professor of Pathology at Cambridge, 1884-1897 (H, VII, 213, n. 5).

[227] Karl Wilhelm Ludwig (1816-1895) was a German physiologist and inventor of the sphygmometer (H, IX, 281, n. 6).

under the shafts. I took this first as an explanation of why horses wear blinkers and then reflected that one habitually sees what is in front and therefore in the case of danger one habitually starts *back* and it seems, does so still when the danger is seen at an unaccustomed angle. This led her to say she had an exceptional power of seeing out of the corners of her eyes and used to dispute with him about the dictum of physiologists that you can only see colours with a certain part of the retina and that what is behind is *seen* black and only *judged* to be coloured. She was very beautiful and let me give her dear cheek long clinging kisses. I said, looking at the letters she was writing—did she not want a Secretary—she said Charlie was unhappy because she would let him do so little for her and would break his heart (I doubt it) if she let anyone else do anything. She said she must keep her faculties from stupefying and met my half uttered prayers by saying I had quite enough to do, I should attend to my own business— whereto I, Yes, but one coveted a little pleasure too—it was human nature; She owned human nature did crave (in reference to our mention before of the dangers of Boxing day) its taste of gin—I said and kissed her crape—was not mine of an innocent sort and then went away. She asked me about Mr. Overton and said he had elected Mrs. Congreve as his director after 5 minutes discourse and had shown the Ms of his book to her first of any one: it represented I heard elsewhere the work of 3 years Sundays. I left her cheered and comforted. It seems wicked that my love is more contented now than in her happier days and yet it is not all wickedness, for I am content to ask less, as well as more content to receive less than I would fain have asked, when the check on her power of giving does not come alone from my unworthiness. It is unspeakably sad to feel that she is worse off than I am, and the feeling comes over me like a remorse or shame, when the unchangable sweetness of one's love for her fills one's soul with the inextinguishable pleasure of love not yet bereft: as I watch her beautiful courage it seems like a warning vision of the impossible duty that will be mine when I too am left alone: yet it is a present help and blessing too—Inshallah![228] it shall not die with me. Dear, dear Love!

December 25, 1879

I am thinking of trying again tomorrow—a day other people are not likely to trouble her: if all went well it could be a great and precious pleasure. I think I could bear a disappointment. My thoughts of her have the same happy peacefulness of delight in her being as in the happiest moment of the old past, and yet—I go to sleep thinking of her—last night I could not sleep, only sob again and again with fresh realization of the utter sadness of life, her life, to which love itself can bring no comfort—only the will and power still to care for other sadness, to solace other lives. There is something in the daylight darkness—it is noon and I cannot see without candles—which adds to the sense of depression, but life is hard—on all or most and action difficult for any, one's happiness is only to feel now and then as if one were acting on the right side, in the direction which—if all took the same—might lead to an easier lot for the

---

[228] Arabic for "if it pleases God" or "if God wills"

many. Meanwhile in my dreams of quiet, slow converse with her I find myself trying to explain, better than before, how it was something in me, not in any word of hers that made me feel at times as if she was playing the devil's advocate in my soul, appealing to a side of me which I had been wont to discourage and disapprove. Say I pride myself on having no enemies and enjoy the influence I can use over others—through their understanding, not their feelings: why should one not be content with that, one's own gift, instead of moaning because one is not much beloved by anyone in particular: I never knew the passion of covetousness or discontent save in my longing for her love. I never knew—could never know—the sweetness of any human passion except my love for her. It is intolerable to me to accept, like a Calvinistic destiny, the doom of a life less than the best possible for me, any other is to me accepting death not life. I feel with her all the hardening, narrowing tendency of life in action which outstrips the pace of possible personal feeling; I saw this *a priori* when one choice was as little in my reach as another, and I rebelled against the thought of being enslaved by my own deeds even as I shrank from the imagination of bondage to a lifelong passion for one. I welcome the word she lets fall in recognition of these real conditions of difficulty all the more because in the days of my difficulty it seemed as if she thought only, and with contempt, of the weakness I had—did nothing for fear of becoming entangled in doing and yet complained of the pains of idleness. I recognize the double difficulty still. If life had brought me, not her love but better chances of work outside, I might have learnt to forget the first dread just when its safeguard grew needed. If life had brought me—what I knew it never would—the absorbing rapture of an answered, answering love, I know I should have fallen a prey like others, have lived on my happiness while it lasted and have let life end with its death. Had one had this choice of good gifts, strange as she would think it, my bent would always have been to choose the first limitation—I would rather do than feel, rather act on others' feelings than be myself the outlet, the channel, by which human passion passes from feeling into nothingness. But fortune has given me neither gift in dangerous completeness, and between the two there emerges for me a vision of the ideal among the real possibilities of arduous life. I see Samuel Wilberforce[229] writes—when younger than I am,—that he dreads "being scourged into devotedness"—to me it is a desirable doom, if only more devotion would follow acceptance of the scourge. I have said elsewhere, with half-veiled meaning, why it is abhorrent to me to accept the impression of a diseasedly imperfect life, and I think now it was the strength not the weakness of my nature that made it impossible for me to accept her ideal rather than my own. It is curious how bit by bit I find myself as it were possessing just the place or character I had dimly coveted long ago:—it was only a trifle, and I attach the *minimum* importance to it, but still it is just a coincidence, that the favorite topic of my friends at the School Board election meetings was my admirable combination of speculative and practical ability. Of

---

[229] Arthur Rawson Ashwell (1824-1879), *Life of the Right Reverend Samuel Wilberforce, D.D. (1805-1873)* (London: J. Murray, 1880-82). See December 31, 1879.

course I know better than they the middling success of the practical part, but it would have been perverse not to feel slightly flattered at being praised for the very thing as to which one had a little vanity in one's youth. There is this too to be said for one's preference for the active life: as a matter of merely subjective contentment, whether one is occupied with work or passion, the time of discouragement comes equally—the work passes time—on the whole contentedly—but when *we* are discontented, it is only too easy to see how little objective fruit we have to point to—and one has worked too hard for the average earning of contentment to seem reward enough. It is the same no doubt the other way; the soul that has spent itself in loving must at times take comfort only in the thought of "other lives that could have been worse without me," and that is as much outside and objectively no larger than the trifling real fruits of all one's active labours. But the true, full, secret of my resignation now is that I have as much of the second life of loving passion as one can have without the happiness that makes the happy bondage of a lifetime. God knows I had accepted gladly all bonds of filial duty to her or them, but since she could not have it so, what might have been pleasure is released as energy—I want Trübner's Catalogue on Egypt and Assyria.[230]

December 26, 1879

She was alone; said it was rare for her to see no one all day as was the case the day before. She was reading, or rather cutting a new book. I apologized for coming so soon again, that I felt always guilty because instead of bringing her useful or entertaining information my own ideal was just to hold my tongue at her and be comfortable, she deprecated the useful information and the silence alike: then reflected she had not returned my kiss, and did so—she thought it such a horrid habit of people to put their cheek and make no return, the little niece from Natal does so (and she is called Marian!) while the little boy puts up his lips. I said should I go, having had the kiss I came for, She said she wasn't so easily tired. She had heard from Elma, who had been ill and was sorry, not surprised that Roland had not passed;[231] I failed to explain myself about the absence of the maternal instinct in Elma. She said with all her admirable generosity and so on she was a strange person and quoted some one, perhaps Mrs. Charles Lewes, who found it difficult to get on with her. I was vexed with myself for seeming to be judging her, though Mrs. Lewes was doing so also by her regrets that Elma had planned everything in such detail to her own mind that she could not but have been disappointed. Then we got on to politics—Lady Strangford and her Bulgarians,[232] whom she doesn't think half as wise and good as the Turks.

---

[230] One of a series of Catalogues published by Trübner's publishing house.

[231] His examinations for military college (H, IX, 282, n. 7).

[232] Viscountess Strangford was Emily Anne Beaumont (d. 1887). After her husband's death in 1869 she underwent a four-year hospital training as a nurse and started the National Society for providing Trained Nurses for the Poor. In 1876 she took a leading part in organizing the fund for the relief of the Bulgarian

Disraeli—she scolded me much for calling him unprincipled—she was disgusted with the venom of the Liberal speeches from Gladstone downwards. I tried to justify my use of the term as a slowly formed sincere belief, referred to his books, which she thought wonderfully clever; I said look at the Truck System in Sybil[233] and his indifference to the obscure useful acts upon the subject. She admitted that was a real charge and implored me only to make *such* real concrete doings or omissions the ground of attack and to refrain from judgments on the whole man. Then we mixed in the Cornhill on Tennyson, which she got to refer to the one parallel passage which showed a really interesting resemblance (a poem of Lord Herbert of Cherbury to In Memoriam).[234] She said men's characters were as mixed as the origins of mythology. We went back more than once to the question of "principle." I said I used to hate L. N.[235] and she said Yes—one was tempted to call the author of the Coup d'Etat a *bad* man, but she believed he was only willing to do one bad action as a means, and then meant to do good ones. Dizzy[236] was unprincipled therefore ambitious, not a fool, and so he must care for a place in history and how could he expect to win that by doing harm? I said he would be satisfied with such a place as Wolsey[237] or Richelieu[238]—whereto She

---

peasants and educated several at her own expense in England. In 1877 she went to superintend a hospital she had established for Turkish soldiers and was at Strigil when it was occupied by the Cossacks (H, VII, 235, n. 8). She edited her husband's letters and papers and wrote *Egyptian Sepulchres and Syrian Shrines* (London: Longmans, Green, 1861) and *The Eastern Shores of the Adriatic* (London: R. Bentley, 1864).

[233] In depicting the miners in *Sybil, or, The Two Nations* (London: H. Colburn, 1845, bk. III, ch. I), Disraeli, who depended on the Blue Book reports of the employment of women and children, passed lightly over the horrors of their drawing trucks of coal through the mines (H, IX, 282, n. 8).

[234] In "A New Study of Tennyson (Part I)" *Cornhill* 41 (January 1880): 36-50, J. Churton Collins compares six stanzas from "An Ode upon the Question, Whether Love Should Continue Forever" with stanzas of *In Memoriam* (H, IX, 282, n. 9).

[235] Louis Napoleon (1769-1821) executed the coup d'etat in 1851 (H, IX, 282, n. 9).

[236] Nickname for Benjamin Disraeli (1804-1881) according to André Maurois, *Disraeli: A Picture of the Victorian Age*, trans. Hamish Miles (New York: D. Appleton, 1928), 74.

[237] Thomas Wolsey (c.1475-1530), English cardinal and politician, was for a decade one of the most powerful men in Europe.

[238] Armand Jean du Plessis de Richelieu (1585-1642) was the French cardinal and politician who helped to establish French supremacy abroad.

and the Positivists are setting to work to idealize Richelieu, so what then? But here she stopped; it was enough not to idealize the evil, she did not wish to idealize the good out of knowledge. I said no, because hero worship was an indulgence, there was self-denial in not insisting on it, and then I lapsed into some of the fond folly which always provokes her.—*She* had never known anyone perfect and worshipped none the less. Then for the twentieth time I prepared to go and said she had been scolding me for the nearest approaches to good points I had—I thought she believed me to be at least charitable and veracious, she startled me by some little outcry at the last word—had she ever said I was veracious—that was a rash thing to say of any one, it was so very difficult to attain perfect truth—nay more, it was a virtue that might be overdone and on the whole she elected to scold me rather for imperfect veiling of unpleasant truths, as when I didn't like any one—(here I burst in that I never did dislike any one, and she quoted my letter from Dinan, as if had said then love-making bored me). Still she didn't deny I was indifferent honest. I said, she must tell me if she ever thought otherwise. She said, after half a pause, would I really rather she said anything she thought—would it hurt me—my heart sank fathoms underground and tears came into my eyes—if she said she did not like for me to call her "Mother"—I gave a sigh of relief, if that was all. She went on, she knew it was her fault, she had begun, she was apt to be rash and commit herself in one mood to what was irksome to her in another—not with her own mother, but her associations otherwise with the name were as of a task and it was a fact that her feeling for me was *not* at all a mother's—any other name she did not mind, she had much more "respect and admiration" for me now than when she knew me first, but &c—she hoped I was not hurt. I tried to say that the only name natural to me was darling and that I took the other as being less greedy, more dutiful. I sat up late last night writing (to post tomorrow) a short reassurance that I am not hurt.

December 28, 1879

But on the contrary—as always—braced and comforted by the glimpse of her sane large ideals. It is good to feel that one cannot satisfy her real and reasonable demands, and that one has no right to dreams of semi-ascetic perfection till one has.

December 29, 1879

I hope in writing to her I did not seem to claim any preeminence in love though I was forced to say that I indeed *did* love her—once and always—as a mother, and yet I knew—how show without saying—that I knew uncomplainingly—her love for me is not—as she said, the love wherewith a mother loves her child. I said and wrote that I was not hurt, in good truth after these days I ought to add—not hurt at her saying this—that it should be true is too old a hurt to count. But I must not risk myself too much in much of this kind of meditation; it would be more useful to ask how—by what arts of self-discipline one is to keep one's mind fixed and sufficiently concentrated upon "appropriation" to give an intellectual backbone to one's existence, without which moral effort is apt to stagnate and evaporate in purposes. The first thing is clearly to polish off the business at the firm as zealously as may be, so as to be free to work that School Board and one's reading move orderly together. This heartache is a holiday sort of a luxury. It is an unspeakable comfort to see her so much better in health.

December 31, 1879

Read a little more of Mr. Wilberforce's life. Cobden[239] said of him if he had not been a priest he would have been prime minister and I am inclined to think it the only flaw in his character and destiny that he was not of the two the latter. He speaks (with admirable candor) of "Secularity" as his temptation in public life; and I ask whether it is well, given all the unavoidable snares, for a man to add any shadow of conventionality to the weight of duty—secularity is not a sin in ministers of state. And yet even without the claim of a religious profession, one is always forced to make a similar charge against oneself—how can one keep one's mind and feelings set constantly and with practical effect upon the higher and not the lower level? I know, I *know* there is no way but this to seize at every turn the chance of good or best, to do or try, there no easier rule, no more compendious discipline.—Dearest, dearest every glimpse of the true truth turns to after glow of grateful tenderness and the sweet worship of love.

January 2, 1880

I won't say anything about Mr. Fitzgerald, whom, rather late in the day, I proceed to identify with Elma's "old Fitz."[240]

January 6, 1880

Am glad to find the identification was wrong. I went to her this afternoon; she was alone again and I stayed for an hour, talking pretty freely about Elma and my worship for her, which I justified so soberly that she ended by laughing at me and recognizing that I was apologizing for my good opinion of her, in reply to which she offered to concede, as the servants say, "There's a many worse"—than her sweet self. She implored me not to get into the way of a too constantly moral intention of questioning "am I right?" "is he right?" or—with an expressive gesture "oh dear how wrong of me!" She spoke of harsh judgments born of incapacity for special errors—I spoke of feeling wide capacities for sin and she demurred, was inclined rather to place me with the virtuous. She mentioned Mrs. Congreve again, and said I should like to know her. She offered to show me her favorite passage in the "Imitation." It is one I have hung upon often—in "magnum valde magnum"[241] when there is no solace

---

[239] See December 25, 1879.

[240] Edward FitzGerald (1809-1883), *Rubáiyát of Omar Khayyám* (London: Allen, 1859).

[241] "no cost too high" or "no price too great"

in heaven or earth still to abide in faithfulness to the spirit of love. I said as I was going away I had meant to ask her to scold me for laziness—but with the contrarity that she is inclined to with me just now she observed that if I did all I was obliged to do I should have enough on hand. I hate myself for one thing—and dread lest she should ever feel any hint of it—I can speak to her more freely when one meets again and again alone; and I hate myself for the delight it is to me just to be with her and I am half ready to beg rather to mourn with her than have this solitary joy and then one does mourn with her at the thought of his generous delight in his happy love for her.

January 12, 1880
Wrote to her yesterday—but did not send the letter—for no reason in particular. Friday or Saturday I will go again.

January 21, 1880
I did go on the Friday (16th) with the pretext that Mme Bodichon would like to have the latest news of her. Somehow I was stupid and bothered her, I think with long silences; and then made things worse by raising the to her painful question—would she reprint any of his Articles. She was able to a certain extent to discuss the question freely—that his early papers had an historical interest from the precocious justness of his appreciations, but still they were so different from his later writings, the best of him was in these—anyway she could do nothing now; she had no word or hint from him to guide her, and then in a tone of distress, she must judge for herself, I must not speak to her again about it. She said too that I was speaking for myself only, not thinking of the general public, and it was hard for me to explain that it was just for the more careless readers who will not approach his problems that I thought miscellanies might form an attractive introduction. Her strongest feeling was, I think, dislike for a publication that she did not herself desire and which was only likely, in her apprehension, to elicit "something nasty in the Athenaeum." I was painfully affected by an impression of half-formed gestures, deprecating a near approach, and yet how can I have anything but sympathy for much stronger repulsion or irritability than she ever allows herself to feel or show? I came away much saddened, cried on the way back, but not with the same altogether absorbing despair as after similar grief before. Why cannot I silence my own cravings and bring before her only small matters with a possibility of pleasurable interest. The next day I went to Scalands, for 3 days with Mme Bodichon; her kindness, the trees and birds and sunshine were pleasant. I spent one evening in writing to tell Her so, but did not post the letter and am in doubt still whether to write or call at the usual interval.

January 24, 1880
I did write and shall call the end of next week. The foolish feeling will have worn off by then, and with it the longing to bother her with foolish talk. My poor darling! it is strange that since she said that, I have often had to check myself on the verge of the forbidden address—I hardly knew how natural and dear the name had become. I liked to hear and speak of her at Scalands.

"Barbara" sympathized with what I said of the delight of not having to make allowances for her; said Charles had been good to her but he couldn't understand; agreed with my half-spoken regret that no one could be any comfort to her—she asked if Mrs. Congreve was or Johnny Cross. Tennyson, and Johnny and some one else[242] came to the Heights while she was there. She herself spoke of a neighbour having introduced Kate Greenaway.[243] It is only by thinking of her lot that I compel myself not to say—I cannot bear the distance—. Mme Bodichon told me how she said to "Marian" in the earlier days "I do *not* like Mr. Lewes" and was answered "You do not know him": but, she went on to me, he was not then as we knew him later, her influence, all agree, improved his character, though she must have seen in advance all that was to be—and was her justification. I hinted in my letter at the latent doubt whether it was rule enough to "do everything I was obliged," and today was better content than usual thinking first about Educational Endowments and Sites, then attending to Mortimer Street and then reading Appert[244] with result at the museum (by the electric light, which I had not seen there before): read reviews after dinner and at last was tired—which does not matter when one has not time enough left to realize that it is with the spirit as well as the flesh. The only thing that makes me doubt if it would have been good for me to know her sooner is the doubt whether she would still have given the same advice—for it is barely conceivable that had I loved her at 20 and been referred by her to other possibilities of love—it is barely conceivable that I might have accomplished an unhappy marriage.—She would ask, why not a happy one, to which the answer is that it is not given to me to inspire the true ideal passion in anyone for whom I can feel it.

February 1, 1880

I had meant to call last Friday, but by ill luck forgot a school engagement that had determined me and went instead on Thursday. Young Johnny and Eleanor Cross were there when I arrived and outstayed me. I listened while the latter talked music, and looked at her, she was well and beautiful. She had been to the Old Masters and the Grosvenor (with whom?)—she said "we"—I don't know why I should have been surprised. I had thought she would never go to the Saturday concerts again, perhaps she will. I suppose I should have been pleased enough if she had proposed to go to the Grosvenor with me—but it was probably the Burne-Joneses, as she spoke of his reluctance to sell his drawings. They being there I could not ask about the girl. I think perhaps what wearies her least is the ardour of a single-minded youth—with which she has some natural sympathy and at all events can feel a dramatic interest. I was fool enough to come away in tears again, shall I never reach the end of this disappointed

---

[242] Tennyson and his son Hallam called September 26, 1879 (H, IX, 287, n. 5).

[243] Kate Greenaway (1846-1901), illustrator (H, VII, 203, 215)

[244] Georges Appert, *Ancient Japan* (Tokyo: Imprimerie Kokubunsha, 1888).

covetousness. It is true I can always silence the craving of my own soul by thinking of her solitude, but she has a spring of vitality within which makes her winter less barren than my prime. She told little Marks[245] that she was doing conic sections every morning because "she didn't want to lose the power of learning." I am afraid I wished she would spare some of those hours for teaching. It is unreasonable of me to keep chafing in this way as if I were asking in vain for something needed. I have almost accepted the knowledge that our lives are to be shaped apart and independently, that her days will never be happier or the easier through me, or mine the less sternly replenished with "agenda" because of any sweet respite from her love. It is something known, lived through and unalterable that my life has flung itself at her feet—and not been picked up—only told to rise and make itself a serviceable place elsewhere.—So be it—so it is. I have said, I have sworn to myself, again and again, I do not, I will not complain. I will take the life she points to, lose myself in it and leave a few impersonal footprints—only then I cannot yet quite bear to think that she has more sympathy with a life in which the I is not quite lost—in which a living I appeals joyously, hopefully and not in vain for love and sympathy and full approval. But then—is it my fault that every wholesome, natural reasonable passion I have felt, from the young ambitions of the tomboy to the fierce worship of Her lover—is it my fault that all without exception have been choked off by a churlish fate and I hurled back upon the one inexhaustible gospel of Renunciation? But this is an old story,—and after all I suppose the mind never does quite accept the prospect of an unrelieved black shadow, and perhaps the secret of my hankering still after leisure for my own work i.e. the "History" is that I am learning *not* to look to her and love for the almost indispensable breathing spaces of consoling rest, but again and with better hope than of old, to the dispassionate regions of pure thought and solitary meditation.

February 7, 1880
Auf! let us learn to live without looking anywhere.

February 8, 1880
Wrote last night a letter that it seems useless to send this morning; I thought of writing and then not going to see her for another fortnight—from Friday to Friday is often the only chance now, but after all there is no reason— and—though it is a selfish bit of forethought—if I were to stay away so long in a fit of self-mortification, I should be just as likely then as sooner to stumble upon such visitors as last time, and that would be hard to bear. Say I were to call once a fortnight and not go in if anyone else were there? I won't post my letter. It is no comfort to be always tired. "Appropriation" makes no way and I don't think will. We live and learn and I take it now that for me to write a book above mediocrity, I should have to give my whole mind to the subject and moreover the mind would have to be sustained by beneficent fate in some degree of cheerfulness.

---

[245] Phoebe Sarah Marks, later Mrs. William Edward Aurton (H, IX, 293, n. 9)

February 9, 1880

—Which mine isn't. It is enough perhaps to justify a more than normally strong sense of defeat that between Saturday and Monday 2 editors decline with thanks—one with and the other without reading—my solid article. That Mary is bent on giving up dressmaking as a failure, and that Lyulph Stanley is as insolent as usual and one can hardly be very useful on a committee when one's very existence is openly resented. I don't care about the article as an author—it wouldn't break my heart to give up for good ambition that way, but I wanted to earn money for the notice B cases and other necessary expenses that come from being on the board—and—hang it! for just once I will let myself say—I *have* rather hard times all round. Sometimes I think it was only wise not to meddle with reforming tricks—as I used to refrain deliberately because I knew I hadn't the money for the luxury. But in owning to defeat all round I don't lay it upon fate—it is I that am incompetent—to do three or four difficult things all or even one well at once. And as I cry out under it—I *have* been crying and this time I don't think it was only because of the older standing failure (in the matter of her love)—I do distinctly realize that the objective misfortune constituted by my failure is in no way magnified because the failure is mine and I have the sense of its extent—if somebody else failed just so far as I suppose I should expect the world to display a philosophic resignation. This evening I have been wallowing in S. B. reports—if nothing else is in reach one is called upon to be an industrious and well-informed member: Amen, amen, but it doesn't lessen the present feeling of discouragement that there is no one to whom either one of the four defeats is known or would be intelligible not to say interesting. I hate to think of the possibility of one's heart closing toward her—that indeed can never be, but there is one great cause of distance between any two people who live so that neither knows anything of the other without being told. It is an immense disadvantage to have nothing known of one but what one tells oneself—in despair one tries to tell what one neither can nor should, and will anyone make allowance for one's choice of evils, when somehow or other it has to be told or a fresh misunderstanding risked? I have tried to tell my own story before—and failed badly, and now I shrink from trying to tell,—and then what has one to see her for? As aforesaid I am dead beat—all round—and that being so; of course I can't go and see her. I will go to him instead—dear fellow he would forgive one for mourning several griefs together—knowing always which is the bitterest of them all.

February 17, 1880

Last Saturday I went rather too early; but was told she was in; had a headache and the day was too damp for her to drive. Johnny was there—and she said to me, how did I guess she would be in. I said I had expected her to be out, but called just to know how she was because I foreboded being unable to call all the next week. I did not stay long, or outstay Johnny, but ventured to kiss her cheek in farewell and wrote on Sunday before speaking to a very few Radicals about "Common Ground." I have been to a few schools, perhaps the members are getting to hate me less—but it is all hard work—I am ready to give up. . . .

February 22, 1880

Nearly the last straw in my present state of depression is the way people insist on taking me for a virtuous person given up to good works—I could hardly keep from crying the other day when—said she hoped it would be said of me "Twas much and you did it" i.e.—I am much bothered just now—what with Hamilton and Co, notice B cases and promised subscriptions, I am horribly in want of money—the other day I walked back here from the Temple, and again back from Victoria Station at night because I hadn't a sou to pay the fare. I should be content enough I fancy, if only I could decently earn £50 a year by scribbling; or I could make shift without if She thought the spare time was better spent upon posterity, but as it is, I am habitually worried by the need to do somehow, something more or different from what I can.

February 26, 1880

The day before yesterday—Tuesday—I went to see her and had an hour alone with her. The 16 year old child was not unhopeful—anyway the darling had been pleased by a letter of thanks from the mother for the result of her counsel. I risked the opinion that it was dangerous to refer a girl to the thought of marriage as a solution of the life problem. She accused me of an ascetic contempt for marriage which I rebuffed in some detail, and I suppose with success since she said laughing the next minute á propos of something else "Since I always meant just the opposite of what I seemed to say!" She was very dear.

March 9, 1880

From Tuesday to Tuesday there is nothing that needs saying. On Sunday I went to Wimbledon, walked across the common and saw the Bretts'[246] house, his children and the fascinating photographs of them; the next stayed at home preparing a lecture for the Democratic Club, and delivered same at night, for the rest, School Board and Mortimer Street. Yesterday was not idle; had a cup of tea in bed, reached Mortimer Street at 9, looked round, then to Hart Street to see about pupil and assistant teacher, then to Vere Street for drawing examination—surprised to find that the second step included geometry: then saw the visitor and received report of street cases caught by other visitors, managers meeting, made Mrs. Buxton's[247] acquaintance, then set off for the Rota, Works Committee and Educational Endowments, Industrial—home—reading Blackwood en route, wrote several letters and read beginning of Froude's History of Henry VIII[248] for another Club lecture.

---

[246] John Brett (1831-1903), landscape painter and astronomer (H, IX, 298, n. 5)

[247] See November 30, 1882.

[248] John Anthony Froude (1818-1894) *The Reign of Henry the Eighth* (London: J. M. Dent, [n.d.]).

—All this with perhaps a dim idea of earning the right to go and see her today. I got there a little before 5; she had just come in from her drive and came down after a few minutes. She was looking well and I began to talk about the Bretts' children—her recollection of them was as "fit to eat." Then Mrs. Lankester and a daughter[249] were announced. The former was appallingly voluble and I felt for my darling, and indeed did her some service later, when she turned to me, á propos of a mention of Miss Bevington—the latter was said to take a melancholy view of life and Mrs. Lewes referred to me as despising all prospective consolations as "a gambling speculation." It was questioned whether Miss Bevington would be consoled by marriage or if it was too late. Mrs. Lankester was comparatively reserved while the conversation wandered among abstract themes—they stayed a good while, then the daughter moved slightly and I rose to encourage them, but the darling said graciously to me to wait a little longer. I said presently it was hard at the end of 7 years to feel I had not yet explained what I meant by the "gambling speculation." I recurred to what I had meant by the "danger" of referring young people to the satisfaction of emotional affections—I said all one's normal appetites were sane and lawful in themselves, but just as she insists on the danger of seeking for pleasantness in the outer life—I hold it to be a danger to seek first for pleasantness in the inner life. She said one could not empty oneself of all desires and impulses. I said, was it not better to attack the objective sources of evil, rather than await in patience their possible diversion or drying up. At last she was content to leave it as a matter of temperament—that some may be more cheered by words of fortitude than hope. She moved to a low chair opposite the fire to warm her feet and I ventured to kneel by her side. She was a little tired by the discussion and said I had taken it up too seriously, she only spoke in play. I said it was ungrateful to complain of one thing she had said when all the rest had been full of consolation. She answered, Nay she had given up all thought of consoling me. I kissed her again and again and murmured broken words of love. She bade me not exaggerate. I said I didn't—nor could, and then scolded her for not being satisfied with letting me love her as I did—as a present reality—and proposing instead that I should save my love for some imaginary he: She said—expressly what She has often before implied to my distress—that the love of men and women for each other must always be more and better than any other and bade me not wish to be wiser than "God who made me"—in pious phrase. I hung over her caressingly and she bade me not think too much of her—she knew all her own frailty and if I went on, she would have to confess some of it to me. Then she said—perhaps it would shock me—she had never all her life cared very much for women—it must seem monstrous to me,—I said I had always known it. She went on to say, what I also knew, that she cared for the womanly ideal, sympathized with women and liked for them to come to her in their troubles, but while feeling near to them in one way, she felt far off in another—the friendship and intimacy of men was more to her. Then she tried to add what I had already imagined in explanation, that when she was young, girls and women seemed to look on her as somehow "uncanny"

---

[249] Mrs. Edwin Lankester, mother of eight (H, IX, 298, n. 6)

while men were always kind. I kissed her again and said I did not mind—if she did not mind having holes kissed in her cheek.—She said I gave her a very beautiful affection.—and then again She called me a silly child, and *I* asked if She would never say anything kind to me. I asked her to kiss me—let a trembling lover tell of the intense consciousness of the first deliberate touch of the dear one's lips. I returned the kiss to the lips that gave it and started to go—she waved me a farewell.

I am glad that she does not care much—individually and selfishly—for the fair type of admirable womanhood. God knows I have wished and tried and moaned over the failure of wish and effort—to remodel myself upon that type. I couldn't and I have called it election to damnation. I would have sold my soul for the mere appearance of approach. I am glad she does not care—I needn't wish to sell my soul since the sin would have been its own reward and she no less indifferent than before. What love she has to spare she shall give to me—"me, myself, me"—not to a fair and gracious type. I came back in smiles, not tears.—Dear fellow—would one could send him word that she is well and brave.

March 18, 1880

I had a pretext on which to write to her the next day; she answered as usual promptly and with a word of apology for the absence of any answer to the unpractical part of what I had written. She says one cannot empty oneself. I think one can. What else is it to continue an active, industrious link in the social machinery, continuing to mark results in what one has no concern save in a calm approval of the distant image? At the Bylaws Committee today: Am getting very tired—and the lines on one's face are very deep; I am well-pleased to see. A thought more out of spirits than usual, perhaps because it is so easy to be kept from doing anything towards "Appropriation," or perhaps because I haven't yet gathered any assurance that she would think it mattered much whether or no. On Saturday I should like to go to Highgate, then to her, then I would ask if I might come once more before going to Sark.

March 19, 1880

Dreamt last night my mother died—and I did not cry, or wish to write to Her:—I mixed up in a curious way my own ordinary state of "detachment" with Mrs. Murphies' matter of fact resignation to her good old husband's death. Seeing how hard it is for people to stay alive till their natural death, how can anyone even think they wish to be immortal. In the last fortnight I went to the last of Mrs. Wartsake's "at homes"—She would have been affronted if I hadn't—and I dined with Miss Williams once. It is always slower than slow to see one's fellow creatures.

March 26, 1880

I went yesterday and had 5 minutes alone with her, enough to hear she had not been well, was tired, and thought "she had done her duty" and might leave town the end of April or beginning of May. Then the bell rang, and before the new visitors were announced I kissed her and left. She said I should go to the Channel Islands—I was looking pale and overdone. I cried—or half—on the way back—wished to write to her to say I loved her enough to let her go—tried to forget my own loss in the thought of hers and felt in truth ready to give up all for myself if only her life might be made easier. And then I stopped—how would my saying this help her—if I say nothing she will not trouble herself to imagine whether anything painful might have been said.

March 28, 1880

This is my real Easter holiday, Friday, Saturday, today and Monday I am peaceably and idly indoors at home. Yesterday I read through my private journal from May 74 to the fatal March—I don't admire myself on the retrospect and I can understand the "exasperating" effect on her mind of my alternations from the tone of rapturous delighted adoration and devotion to still unsatisfied questioning. But no kind of folly is unmotived and I still understand my own feeling of irritation, when under difficulties, I had started on the effort to be "good" that she should take for granted, one was satisfying one's own gnawings by the effort—and—this was the implication that vexed and puzzled me most,—her eagerness to congratulate on this supposed advance seemed to assume that after all one's own content was the real aim or test, and as that was as little as in sight as ever I fell back into the discouragement caused by most of her auguries—the old idea of a false prophet was one who prophesied smooth things. I have thought, the last few days of writing a little book of "Vignettes"; I shall sound the boys and Annie at Sark as if it were written, I should not like my own people to guess quite how much autobiography there might be in it, and also I could imagine the boys each contributing a scene or two that would increase one's dramatic range. On the other hand, it would be nothing if not finished into very classical perfection and it is hard to be sure. As to ulterior motives, I should be glad of a chance of delivering myself aloud as to divers conclusions upon life and morals, and I want before giving up the ghost of ambition to have one—or two—more shots at my neighbours' ears. It is still a question whether one is to write for money or antiquity.

(Haight includes in Volume IX on this date the letter which is found inserted between the pages at the end of the Ms.)

Sunday, 1 Douro Place
Victoria Road, W

My own Darling

There are no posts in particular at Sark and as I am going there especially to be out of temptation to torment you, I want as a reward, leave for one more last caress. For my own, you have "done your duty" to us, and as I can't forget how hard that is, I can't help loving you even more and more dearly for the sake of the sweet patience that bears and does what is so hard. And therefore darling, I do want you to leave us before you are quite outworn, and I ought to be able to let you go without moaning, that it is like dying once a year, and that each year it is harder than the last.—

It seems horrible that I should be better off than you, and yet while you are here, I cannot help being happy for every moment in your presence. A word you let fall on Thursday makes me want to say one thing—you said some people wrote to you more freely from thinking you were alone. Darling, just because my love for you is the one great joy and blessing of my life, I should like you to know that if you had been alone seven years ago, I should not have ventured to let the love I felt have all its way. I dared to love you like this and to tell you so because he liked for you to be told, and all one's love could not be more than he thought due, than he liked to have poured at your feet. He delighted in sharing the blessedness of loving you and but for the sweet memory of his generous welcome I could not bear to be glad in feeling your dearness now. All my little bits of good fortune seemed to come through him, and the thought of him is never more vividly present than when I am happiest in your love. If it were not so, it would seem a disloyalty—as it is I often half hate my self because your happiness is dead and mine because of yours—I must live while you do.

One more little confession: it does not hurt me in the least not to say it, but "Sweet Mother" has come a hundred times to the tip of my pen since it was told not. Do you see darling that I can only love you three lawful ways, idolatrously as Frater the Virgin Mary, in romance wise as Petrarch, Laura, or with a child's fondness for the mother one leans on notwithstanding the irreverence of one's longing to pet and take care of her. Sober friendship seems to make the ugliest claim to a kind of equality; friendship is a precious thing indeed but between friends I think if there is love at all it must be equal, and whichever way we take it, our relation is between unequals.—It is a quite unpractical trifle, but I am impelled to say this because any change in one's speech seems to imply a change of feeling and there has been none in my feeling for you except a growing desire not to make any burdensome claim, not even to weary you with the boundless, grateful love that must still and always be yours— as I am.

Edith

7 kisses are launched upon the foggy air. Goodbye darling.

April 4, 1880

Sark has not proved inspiring so far. Holidays are a mistake; I adhere to it,—for some people.

April 23, 1880

Last Saturday (the 17th, just a week after we got back from Sark) reached the Priory at 1/4 to 5; she was, according to Brett, "very well"—still out for her drive. Came back rather depressed—an effect that was confirmed yesterday by proofs of an article written hastily to order for Morley—Decidedly I have grown stupid. I didn't write to her from Sark, either about the *Chef Plaint*[250] or my own woes. Shall go Monday or Tuesday again, and see her, perhaps, for the last time but one.

---

[250] "major complaint"

May 2, 1880

Last Monday I left the Works Committee early and got to the Priory a quarter or half past five. Asked how she was and Brett said she had a very bad cold, would ask if she was well enough to see me. She was lying down and rather miserable with violent influenza cold; I had only been with her two or three minutes when Mr. Pigott was announced—she said, to ask him to wait five minutes in the dining room, she had not seen me for so long, but he was such an old friend she did not like to refuse him though she wasn't fit to see any one. Before this she had taken away my breath when I spoke of her leaving London by saying she was going abroad for two or three months—she would write to me about her plans—she was not going to Witley before. I was rather stunned—glad in a way of every sign that she has not done with life and only hurt in an unavoidable way by the feeling how far away all the determining conditions of her life are from me, and a rapid thought that it was an irksome task to her to feel bound to give so much account of her doings because my love was covetous. I wrote a few lines that night to excuse my silence at the news, went the next day to the Shaftesbury with a party of members and felt as if the Vice Chairman and Mr. Sardton were more amused by my remarks than any other. Killed time with S. B. business Wednesday and Thursday, stole an hour the latter day to rush round and leave some cowslips and forget-me-nots at the Priory, heard she was no better— saw a bag and sunshade in the hall. That is only a half-absurd remark. Yesterday morning had some kind lines about cowslips and "Fortnightly" article. "Oh me, oh me, what slender cheer". . . Happy thought! I will leave the Board early enough to call at the Priory on Wednesday, as I can't any other day. Monday I am to see Knowles[251] about the Nineteenth Century where I offered to protest against the term "Agnostic."

May 7, 1880

Yesterday morning She was married to Johnny Cross and they went abroad. Charles Lewes came immediately after to tell me, and made an appointment for this morning. He tried to "break it to me" and then to explain and reason. I said I was not surprised. I could hardly say anywhere but here that the conception had in some dim form or other crossed my mind. I need not explain to myself how it was. Of course she suffered much—Charles said she had twice broken it off as impossible—had thought of all the difficulties—the effect upon her influence and all the rest: then she had consulted Sir James Paget, as a friend, her physician and impartial. He said there was no reason why she should not. Charles thought it would be well for the world as she might write again now. He had told Mrs. Peter Taylor and dreaded telling Mrs. Congreve— Harrison and Beesly had been told. Mr. Hall was to delay the announcement in the Times till Monday. She herself had not been able even to tell Charley, she had made Mr. Cross do so. I was not pained—you see with the utmost readiness for selfish complaint, what could I complain of—having nothing to lose. I could not trust my voice and eyes, so rushed into the streets as soon as he was gone,

---

[251] James Thomas Knowles, founder of the *Nineteenth Century* (H, VI, 362, 364)

went fiercely from school to school, and through the evening fought off the tears. If I ever write another book I shall dedicate it to the loved memory of George Henry Lewes. As soon as I came in I wrote to Miss Cross saying I was glad and asking her to forward the note to him. In this I enclosed a few lines to her and asked her to say what I wanted her to know before reading—I thought so she would be spared the painful moment in which one grasps the closed envelope, fearing what it may contain.

May 8, 1880

A postcard from Mrs. Lawrence: "Is it true?"—news travels fast.

May 9, 1880

I think the day in March—two months ago she came near to telling me. I am glad that I said nothing that could hurt her; I hardly know whether to wish I had induced her to tell me all, for I think she could hardly have done so without afterwards wishing that she had not.

May 12, 1880

On Sunday I wrote to Charles, to say I felt his goodness and consideration for her, and to suggest when he saw Mrs. Congreve he should say I would like to know her. A kind answer yesterday, saying he had already seen Mrs. Congreve. This morning a note from Eleanor Cross, who speaks of receiving a "delightful letter full of happiness." Strange how differently the same fact appears when the point of view is changed. I had thought of this family as the favorite of fortune and knowing all its bliss, that the sisters could only rejoice, for their brother first and then for themselves in being brought into nearer relation with her: and now there is a word in Eleanor's letter—reasonable enough in its way, but just a little surprising to me, they can "rejoice in giving her the best they had"—of course they had something to lose in their good brother.

May 13, 1880

I wonder a little how her feeling toward me will be affected by the change. I wonder disinterestedly for I do not see that I can wish. It seemed so natural and comprehensible that she should not write to me as "dearest" after his death; it is plain enough how the filial tone of my writing jarred upon her in the spring. There is reason in that unhappy letter which disclaims the power of "giving" in friendship, when she was "a wife with a wife's supreme and sufficing love" as there was reason in the chill of all other feeling following the great bereavement. Whatever happens now will be reasonable and natural too; but I cannot quite foretell—having no wishes I have no fears; surely no unforeseen calamity can break? I am not afraid but long experience forbids one ever to be quite sure that nothing unforeseen will happen or that the unforeseen may not be unexpectedly terrible.

May 16, 1880

Have just been looking at some of her letters. Somehow I can hardly realize that so much more time has passed after, than there was before that painful letter; it was the letters before that I used to read again and again night after night till I knew by heart the face of each envelope. A quotation has just occurred to me; it will be amusing and neither inappropriate nor unpleasant to let her know

"I think with joy
That I shall have my share, though he has more
Because he is the elder and a boy."[252]

She has been happy for eleven days. Good be with her! It is a comfort to remember that she is no longer desolate. It is a pale sort of comfort to remember that the moments which in times past I have longed to forget cannot or could not have made much difference after all. I have a sure protection against indiscretion now. It will be very difficult to me to speak or write of her as "Mrs. Cross," and so I shall be safe from the temptation to thrust myself upon them uninvited. I was the more anxious to write at once to express my full acceptance of what had happened because I did not wish her to suspect me of any lurking jealous resentment if I held back afterwards a little more than of yore. I shall remember to be more scrupulously courteous to Johnny than I ever was to my dear lost friend, but I can scarely wrong him in not expecting so sweetly generous a friendliness.

May 23, 1880
Have been scribbling off and on at "Vignettes." Hardly know whether they will come to anything. Am positive not to publish unless they are likely to be really good. Have not been unhappy about her, only just a little uneasy as to whether I may have said or thought too much in answer to her unspoken doubt about our feeling—mine with that of others. It was honest not to ignore the existence of the question, but was it possible to answer it in a way that should save the fact of its having been asked from causing any pain. I love her just as before: involuntary kisses form themselves and it is an unmixed pleasure to me to think of her as having life made easier again. But this has come of the repeated checks on such close dependence as my soul desired,—the help I might not have has been done without, and the impulse to seek it is almost extinct. I feel now as if it would not be too costly a risk to ask her, if the need arose, whether it would be for her happiness to let our intercourse drop into casual and rarer shape.

May 29, 1880
Yesterday came in—with my mind full of her—to find a dear letter from Milan. I had said nothing unwelcome, she was well and grateful—to me and others: there is something very touching in the way in which her lovingness disarms the pride that would resent external judgments.

---

[252] GE's sonnet sequence, "Brother and Sister," II, 6,7,8

May 30, 1880

Her letter ended with one of those—to me vexatious—hints at what I feel to be false prophesying and I have spent today and yesterday in trying to shape an answer that shall say what I mean without betraying any ungrateful irritation. I hope I have succeeded. I am able now to think with unmixed content of the change in her life. I did not even feel tempted to resent the restored "dearest."

June 1, 1880

The memory of her letter is still pleasant to me. I think of her caressingly and without impatience; I am not expecting any answer to my letter, and there is nothing it is necessary to my happiness to say to her now. For the next two or three months I can putter over schools and "Vignettes" and when I do hear from her again I shall be glad.

June 5, 1880

"Vignettes" are the resource when I have nothing else to do. More or less troublesome interviews and correspondence take up the time with School Board work. I think of her without pain. My mind seems to have recovered its independence. I can live alone, and being alive the independent pleasure of loving her is a sweet superfluity, a luxury which as such is satisfying, though taken as the one necessary of life it seemed more like hunger than food. Am a little anxious about "Vignettes" lest I should anywhere let slip what might be too plain a confession to her, if she saw it: but I suppose there is little danger. The one I call "At Anchor" is pure reminiscence—of the Solent from the Needles the summer after "Natural Law" came out, but I don't think she will guess this. Augustus thinks there is great "force and distinction" about the bits he has seen, but feels them to be queer and does not know what people will make of them. A fair criticism is that the intense and vivid feeling is all *á propos* of something off the general track. This is partly intended, and has to do with my theory of the *homologies* of life, the secret of dramatic, and in a degree of all artistic effect is that a particular presentation calls up a feeling wider than that proper to itself. My mother thought I was not at all like "Reuben" in any way.—

Have been reading her early letters through on end and I seem to see daylight now. What seemed to me a hard inconsistency—perhaps I might tell her so some day—was that she began by telling me to let feeling have its way and trust myself to love. I did love her—who could help it and then once and again I brought on myself her warning, not to love covetously and make unreasonable claims. I struggled with my covetousness and tried to be reasonable, but there was a heartache left for me to struggle with, and it was more than I could bear that while I was trying to do without what I wanted most, she should be always ready to congratulate me on getting what I didn't want or to scold me for not wanting something else—that I could get as little as what I wanted. I think this was the key to all that happened till her stern letter.[253] Then I was thrown back

---

[253] Haight and McKenzie say this refers to March 1876 (H, IX, 313, n. 2; McK, 88). See July 24, 1880.

upon myself. I might neither live with her nor without her, so I held my life in suspense—it was a period of suicide. Then came her eloquent silence about the book—and I have never wished passionately for anything for myself since. I have felt deeply what has happened but from then onward though I have wished to do what might be right or most nearly right, I have never cared passionately or wished that one thing rather than another might be most nearly right.

June 10, 1880

It is always rather curious to me to be writing diligently "out of my own head." I am going on with "Vignettes" in fragmentary mornings and evenings and hope soon to feel the pulse of an editor as to the least compromising of the single bits. I wonder whether they can be good: if so there will be about the right proportion of literature and doctrine to pacify my conscience in making the book.

June 13, 1880

What used to hurt me in her references to that imaginary future was my feeling: If nothing but just that seems satisfactory to her good wishes then no real and probable life of mine will command her full and loving sympathy. How can I make her understand that it is not the missing of that future I regret only the warning that she does not care much about any other. One can teach oneself anything, but I do not want to have to teach myself to do without trust in her kindly interest. I am not proud she knows, but it is rather humiliating to me to be told again and again that the association called up by my name is always that of a woman who might find a husband if she would take a little more pains with her dress and drawing room conversation—and this in the mind of some one that I love. I have digested so many worse rebukes that I could put up with a simple criticism of my manners or appearance if it was without *arrierè pensée*,[254] but I cannot feel that I *ought* to allow weight to a suggestion that urges me to seek the meaning of my life in the solicited good will or good opinion of strangers. I don't think so meanly of the men I meet as to assume they have nothing better to do than be persuaded to think me "charming." Without your encouragement, I should hardly think so meanly of myself as to say my life was worthless unless I could achieve that triumph. The charm that I revere and love is one that springs unconsciously and inevitably from a sweet nature and a whole life. Dearest, how contentedly I should love you if your urgency were towards the possible doing and being better without wretched sidelong glances after someone fool enough to love one's wretched best. It is not only I that feel humiliated, I am more pained by the shadow of something almost like insolence in you—"Let some one else love what I have despised." And if you do not despise me, Darling,—God knows I am loth to think it—then spare me these words which make me despise myself!—as if all that I am, all that I can wish or strive to be is as nothing in your eyes unless my outer shell finds favour in the eyes of men! [and besides, what right have you to assume that I am not on terms of satisfactorily friendly intimacy with the few men that I am naturally brought in contact with?] I will say no

---

[254] "a second thought"

more. I don't want to be angry about this, or to say that such allusions are "unfruitful of everything but an unpleasant impression on my mind, and that I must beg you to give them up or to give me up." But I have no choice but to feel hurt or angry if I let myself feel your words at all, and I do not like to teach myself to receive any words of yours with indifference; like the speech of a mere stranger that has fallen wide of its mark. This is unjust and ungrateful. It is not what I should choose to say to her, but it is what I naturally feel—a feeling as little appropriate to her meaning as that answer of hers was to mine, but I ought not to leave her in ignorance—if I can help it, of my real feeling. Perhaps I ought to say to her that I do not, like Adam Bede, express my doubt more strongly in the hope of eliciting reasons on the other side.

June 17, 1880

You see my experience has been on this wise. I was called upon to bear the knowledge that she could never care very much for me in the way one covets for oneself by the natural instinct of self-preservation or self-pleasing; this could be learnt but behind it was left the harder task of bearing to know, not only that I could win little gladness from her love, but that my love could never be of much or any use or comfort to her: this too has to be borne, but one cannot wish ever to cease to feel it as a pain. One loves all the same and chooses—since it must be so—to have the pain to bear. It takes all one's strength to bear it without bitterness. And then she seems to say—you are wasting this love upon me, who do not want it—why do you not find somebody who will consent to want it and give it all to him? This touches me like a reproach—it is my hardest grief that the love I bear to you is fruitless for your good but—oh my love! is the fault of that in me? Should I not have served you with eager faithfulness and glad devotion through a life of love if fate had left you in my arms?—if you could ever have been content to rest in them? That might not be but is it for you to reproach me because everyone else, like you, finds his happiness, if at all, elsewhere,—what have I done that you should call on me to go out into the high ways and hedges and beg amongst the starving beggars for a pauper mate, because the king has no profit from his subjects' love? Let those who must or may love once or twice or thrice, let their happiness be born again when it is dead, but earth hath only one joy for me and that is dead and my love still worships at its tomb and though my Love himself came back to chide me, I could say no other than that I do well to love and worship mournfully.

June 20, 1880

I have put the above sentiment into a "Vignette." Yesterday had the Westminster Teachers to tea; Sidney[255] came and showed himself quite reconciled in discourse to my mother.

---

[255] Sydney Buxton supported the Women's Trade Union Association. See March 9, 1880 and November 30, 1882.

June 23, 1880

Nearly a month since her letter came. In another 6 weeks or so she will probably be back in England. I think of her constantly, with a caress in my mind; but I am not unhappy about her one "perversity." I feel as if I could reason with her on the matter without drifting even into as much melancholy as in my last letter.

June 26, 1880

One feels rather tired of living from day to day without other purpose than that of just getting innocently through the day's work and I am resolute not, if I can help it, to disguise the void by living in hopes that the next few weeks or months will be lived through in time and make way for a momentary meeting of a mouthful of written intercourse. Shall I ever tell her that in some ways she has done me harm? My native idleness wrests to its own use her praise of sympathy if all good is to be done by the help thereof—failing the sympathy is one to blame for doing nothing?

June 27, 1880

Looking back is uncomfortable—all sorts of grievances are easily revived in memory but I have no fears in looking forward; when I see her next, instead of hungering for her welcome, I want to welcome her with love and the whisper of my gladness in thinking of the love that waits upon her steps. I must not—I will not be tempted again into coveting for myself. It is not pride. God knows I should be ready enough to gather the crumbs that fall from any table she has spread for others,[256] but I know it is best for her, she is less troubled by any care for me, when I have schooled myself in self-denial and wait on her with love that asked for nothing again.

June 30, 1880

I hear today at second hand that they have taken a house in Cheyne Walk. I hope it may be true. I had a horrible dread of having to welcome Johnny in the place where I had known Lewes. And yet I feel robbed—as if I had lost something irreplaceable—now I shall never see that room again—it is taken from me without so much as a moment's farewell. She wrote to Mrs. Burne-Jones and to Blackwood the night before. The things that are said of her hurt me. They go back to the old story. I cannot believe that she built her happiness upon a separation,[257] that but for her need not have come. No doubt she let her own feeling count for something, but I am sure the controlling motive was the thought for him. The only difference this has made in my feeling is to give me courage to blame myself less where she has been apt to blame me for not being like herself.

---

[256] An allusion to the story of the rich man and Lazarus (Luke 16:19-31)

[257] The gossip of 1854 that GHL had run away from his wife and family (H, IX, 313, n. 3)

July 3, 1880

I have found June rather long. I am tempted to think whether I ought to renounce the intercourse altogether when I feel how it makes all the rest of one's life seem barren and provisional. It is a sort of instinct to cut one's throat and have done with it that drives to wonder whether I had not better—if there is no chance of a more healthy, normal relationship growing up now,—make up mind at once not to hope or expect anything at all. It is like that assumed "poor child": I am to be pitied if she does not care for me;—if *she* pities me—I am to be pitied indeed. If she thinks there is no satisfactory life possible to an unmarried woman—there *is* no satisfactory life possible to me who can conceive no satisfaction but in her friendship for me unmarried. Look at it this way my Darling! You, the embodiment of the good I desired and could not have, you did nothing but scold me for not enjoying the possession of life's good.

July 6, 1880

All this is only the fractiousness of hunger, it is not I, only the wolfish hunger within me that utters these incompatible plaints. I am not going to inflict my hard won place in her regard by mere follies. I look forward rather to rejoicing in her happiness and wooing her playfully to believe in mine.

July 11, 1880

Yesterday I was startled by the question "Is Mr. Cross any better?" and then a rumour that he was ill—or like to die—of typhoid fever at Venice. It seemed too horrible to be true and yet I hardly dared to doubt it. It was bad enough at best to think of her alarm if he was ill at all. I tried to harden myself shiveringly, as I went up to Hampstead to seek news from Charley. He had gone to join his wife and children at Witley—I asked the servant if she knew how Mr. Cross was and she said getting better, when she heard them speak of it last—they were talking of coming back to England. This did not tell me what the worst had been and I tried again at the Priory where the woman in charge had heard nothing. It seemed the first report was exaggerated, but I could not help feeling besides the moribund anxiety for her a dull pain at the thought that her anxiety might have come and gone without my knowing.—Shall I run down to Weybridge this afternoon and see if it was true his sisters had been telegraphed for—the servants there at least will know all about it.

July 12, 1880

On the whole, after some hesitation I went. I took a 3rd class return from Clapham Junction and arrived just before 6. Eleanor and Florence were alone at home. Three weeks or more before he had been taken ill, she telegraphed at once and Willy Cross went out; for a week he was ill—if not in danger, and then, very weak, they carried him by slow stages out of Venice; Munich did not suit him, but he was out of danger now, had written one letter himself, they were going to Wildbad, and likely to be back as proposed the end of this month. I was very glad I went. Eleanor spoke a little about the marriage, hoped I was glad for her as well as him and said, as Charles Lewes had, that they had been very anxious before their marriage, he was so worn and ill. He had to continue all his business to the last because she would not let anyone be told and he shrank from the responsibility, if her friends were likely to take it as she thought they would, of coming between her and them. She had said to them— "Edith would disapprove." I was glad I went. It was a great comfort both to know he was better and to hear them spoken of. Poor Johnny! As I guessed, he knew somehing of the bitterness of that recurring exile from her presence. I am heartily glad to think of his happiness. It is happiness to me to think of her with love, though my heart aches afresh as with an open wound as the vision of the next meeting makes way for the thoughts of how one passes into the chill anguish of exile when the short sweet moments end.—At least that is over for Johnny. My darling,—might I reproach *you* for not having known that in doing this I should understand—that even if you could ever do aught I could not understand, now, then and always I must love you unchangeably, my sweet. I opened a copy of Theophastus and read an inscription "to my dove-voiced Mary, from G.E."

July 17, 1880

Last night and this morning I have been reading through her letters and feeling afresh the possibility of explaining, without querulousness, how we have been a little at cross purposes all these years, when I wanted her to help me to be content without the gratification—first of personal desires and ambitions and then of comparatively unselfish ones, and she would do nothing but bid me hope—even selfishly—for the good I knew myself to be called on to renounce.

July 21, 1880

Have a nervous restless feeling. The moon has come back to full brightness looking in to my room at bedtime which reminds me always of the July when we first settled here—in 1872 when I was reading Middlemarch and as yet knew her not. The eight years have been sadly wasted—not more so perhaps than the eight years before them, but then the waste was only just common idleness and helplessness, not a lost opportunity of divine rarity and sweetness. I cannot keep myself from looking forward to her return with a dim hopeful expectation, though I know with the certainty of sevenfold experience that it can make no difference, that it will only make a painful difference if I let my hopes build on it.—I won't, but I am restless and uneasy.

July 24, 1880

I have been thinking lately of that day in March 73—three years before the fatal March. She said to me then, when I tried to tell her of the strange feeling of "conversion"—"Why should one expect the truth to be consoling?" Why indeed?

July 30, 1880

A letter came last night and pleased me by some—*freilich*[258] rather scant—concessions in reply to my letter sent to Venice. They think of staying at

---

[258] "admittedly"

Witley till November. Since the 9th of March I have only seen her twice for a short five minutes—that makes full 8 months out of the 12 an utter, barren blank. Yet I am cheered by her letter—even while I smile at myself for being nourished by such slender consolations. She is very dear—I must not tell her how much she has herself done to kill the ambitions to which she now appeals. If I were to tell her I am less at my ease with her than any one else because no one else thinks so ill of me (with reason)—Is there any one else she loves of whom her good opinion is in proportion to the reserve shown? Well, well,—it is over now; I have answered her letter and it is likely shall feel no impulse to write again.

August 8, 1880

A pretty love letter wrote itself—in the air, not for sending—last Sunday when I was alone and should have been writing a paper on Education for an American "Social Science." In the last letter I had sent, I think as usual, there was too little and too much said. I have a recollection of words with an uncomfortable ring—I spoke of self-abasement to send such a letter as the one of love would be an insincerity, seeing how much else would have to be said to let the message carry truth. I do not know whether it is mere suicidal mania, but I think again and again of Mrs. Compton's[259] renunciation and I wonder whether I should do something of the same—unless indeed the relation could become more natural and wholesome.—I wonder whether I should put it to the test and ask her to come and see me when they are in town again, and if she declines then identify myself with the despised family and no more seek the unattainable visionary delight beyond: I hate myself for these passages of unloving resentment and yet—is there not a cause? Any way for the present I am silent, and I think the longer the wiser.

August 29, 1880

Last night I thought so again and my heart was sore and angry and I could not sleep for love and pain. I did not want to write to her, but then I thought if my silence began now, she would feel a silent hurt as if I had changed to her because of her changed life: and I thought I would write once and give some other explanation of my silence in future. My heart aches as venomously as ever. I must either live without her or come nearer.

September 6, 1880

I wrote last Sunday, sending the second of two letters, in which I hoped there would be nothing to jar on her. I dreamt of her on Saturday night. Yesterday as I lay in the hammock, in the intervals of skimming an imperfect novel and scribbling the "giant with no heart in his body," I had dim visions of confiding in Mary Cross,—telling her how I thought now I might withdraw unmissed, not that I wished to withdraw—I wish it as little now as ever, but telling her how the hanging from day to day and week to week upon the hope of some word or sight of her paralyzes all one's strength and holds one's life in

---

[259] Lady Alwyne Compton, see December 5, 1880.

suspense,—it is not as if I knew what she would have me do.—Why shouldn't I tell her that the only thing that amuses me in the least—if that were to count for a "leading" is to write stuff out of my own head,—about Ethics, Egypt, or Eieiaio.[260]

September 9, 1880

On Monday I heard from her, in prompt reply to my last which had only just reached her. She speaks of love and tenderness that do not prevent her feeling sometimes as if she had woke in an unremembered state of existence and almost wished she were dead. One felt all the difficulty; she will miss the active intellectual companionship. The "family" is all very dear and good, but of old she did not depend on them alone. Then before the marriage between her and Johnny I think the sympathy must have been complete: now he cannot in any way lighten her feeling of a divided duty. She must remember what is lost and yet for his sake it would be well if she could sometimes forget. At least it is not now the time for me to go and hide from her; it is possible that my love staying still the same through the other changes may furnish something of momentary comfort and confirmation. And I should not feel myself to have lived in vain, if for a single moment of her life she had ever felt for half a moment as if a pain were soothed or a want supplied by my love, always watchful and ready to her call.

September 12, 1880

Am getting on with "Vignettes."—I don't think they are good. I hope she will write to me by the end of the month.

September 24, 1880

Not quite without purpose, but mainly to satisfy the mere craving for the sight of her dear face, I took my life in my hands and wrote to ask if I might come down and see her. I posted the letter on Tuesday. Yesterday evening an answer came from Johnny: she was not well but if better would write next week and fix a day. On his part there was no dearth of kind expressions, but I am answered as to my chief question, whether I might call uninvited, just once or twice in the summer to keep myself alive. I had not for a moment anticipated a purely pleasant answer. Like a brute I am only half sorry she is unwell—it seemed impossible that she should be wholly kind and I should not have liked her to have a less sufficient reason. This morning I thought I was content. This evening I have been crying a little and thinking again of confiding in Mary Cross.

---

[260] The Patagonian giant in "Love and Friendship" who allowed his heart to be charmed out of his body by a cruel princess. This "Vignette" was originally published in *Fraser's Magazine* 21 (October 1881): 448-461 and then as one of the *Episodes in the Lives of Men, Women and Lovers* (London: Trübner, 1882).

October 4, 1880

Last Wednesday went to see Mrs. Anderson[261] about a trifling ailment and was told that its usual subjects were half-starved slave-driven maids of all work! Mrs. A. seemed to think it would account if I had been writing any more philosophy the like of which made *her* legs ache to read. Yesterday morning read all her (not Mrs. Anderson's) letters through on end. I get a rather different impression each time I go through the series—this time curiously enough—I only just read through the words. My impression was as if there was very little in them at all.

October 9, 1880

In another four weeks or so, I suppose, she will be back in town. It is not quite a fortnight since I had a note from her—4 days after Johnny's—saying she was still not well, and he wanted to take her away. My head is a little stupid (with quinine I think) so that I can't spend the interval in which, Mrs. Anderson tells me to "rest a good deal," in any kind of distracting writing. I am therefore rather cross and dismal.

October 10, 1880

But as usual that mood does not last quite unbroken. Last night my heart was yearning after her with pure tender love and I imagined myself saying to her between long happy looks and sweet caresses that I could and would bear even her absences if only I knew in absence what and how she would have me do alone. Nothing is less likely than that any publisher should give me money for "Vignettes"—*if* however that unlikely event befel, I should think about buying books enough to get on with "Appropriation" at home, while keeping up the board and giving a very little time to Mortimer Street; otherwise I am bound to be either viciously *idle* or physically over-fatigued. But I don't care as much as I used in the days when I worried her about my anxiety about the horns of the impaling dilemma. I am not young enough now to care much about anything (except her).

October 16, 1880

Though I have no immediate expectation, I feel an anxious suspense after every postman's ring until the uninteresting bill or school board packet makes its appearance, and I remind myself that I expected nothing more. In another two or three weeks I shall hear something. I hope she is not unwell tho' I am sometimes a little uneasy in remembering her "you will be sure to hear when I am better": but I comfort myself that she will not remember that to the extent of feeling bound to write. Though I have the same longing to see her again, it is without the joyous anticipation: I look forward to nothing but the pleasure of welcoming her with tender love. She has told me again and again she had

---

[261] Dr. Elizabeth Garrett Anderson (1836-1917), along with Elizabeth Blackwell, was one of the first women who dared to be medical doctors.

nothing to give—why should I contradict her when my heart has done little all these years but ache an echo to the truth.

October 24, 1880

Am still waiting and watching. If I had known where they were going (as anyone else in my place would) I should have taken advantage of the doctor's recommending change of air to steal down and lodge in the same place and enjoy delightful meetings. But that is not my luck. I don't want to go away anywhere else lest I should lose by a post the first intimation of her return; of course I cannot write to her—though it is 4 weeks since I heard,—as I do not know where to write to: it is a kind of persecution to send letters always "to be forwarded."

October 25, 1880

A note from Johnny this morning: I gather she has not been well enough all the time to leave home, and last Sunday was worse—I fear with the old pain. They will come to Chelsea as soon as she is well enough to move.

October 28, 1880

Have been much distressed this week by the death of Mr. Rodgers on Monday evening.

November 7, 1880

No further news of her and I have not liked to call at the house for news. All last week have been busy over pacific diplomacy at the board. I am not feeling well, and am unprincipled enough to be glad when I can decently claim not to be well enough to do disagreeable things.

November 13, 1880

Last Tuesday I went round by Cheyne Walk—looked at the outside of the house and argued from its aspect that they had not yet arrived. Hadn't courage to call and enquire. Am feeling seriously anxious now lest continued illness should be the cause of their delayed return. I am all right again now—i.e. as usual in health and beginning to want some work. There is something painful in the effect on one's feeling of these long separations: one does not wish to be able to live without her and it is horrible to feel oneself—if not living, at least existing *by force*, through days and months—growing to years from which she is altogether absent.

November 19, 1880

Again last Tuesday I went to Cheyne Walk, driven by growing anxiety. The house was not ready or furnished; the man in charge wished to show me over and said Mr. Cross was coming up with furniture midday. I wrote to her in the evening and last night heard in reply that she was better, but not to be in town till the end of the month. The physical alienation makes some way. An absence of nine months, which she could have abridged by a cheap word, makes it impossible to ignore one's fate—to live a long way off.

November 27, 1880

I answered that last letter with perhaps too much accent of complaint, but this I hardly regret. I shall perhaps regret it if—as I still refuse to expect—poor Maria does not recover and turns out to have left me any money. This will be known before long: and it can not really be much longer now before I see her again. My longing has got partly quenched. I wish on Tuesday to go to Highgate.

November 28, 1880

December 5, 1880

Thought about writing last week and then stopped short. I was not able to go to Highgate—at least I should have had to go empty handed which I did not wish. Went to see Mrs. Compton[262] yesterday; she thought husband and children were very well, but one wanted friends besides. "Could not help being sorry about—Mrs. Lewes." Said something about her having been to Brighton—perhaps that is since I heard. I am getting rather hardened. Can friendship survive 9 months needless separation? Poor darling I wish she were happier and stronger than I guess. It seems Maria[263] has left Will her executor, with Henry. The good Emma is either huffed or considerate in not sending word of the substance of the will, since she knows it. If it were to contain no dispositions in favour of either of us, it would be, perhaps, a pretty freedom from *Schadenfreude*[264] that disinclined her to communicate the fact.

December 12, 1880

I have written today a letter to await her at Cheyne Walk, I went round by the house yesterday and thought too many blinds were down for it to be inhabited. The days are wonderfully bright and not cold; I hope she is at Brighton. The existing Will leaves £200 to most of the nephews and nieces and an odd thousand or so to Will and Henry. Wrote to Ian Blackwood the other day. Am rather used up so actually encourage the idea of going to Ilfracombe for Xmas—I think a fortnight's thorough change and rest will be good for me. The School Board would be less depressing than it has been if I were less dismal otherwise, as I am getting to find it less impossible to make my influence felt.

December 17, 1880

An answer came next day,[265] speaking of herself as "hunted" in appearance. I answered immediately saying I would not join in the hunt, nor

---

262 See August 8, 1880.

263 Maria Sharwood, see November 27, 1880.

264 literally "gallows humor"

265 In MS something is scratched out.

therefore seek her this week. I think I shall go Sunday afternoon. I would rather see her with other people by my own choice than try for a private interview and risk a chance rebuff. I can't help feeling that this is the first time in all these years that I have not known of her return for "a week and more," still last year she did not write to me, I only ascertained the date by enquiry at the house—as indeed I should have done this year, but for the unlucky snub about the caretaker. Was rather ashamed of myself the other day in reading Pollock's Spinoza.[266] It is weak to surrender all aspiration because of a disappointment in love—which is practically what it comes to, but I'm afraid I'm at the end of my strength—to the point even of being disappointed at losing a fortnight at the sea-side this Christmas. I thought perhaps the rest would revive one's energies.

December 19, 1880

A short and sweet—quite sweet—note came last night asking me to go this afternoon: she hoped no one else would be there. I don't think it likely that no one will but of course would rather go invited than not. The Ilfracombe plan is off, my mother and Augustus go down to Weyhill to talk about Will's executorship. I shan't care about that if she is kind to me! I shall know in 4 hours and 10 minutes!

December 23, 1880

She was alone when I arrived. I was too shy to ask for any special greeting—only kissed her again and again as she sat. Mr. Cross came in soon and I noticed his countenance was transfigured, a calm look of pure *beatitude* had succeeded the ordinary good nature.—Poor fellow! She was complaining of a slight sore throat, when he came in and touched her hand, said she felt the reverse of better. I only stayed half an hour therefore; she said do not go, but I gave as a reason that she should not tire her throat and then she asked me to come in again and tell them the news. He came down to the door with me and I only asked after his health—she had spoken before of being quite well and I thought it was only a passing cold—she thought it was caught at the Agamemnon.[267] I meant to call again tomorrow and take her some snowdrops. This morning I hear from Johnny—she died at 10 last night! On Tuesday I was struck, as something ominous, by a sentence in a novel—"There is only one remedy for a chronic misunderstanding—Death." One slender comfort is left me—that I saw and kissed her so near the end. I thought—though I did not say—God grant I may die after such a meeting as this—and it is she that is dead. Now all is over. I have nothing more to wait and long for—Alone for evermore! Poor Johnny—it was good of him to write to me at once. He says "Pity me"—I should think I do. No one knows how deep my need of pity. But to her what can death be but the

---

[266] Sir Frederick Pollock (1845-1937), *Spinoza: His Life and Philosophy* (London: C. K. Paul, 1880).

[267] The Crosses had a box for Aeschylus' *Agamemnon* given in Greek by Oxford undergraduates at St. George's Hall on December 17 (H, Biography, 547).

order of release. I feel almost as if the bitterness of death had been past for me when he died. One's power of grieving gets dulled by use. By a merciful chance I am alone in the house and can cry unchecked, but two years ago there was her living sorrow left to mourn for and I have wept for her and for myself till grief seems an old dull story—death itself nothing new or strange, familiar like my own hopelessness. I will remember nothing but her last sweet note: if this time she did not return my kiss, it meant only that she was suffering and weak; most often the renunciations which have pained me had that cause. All is over now; one has to begin life again "at a lower level of expectation." This book will be closed or grow objective. My heart's life is ended.

December 24, 1880

And yet—is it? Surely the life of these past years have been my love for her: why should that die because the hopes that mingled with my love are dead. In thinking of her, kisses used to form themselves instinctively on my lips—I seldom failed to kiss her a good night in thought; like the ghost of a ghost the old habit haunts me still. It is vain now to stretch out longing arms toward her distant presence, but the love that made the longing and molded the caress— shall that too feel the defacing hand of Death? No—No. Dearest—far off like the worshipped gods of others you shall live unchanged, unchanging in my heart—it is not I but you that shall henceforth be diligent, tender, patient and yet zealous for all good—what is left me but that—but you—still now and evermore—my wise, gracious and undying love.

December 25, 1880

I dreamt insanely of seeing her and that she repelled me, for I know not what phantom reason. If only I had said something to her—fonder than my selfish kisses, I should have liked to remember her acceptance. But I will not use myself with idle regrets. I do not think she ever asked from me in thought more love than she knew I gave—at least in May she was glad my love rang true, and for me, if I remember all her sweetness, all her loving looks and the dear cheeks' sweet caress, the fortunate hours of free intercourse and the abiding place she gave me among her few nearest friends, remembering all that I cannot moan as destitute. As poor Johnny writes—I, was the last friend she saw—even that foolish plea of jealousy escapes me. One grave may hold the hopes of love's small triumphs and the base complaints of covetous envy. Most Beautiful and Most Beloved—ever so dearest shall live while I do—while all of me that loved you lives; the fault was mine if one feeling found room within me that was not utter love. The sweetness was yours, the bitterness mine, I never doubted this only I wanted more sweetness still. Nature's grim judgment now bids me rest unmurmuringly content with the memory of the good which, while possessing I dared to murmur at, as if it were not good enough. At least I was not always ungrateful and she knew more of the gratitude than the murmurs. Content is a cheap virtue now when there is nothing left worth murmuring at—and then one breaks down into simple childish tears of simple unmixed grief and love—loss eternal as death and life. Darling, as in past years the thought of having to live without you seemed impossible at a distance—now face to face I do not know

136

how to believe that you—the incomprehensibly dear you clasped so often in my arms—are gone, gone wholly and for ever out of the reach of living love. I profane your memory, dearest, with no impiety, I hope dimly to build your monument in the bettering of words and deeds to come, but the dead love is Sorrow and the living Joy—thank heaven your life, my best one, knew that joy and now all your sorrows have fallen asleep. To my love, Darling, death will be the glad end of our parting. I must write no more or the life between will seem too hard.

December 26, 1880

This morning I ventured to look again at some of her letters—all dear and gracious and full of sweet acknowledgment of all my love. Mrs. Anderson came to see me this morning—was very kind: wished to know when the funeral would be—spoke of people having spoken of Westminster Abbey; she seemed to understand about the dear one—thought she must have had Bright's disease and would have suffered more if she had lived. She asked if I was going to the house today and on that instance I did—hoping for some chance to save me from ringing that bell again. I met Florence coming from the house; she could hardly speak; her brother had gone out for a walk with Mr. Druce. He loved the house where she had lived just 3 weeks. I turned back with her we exchanged few words—I learnt their address (3 Percy Villas)—later Miss Helps called—to ask Charles Lewes's address and also about the funeral. This reminded me to write to Charles.

December 27, 1880

I have forced myself to read continuously—Trevelyan's Fox,[268] Duffy's Young Ireland[269] and O'Brien's "Parliamentary History" of the Irish land question.[270] If the family approve I hope to go away on Saturday—first to Nuneaton, and perhaps thence a little among the nail-makers—I saw a paragraph in the Pall Mall that the Sedgley schools were being opened free by the Board there. I must write to Bramley to ask how much of the City guilds' funds are derived from their Trust Estate. Mind and body are quivering for action. The moral of "Some one had blundered" finished itself this afternoon by a thought—the solemnity of the political necessity, One *cannot* be right alone. There can be nothing now to wait or hope for—no unearned delight: that sweetest

---

[268] Sir George Otto Trevelyan (1838-1928), *The Early History of Charles James Fox* (London: Longmans, 1881).

[269] Sir Charles Gavan Duffy (1816-1903), *Young Ireland* (London: Cassell, Petter, Galpin, 1880).

[270] R. Barry O'Brien (1847-1928), *The Parliamentary History of the Irish Land Question from 1829 to 1869*, 3d ed. (London: S. Low, Marston, Searle, and Rivington, 1880).

happiness—of loving her—could not be earned, but now to that it can no more be given, each day must live by its dole of labour. Henceforth instead of that vile maxim—to do nothing but what one must—I have rather to hope and pray and labour to attain that no moment shall be left without a chosen or invented task. A hint from the life of Fox moved me wholesomely, even his failing genius needed the food of industry. I don't try to harden myself—the kind words and letters from Mrs. Anderson, Miss Orme and the rest are truly welcome—I don't try to forget—how could I ever? only I dare not give all the time to remembering. I give more to grieving—uncontrollable tears take their share—oh my Love! My Love—My Love—

December 28, 1880
  Nothing will ever extinguish my regret that it was not my fortune to learn to know her in 1864, when we were at Bonchurch and I was 20. It would have been 8 years more, just double one's short lease of love, but that is not all— those eight years were stationary or worse for want of an outer life to match one's tastes and impulses. She would have made me study seriously and as I was quite as clever then as later, she would have thought the younger cleverness more hopeful—and I shouldn't have been handicapped with the leaden weight of wasted years. It is urgent in more ways than one to help the young—and especially young women—to harness their fresh impulses and enthusiasms.

December 29, 1880
  This day stands alone. I am not afraid of forgetting, but as heretofore I record her teaching while the sound is still fresh in my soul's ears. This morning at 10 when the wreath I had ordered—white flowers bordered with laurel leaves—came, I drove with it to Cheyne Walk, giving it silently to the silent cook. Then, instinct guiding—it seemed to guide one right all day—I went to Highgate—stopping on the way to get some violets—I was not sure for what purpose. In the cemetery I found the new grave was in the place I had feebly coveted—nearer the path than his and one step further south. Then I laid my violets at the head of Mr. Lewes's solitary grave and left the already gathering crowd to ask which way the entrance would be. Then I drifted towards the chapel—standing first for a while under the colonnade where a child asked me "Was it the late George Eliot's wife was going to be buried?"—I think I said Yes—Then I waited on the skirts of the group gathered in the porch between the church and chapel sanctuaries. Then some one claimed a passage through the thickening crowd and I followed in his wake and found myself without effort in a sort of vestibule past the door which kept back the crowd. Mrs. Lankester was next the chapel—I cannot forget that she offered me her place. I took it and presently every one else was made to stand back, then the solemn procession passed me. The coffin bearers paused in the very doorway, I pressed a kiss upon the pall and trembled violently as I stood motionless else, in the still silence with nothing to mar the realization of that intense moment's awe. Then—it was hard to tell the invited mourners from the other waiting friends—men many of whose faces I knew—and so I passed among them into the chapel—entering a forward pew. White wreaths lay thick upon the velvet pall—it was not painful to think of

her last sleep so guarded. I saw her husband's face, pale and still; he forced himself aloof from the unbearable world in sight. The service was so like our own I did not know it apart till afterwards when I could not trace the outlines that had seemed so almost entirely in harmony with her faith. Dr. Sadler[271] quoted—how could he help?—her words of aspiration, but what moved me most was the passage—in the Church Service lesson—it moved me like the voice of God—of Her: "But some man will say, How are the dead raised up? and with what body do they come? Thou fool, that which thou sowest is not quickened except it die. And that which thou sowest, thou sowest not that body that shall be, but bare grain—but God giveth it a body, as it hath pleased him, and to every seed his own body." Awe thrilled me. As at the presence of God. In the memory of her life bare grain—oh God, my God. My love what fruit should such seed bring forth in us—I will force myself to remember your crushing prophesy—that I was to do better work than you had—that cannot be, my Best! and all mine is always yours, but oh! Dearest! Dearest! it shall not be less unworthy of you than it must. As we left the chapel Miss Helps put her arm in mine, but I left her at the door, to make my way alone across the road to the other part where the grave was. I shook hands silently with Mrs. Anderson and waited at the corner where the hearse stopped and the coffin was brought up again. Again I followed near, on the skirts of the procession, a man—Champneys[272] I thought—had a white wreath he wished to lay upon the coffin and as he pressed forward those behind bore me on, till I was standing between his grave and hers and heard the last words said: the grave was deep and narrow—the flowers filled all the level space. I turned away with the first—Charles Lewes pressed my hand as we gave the last look. Then I turned up the hill and walked through the rain by a road unknown before to Hampstead and a station. Then through the twilight I cried and moaned aloud. I have written letters already; sloth does not seem the worst temptation; it was idleness while she lived to trust to her to order or forbid. Now seeing that she is to gather the fruit of her labours from my life, I must choose for myself to labour only where I may do so with most hope of fruit.

December 30, 1880

I am thankful to know that her brother[273] wrote to her, after her second marriage. His son had called on her after Mr. Lewes's death but she did not see him. I am glad above all things that she should have had the comfort of that

---

[271] Thomas Sadler (1822-1891) was minister of Rosslyn Hill Unitarian Chapel at Hampstead; he also conducted GHL's funeral. His address was in the *Daily News*, December 30, 1880.

[272] Basil C. Champneys, architect who oversaw alterations and decorations of the Priory in 1875 (H, IX, 324, n. 7).

[273] Isaac Pearson Evans (1816-1890) refused to communicate with GE after she began her life with GHL in 1854.

reconciliation. Her brother—his name is Isaac—and his son a clergyman were at the funeral: apparently he lives still at Griff—her old home. There is a miniature of her father. She had yielded to Johnny's prayer and was going to have her portrait painted. It was like her to consent to him—she had always refused Mr. Lewes who was never likely to have survived her long. Mrs. Anderson wrote and came again today—she was very kind.

Nuneaton, January 2, 1881

"That sad patient loving strength which holds the clue of life."—I hardly know which is hardest to know that while my darling lived I never quite conquered the impatient longing that she should love me more—or to know that it is too late for the most utter patient and unselfish devotion to reach her from me now. If at least one had loved her better! To love her even as I could was the happiness as well as the best good of my life—*it was sweeter to love her than anybody else*—shall I be able to go on loving without her to show me how? She had but to live and I *must* love fondly, passionately and with sweet, pure delight. The worst loss is not having her to love. I came here yesterday about 2 and started straightway unincumbered towards her old home:—With little trouble I was set upon the road; a little out of the town the road bridged a canal. I welcomed the downy path like the friend whose invitation brought me. It was a sunny winter's afternoon; the low western sun dazzled me, the sloping fields, the tops of little mounds reflected in the still water, the golden straw of a waggon standing at ease by the rick, all these shone with an unaccustomed lustre, as it seemed to my city-blurred eyes, shone with a glad radiance that would have struck one cruelly if one had not known too well that she would have one find consolation in the thoughts of gladness and bright sunshine left for some. The walk by the "brown canal" was wonderfully still and peaceful—soothing like sweet loving thoughts of her:—I was glad to have come, doubly glad to find all that she loved so little changed. This morning a grey rosy mist came between the outlines of ploughed fields and leafless trees making the dull road pleasant and the wooded corners, the water and every quiet bit of country life enchantingly lovely. I heard her nephew preach—perhaps if Mr. Irvine[274] had been a young man now, he would not have preached very differently. There was little (or no) doctrine, kind references to politics and the range of public duties and most of all—was the young man preaching to himself, as he very frankly confessed he thought preachers should,—he dwelt on the duty of bearing cheerfully the allotted ills—since ills there must be until every one had sought (and found the reward for seeking) first the kingdom of god and his righteousness.[275] I wandered in a sort of figure 8 from Bedworth church to the canal and a new lovely bit of stream to Griff Colliery and Coton church—where no service was;

---

[274] Adolphus Irvine is the Anglican rector in *Adam Bede*.

[275] Matt. 6:33

then to the gates of Arbury Park,[276] where had a chat with the lodge keeper who had been there 28 years and lived at Coton before; her husband worked on the estate under Mr. Evans; "when he gave the business over to his son" he went to live "retired" at Foleshill. Hence probably the fruitlessness of my roamings round the churchyard at Bedworth and Coton. I hardly know whether my days of long pleasant walking in search of kind fatigue are the best way of conquering one's sorrow—they fight off the consciousness rather and at night the grief comes back and I seem to have less physical strength left. Yet I am glad—I think it was wise.

She told me once to be thankful—to think myself the happiest of mortals if I had never been the cause of misery to another. My love for her has made me understand such temptations as Maggie's[277]—have I not again and again wished for anything, for anyone whereby I might buy the longed for blessing. I felt always that it was by no choice of mine that I was doomed to woo her only by trying—oh how vainly!—to "be good." I must—I do—try to be thankful for what I have had, to think of that rather than of what I have wanted. It *is* a blessing that what was abnormal in my passion caused no pain or grief to her—bore nothing worse than some denial for me. And one can only know one's worst sorrows once. I fear I shall never be tempted to break my heart over anyone else's caring too little for my love; but at least let me hope I am like Maggie in this: has not something been taught me "by this experience of great need"—"a secret of human tenderness and long-suffering, that the less erring could hardly know." "Oh God, if my life is to be long, let me live to bless and comfort—." There is no great background of all suffering love—the more need to "grasp my morsels."

January 4, 1881

Yesterday walked through Arbury Park to Astley Church and Castle—the Castle has a real Moat; the church, besides the apostles with didactic ribands and coats of arms on walls and ceiling, had quaint epitaphs—one on a 17th century baby that died in convulsions, which grief perpetuated in its parents' hearts—also a spinster lady, who having "lived handsomely upon a narrow income" merited that a Newdigate Armiger: should communicate the interesting fact. So far the walk was very pretty—absolutely so in itself. I like best this quiet country just around her home, within the range of her earliest, most frequent walks. Sought the rest of fatigue by cross country tramping to Foleshill[278] to see what manner of dwelling place was saddened to her by her

---

[276] The Newdigate estate where Mary Ann Evans was born November 22, 1819, and lived until the move to Griff in 1820.

[277] *The Mill on The Floss* (1860)

[278] GE and her father Robert Evans moved to Foleshill near Coventry March 17, 1841, when her brother Isaac married.

141

father's death. Last night I wrote to the Rector of Bedworth. Today have been at Leicester, visiting stocking seamers and Board Schools. Was pleased because the little boy of the Society wanted me to kiss him when I left.

January 6, 1881
Yesterday to Bedworth. The Rector was not unkind; told me where to find her father's grave—a vault that had escaped me on Sunday at Coton; and gave me a clue to the whereabouts of the moat and the "rookery elms"—or rather oaks. He said she was at school in Coventry—only a short time at Nuneaton—and as it was with "non-conformists" no doubt that was the school of which she told me. He spoke of a young man of the town who had been sent to Germany to study theology as having brought back Strauss[279] and perhaps introduced her to that line of thought. He did not know if it was the Hennells[280] as I guessed. His father was away and his mother ill, his sister (I forget what) so he regretted that I could not see the house, but said the outside was unchanged, and asked if I knew "Mr. Scrivenes"[281] who had written about her in the Nuneaton Observer. In the family bible she is entered as born in 1819 not 20, and he mentioned one legend of her that at Griff, one night robbers came into the house when she was up, but so engrossed in her studies as to hear nothing. Today was cloudlessly fine so I went again by another route through Arbury Park to Astley and back by Bedworth and the canal. The sharp wind had fallen with the sunset, and the still evening by the canal was a memory to carry away. In front, for I was walking away from the sunset, there was a pale red haze above the low hill, and the low trees and hedges, and the still, pool like water reflected the dim hues, but again and again I looked back upon the unspeakable beauty and calm of the western sky, with its ever varing reflection, at one moment, a glassy surface streaked with colour like the ghost of a rainbow (not of despair) sometimes the rose and beryl of the sky showed plain in the canal as they did above the clump of firs, the bridge, or the nearly level field with a fringe of feathery dry grass; and overhead the blue seemed to deepen almost to violet and a crescent moon shone out with the tiny evening star. At mid day as the sun shone brightly—it was on a common bit of road that the reflection seized me—I seemed to see how human life goes on

---

[279] GE translated *Das Leben Jesu* by David Friedrich Strauss (1808-1874) during 1844 and 1845. First published in 1835, her translation appeared in 1846.

[280] Sara Hennell (1812-1899) was the author of *Thoughts in Aid of Faith* (London: G. Manwaring, 1860) and *Present Religion as a Faith Owning Fellowship With Thought* (London: Trübner, 1865), a dear friend to GE and a constant correspondent; Caroline Hennell (1814-1905) married Charles Bray in 1836; and Charles Hennell (1809-1850) was the author of *An Inquiry Concerning the Origin of Christianity* (London: Smallfield, 1838).

[281] Alfred L. Scrivenes co-founded the *Nuneaton Observer* with William Wilson in 1877.

its course; our happiness comes and goes apart from the still recurring sunshine, which is a good for those who have no other, but as the sunshine never wholly fails, so there is always happiness for some; if we were always all quite good, how much more cloudlessly the common sun would shine and though there will be always irremediable griefs like this, we ought to have gathered in the sunlight strength and endurance to bear our dark bereavement, and struggle still to "lighten the darkness" of our brethern. The other night when I could not sleep, and was thinking of Johnny and poor Elma, searching in my mind for any words that might be of comfort, I understood as I never have before her feeling that resignation or at least submission must follow from the sense of fellowship in suffering, that angry rebelliousness ceases just in so far as one is able to realize that others share our pain, that they too are ready to cry out, how for very shame can *we* cry out, fill the vault of heaven with angry outcry over my one pain, when all those around me have an equal grief; there is no providence for me to rebel against in the name of all, besides, how will cursing help them? One might have a right perhaps to embrace despair and forswearing help for oneself, curse the universe and die, but the patient sorrow would still be there unhelped—how can we leave it when we know how bitter sorrow is?

After the sunset I went (Mr. Evans had asked if I knew him) to see the Editor of the Observer, hoping he might have known her father, and have written from recollections of his own: found instead a newspaperish little fellow with only secondhand knowledge; still I learnt from him one thing; that they went to live at Foleshill in 1841 and that Mrs. Evans had tried to arrange for a Signor somebody to come over from Leamington so that her daughter might share lessons in language with other girls—whose mothers did not see it equally. All these scraps help me to piece out a vision of her life. The years she spoke of as partly wasted "for want of a fuller objective life" were from 17 when she began to keep her father's house, to 29 when his death left her solitary and the 4 or 5 years after that before her life joined Mr. Lewes's.[282] It is strange that with her early understanding interest in the broad passions of common human nature that she lived for so many years in comparative aloofness from her kind, and yet hardly strange, for after all the real and the ideal do not quite touch; she brought the ideal into being because she understood the spirit of the real, which is apart from its ephemeral and grosser body.

January 8, 1881

Yesterday was spent in Coventry: I was much taken care of. First walked through the town; went into St. Michael's and Trinity Church and St. Mary's Hill, bought a local paper and asked as I paid for it if it would tell me where "George Eliot" was at school. The young man told me the street and house. I went there straight; an old-fashioned 5 windowed, Queen Anne sort of looking house, with a shell shaped cornice over the door; the street not dingy, though a timbered, almost cottage was opposite the school; two doors down a

---

[282] GE met GHL in October 1851; they left London together and travelled to Germany, July 20, 1854.

quaint brick and timber building with an oriel window built out on wooden buttresses. Then I took the Foleshill Road and very shortly, came to the boundry between Coventry city and that parish: I turned back and saw what manner of house it had been and then took a foot path which I thought was likely to have been her favorite way into the town. Stopping then to look at the Coventry papers I saw "Miss Sara Hennell writes to us from Coventry"—clearly then I could do nothing better than find my way to Sara. The Post Office gave me no clue, the friendly newspaper office again held out hopes of information when Mr. So and So came back from dinner, meanwhile I to the station to get the pocketbook containing cards from my bag in the cloakroom; hung about a little shyly and then went in again to ask. The Proprietor did not know the address but said Mr. Bray would know, and when I still looked disconcerted, suggested that the "Herald" a little further up the street would know—as sure enough it did. I felt agitated as on the border of a discovery when I found the house and had rung the bell. A maid servant peeped out from an area door and then slowly came to open the door. Miss Hennell was in. I sent up my card and presently a little grey haired pleasant faced old lady came in welcoming—so glad to make my acquaintance &c. She was willing to talk to me of the dearest, but old close intercourse of long ago is not the best foundation for narrative or description and so I gathered more in the way of impression than information. She came to know them soon after her father came to live at Foleshill. Apparently Mr. Hennell, the brother, and Mr. and Mrs. Charles Bray (the latter a Hennell) lived at Coventry and she was constantly with them, called Sara and Carrie her sisters: they showed me a sketch of the garden where, sitting under an acacia she read "Hyperion"[283] aloud and where almost daily invitations to "the bearskin" brought her there for talk or books. Mr. Bray[284] used to walk with her almost daily. Hennell—I must see what book he wrote—was a Unitarian turned heterodox and it was to please him she translated Strauss—hating him or it all the time. They quoted a fine sentence of hers that whenever Strauss comes to one of St. Paul's outbreaks of fiery zeal or charity he "fizzes" like water on hot-iron! They were good creatures and the society they introduced her to no doubt was pleasant and useful to her but one understands that she felt it a meager life; they said all the entertaining at home—farmers and so on—was most irksome to her, though she did it all scrupulously: then her relations, the brother I suppose most, cooled when she began to leave off going to church &c and so when her father died she was altogether alone. They took her abroad and left her, by her own wish at Geneva; then she lived with them for a year till Dr. Chapman[285] persuaded her to

---

[283] John Keats (1795-1821) composed "Hyperion" during the winter of 1818-19.

[284] Charles Bray (1811-1884) was a prosperous ribbon manafacturer at Coventry, a phrenologist, and author of *The Philosophy of Necessity; or, the Law of Consequences as Applicable to Mental, Moral, and Social Science* (London: Longman, Orme, Brown, Green, and Longman, 1841).

[285] John Chapman (1821-1894) met GE in 1846, when he published her Strauss; she became his assistant editor for the *Westminster Review* in January 1851.

come to London and help him with the Westminster—doing a better work than he knew. This helps to explain what was as incomprehensible to me as the Strauss—her coming up by choice as an adventurer in letters, and one feels too how painful the solitariness of this life must have been to the darling—a thousand blessings on her husband's memory. They showed me a photograph of her, done in 1858—and oh! so like—her dear sweet look: there was a silly little coloured sketch done when they knew her first, just showing her dress and attitude, perhaps something of the eyes and her hair done in curls. I saw some of her early letters. Some to Maria Lewis,[286] a Governess pupil at her Nuneaton school even as early as 36—she had asked to have them returned in the Strauss time and gave the packet to Miss Hennell who had left them unopened till now. After a while she calls this friend "Veronica" and signs herself "Clematis."[287]

All these letters are full of humility and self-reproach. At 19 she calls herself a "cumberer of the ground:" The poor sweet darling!

January 11, 1881

She wished to be as faithful in her small obscure station as heaven knows what missionary whose life she had been reading, was in his exalted place. In one letter there is the most frank and confident disapproval of oratorios—she thought it blasphemous to have—I forget what passage—sung, and "by Brahms too (a Jew!)." A kind note from Johnny yesterday and Elma keeps writing long letters as of old. I am finishing "Sat est vixisse" on the lines of the first draft—I wanted to get it done before anything discouraging comes from Blackwood.

I went last evening to see the Crosses; Mrs Congreve had just left them. She was the daughter of the doctor at Coventry who attended Her father in his illness. A cast was taken. Florence said Mr. Cross thought of publishing "the letters" separately from the life.

(In the Ms this is on the page opposite the entry for January 11.)
January 13, 1881

I see I have not described my visit to the "homestead" and I fear lest memory should let any features slip—I had many times looked over the field and garden gate, the drive and lawn were trim and neat, the house large and ivy grown; but after seeing the Rector of Bedworth I ventured to enter a gate out of the Arbury Drive just beyond the farm buildings: a thrashing machine was at work and through the hedge when past the farm yard, I saw the gardener at work among the laurels. Then a gate led into another field, to the right, joining the

---

[286] Maria Lewis (1800?-1887) was the most important of GE's teachers beginning in November, 1829, when she was sent to Mrs. Wallington's school at Nuneaton.

[287] In 1840 Martha (or Patty) Jackson, a schoolmate of GE, discovered a dictionary correlating plants with mental or moral qualities. She took the name Ivy (constancy) and assigned Clematis (mental beauty) to GE (H, I, x lix).

garden on the other side, only separated from it by a railing with a gate and footpath coming down to where I stood. In this field stood the "rookery oaks," with their turfed and mossy boles and to my left again the little remnants of the "Moat" where rushes grew, where now a green holly stood and the ground was dry and brown with withered oak leaves—I gathered a twig of holly and the leaves opposite. [288] Then a stile, by the end of the water led across another field and then I think the tiny rivulet, but a broader bridge was made and the water trickled with scantier forest of forget-me-nots, through a little arch of brick and so one emerged on the towing path by the Griff hollows canal. That day I gathered by canal and river withered grasses and flowering nots, yew and ivy—bits of gorse in bud and the red wild rose berries. I shall keep the grasses always—perhaps the rest,— when they are withered, in some hiding place.

January 14, 1881

Wrote yesterday to Mrs. Congreve, asking if I might come and see her.—A very nice answer today—she loved her "passionately." I must go and see her Monday.

January 16, 1881

Have been writing a little "Sat est vixisse" and wondering at my own calm. She used to ask me what I loved her for. I seem to know even more plainly now than then. What fascinated me was the vision of a wholly *natural* nature, full of all manner of primitive passions of irresistible strength, but so beautifully ordered and inspired that her impulses were in fact more righteous than another's laboured resolutions. To my slow vacant nature this might well seem the divinest beauty; my dull unchanging constancy is a good vantage ground from which to reverence the fulness of life and loving energy that could not accept a lot made of negatives.

January 18, 1881

Went yesterday to see Mrs. Congreve. Learnt with a sort of pleasure that she had loved my darling lover-wise too—too much to repeat much of her words, but she told me how on seeing her again after an interval, her heart was palpitating so violently that to avoid a painful breaking down she forced herself into a calm that seemed cold: she tried to talk in common fashion, Mr. Lewes was there, and then—the Darling, my sweet Darling rushed out of the room in tears. Mr. Lewes signed to Mrs. Congreve not to follow her and with a breaking heart she sat through his call, and afterwards, though she guessed the Darling had been pained by her seeming coldness, she dared not ask her for she thought too she did not wish it to be thought. After a while she, the dearest, spoke of it and then it

---

[288] Two oak leaves and a twig of holly are pressed in the journal on the page opposite.

could all be told. I said, were you not very happy to think that she could care so much for your love? The Crosses seem not quite to have understood her—or I them. She only saw Her once at Coventry when she was a girl of fourteen, but she remembered every detail—how she heard the piano approaching the house, the contrast between the open piano and books and her father's appearance, and then walking with Her in the garden, and being set at her ease and drawn out to say how she wanted to learn German and so on. Then she did not see Her till 22 years ago when both were married and living at Wandsworth. She remembered hearing her father say, and understanding by a kind of intuition, when people were speaking unkindly of her and Mr. Lewes, that he was certain by what he had seen of Miss Evans that she had done no wrong, that she could not have done anything she did not in her conscience feel to be right. She spoke of that as the time when friends wrote you letters of six sheets to remonstrate with you for going to see her. In those days they were very poor; she said they had not even enough food and then explained it by a story that one day when they were having luncheon,—for economy bread and butter only, their landlady who had had a present of game sent them up some partridges, and after eating it they felt so much better they agreed they could not be having enough to eat. And they were troubled with servants, till a certain "Gene and Amelia" came, this perhaps at the Priory, but between they had lived at Harewood and Blandford Square:[289] after the first years she had had everything she needed—but I thought the years were not a few—at least 3 or 4 from 1854 to 59. One thing else she said that seemed to help my vision; that her vehemence in those days made her formidable to many women—one can understand her passionate utterances—repented when unanswered; and if not shy, she was very timid and the "appealingness" of her look, which in later years had turned to graciousness was, she said unutterably touching. And even then, in those earlier years of the marriage, she had a look of sadness, like discontent "though one knew she was only discontented with herself." She said the face was more beautiful at last. My Darling too was never dearer than when I knew her—only one would have liked to be in time to comfort her with love when love was less abounding.

January 19, 1881

Mrs. Congreve had only kept a few letters later than 13 years ago, when she came back from India, but those she had destroyed were mostly notes; yet Her least notes, she said, were not like other people's—she did not say "Come" but "I love you to come," or something of her own like that. I wrote afterward a note of thanks and something else to Mrs. Congreve, who answers, very answeringly, and ends "surely we shall be friends."

---

[289] GE and GHL lived at 10 Harewood Square from September 26, 1860, to December 17, 1860, and at 16 Blandford Square from December 17, 1860, to November 5, 1863 (H, index).

January 20, 1881

Mr. Cross came this evening—calling twice as I was out at 5. He stayed over half an hour telling me that he had made up his mind to write the life himself: the resolve was quickened by the thought that if he did not some one else would and he had this warrant: as they were walking one day at Whitby she said he ought to do some one work—a contribution to the world's possessions: she was sure he had the power. He said half playfully, he did not know what he could do, unless it were to write her life if he survived her. She smiled and did not answer—did not protest. He said of course magazines would have articles—one could only hope they would be done well and by those she would have chosen. Grove[290] had asked Mary Cross to write "of course she could not"—he had said I was the only person he should like, and asked me if I had been asked. If I could do it, he thought it would be right to make some sacrifice, as she would have preferred for me to write. He was going tomorrow—if the line was not blocked with snow—to Coventry, asked me what I thought of the photograph, what Mrs. Bray was like—she was the chief friend of the sisters. Then he was going to Sheffield to stop the publication of her letters to her aunt, Elizabeth Evans. He said they had legal power to do that—not he, her will did not affect him, Charles Lewes was her residuary legatee, but he would do whatever he was asked. I mentioned the chance of American letters being published: he said she always wrote guardedly: Mrs. Stowe[291] was the only person likely to have many letters, and she had a very deep feeling for our Lady. Apparently she had told him very much of her life: he looks forward to travelling to all the places where they had been—or She alone; he spoke of someone at Geneva (? where she stayed in 1850)[292] and he was anxious to gather quickly all that was remembered by friends no longer young. He mentioned Mme Belloc,[293] and Mrs. Peter Taylor,[294] Mr. Spencer and Mr. Pigott, who used to spend every Saturday evening with them for a long time; these with Mme Bodichon, Mrs. Charles Bray and Mrs. Congreve (and Mr. Burton) seem to be most of the old, constant friends. He spoke of taking Frederick Pollock's advice about publishing the

---

[290] Sir George Grove (1820-1900) was the editor of *Macmillan's Magazine*.

[291] Harriet Beecher Stowe (1810-1896), American author of *Uncle Tom's Cabin* (Boston: J. P. Jewell, 1852), was a regular correspondent of GE's.

[292] GE stayed with the D'Alberts from July 1849 to March 1850 (H, index).

[293] Bessie Parkes Belloc (1829-1925) was Bessie Rayner Parkes the friend of Barbara Smith Bodichon. She was a poet, co-editor of the *English Woman's Journal*, and champion of women's rights.

[294] Clementia Doughty Taylor

Ethics. Leighton[295] will try to do something from the "Mask"—as he called it—taken after death and the photograph if he could see it: but he is diffident and promises whatever he does shall be destroyed if it is not satisfactory. I asked if she had left any Mss that could be published. He burnt—I suppose it was right, I could not have done it—the beginning of a new story—only begun two days before, a first chapter and a general sketch. There are many books of Ms notes &c containing full materials too for the life, but of these he said, as a reason why no one else could write this that there was much that only he ought to read. I cannot help being envious. Mr. Cross was very kind, said to me of everything that it was in sacred confidence. My own darling—he was struggling into a sealskin coat—I helped him on with it, thinking of you. He spoke of wishing to go to Malvern to see Mrs. Stuart. He did not know how long he should be away now, would come and see me again when he was back. The embarrassment was a little taken from the first meeting by my having only just come in, and coming downstairs just as he entered the room.—I am moved to record that the thought of a feeling does not necessarily generate the feeling. Maria Lewis is living still. She sent her a cheque (as she did every year) only 3 weeks before she died.

January 23, 1881

I must not dwell on the saddest memories, which are not of present lost but the sense of past separation. I ought not. In single instances, when I appealed or protested she answered reasonably and with allowance. It was no fault, no fatal, final calamity of mine that her mind naturally and necessarily reverted with the lapse of time to its habitual attitude and she judged for me as she would have for herself. No wish or feeling of hers could have altered the nature of things: I know she felt that "my divine Mary Cross" had a second best life. No feeling of hers could alter the fact that *my* life is practically only within reach of second bestness—if that. Even if I did succeed by and bye in making the History of Appropriation into a classic with good moral tendency—it is not happiness to have to struggle unhelped, uncheered, with every obstacle within and without; to see failure always near, or present and to know that even success is barren of comfort to one's aching heart.

I think it would be a culpable weakness to betray now, even to Mrs. Congreve, the secret of my love sorrows: it *is* hateful to me to find myself right, when she was not right—yet, I attach exaggerated importance to it—I am as miserable because she wished me to be married as if I had wished it in vain. But it is foolish and selfish to dwell upon this now. I am anxious to settle into a routine of work, but it is not easy quite yet. It is discouraging to remember that I was thinking of Appropriation more than two years ago and am no further on than then.

---

[295] Frederic Leighton (1830-1896), artist and sculptor, was the illustrator of *Romola*.

January 26, 1881

Triste[296] last night: vexed on apprehending physical causes. Am divided between the impulse to seek encouragement and the thousand and one reasons for reticence and self-command. Am easily tired, and feel done up though I never go near Mortimer Street. I must really try for a month's real pleasant rest at Easter.

January 28, 1881

Have written to Elma and Mrs. Congreve—the latter writes very pleasantly: in answering her I partly got away from the wrong thoughts of discouragement.

January 30, 1881

Eleanor Cross came yesterday afternoon. Shall see Mrs. Congreve on Monday: I hardly know whether it will be possible—but what I should wish is to make the history a standard statement of fact and a new authoritative exposition of principle—at least that new principles should detach themselves from the statement. But—

February 2, 1881

The rather grudging or cowardly articles in Cornhill and the Contemporary[297] did not pain me—I feel always as if one more miserable criticism the more was a matter of slight account. Indeed the Contemporary did more to rouse and comfort me than Mrs. Congreve's true suggestions. All that Miss Wedgwood[298] (if she it was) half-complains of reminded me of all that I rejoice in—when others demur or doubt, I am stirred to take my Darling's part— to prove by word and deed how truly, wholly right she was. Indeed except that small, entirely presonal half-grievance of my *own*, what was there I ever asked from her in the way of guidance she did not give. I felt with her on every point— she thought with me—once when I hinted at disagreement she said she had never differed from anything I had written on the point where I nervously dreaded difference most. I wrote to Elma and to Johnny in protest against the Contemporary—a grateful answer from the latter this evening: I shall understand better soon what gave him his place with Her. I met Miss Helps on Sunday evening—she mentioned a kind little word. The dear one spoke of me. Mrs. Congreve said that it was most in the last year or two that she spoke of me, before it was mostly Mr. Lewes, who was pleased with my worship of Her. I was a little

---

[296] "sad"

[297] Leslie Stephen, "George Eliot," *Cornhill Magazine*, 43 (February 1881): 152-168 and [J. Wedgwood], "The Moral Influence of George Eliot," *Contemporary Review*, 39 (February 1881), 173-185.

[298] Julia Wedgwood (1833-1913)

glad of this—as if it was to herself as well as to me that she spoke of holding me in more regard. I believed all her dear words but still wondered sadly sometimes whether the earlier years did not hold promise of fondness, which perhaps I liked better than esteem: but oh! if I could only feel that she had approved—oh my dearest—my love—Darling—Darling—

February 5, 1881

I have been dreaming today, and wake to the lasting grief.—She would have had me be something different, lead some other life—and I do not know, I never knew *what* she would have me do or *be* except the impossible which she owned was not perhaps quite always the one thing needful. I know what she called a "blessed lot"—I can do without that—but it is hard to have to live and wonder always what she called an "effective" one—it is little comfort to think that perhaps she spoke the words without any image for my guidance behind them. My only help from her is this: the grief is bitter, but it is only mine—it hurts no one else and even I must not dwell on it—not "indulge" in the sad luxury of grief.

February 16, 1881

It is a real gain to have learnt to *feel* that. It helps me in the night when I cannot help lying awake to cry. I went to see Mrs. Congreve last Wednesday and tried to speak of other things than the one. Yesterday I went to Highgate. The large withered bouquet still lay there—a small wreath of later date—some one had brought a pot of heath and most lately of all—a small handful of flowers, while a few cyclamen lay displacing my dead violets at the head of Mr. Lewes's grave. I was struck as I never had been before, in entering the cemetery, by the crowd of graves, like a grey stony army. I have been much cast down—I feel rather shaky in body, and have hardly drive or strength to do much towards "Appropriation"—and I have no external encouragement to believe that the result of my work if I could do more, would be objectively such as she would have thought worth having—I mean what she would have valued for its own sake, not merely as a harmless occupation for me.

February 18, 1881

Last night on coming home at 11:30, from an unprofitable Board meeting I found a pleasant note from Mrs. Congreve, speaking of the feeling that we share; it was welcome to me as breaking in upon the solitude I feel. Curiously a note (by return) from Longman—expresses willingness to consider "Vignettes" for Fraser.

February 20, 1881

Since writing to Mrs. Congreve I have felt nearer and more loyal to my lost Darling. I have been reading through my old notes, wishing to find the verbal record of her description of her old school days: I think it must have been in the spring of 77: An interview of which I kept short record: she spoke of Miss

Martineau's autobiography,[299] of a visit she had paid to Miss M. and either then or some other time she spoke of her school days: the girls used to call her "little mamma" and swoop down upon her—"I want to kiss you little mamma, but I mustn't tumble your collar"—alluding to a phrase of her, for she did not like to be ruffled or made untidy. I was a goose not to write this at the time—I remember it so clearly that I always thought I had. It was a Methodist school and the girls used to get up prayer-meetings in which she took a leading part, reproaching herself when she found she could not be carried away like the others. And then she told me how she used to fasten upon any book—such as Paley's Evidences,[300] or scripture commentaries, which promised to give a rational basis for her belief and how she used to carry poor Paley up to her bedroom and devour it lying upon the floor alone.

In the search for this record I have read through a good deal of my old "experiences"—now that I see my way to the answer that I wanted, it does not distress me that I never received it in so many words from Her. Her answer was to make me feel differently. Thank God—thank Her! I *do* feel differently. I hate the selfish limitations to my love for Her: I am shameful that I checked the outer signs of them, so that of late years she thought I loved her as perfectly as by her grace I do and will henceforth for ever. I have no reason now for writing here except when a fit thought is in my mind. I think I will resolve not to open this book merely to set down the foolish changes of one's mind. This next week I will give to schools or writing and then set to work at Assyria.

February 26, 1881

Did not see Mrs. Congreve for long alone and could not speak much of the Dearest—Mrs. McCall Saul[301] is another sister of Hennell's—it was she who had begun Strauss—the Darling was her bridesmaid in a first marriage. Poor Elma is very ill and losing hope. Longman wrote yesterday asking at what price I would sell the copyright of Vignettes for magazine use and reissue and sent him the remainder yesterday.

---

[299] Harriet Martineau (1802-1876) was a didactic writer and champion of women's rights; her *Autobiography* was published in 1877. She believed education to be the key to equality and supported women's suffrage movements and working men's groups.

[300] William Paley, *A View of the Evidences of Christianity*, 2 vols. (London: R. Faulder, 1794).

[301] According to Haight this is Elizabeth Rebecca Brabant who visited Coventry and began the translation at the request of her husband Charles Hennell but decided the work was beyond her. Charles died in 1849; she married Wathen Mark Wilks Call in 1856 (H, Biography 47, 79, 242).

March 3, 1881

Last Saturday and Sunday began to write something about Her. Sunday wrote to Mrs. Congreve asking to be confirmed in my own impression that I had better not write. Had a corresponding answer so dropped the Ms. Want next week to begin reading at Museum for Assyria. I force my mind to rest on the memory of my love—on its continued unchanged force to the exclusion of all sadness that might come from thoughts of our being parted before the perfect union I always longed for had been quite reached.

March 8, 1881

I must not dwell on painful recollections. They rend my heart and put pain in the place of love. I have been wrong in looking at "Natural Law" and wondering why some sentences failed to meet with answer. It is doubly wrong of me to waste my failing strength in useless sobs because I have no doubt that the only chance of a life which she would not have thought an utter failure lies in writing—if one could—an acceptable and influential book on the subject I wish to write about. And then one wonders—can it be possible without any help—without Her help. I remember the tone of mind she referred to in speaking of herself before last May as "growing rather bitter"—how can I build sweet, wholesome industry on this foundation if—oh there are things she would never have said if she had thought how they would torture me now—I must not dwell on them—but they were said—nothing was said that could neutralize the fact that they were said. I have sobbed and cried aloud and when all one's tears are shed it seems as if the fault were in oneself—as it always was. My refuge from too much longing for her love was always to love her more and more and that refuge is open still—one's love must show itself in act. I saw Mrs. Congreve again yesterday and asked when Her first interest in Positivism began. Not she thought till '60 or there abouts—She had not read Comte when they met first, and Mr. Lewes was controversially full of him. She also said in reply to something of mine she had never been able to feel at the time as if her friendship had been any help or comfort to the Dearest.

It is hard but one *has* to live one's life without other comfort than effort.

March 20, 1881

Have been at Malvern with Elma for a week. Was very "good and gentle" with her and would not be deterred by her occasional signs of thinking that it was something new. Speaking of the Madonna used to end by bringing back upon me the awful sense of loss, and I was silenced, turning away to hide the tears. Elma read me Her three first letters, and at my request the one about Mallock. The first were what might have been expected,—with much reference to Mr. Lewes, who it seemed, opened all her letters, especially I imagine those in unknown handwritings. The point of the latter was the suggestion—put cleanliness in place of virtue throughout M's argument and judge how far your feeling about that formed habit could owe anything to the existence of a God or heaven. Two other fragments of E's recollections I annexed. Mr. Lewes, dear fellow, used to go down and order the dinner if she was busy writing and once she told, with tears streaming from her eyes, how her jealous anxious nature would have taken alarm at even less than apparent jealousy, at anything short of the complete unmixed delight with which Mr. Lewes followed her writing and its success. I looked covetously at the letters in their case, and would fain have read them all though I had more of my own; but I did not feel jealous of Elma's place in our Lady's regard—where it was different from mine it was because of qualities I have never much coveted. She saw a good deal of the Madonna this last spring, the dear one used to go often to see her, and partly no doubt owing to this, she asked in April whether E's love would hold even if She did something unexpected—. She had already spoken of going abroad and Elma's answer was a hope that she would go with someone who would take care of Her, see she had eatable dinners and kept Her feet warm &c—all in an encouraging commonplace tone, which made it possible to the Darling to tell her by word of mouth. I am thankful she had such comfort, thankful to know that she could speak to others of Her happiness with Mr. Cross, but yet, I would rather have been the one to whom the inward sigh was uttered—since Her life could not be all gladness. Elma urged me to write, on the ground that most people are fools and believe what they see in print, and therefore the Cornhill and Contemporary should not be allowed the last word. I showed what I had written to Augustus and as he says it will "lead a good many people to share my feeling," the duty seems plainer again.[302]

April 24, 1881

We have been for a month at Perranporth, where I finished what I had written—with shame and grief that I cannot better say what is in me. I feel as if the habit of self-suppression strangled even here the utterance of that "passion" she used to wish for in my writing. There is one thing I must write before preparing my "Sermon" for this evening. Last Thursday afternoon I was walking or roaming alone among the sand hills, the sky was overcast with grey stormy clouds, making a dark blue leaden sea, the ghostly white of the sand and the grey white of the dry grass made a fit foreground for one particular patch of sea, where the black shadow was broken by a golden line. I had been fretting and chafing rather wickedly before but that afternoon there came back to me her words "I can trust you now for all the forbearance"—should one's forbearance end with Her dear life? Then, with a sky clearing and growing to a fair rosiness I came in: Augustus was not yet home and I went out again for a few minutes to watch the sky from the west cliffs—and also if it might be to fight off the tears that were springing irresistibly. There among the chill gusts, something else came to me. I said to Her, of course Darling it would have been good if the greatest happiness had come to me; I am not wrong either in feeling some pain where the sweetness might have been, or in feeling that if it did not come I ought still to be able to live worthily without it. But, Darling, come what may, I am still and have been richer than most,—to love you, my own, is the best good—but one, and what was I to deserve more than the sweet glimpses I had of that? Darling! It was the future

---

[302] "George Eliot," *Nineteenth Century*, 9: (1881): 778-801 reprinted in *Littell's Living Age*, 149: (1881): 781-805.

terrified me—could I—can I—live worthily of You without your dear sweet help? And then I thought—and thought it would please you for me to think—Let me live always in Her sight. Day by day let me begin and end by looking to Her for guidance and rebuke, plan the future by what She would have thought best, and make a dread rule to myself out of the vow that every night what has been done ill or ill left undone shall be confessed on my knees to my Darling and my God—One cannot but smile through one's tears in thinking it is as my Darling would have liked to be remembered; and if this vow is kept—as I swear by my Love it shall be—I swear it kneeling, not boastfully but in prayer—Dearest that your love, your goodness will take care of me still and let me keep the blessed vow, then surely the monument, small as it is will not be quite unworthy of you Darling and your immortal sweetness. Your written works, are an immortal memorial, and so is the memory of the lives to whose happiness your life my Dearest was wholly devoted. But, my Own, it was something more than earthly happiness that you had to give to me and if it may be so hereafter—your own Edith—"rescued from self-despair, strengthened with divine hopes and looking back on years of purity and helpful labour"—may sink to rest with you not uncheered by the thought of your goodness living still in other lives to whom you shall have sent some image of it through me. If my own work is always too unworthy of you, who knows but what, in spiritual as in natural generations, genius may run underground for one life "like the fresh rivers," and some spiritual child of mine be worthier of you than I was—and that too would be your work.

On this side of that line shall come, by my will, no thoughts of you, or what has been between us save of love and gratitude, penitence and resolution. There shall be no selfish regrets and visions,[303] only sorrow, (I thought that tear was dry), for what has been wrongly done or said or wrongly omitted so to be; and visions of what one may rightly do or say in atonement or of one's own motives—for Her service and honour. The ready courtesy to strangers that she wished for is to be cultivated—for her sake too, such outer graces as may be, and for the rest earnest work—no trivial vacancy of mind or action—no shirking of the proposed task, only prudence and caution in not attempting what cannot be done as it ought. With these—prayers rather than resolutions—and all I know to be implied in them—I would close this page of my life—the love that had some selfishness in its longing and its joy, and the sorrow that was bitter as well as deep and loving. God—my God—help me to be good!

May 7, 1881

We have not been back quite a week and each day I have done part, not all, I ought. Mrs. Congreve, Elma and the Crosses like what I had written, and two—or perhaps 3—strangers have written to me with thanks—I am therefore

---

[303] A large smudge on the Ms indicates where the tear fell.

less unhappy as to any apparent want of appreciation—only keep my own knowledge of how much more and better might have been said. I have almost made up my mind not to stand again for the School Board. The remaining year and a half that one has to serve on it I want to spend in quite mastering the work, training a successor, practicing speaking on subjects I care about much, and collecting myself for "Appropriation" by always reading and making notes more or less towards it and for the rest, my Darling, let me be "resolutely content" to be as human and as humanly good as I can.

May 13, 1881

Confitesr.[304] Darling, every day gets along somehow, pretty innocently, but I do nothing for you that will last, nothing worthily immortal—I wonder—can you forgive me? I cannot forgive myself, if that means some shade of disappointment in your thought.

May 14, 1881

In the matter of religion—when some one we love has gone from us, our feeling towards that one lives still—and the object of any feeling lives too.

May 19, 1881

Darling—one can do so little for you, the only thing possible that has come to me was very small, but without you it would not have been done. Mr. Green is very ill and when I saw his wife she spoke of pining for fresh air: I proposed to call and fetch her for a little walk. Sunday morning I made her walk a little round their garden till she proposed to go beyond it and on going to put on her things found he could not spare her. Yesterday there was a slight turn for the better and she was glad of a turn in Kensington Gardens—the better for the change and very grateful for the thought of her.

May 21, 1881

Dearest—it is better to say than be haunted by the thought—the feeling of my irreparable, utter loss comes over me crushingly, with a death-like hopeless pain. You cannot hear so I may say now—I never had my heart's desire and now I have lost everything and I am tempted to feel bitterly that my greatest loss is of what I never had. It is ungrateful: I was always so when I had to do without you long: how can I bear it for all the years?

June 5, 1881

By the memory Dearest of your past sweet goodness to me. I was always very jealously exacting, but the sight of you, the sound of your voice, a written word, always made me sorry and grateful. After a period of sadness your own words have cheered me: in a generous mood I offered to copy for Elma all that was common property in your letters and in doing so I drew out a picture of

---

[304] "I confess": the first words of the prayer of confession

all your goodness to me and indeed I ought not to be ungrateful. I have a wholesome discipline of hard dull work for this Whitsuntide, then, till the autumn holiday which will not be far off, I would look after schools and Board work and then have a spell at "Appropriation."

June 9, 1881

I wrote to Mr. Cross a little reminder of one's existence, and friendly feeling on Monday and today he came to call, stayed an hour or more, talking as if with a view to becoming acquainted, or perhaps I only lend him my motive.

June 21, 1881

Mary Cross came on Saturday. Yesterday I saw Mrs. Congreve and am to dine with her tonight. These are the landmarks it seems in one's life. A week ago I went with a "bush of syringa" to Crown Street and with a handful to Highgate, where there were pretty pinks, pansies and forget-me-nots and mignonette: the flat space was turfed, of which I was glad.

July 5, 1881

From Friday to Monday was with Mme Bodichon—whom I found very charming, throughout her illness. She saw the Madonna first in 52, at Mrs. Jameson's[305] and thought her very charming and wonderful, and then saw Her again when she lived in Cambridge Street after leaving the Chapmans. Then she went to Germany with Mr. Lewes while Barbara was out of England and when she came back all her people exclaimed: but she put on a calm face and went to see her—without telling her younger sister, but she thought she was old enough to judge for herself: and whatever she went through at home on that account, the darling never knew. She herself gloried in suffering reproach for Her Sake and exulted over the unbelievers when at last all the world knew. There was an inscription in her "Adam Bede" to the "friend who first recognized me in it" and her delight &c. She said no doubt She had said to me—as to Her—what She never did say—for its needlessness and other reasons—that She thought She had a right to do as She pleased if She chose to accept the penalty—the outlaw—my poor sweet Darling! After Mr. Lewes's death, Mme Bodichon asked Her to come and live with her, and be saved all trouble, have Her own rooms and servants, &c—I doubt if she could have done it even if Barbara had been well—She said she meant to keep on the two houses and thought She might be of use by living in London and seeing people.

July 12, 1881

Mrs. Congreve told me yesterday that Barbara was the first to go and see them at Richmond—happy Barbara! Mrs. Congreve was counting on my

---

[305] Mrs. Anna Brownell Jameson (1794-1860) was an essayist, travel writer, biographer, literary and art critic. With Bessie Parkes she helped to initiate the *English Women's Journal*.

visit—which pleased me. Mr. Cross and Mr. Hall came on Sunday—the latter looking as ever very good. On Saturday I had a replica of my own foolishness to give counsel to, and have had letter since in the same strain—would I were as well worth loving by *anyone* as my Darling was by all. At least I cannot for very shame be wanting in patience and tenderness.

July 23, 1881

Winifred has been staying here since, and I have resumed my "directorial" duties. Yesterday had 3 experiences—or one might say 5. In the afternoon I was one of a deputation sent to the Home Secretary, Sir William Harcourt,[306] to explain to him why the School Board wished to revert to imprisonment instead of distress warrants as a means of enforcing the payment of fines. I went with the Chairman and 3 other members; we met Mr. Lucraft[307] and Mr. Croud in the lobby. Mr. Buxton claimed admission beyond but was not allowed by the police to carry his deputation through, though Croud showed the letter from the Home Office summoning us. We were not kept waiting long and reached the Home Secretary's room, when he was alone, *via* a nice wide carpeted corridor lined with bookcases full of Parliamentary papers. He began, as we entered by saying, he had asked for not more than 6, and subsided when told there *were* just 6, including the clerk of the Board. He began "So you want to send every one to prison"—called himself an "Old Whig," a believer in the liberty of the subjects, and when the Chairman quoted the unaminity of the Board, the most Democratic body in the country, he thought it clever to respond—Democratic bodies were always tyrannical! forgetting that in this case it is over themselves that our constituents wish us to "tyrannise." Old Lucraft was set on to instruct him about popular feeling—as to which he was ignorant—even for a Whig—while as to the business of his department he was ignorant—even for a minister! After a while a division bell rang, upon which he asked to be excused; promising to come back. While he was away we rapidly discussed the chance of influencing him at all, but when he came back, he professed to have consulted Mr. Truter and to have his authority for saying it was impossible to "go backwards." Then he made a mistake. Lucraft told a story of a man who drowned himself on coming out of the workhouse, his goods having been "sold up for 26/." Harcourt said Was this a School Board case?—We: no, we did not choose to risk having such an one. He—that we had better not, the fact was we were going too far, he had been talking to the Magistrates (!)—we should be careful not to go too fast—they complain that their courts are blocked with our cases, (The Chairman of the Board, the present system makes twice or thrice the claim on their time that the old one did), he thought we were going on very nicely and we should be content; our attendance was increasing yearly: The Chairman—yes, with the increase of population, our percentage had fallen off

---

[306] Sir William Vernon Harcourt (1827-1904)

[307] Benjamin Lucraft was a member of the London School and a representative of the working people.

since the act. I was irate by now and ventured to state the case rather crudely: We complained that the present arrangement hindered us in the attempt to force the children of reluctant parents into school: we had assumed that if we made out the fact he would wish to help us: did he mean to say in answer to our complaint that we were hindered in the work of compulsion—and a very good thing too! After this we left, and I reflected in passing through the privileged corridors and lobbies, (where the men did not seem to notice my presence as at all odd) that probably the house would resign itself without very much difficulty to its first "lady member." I was rather excited with this interview, and at once determined that our line must be not to press for distress in unsuitable cases and to appeal to the public, taking them to witness that it is not by our choice the step backward—of not dealing with the poorest and roughest—is taken, for the moment: a local authority cannot enforce the law without the support of the legislative and executive power: and I turned over in my mind the possibility of getting the Trades Congress to take up the question and discoursing to my constituents in Portcullis Hall. I walked from Westminster to Chelsea, thinking of all this and as I neared Cheyne Walk, felt the same reluctance as before to come to the house, but would not give in to it. Brett answered the door, looking thin and older, with dark eyes—like her dress—Mr. Cross had gone out five minutes before: I was in fact rather remiss in my expressions of regret at missing him and told Brett I had wanted to see her. I could not quite keep back the tears—could not speak of Her. Brett said it was nice to see one of the ladies (who used to come to the Priory): she had seen Mrs. Congreve and Mrs. Burne-Jones—the latter a very nice lady.— (I was glad to hear she had been) they and I were the three great friends:— Coming away I had to hold the sunshade close to my face, I was crying helplessly.—My Darling! one's anger with Sir William Harcourt melted—Oh My Love, My Love! Just after I had come in Miss Williams called. My mother betrayed the fact we were just going to dinner and asked her to wait for me. We began conversation and were just started when she came again to fetch me. I was put out at the discourtesy and interference and bolted half a dinner, fidgetted for an interval and returned. I *hope* I was not to blame—of course I was in some way—the poor creature professed a feeling for me different from what she had ever had for any one, it might make her happiness if I could return it; and then she said—"Imagine what it is to have that feeling and to be obliged to go away from you." I did not feel any unkind dread—what would it be for her *not* to go away—but I thought of my like love and urged upon her that *I* did not deserve such love as I had given *to* Her, it pained me like a blasphemy—I suppose I was wrong to say this—it hurt her and she had not the readiness to seize the confidence as a proof of kindness. She said I was very philosophical and a little cold—one of the Walworth Free Thinkers answered my praises of Enthusiasm by saying I had very little—and she went away a little hurt, though I rather wooed her at last. The only thing that checks my impulses of tenderness is the fear lest there is some flightiness and want of moral balance in her nature—a want of the fixed points, to which one needs to appeal. She went away and I came down to the waiting family and told my mother something of it to pacify her and excuse my irritation and then the thought of my Darling came over me and I cried again and my mother tried to comfort me and so the evening was ending, but Winifred called to me when I left my mother's room and had quasi confessions to make—her faith is troubled because she thinks I am not as big a sinner as I ought to be without God's grace! It is the sort of joke that would have amused my Darling not unpleasantly, though She would have been severely conscious that my merits were not marked enough to make a very large religious difficulty. At 12 I went to bed. To complete the day's record: in the morning I was correcting proof of Norié[308] and digesting the figures on which arguments for Sir William Harcourt might have been based, had he wished to hear any: at two I saw our clerk Harcourt about the draft report on letting schools and at 2:30 began the S. M. Committee.

July 29, 1881

After this Mr. Cross wrote regret for missing me and I a half proposal I come again—he said any afternoon but Thursday, I—to avoid such endless notes—did not answer but went on Wednesday: he was not in, having expected me to write and propose a day. I was not sorry for I waited half an hour or more in the drawing room—knelt at Her chair and kissed the arm of it, read again the inscriptions in all the Mss (which I was glad to find Mr. Cross had kept) and for the first time—I think, that of Daniel Deronda, which had the most pathetic lines from Shakespere's 29th Sonnet. Theophrastus Such was bound—there was no inscription. Bridges' First Volume of Comte[309] was lying out—some few pencil notes of Hers. The white "Imitatis"[310] published last year by Kegan Paul was out—"Mrs. Cross from C. K. P."—it was marked—by the dear Hand.

July 30, 1881

Saw Mr. Cross yesterday. On the chimney piece was the portrait taken by Monsieur D'Albert. A rather round, fair face, with too blue eyes and too light hair, lips rather full, but sweet—not like Her, but not wholly unlike Mrs. Bray's little sketch, hinting at the same sort of pathetic look; the hair was not in curls, braided, rather fluffily; the dress pretty; black velvet with long pointed bodice, open nearly to the waist and a lace stomacher with cord laced across it. Mr. Cross was rather silent, looked thin. Said She never mentioned Feuerbach to him; thought She began to read Comte at least when Miss Martineau's volume came out—or in 51 or 52—but that She might have gone back to it in a new spirit when She knew the Congreves. Mme Belloc saw Her first at Coventry, in Her father's life. I wanted to ask Mr. Cross to let me see if there were any pencil

---

[308] EJS was writing the Prefatory note on December 5, 1878. See December 5, 1878.

[309] John Henry Bridges (1832-1906), *The Unity of Comte's Life and Doctrine, addressed to J. S. Mill* (London: Trübner, 1866).

[310] Thomas á Kempis (1380-1471), German Augustinian monk who composed the *Imitation of Christ* (1441)

marks in "Natural Law"—but I did not venture. I am glad I have been, but do not think it is my mission to go again. As I was leaving I said something about the work: and he said it was going on; he did not think anything should be published for some time; he wanted to "avoid precipitancy," to have the whole life before his own mind: he had intervals of despair, and then moments in which he saw his way. I said when he was despairing he must turn away—to some of Her books—: he said, there was no turning away from a mood—it would come in between the lines. But it was wrong—he felt that very strongly,—did not I but give way to these moods. I quoted Her about indulging in such thoughts—"Why do it if it isn't an indulgence?" Strangely, I never knew till now that there were 3 new poems in the Cabinet Edition of Jubal. Two touch one to the heart's core. "Sweet evenings come and go Love" is a beautiful little song, but, My Darling, the last lines are cruel: there cannot "better souls be born"—and whether, Darling, you wished it or not, you were the Best, our Best, and we have lost you and our lives are forlorn—save for the willing pain of ministry. See, My Darling, Life had brought me the gladness and the gratitude of love, for its dear sake I accept the unsought fate, but Darling, you have left me a special and a heavy cross: the joy in having is to impart—but—I never had—what you count as having and to my sore and aching heart, it seemed as if you said that was my fault. And so no doubt it was: You would not have had the feeling that you were giving me nothing if I had not seemed to ask sadly for more than you could give. I do not, I will not "indulge" in these sad meditations: as I vowed to you in your sadness, the wound I have to carry through life shall not weaken me by its pain— only make one more tenderly responsive to every other's pain: so after years maybe the blessing of your spirit will come to me, if not, thank God—My Darling!—this agony is only mine.

August 18, 1881

Since last Saturday, I have been with Elma, trying not to make myself too disagreeable, recognizing my failures with a constriction about the chest and left side, and concluding that the recurring pain is not to be shirked by any despairing flight, but endured meekly and one's own share in the occasion struggled against still; all pain that comes to us in the course of a "loving, resolute life"—even if it is born of one's own short-comings to be borne without complaint or rebellion. Elma quoted to me Her saying—the first time she saw Her after Mr. Lewes's death: "Joy was not a duty, but cheerfulness was." And in the book of Main's "Sayings"[311] I found a welcome oracle: "There's many a good bit o'work done with a sad heart." It must be that the love which has had such power over my whole life and soul has not yet spent all its power—strength and light are still to come, for—Oh My Darling!—I love you with unchanging tenderness and faith. I would fain, Darling, love you with a purer, more entire devotion each day that comes—or if I cannot love you more—at least serve you better by my love: judge, Darling, how much I love you since I do not say now—

---

[311] Alexander Main, *Wise, Witty and Tender Sayings. Selected from Works of George Eliot* (Edinburgh: William Blackwood, 1872).

that is all I have to live for. But whatever other life I have is yours, your gift, not mine and all that comes of it will be always yours alone.

August 20, 1881
Here is another hopeful word from my oracle: "All passion becomes strength when it has an outlet from the narrow limits of our personal lot in the labour of our right arm, the cunning of our right hand, or the still, creative activity of our thought." I welcome too the implication of another passage, that it is imbecility to "reach middle age without the clear perception that life never *can* be thoroughly joyous." Yes, Darling, "loving resolute life" is possible without joy, without the personal happiness born of the contentment of one's own desires. It would please you, My Love, to know that indeed you have not left me forlorn, that my love for you is as strong and warm as ever—that it fills my soul to overflowing with a yearning tenderness that must make objects for itself, that, Darling, you have indeed taught me just what you felt I needed most to learn, the longing to impart.
The Church Quarterly Reviewer[312] is wrong on a good many points, among others about Her ignoring the possibility of "conversion"—except in Janet's Repentance[313] and the assumed fact that "conversion" is inconsistent with Her doctrine of the inevitableness of consequences. The susceptibility to the impression which at a given moment revolutionizes the life and the character is itself a product, and may prove itself the most precious product of the whole past life.

(In the Ms this note is slanted across the page opposite the last part of the entry for August 20.)
á propos of self-abandonment to emotion—intricacy of feeling—notably a married woman's—who feels, but dares not give herself up to the feeling which incapacitates her from responding to another's feeling.

September 14, 1881
From Malvern went for 2 days to Birmingham where ran about to Board Schools, then to Longton for 10 days, one afternoon to Parkhall—Mrs. Boyd's Tower, and then to the Russells at Innellan—a day down the Clyde to Inverary and home by Malvern. This week the Trades Congress meets and I had men and brethren to dine at Mortimer Street. Mr. Burnett refused to admit the hypocrisy of calling it "lunch" and the men today seized the opportunity of praising the fare and the cooking to insinuate that *there* "woman's mission" lay. Miss Williams's soul lays heavy on my conscience; have been glancing at St.

---

[312] *Church Quarterly Review*, 12: (1881): 242-267.

[313] The last of GE's *Scenes of Clerical Life*, first published in *Blackwoods Magazine* (July-November 1857).

Ignatius's Life[314]—I wish I had the power of constraining souls. I must read the "Spiritual Exercises."[315] I have a vision of constructing a book of practical devotion—borrowing all I can and someday daring to write what is wanting.

September 18, 1881

I am not pleased with "Sat est vixisse"—without being less artistic than the rest, I want it to convey a plain conclusion and appeal: ought it to be as personal as the rest? I have been feeling, again, more at peace in my love. This is the first summer that has passed—since 72—without my having any thing to look forward to in its course or at the end; and I felt as if it had been ungrateful in these past years to look always forward, as if what one had had—while it was still a living fact—were not enough. Now that one has nothing more to hope for, one dwells upon the past with a sad content. The lasting blessedness was that She is so good and dear and I loved Her beyond words, the wildest, fondest words. That remains—how fully and with what blessed power, I wish She could have known—but the personal longing, the vision of a selfish pleasure, of which the death agony began when death first made her desolate, that longing and that vision have left me now; and the bitterness which used to mix with renunciation has—thanks to You My Darling for this also—left me too; I accept my life, "far-sent, unchosen mate," I accept gratefully the scraps of kindness and opportunity which it brings me, if it brings any thing worse, I would accept that patiently, but it brings me I think nothing worse than what I bring myself, feebleness, indolence, irresolution and dulness of heart.

September 23, 1881

There are bits of practical wisdom and acumen in the "Spiritual Exercises," mixed however with a good deal of not quite edifying "Methodism." The essence of the Method is to form a vivid mental picture of places and events, as a prelude to working up appropriate feelings. It is obvious that any one who both could and would "do" the Exercises must emerge with the power of control over his mind and feelings immensely strengthened and developed. The only counsels I feel much impelled to annex are based on a sound estimate of human frailty. We "fall on the leaning side"—therefore the saint advises to redress the balance by leaning deliberately as much as is miscast the other way in our actions. Again "desolations" are synonymous with temptings of the Evil One;—a resolve made in times of consolation, therefore should not be set aside in a period of desolation. My thesis would be, that rationalists have just as much need as anybody else to try to cultivate the art of "being good" and this as systematically as Methodists or Jesuits. I have felt a little hunted since coming back from Scotland—what with the Trades Congress, Mortimer Street, Elma and her trouble about Roly, Miss Williams who however gave me a hopeful moment the other

---

[314] *Life of St. Ignatius, founder of the Society* by Dominique Bonhours (London: Henry Hills, 1686).

[315] "Spiritual Exercises" by St. Ignatius of Loyola (1491-1556).

day and various other small outer matters which together give my slow brain the sense of being much occupied.—So much so that I had a new illumination on the subject of my standing difficulty: *Was* it my fault that I didn't wish to be married in general and that no one in particular wished to marry me? Would it really be a "higher life" to throw overboard all such of one's engagements as would not combine with the overpowering devotion of one's life to one? If there had been any chance of devoting my life to Her, there would have been no question—right or wrong I could no more have helped myself than the spring tide can help rising. But otherwise—honestly I don't think one is a monster for not having that uninvited yearning twice. A case of conscience *might* arise if a particular man's life came before one, appealing to have a want supplied, but my imagination breaks down in the attempt to picture such a contingency, the attempt revolts me as an impertinence of the vainest sort. If I had to make my life over again under totally fresh conditions, I would hope to be able to do so—though it might and would be difficult,—but I don't think I ought to wish to have this particular difficulty to overcome, while, without it I have more than enough to occupy my thoughts and affections. Granted that I can imagine more satisfaction to my affections than I exactly enjoy—the fault is mine and,—thanks be to God—my God!—not wholly irreparable. I am less desolate now than of old—which is surely a sign, Darling, that you are not displeased with me . . . . And then, Darling, to prove my happiness, I burst into tears, for love of you, just as of old.

Now for an Agenda memo: Tomorrow, Sunday, sort letters and S. B. papers. When that is done look at Her letters: write to the Democratic Club to offer remarks on University Extension. Monday? *finish* Balance sheet. Then Industrial calculations about salaries—perhaps this really ought to precede the clearing up of paper—and I am less likely to idle over it. Then I have to place, and choose books for, my domestic economy girls. Then prepare discourse on "Higher Education," and write paper on "Industrial Training" for girls by the 25th . . . while in less than a fortnight I shall have both Board and shop to manage at once. And I wanted to re-write *Sat est vixisse*—And with all this to do—yet I am often idle.

October 2, 1881

My mother and Augustus went to Oxford just before the last entry; since then I have been busy in mixed fashion, Monday, Shop, Miss Williams to dinner—Tuesday, Board and shop again till 10.—Wednesday shop morning. Will and Annie to lunch, National society for books and University Extension, at 5, Swimming competition at 7, home 10:30. Thursday, shop, Friday, Industrial, beginning with a call on Frith[316] at his studio in Bayswater, as "Miss Hamilton" who was to advise him about the dresses for two aesthetic ladies in a coming picture of "Private view day at the Academy," and ending with auditing the tailoresses accounts at 36 Queen Street with Mr. Sadler of the Democratic Club

---

[316] William Powell Frith (1819-1909) was a well-known Victorian painter. Haight identifies him as a landscape painter who painted Dickens' portrait (H, III, 114, n. 2).

and the Secretary. Saturday, first household affairs, then long visitation from a head master who is in hot water with the head mistresses, the shop, then back and call on Elma, bust of Mr. Lewes not very like, evening entertain Allen Hutchinson—26—went to sea at 15—then taken away and allowed to go to New Zealand, where has been on his own funding for nearly 10 years. Now wants something to do in England. This morning wrote many letters, this afternoon went to see Mrs. Congreve, who told me of a trouble I need not record here. I was sorry for her—all the more because I could not give very hot sympathy with her anger. It is very difficult to judge what is an unpardonable and when a pontiff is *in loco parentis*—I could only be sorry. She asked me if I was able when away from home to throw myself into other lives; I said I had no life of my own; she gave that a laudatory turn—if one could conquer self in daily life: I have felt indeed just of late as if she would not be too much displeased with me:—as she once said "There is some possible and some certain good in reach of every one"—perhaps I have tried to reach my little—and in this effort there is a kind of rest. It has been given me lately to feel—even in the midst of the sore aching of a desire that has not been and now can never be contented—to feel that this sense of pain can be conquered, not destroyed but overcome, that the grudging sense of effort, in caring for one's life as it is instead of as one would have wished it to be, will grow less as the effort is made more and more heartily; until at last I shall not say "I have no life of my own," for all these that are near me will indeed be mine, a part of me. Even as I write this, I do not quite know, oh She would blame me because I do not care more. Darling my punishment is heavy—you can never unsay to me the judgments that I labour very humbly, Dearest not to deserve now,—or to deserve less: I have left off asking if I ever deserved them quite:—And you were always good to me—as good as if I had been better. The hardest is not to be able to pay you in the thanks you would have liked best.

October 10, 1881

Another week has gone much the same way. I have had a warning or two to beware of small neglects and self-indulgences. It may be one's reward for trying to "be good" that omissions which would else be harmless may turn into wickedly lost opportunities. I am wicked because I recognize the danger more with my understanding than my feelings. Went to see Mrs. Congreve this afternoon. She had "to thank me for a very sweet note." It was rather amusing to me last week to find myself mothering the young brother and sister in the most natural way. Yesterday wrote to Sully about "Scientific Optimism" a 19th Century article[317] in which he quotes me as one of the Optimists. Sent Longman

---

[317] James Sully, "Scientific Optimism," *Nineteenth Century* 10 (October 1881): 573-587; in speaking of those who have begun to use the Darwinian theory as a source of comfort: "As Miss Edith Simcox well says, 'The irrepressible optimism of humanity comes back, though we drive it forth with the pitchfork of logical dilemma'" (*Natural Law*, p. 183) (577). He alludes to EJS (580 and 586) in discussing the way certain systems of theology have sought to satisfy the need to know why humans must suffer: "It is but a poor retort to say with Miss

the other "Vignettes" as he thought of printing one more. Prepared notes for a lecture—delivered same without looking at them once.—Middling. I am not "all here" in any part of my work.

October 12, 1881
Have ventured this evening to look at Her last year's letters. I was crying in bed last night—my heart is sore with the old pain. I can only try to recal how once to her I promised that my life's grief should not weaken or embitter—only keep one's heart more tender. I love Her still as always: there is no one to cheer me by saying—She loved you too a little.

October 30, 1881
All this has to be accepted—it is no use dwelling for ever upon what it might have been well to change—if one could—as if everything certainly *could* have been changed that it was reasonable to wish to change. I have been rather *triste*[318] of late, but not actively malcontent. A doubt occurs to me today about the S. B. which I had thought myself obliged to leave, without question, because of the cost of an election. Now it crosses my mind whether I might stand *passively*; write a little address, saleable at 1, and say in it, I don't want to be returned again, but you may do it if you like. To make my exit an experiment in the way of reform. When I have cleared up arrears at Mortimer Street, I may be free for a little "Appropriation"—it will be difficult to take up again if I let too much time slip. I was pleased to note, though, that Grote did not accomplish any of his History[319] till after he had retired from the Bank. Was a little amused—hardly annoyed—to hear last Monday, when I had a note from Mr. Cross; that some asses had arranged an "engagement" between us. I must be rather a monster, for my feeling about that and the other canard of the same sort is less of personal annoyance than a kind of compassion for the other poor fellows whose names are taken in vain. No one can know as well as I do with what effort they only just succeed in being barely civil. As to Mr. Cross it might console my vanity—if I had any of that sort—to imagine his unresponsiveness to *my* laboured courteous to be owing to a more vivid imagination of the world's wickedness. It puzzles me, I confess. I don't know any other woman who wears spectacles and doesn't frequent "society" whose name is made free with in that way.—I only know that it is more than unprovoked: at least it is impossible that any one but Mr. Cross should have known,—or that he should have

---

Simcox, 'Is the good of life less good because it is unequally distributed?' Of course not."

[318] "sad"

[319] George Grote (1794-1871), *A History of Greece from the Earliest Period to the Close of the Generation Contemporary with Alexander the Great*, 2 vols. (London: J. Murray, 1867-70).

misunderstood,—my desire to atone for the incivility She once imagined. Darling—I don't wish to die before my time, but I shall be very glad when I am dead.

November 6, 1881

Yesterday at the British Museum I read the three Westminster Review articles—on Cumming, Heine and German Life[320]—which I had not known of in the spring. On my way home I bought Scribner—and read it walking across Hyde Park in the twilight, which had changed to darkness as I came to the passages from Her own letters. My Darling—I have more to be thankful for than almost anyone:—I think I understood you wholly, knew you just as you were and loved you wholly, because you were just that. I feel deep pity for those who had just a thought of reserve in their admiration, of limit in their love. I might easily have been more fortunately intimate, but no change in you could have made my Darling anything but less divinely dear. The writer (in Scribner) has not understood that an infinite human love gives real life more than any hope of heaven or life to come can give in the life that now is. All do not taste the fulness of this supreme joy; I have tasted it in part and I know that my life is richer than that of thousands who have not lost their greatest happiness—which is less than mine. Darling, for your sake I have striven against the hard pride which is content to stand alone, but indeed I think I am right now to be as strong as I can, and not appeal for help—save to Her dear memory. Let me be strong and not hard. My difficulty is this—in trying to say the thing that will help and not wound, perhaps one does not say what comes first as one's own feeling—hence a degree of remoteness—of impersonalness in one's sympathy: but if one speaks just what comes—one must be wiser and better and kinder than I to make sure that this *will* help and not wound. It is harder for me to reach perfection than for Her: She had impulses to control—I should have to develop intuitions, and after all there is a physical substratum in the qualities that make a sympathetic nature. But it is vanity to complain, as if it were not worthwhile to try and be the best one can because one's best will still be middlingly bad. The passages from Mr. Myers' letters promise that Her published letters will be of unspeakable value.

November 24, 1881

Last Friday a card from Mme Bodichon brought me down to Hastings next day. She had reclaimed her letters from Mr. Cross (who, by the way, writes and signs to her as he does to me, not as he does to Elma) and on Monday she showed them me and accepted the offer I made in my last letter to her. Since then I have read I think all the letters through just once—earning some sleepless hours and passionate tears over them, yet finding pleasure beyond the pain in the vision of Her dearness through all the years, Her faithful friendship, and Her

---

[320] "Evangelical Teaching: Dr. Cumming," *Westminster Review*, 64 (October 1855), 436-462; "German Wit: Heinrich Heine," *Westminster Review*, 65 (January 1856): 1-33; "The Natural History of German Life," *Westminster Review*, 66 (July 1856), 51-79.

repeated assurance to Her friend of Her great and growing happiness. Mme finds Mr. Cross "very pleasant"—likes him better than she used, when he was only a nuisance, coming *au tiers*,[321] but still she did not understand, could not think of him with Her: Mme Belloc however has a higher estimate. The having all these letters in my hands is an unspeakable, infinite delight.

November 27, 1881

All the same after the first night of reading them, I felt miserable,— envious I think especially of those who had a friend like Barbara to speak well of them to Her,—instead of such an enemy as I was to myself, to speak ill. But there is one thing I have to envy no one. She asked me to be content that others should love her as well as I did. If it had been possible I would have rejoiced for them to love Her better.—But I do not find any one who does. It was and is my great blessing to love Her *wholly*, without reserve or limit, doubt or check, to delight in Her, just as She was, and to my love, is, everlastingly. All the small words that gave me pain in the days of my covetous, selfish passion, were in themselves kind and sweet, they do not pain me now; and later, when I vexed Her once or twice, She would not have been vexed if I had been able quite to explain; and then as now, I was always able to understand Her, and if I lost a little of Her love by my stupidity, that She was so loving to me notwithstanding gives me all the more reason to love and worship. Mary Cross was in a curious mood yesterday. She had loved other people more than our Lady and was quite angry when I said even her dear brother would have grown more perfectly good by being with Her. I had sent Charles Lewes some sweet words of Hers, for a birthday present and he came this afternoon in answer. Some of Her Westminster Articles *may* be reprinted. She also wrote at one time in the Saturday, and the Pall Mall. There are also some poems, and notes—or as She seems to have called them "quarries" for some of Her books. I shall not copy for myself any of Her letters till I have Mme Bodichon's leave, but for the sake of measuring Her writing and because it is a passage that I may certainly keep, I give two pages of Her note paper over leaf. It is written from Torquay—1868. I allow myself also to quote two or three passages that are of special value to me—as on the whole I will not copy the letters to keep for myself.[322]

(In the Ms this quotation from GE's letter is on the page opposite.)

"What I should like to be sure of as a result of higher education for women—a result that will come to pass over my grave—is their recognition of the great amount of social unproductive labour which needs to be done by women, and which is now either not done at all or done wretchedly. No good can come to women, more than to any class of male mortals, while each aims at doing the highest kind of work, which ought rather to be held in sanctity as what only the few can do

---

[321] "as a third party"

[322] H, IV, 425 on March 28?, 1868

168

well. I believe—and I want it to be well shown—that a more thorough education will tend to do away with the odious vulgarity of our notions about functions and employments, and to propagate the true gospel that the deepest disgrace is to insist on doing work for which we are unfit—to do work of any sort badly. There are many points of this kind that want being urged, but they do not come well from me, and I never liked to be quoted in any way on this subject."

December 4, 1881

I wonder if it is at all significant of character—I am sometimes afraid that in writing letters I am too apt to use this nominative—"I think," "I believe," "I am sure," &c &c , on the other hand, the objective *me* is conspicuous by its absence, its place being taken, too often for good English, by the shy, ambiguous "one." In Her letters, the nominative is rare, and the objective frequent. The last weeks have slipped by very rapidly.

December 26, 1860[323] "The bright point in your letter is that you are in a happy state of mind yourself. For the rest, we must wait and not be impatient with those who have their inward trials tho' everything outward seems to smile on them. It seems to those who are differently placed that the sense of freedom from strong ties and urgent claims must be very precious for the ends of self—culture, and good helpful work towards the world at large. But it hardly ever is so.—As for the 'forms and ceremonies' I feel no regret that any should turn to them for comfort, if they can find comfort in them: sympathetically I enjoy them myself. But I have faith in the working out of higher possibilities than the Catholic or any other church has presented, and those who have strength to wait and endure, are bound to accept no formula which their whole souls—their intellect as well as their emotions—do not embrace with entire reverence. The highest 'calling and election' is to *do without opium* and live through all our pain with conscious, clear eyed endurance." . . . . "By the way, we have consulted a barrister, very accomplished in foreign and English law, about that matter broached by your friend Mrs. Brodie.[324] He pronounces it *impossible*. I am not sorry. I think the boys will not suffer, and for myself I prefer excommunication. I have no earthly thing that I care for to gain by being brought within the pale of people's personal attention, and I have many things to care for that I should lose—my freedom from petty worldly torments, commonly called pleasures, and that isolation which really keeps my charity warm instead of chilling it, as much contact with frivolous women would do."

---

[323] H, III, 365-366

[324] Mrs. Brodie is the wife of the chemist Benjamin Collins Brodie and the daughter of John Vincent Thompson, serjeant-at-law. Apparently GE had consulted her about obtaining a divorce abroad (H, III, 366, n. 1).

December 25, 1881

I have finished copying Her letters and have only some passages from Mr. Lewes's to add. Mrs. Congreve let me read one of Her letters—from Torquay, in 68[325]—It began "Dear Mrs. Congreve"—I wondered whether she could be the old friend (I had thought she could not be) who when the Madonna sought to escape that formality by addressing "My dear Friend" answered deprecatingly—using the same phrase for once only. "Barbara" was Her nearest friend, the one whose friendship gave most loving pleasure through long years. My term was just 8 ycars and 10 days, just about the length Mme Bodichon would have reached already if I had known Her 10 years sooner. I am glad to know as much as possible of all Her friends. I am not sorry that I do not find amongst them all any to whom She Herself was more than She was and is to me. It would be as unreasonable for Mr. Cross to complain that he was less to Her than Mr. Lewes as for me to regret that Madame Bodichon was more welcome to Her at five and thirty than I could be when She was 53. I do not *indulge* in unreasonable regrets. The sore aching at my heart comes back still, but one can "only know one's worst griefs once": the bitterness of death may pass over us again and again; all my soul's longings were squashed in the bitter waters when Mr. Lewes died; when Mr. Cross was ill I knew the agony of hopeless fear; in the summer's long absence I said over to myself the lesson that perhaps was almost learnt at last, if it is well with Her, what matters how it is with me? And now it can never more be ill with Her, the keenest good and evil seem for me too to have passed away together. I went to Highgate two days ago with flowers, the anniversary of the morning the sadness reached me. It was a bright, white frosty day: the ivy round Mr. Lewes's grave is beginning to grow abundantly.

The Chronology I gather from Madame Bodichon's letters is as follows: They left Holly Lodge for 16 Blandford Square in the autumn of 1860. March, 1862 [326] "Little Inn at Englefield Green," kept by "good Mrs. Bone." Autumn of 63 leave Blandford Square for the Priory. Different summer migrations are referred to in their order.
There is a double letter (Holly Lodge, March 6, 1860)[327] when she is nearing the end of the 3rd vol of the "Mill," in which Mr. Lewes begins by explaining that his "'good Lady' (style choisi!)[328] is reddening her eyes and blacking her paper over the foolish sorrows of two foolish young persons of her imaginary acquaintance"—or as She puts it "I have been crying myself almost into stupor, over visions of sorrow." Mem: to ask Madame Bodichon which of her sisters

---

[325] possibly H, IV, 429, April 4, 1868

[326] H, IV, 21 dated March ll

[327] H, III, 269-270

[328] an obsolete style of address

was "that lucky artist with the streaming hair." [329] He adds that "Adam Bede" was still selling at the rate of 200 a month and that they had refused £4500 for the 3rd edition of "the Mill." The first letter of all[330] says "Come to the Putney Station, not the Wandsworth one, the walk is prettier and not longer."

From Her letters. Holly Lodge, Southfield, Wandsworth. August 11, 1859[331] "I *do* wish much to see more of human life—how can one see enough in the short years one has to stay in this world? But I meant that at present my mind works with the most freedom and the keenest sense of poetry in my remotest past, and there are many strata to be worked through before I can begin to use *artistically* any material I may gather in the present. Curiously enough, á propos of your remark about 'Adam Bede' there is much less 'out of my own life' in that book— i.e. the materials are much more a combination from imperfectly known and widely sundered elements—than the 'Clerical Scenes.'"

December 6, 1859[332] 16000 of "Adam Bede" sold. Of Darwin's "Origin." "So the world gets on step by step towards brave clearness and honesty! But to me the Development Theory and all the other explanations of processes by which things came to be produce a feeble impression compared with the mystery that lies under the processes." "One would like one's life to be born on the onward wave and not the receding one—the flow and not the ebb. Yet somebody must live in the bad times, and there is no reason, I suppose, out of our own esteem for ourselves, why the best things in the lot of mankind should fall to us in particular."

(In the Ms this is on the page opposite.)
>The same letter—one of the longest and pleasantest—
>describes Mr. Lewes's enthusiasm for a new microscope
>which so dimed his perceptions that the advent of a
>"palpable tea chest" (which he had himself ordered a few
>days before) seemed to promise that key to discovery and
>immortality and he began to open the elusive package till
>"at last the obstinacy of the lid moderated his inflamed
>imagination and he began to see the tea chest." . . . "The
>rewards of the artist lie apart from everything that is narrow or
>personal." . . . "Our great, great favorite Molière. I think the
>Misanthrope the finest, most complete production *of its kind* in the

---

[329] H, III, 271

[330] H, III, 59, April 27, 1859

[331] H, III, 128

[332] H, III, 224-228, dated December 5

world. I know you enjoy the sonnet scene, and the one between
Arsino and Célimène. March 11, 1861[333] We are as happy as
creatures can be with imperfect digestions—associating chiefly with
the animals in the "Zoo" where we take our walks continually. "—a
piece of work which had been occupying Her dismissed that very
evening." (? Silas Marner).

November 26, 1862[334] "Pray don't ever ask me again not to rob a man of his
religious belief as if you thought my mind tended towards such robbery. I have
too profound a conviction of the efficacy that lies in all sincere faith, and the
spiritual blight that comes from no faith, to have any negative propagandism in
me. In fact, I have very little sympathy with Freethinkers as a class, and have lost
all interest in mere antagonism to religious doctrines. I care only to know if
possible, the lasting meaning that lies in all religious doctrines from the
beginning till now."

May 12, 1863[335] "The dear Doctor—our image of human uprightness, bodily
and spiritual." At Worthing same year:[336] "Sweet woman's kindness" from Mrs.
Hare—the archdeacon's widow and F. D. Maurice's sister.
Autumn of 1863, move to the Priory.[337]
December 4, 1863[338]—not writing but "taking deep draughts of reading,"
"Politique Positive, Euripides, Latin Christianity and so forth." "In the most
entire confidence even of husband and wife there is always the unspoken
residue—the *undivined* residue, perhaps of what is most sinful, perhaps of what
is most exalted and unselfish." In the next letter I have left out a passage
"Charlie has just returned from his month's holiday[339] and our beloved tête à tête
existence is at an end. We are fond of that dear good boy, but we can't help also
being fond of his absence. That is in the nature of things." (query—was it
wholly?).

---

[333] H, III, 388-389

[334] H, IV, 64

[335] H, IV, 85

[336] H, IV, 101-102, dated August 19, 1863; H has "tenderness" instead of
"kindness."

[337] H, Chronology, November 5, 1863

[338] H, IV, 119-120

[339] H, IV, 14, February 13, 1862, "Charlie has his holiday in May, but we shall
arrange for him to spend it in Geneva with my friends the D'Alberts. . . ."

November 26, 1862[340] "We are very well and unspeakably happy. I know you care to think of other people's happiness—therefore I tell you such private news."

April 13, 1866[341] "We have been going on as usual, both of us better and worse by turns. Yet happier and happier." "We are getting patriarchal and think of old age and death as journeys not far off. All knowledge, all thought, all achievement seems more precious and enjoyable to me than it ever was before in life. But as soon as one has found the key of life 'it opens the gates of death.'[342] Youth has not learned the *art* of living and we go on bungling till our experience can only serve us for a very brief space."

January 7, 1867[343] Letters from Bordeaux en route from Paris into Spain.

Then one[344] from Barcelona en route San Sebastian to Saragossa, 2 nights, Lerida one night then Barcelona. Steamer to Alicante, then to Malaga: ?Granada, Cordoba and Seville.

Home March 16.[345] Cathedral here and Madrid pictures the cross.

June, 1867 [346] "Thou knoweth, if not all things, at least that I love thee."

To Dreseden ? 67.[347]

April, 1868[348] Torquay.

November same year[349] returned from Sheffield and Matlock. "I recognized all the spots I had carried in my memory for more than 5 and 20 years. I drove through that region with my father when I was a young girl not very full of hope about my woman's future. I am one of those perhaps exceptional people whose early childish dreams were much less happy than the real outcome of life."

---

[340] H, IV, 65, same letter quoted earlier

[341] H, IV, 236-237, dated April 13

[342] H, IV, 237, n. 7, Edward Young's *Night Thoughts on Life, Death and Immortality* (London: J. French, 1777).

[343] H, IV, 329, dated January 4

[344] H, IV, 338-339, dated February 2, 1867

[345] H, IV, 351, dated March 18

[346] H, IV, 367, dated June 17

[347] H, Chronology, Dresden July 29-October 1, 1867

[348] H, IV, 425, dated March ?28

[349] H, IV, 488, November 16, 1868

December 12, 1868[350] "G. has been to see his old friend W. B. Scott[351] and is delighted to see his achievements as a painter. Also he (W. Scott) has dined with us and has charmed us by his simplicity and genuine talk."

October, 1869[352]   After Thornies's death[353] "to Limpsfield in Surrey to nice people in an old-fashioned farm house."

About this time, undated[354] remorseful afterthought—"Lying awake early in the morning, according to a bad practice of mine, I was visited with much compunction and self disgust that I had ever said a word to you about the faults of a friend whose good qualities are made the more sacred by the endurance his lot has in many ways demanded. I think you may fairly set down a full half of any alleged grievances to my own susceptibility and other faults of mine which necessarily call forth less agreeable manifestations from others than as many virtues could do if I had them. . . . I wish to protest against my self, that I may as much as possible cut off the temptation to what I should like utterly to purify myself from for the few remaining years of my life—the disposition to dwell for a moment on the faults of a friend."

June 23, 1870[355]   Albert House Cromer. "To me the most desirable thing just now seems to be to have one home and stay there till death comes to take me away. I get more and more disinclined to the perpetual makeshifts of a migratory life, and care more and more for the order and habitual objects of home. However there are many in the world whose whole existence is a makeshift, and perhaps the formula which would fit the largest number of lives is, 'a doing without more or less patiently.'"   . . .   "We are very 'jolly' in spite of weak heads, stomachs &c and have more than our share of happiness."

May 25 [356] Park Farm. Limpsfield. "This earthly paradise."

June 17, 1871[357] Brookbank. "Shottermill near Petersfield."

August 20, 1871[358] "Chervinans," same place. "Our country could hardly be surpassed in its particular kind of beauty—perpetual undulation of heath and

---

[350] H, IV, 494

[351] William Bell Scott (1811-1890) was one of GHL's earliest literary friends (H, IV, 494, n. 5).

[352] H, V, 61, dated October 22

[353] GHL's son Thornton Arnott died of spinal tuberculosis on October 19, 1869.

[354] H, V, 123, dated November, 1870

[355] H, V, 104

[356] H, V, 113, dated August 25 [1870]

[357] H, V, 152

copse and clear veins of hurrying water, with here and there a grand pine wood, steep wood clothed promontories and gleaming pools." . . . "If you want delightful reading get the 7/6 edition of Lowell's 'My Study Windows' and read the essays called 'My Garden Acquaintance' and 'Winter.'"[359] Mrs. Gilchrist the landlady. Haslemere Station. Railway Hotel opposite. Shottermill is 1/2 an hour or 20 minutes beyond.[360]

July 6, 1872 Recommending Deutscher Novellenschatz—specially last 3 vols including "Diethelm von Buchenberg," in which She had been "deeply interested."[361]

September, 1873[362] Blackbrook, Bickley, Kent. 1/4 of an hour from Chislehurst. "The walks and drives round us were delightfully varied—commons, wooded lanes, wide pastures—and we felt regretfully that we were hardly likely to find again a country house so secluded in a well-inhabited region. But the house would not do in its actual state."

February 2, 1874 [363] "Do you mind the conservative majority?[364] I don't."—But she lived to "mind" some of its consequences very much.—

July, 1874 [365] The Cottage "Earlswood Common." "The country around us must, I think, be the loveliest—of its undulating, woody kind, in all England. I remember when we were driving together last, something was said about my disposition to melancholy. I ought to have said then, but did not, that I am no longer one of those whom Dante found in Hell border because they had been sad under the blessed sunlight. I am uniformly cheerful now—feeling the

---

[358] H, V, 153, dated June 17, 1871, also Sottermill

[359] H, V, 153, James Russell Lowell, *My Study Windows* (Boston: Osgood, 1871). These are the first two essays in the volume (H, V, 153, n. 1).

[360] H, V, 178, includes Mrs. Gilchrist, the station, and the hotel in the letter dated August 20.

[361] H, V, 289, GE refers to "a very cheap publication" in her letter; it is Berthold Auerbach, "Die Geschichte des Diethelm von Buchenberg," in Auerbach's *Schwarzwalder Dorfgeschichten*, vol. III of the Deutscher Novellenschatz (Mannheim, 1848) (H, V, 289, n. 5).

[362] H, V, 433, indicates that GE was there but does not include this letter.

[363] H, VI, 13, dated February [9]

[364] H, VI, 14, n. 6, on January 24, 1874, Gladstone dissolved Parliament; in the ensuing election Disraeli and the Conservatives won constituting the first Conservative majority since 1841.

[365] H, VI, 69, dated July 16

preciousness of these moments in which I still possess love and thought."
"About 8 visitors for a day or 1/2 a day at rare intervals." "Irma Hartog's cousin"[366] mentioned. "I daresay you wonder that I have not done more for Girton. The fact is that we have been devoting a considerable sum of late years to the help of individual needs which are not published to the world. More and more of such needs disclose themselves to one—old governesses and other beings having some claims through the memory of good received in one's youth and who could only be helped by such special care. But you will let me know what is to be done for this nice girl."[367]

November, 1874[368] "Please give my kindest remembrances to—or rather, ask her to remember me kindly, for I think our forms of message are very conceited and ungraceful. How do we know that our kind remembrances are wanted? Whereas we do know whether we want the kind remembrances of others."

The Elms Rickmansworth. August 13, 1875[369] Heard last Sunday of Bertie's death on the 29th June.[370]

March 30, 1876[371] "I am well pleased that Deronda touches you. I *wanted* you to prefer the chapter about Mirah's finding, and I hope you will also like her history in Part III which has just been published."

September 6, 1876[372] "From Aix-les-Bains turned northward by slow stages to Ragatz; still kept in E. Switzerland in high vallies unvisited by the English. . . paused in the Schwarzwald at St Blasien, which is a *Luft-Kur*, all green hills and pines with their tops as still as if it were the abode of the gods.". . . "We are both pretty well, but of course not cured of all infirmities. Death is the only physician. The shadow of his valley the only journeying that will cure us of age and the gathering fatigue of years. Still we are thoroughly lively and 'spry.'"

October 2, 1876[373] "My blessings on you for your sweet letter which I count among the blessings given to me. Yes. Women can do much for other women (and men) to come. My impression of the good then is in all unselfish effort is

---

[366] Numa Edward Hartog was professor of French; his cousin was Phoebe Sarah Marks afterwards Hertha Aryton (H, VI, 83, n. 6).

[367] H, VI, 83, includes from 8 visitors on in letter of September 23, 1874.

[368] H, VI, 90, November 16

[369] H, VI, 161

[370] GHL's son Herbert Arthur died of a glandular disease on June 29, 1875.

[371] H, VI, 161

[372] H, VI, 280

[373] H, VI, 290

continually strengthened. Doubtless many a ship is drowned on expeditions of discovery or rescue, and precious freights lie buried. But there was the good of manning and furnishing the ship with a great purpose before it set out.". . . Very interesting letters from Jews and Christians about Deronda. "This is better than the laudation of readers who cut the book up into scraps and talk of nothing in it but Gwendolen. I meant everything in the book to be related to everything else there."

July 2, 1877[374] Witley. "Miss Thackeray is married today to young Ritchie. I saw him at Cambridge and felt that the nearly 20 years difference between them was bridged hopefully by his solidity and gravity. This is one of several instances that I have known of lately, showing that young men with even brilliant advantages will often choose as their life's companion a woman whose attractions are wholly of a spiritual order."

The letter of May 5, 1880[375] I must copy at length, for my own keeping. "My dear Barbara, I have something to tell you which will doubtless be a great surprize to you, but since I have found that other friends, less acquainted with me and my life than you are, have given me their sympathy, I think that I can count on yours. I am going to do what not very long ago I should myself have pronounced impossible for me, and therefore I should not wonder at any one else who found my action incomprehensible. By the time you receive this letter I shall (so far as the future can be matter of assertion) have been married to Mr. J. W. Cross, who you know is a friend of years, a friend much loved and trusted by Mr. Lewes, and who now that I am alone sees his happiness in the dedication of his life to me. This change in my position will make no change in my care for Mr. Lewes's family and in the ultimate disposition of my property. Mr. Cross has a sufficient fortune of his own.

We are going abroad for a few months, and I shall not return to live at this house. Mr. Cross has taken the lease of a house in Cheyne Walk, (No 4), Chelsea, where we shall spend the winter and early spring, making Witley our summer home.

You will like to hear that Charles has shown a quite perfect feeling in relation to this unexpected event, and if you would like to write or in any way communicate to him your wish for further knowledge, he will I am sure readily respond to your wish.

I indulge the hope that you will some day look at the river from the windows of our Chelsea house which is rather quaint and picturesque.

Please tell Bessie for me, with my love to her. I cannot write to more than two or three persons.

Ever yours lovingly,
M. E. Lewes"

---

[374] H, VI, 398, dated August 2, says GE made an "obvious slip" since Anne Isabella Thackeray was married on August 2 to Richmond Thackeray Willoughby Ritchie (n. 6).

[375] H, VII, 268-269

(The Postmark is "July 7." Outside the envelope "I have today found this in a drawer in the desk in the dining room. This explains the mystery." Charles.)

Verona, June 1, 1880[376]

Milan, May 29, 1880 (crossed out)

Dearest Barbara,

The change I make in the date of this letter is a sign of the difficulty you well know that one finds in writing all the letters one wants to write while travelling. Ever since Charles forwarded to me your dear letter while I was in Paris I have been meaning to write to you. That letter was doubly sweet to me because it was written before you received mine, intended to inform you of my marriage before it appeared in the newspaper. Charles says that my friends are chiefly hurt because I did not tell them of the approaching change in my life. But I really did not finally, absolutely decide—I was in a state of doubt and struggle until only a fortnight before the event took place and for a week of that time I was ill with influenza, so that at last everything was done in the utmost haste. However, there were four or five friends, of whom you were one, to whom I was resolved to write so that they should at least get my letter in the morning of the 6th.

I had more than once said to Mr. Cross that you were that one of my friends who requested the least explanation on the subject—who would spontaneously understand our marriage. But Charles sends me word that my friends in general are very sympathetic, and I should like to mention to you that Bessie is one whose very kind words he has sent to me, for you may have an opportunity of giving my love to her and telling her that it is very sweet to me to feel that her affection is constant to me in this as it was in other crises of my life.—I wish, since you can no longer come in and out among us as you used to do, that you already knew my husband better—his character is so solid, his feeling is so eminently delicate and generous. But you will have inferred something of this from his desire to dedicate his life to the remaining fragment of mine. His family welcome me with the utmost tenderness, and they are of the best paste men and women can be made of. All this is wonderful blessing falling to me beyond my share after I had thought that my life was ended and that, so to speak, my coffin was ready for me in the next room. Deep down below there is a hidden river of sadness, but this must always be with those who have lived long—and I am able to enjoy my newly reopened life. I shall be a better, more loving creature than I could have been in solitude. To be constantly lovingly grateful for the gift of a perfect love is the best illumination of one's mind to all the possible good there may be in store for man on this troublous little planet.

We leave Verona today, and stay a little at Padua on our way to Venice. The last two days we have had some greyness of sky and good rain which has laid the dust for us while cheering the richly cultivated plains around us. Hitherto we have had delightful weather and just the temperature we rejoice in. We are both fond of warmth, and could bear more heat than we have the

---

[376] H, VII, 290-292

prospect of at present. We came into Italy by way of Grenoble (seeing the Grande Chartreuse) Chambéry and the Mount Cenis Tunnel. Since then we have been staying at Milan and enjoying the Luini frescoes and a few other great things there. The great things are always by comparison few, and there is much everywhere one would like to keep seeing after it has once served to give one a notion of historical progression.

We shall stay at Venice for ten days or a fortnight, so if you have a scribe or would write yourself and tell me that all is going on well with you the letter would not, as the Scotch say, "go a-missing."

Yours always loving
Marian

Yesterday we had a drive on the skirting heights of Verona, and saw the vast fertile plain around with the Euganean hills blue in the distance, and the Appennines just dimly visible on the clear margin of the horizon. I am always made happier by seeing well-cultivated land.

I ought to have copied in its place part of the letter May 5, 1859.[377] "God bless you, Dearest Barbara, for your love and sympathy. You are the first friend who has given any symptom of knowing me. The first heart that has recognized me in a book which has come from my heart of hearts. . . . I am a very blessed woman, am I not? to have all this reason for being glad that I have lived, in spite of my sins and sorrows—or rather, by reason of my sins and sorrows. I have had no time of exultation; on the contrary, these last months have been sadder than usual to me, and I have thought more of the future and the much work that remains to be done in life than of any thing that has been achieved. But I think your letter today gave me more joy—more heartglow, than all the letters or reviews or other testimonies of success that have come to me since the evenings when I read aloud my manuscript to my dear dear husband, and he laughed and cried alternately and then rushed to me to kiss me. He is the prime blessing that has made all the rest possible to me—giving me a response to everything I have written, a response that I could confide in as a proof that I had not mistaken my work."

January 6, 1882

Was rather painfully touched by a line from Mary—"Mr. Green says there are 2 really kind people in London and my partner is one of them"—The kindness was of the smallest: it gives me real pleasure that anyone should feel I had been kind, but I think sadly of the greater pleasure it would have been for Her to think so—or to feel that others did. Poor Miss Williams haunts me like an exaggeration of every foolishness with which I ever teased or wearied Her. I hope I am not uncharitable in thinking she is more unreasonable and exigiante than I ever was; it is any way a fit judgment that I should feel all the helplessness I can ever have made Her feel. It is perhaps noteworthy that my few day's leisure just now has not had its too frequent effect in making me moan miserably. I have

---

[377] H, III, 63-64

been reading a little Goethe—the "Sprüche in Prosa"[378] specially in quest of a motto for "Some one had blundered": also found a good deal to feel and think about á propos of Watts'[379] pictures at the Grosvenor. I think I can find interests enough in life even apart from the chief matter into which fortune enters, the number and pleasantness of one's friendships. I wish painters such as Watts—of whom there are but few—would not limit themselves to portraits, allegories or illustrations of old far off tales. Why not put as deep feeling into the faces of modern personages,—of fact or fiction—as into Paolo and Francesca?

January 29, 1882. Scalands.
　　　　　Yesterday Madame Bodichon asked me to look through a box full of letters, where it was possible some of Hers might be. I found one almost at once—a strange shock: then a postcard from Mr. Lewes, announcing Her visit: the last day *he* was out. Then I came upon a long envelope containing many letters:—the first She wrote (January 7) after his death, and many of that year. The first ends—"Your loving but half dead Marian."[380]

On March 5 she wrote "the sorrow deepens down instead of diminishing." Her weakness must be excused "remembering that for nearly 25 years I have been used to find my happiness in his. I can find it nowhere else. But we can live and be helpful without happiness and I have had more than myriads."—Her choice of the Studentship was determined "by the idea of what would be a sort of prolongation of *His* life. That there should always, in consequence of his having lived, be a young man working in the way he would have liked to work, is a memorial of him that comes nearest to my feeling."[381]

April 29. "The world, in the shape of kind friends and creatures who have claims on my care, is crowding on me before I am quite prepared for it, though I am now determined to live as bravely as I can." By August: nearly 6000 copies of "Theophrastus" had been sold "so that if he had told any useful truths, the medicine has been taken by many." The last letter of 78 (October 15) speaks of "the poor little man" having visitations of gout and cramp, but being "as joyous as ever, and we are intensely happy in our bit of country." At the end of 69 She wishes Mme a happy Xmas with "the dear Kith and Kin. I cling strongly to Kith and Kin, even when they reject *me*."[382]

---

[378] Johann Wolfgang von Goethe (1749-1832) composed the "Proverbs in Prose."

[379] George Anthony Watts (1817-1904)

[380] H, VII, 93

[381] H, VII, 113-114

[382] H, VII, 144

February 5, 1882

These discoveries were naturally intensely agitating. There were a cluster of letters of 69, after the son Thornie's death, then 3 of 78 and many of 79—some giving rather the impression of an increased need of friendship. The last in 78 was touching in its regret for the past frequent intercourse—and the reference to the difference between old friends and new ones, who were like foreigners, with whom everything has to be told, instead of common meaning and knowledge being taken for granted.[383] Mme Bodichon reiterated her belief that Mr. Cross neither could nor would write the Life, and that the mission would and should come to me. She had been told by someone that Mr. Cross's illness at Venice was not the first of its kind. If this were so, and of course She knew it, it throws a flood of light upon the relation, and on Her previous enthusiasm of admiration for one who led so cheerily a busy, useful life in spite of such impending cloud. Madame Bodichon cried for Deronda, though not for Mirah, and would not allow that such a man was impossible though she could not own him to be actual. She said she believed he was at first meant not to marry (and I recalled a passage that would have prepared such conclusion); she said so once to Mr. Lewes, intending the Darling to overhear, who replied "But you know he would not have married any one but Mirah."

February 12, 1882

It is strange to feel oneself in a way knowing Her better now than when we met. One is tempted to mourn over the "too lateness" of one's knowledge—yet it would be harder if everything had ended: I can hardly realize it is so little more than a year ago. I regret most the unsaid words about Her books. It would have cheered, not vexed Her, if I had pointed to the passages which were so much to me. I was always too stupidly shy and reticent: Madame Bodichon, wishing, I think, to say something kind and having no clear memory to go on, said, the relation to me must have been much to Her; She must have felt that she had done me so much good. Like a brute I never let Her know how much she had done to make me less of one. My Darling! Yesterday the last proofs of the little book came: I think Her preoccupation with "Johnny" began immediately on Her return to London, with the coping of the year of widowhood. People live at such a different pace. What a crowded drama was hurried into less than 5 months afterwards.

February 21, 1882

Heard yesterday from Mme Belloc in answer to my note from Scalands which had only just reached her. Went this evening to see her. She only saw the Madonna once in Warwickshire, at the Brays, in 51, but frequently in the next years when she was with the Chapmans. I want to record what's fresh not so much any new facts she told me as her impression. She said the Madonna was very unhappy in those years, full of ambitions—of a mixed kind, for a woman's

---

[383] H, VII, 71

social supremacy mixed with intellectual supremacy. Justice Parkes[384] admired Her very much and always asked Her to meet his choicest guests, Grote,[385] &c, and Mme Belloc thought she would gradually have won the right place for Herself. I know how little any such place would have added to Her happiness. She spoke to Mme Belloc before She joined Mr. Lewes, and after their 9 months in Germany the latter called Her first day and put his arms round the Darling. She did not like Mr. Lewes but volunteered the conjecture which had always been lurking in my mind.—The first Mrs. Lewes avowed that her last three children were Thornton Hunt's: in the world's eyes Mr. Lewes's chief sin was that he knew this and did not cast the woman off. She said and I wholly believe it, that she thought Mr. Lewes forbore in real kindness, mixed with Godwin-ist opinions. Of course he suffered, and he was blamed for that in which he had not sinned and the more *She* felt him to be blamed unjustly the more irresistible became Her longing to sacrifice everything. Mme Belloc spoke of the storm of horror in London when it was known: her father came in, in a white rage as if on the verge of a paralytic stroke. She likes Mr. Cross better than Mr. Lewes *pour le morals*,[386] but thinks he is too big to be intellectual (also too well dressed) but she had imagined a generous purpose in his desire to give Her his name—so that his big, well-dressed person might stand between Her or Her memory and any venomous chatter of the Yaks and Sala tribe[387] raking up evil tales of Mr. Lewes to Her dispraise. Mme B liked Daniel Deronda best of the books, but thought Deronda was more in love with Gwendolyn than Mirah. But her affection for the Madonna was personal, before the books and untouched by them. It was admirable of Bessie to be true to Her in that day of trouble, all the more, the more she disapproved.

March 6, 1882

Poor Miss Williams is not to be helped.—I do not know that it is my fault, when physical sanity is wanting, one cannot count on establishing a fundamentally wholesome relation, and it was not wholesome as we were. If I made any mistakes, I was not unpunished, for it is not pleasant to me to have quoted to any one those most sacred words of Her to me—still less to have made the sacrifice in vain. Poor thing! I am not very fortunate in my attempts to "play with souls" and have "matter enough to save my own." Feel rather on the verge of the old discouragements, doubt how I shall get on without the grind of the School Board to kill time, though even that does not fill up quite time enough. I should like to have a month at "Appropriation" before the election, to see if I can

---

[384] Joseph Parkes (1792-1865), radical solicitor, was Bessie Belloc's father.

[385] See October 30, 1881.

[386] "for his morals"

[387] African people: the Sala Mpasu of Zaire

take up that sort of thing again. Dined with the Lawrences at Wimbledon on Friday, and Mme Belloc called yesterday so have no right to feel specially alone. Was pleased too last Sunday with the Hutcham Liberals: discoursed on Socialism, ancient and modern: they were familiar with the controversy Individualism vs. Socialism and the Chairman, leader of the former section, accepted my view as offering a common ground. Wished for Her to report, as a symptom of the level of intelligence a comment of said Chairman on my version of Platonic ideal—to be the free citizen of a perfect state: which he offered to amend—"the perfect citizen of a free state." Have not mentioned visit from Mr. and Mrs. Charles Lewes a fortnight ago—He offered me a copy of the etching—I would rather be without it. Thought nothing was being done about a bust.

March 31, 1882

Have seen him and his wife since also heard yesterday from Mrs. Stuart that they said nothing was being done about the memoir, Mr. Cross was forbidden all emotional excitement: one connects this with what Mme Bodichon said.

April 16, 1882

On the 3rd returned Eleanor Cross's call; Mrs. Geddes[388] was there; I mentioned the "Echo's" literary intelligence (that Mr. Cross had abandoned the idea of writing) and gathered that they wished him to be content with publishing letters only; she said they attributed his illness to the strain and anxiety of the book: so no doubt the illness is partly of the "nervous" kind—which seems very strange in a man of that size and sort. Since then have been for 2 days at Weyhill, where everything was bright green and blue, sunlit and flowery: except two middle-aged mothers, Mrs. Smith and Mrs. Davis, who told with tears in their eyes of the trouble of a married daughter—married to a bankrupt clergyman who—for the last two years—had left off drinking;—and an unmarried son— engaged to a girl who was getting better—in a lunatic asylum. It struck me that these were the "realities of life" amongst which She had grown up—feeling the intense reality and pathos from the first—"Episodes" I gather from slight signs will fall perhaps even flatter than was to have been expected, and I am such an unnatural monster that I *really* don't care: was very differently anxious about the Essay in Ethics, nearly 5 years ago. It is not substantial enough for real immortality and somehow I don't ambitionate anything less in my private soul. Have been reading Froude's Carlyle[389]—an infinitely tragic story—to his wife; but Carlyle himself, if things go well with us, will find a place in histories of literature as a curiosity scarce large enough to make his searchings of heart momentous: continue reading other odds and ends of books, more than I have of late years, to get back the habit. I shall, in a way, miss the occupation of the

---

[388] Emily Bury Geddes (1841-1929) lived near Guildford.

[389] James Anthony Froude (1818-1894), *Thomas Carlyle. A History of the First Forty Years of His Life 1795-1835* (London: Longmans, Green, 1882).

School Board when I give it up: but I think it will be best. I would serve on the new municipality, if women were eligible (as I fear they won't be), because I am belike the least womanish of available women, the most available for real business of a detailed practical kind: But otherwise it is time I should try my hand at "Appropriation," before I am tempted to think it is too late to begin a big job: other things, which go against the grain, I think I shall by then have earned the right to drop: but I must not be too idle and unsociable. I shall be released just 10 years after my first writing to Her: little as the years have to show for themselves, they have really been less idle than all but the first of the ten years before. I have learnt to make shirts and manage schools, have written two books nay 3—whereof one unpublished—and lived through the love-passion of my life. Heaven knows I have felt idle enough as the time went by and now I begin to wonder how I shall find as much as that to fill the next decade.—For, you see, *all* this came from Her influence.

April 19, 1882

I think when I get launched in it "Appropriation" will be pleasant: one thing I have learnt from the School Board will maybe come in useful—namely the manipulation of statistics. This is a bit of work I want to do for its own sake—I shall do it as well as I can and circumstances beyond my control will determine whether it is to rank as a library classic for one century or more, or whether it only lives its day as not very readable compilation. It is childish to be always fretting and fuming about the size (or non-existence) of one's own genius. Before I knew Her I did not care at all whether other people cared for my bien traduires[390] or not: I cared most painfully for Her approval, but now that I have not that to long for, I think I care only for what comes, nearest that—namely, an objective influence on the side of truth and righteousness. Books *have* an influence: the political economists are answerable for much: an historical critique giving due weight to economical and moral principles *might* give an impetus to thought.—And yet I idle, instead of using up all moments!

April 22, 1882

Begin looking up "Appropriation" notes, in the abortive book, &c. For Thy sake, my sweet one, I will really wrestle masterfully with my great subject. My mind is not incapable; methinks I know what to make of facts when I have taken the trouble to acquaint myself with them. I have allowed myself to look down on Darwin's thinking power—which he, admirable creature! never cackled about—and I ought as a penance to try humbly to imitate something of the adorably patient intelligent industry, whereby he has really done so much for thought as well as knowledge. If I were half as industrious! A small good omen: the "Literary World" praises "Episodes" without complaining of obscurity. I don't believe the "general reader" is as big a fool as Editors and publishers make out, but any way it is an encouraging sign that I can make myself understood of

---

[390] "good sentiments"

the people that this obscure reviewer talks about "bright," "freshness" &c notwithstanding the distinct gloom of 3 of my subjects.

April 30, 1882

A propos of Emerson's death the "Times" notes that the places of well-known men are not filled up as fast as the last years have emptied them. The more need for the great work above I considered. The Academy reviewer (of Episodes)[391] raises in my mind the question "What is imagination?" Is it anything more than keen and intense sensibility, with the power of expression? He talks of my "imaginative power." Now I have distinctly none. Barring the Introduction which amounts to little, every scrap of insight or feeling is taken direct from my own experience. I don't choose to say, or wish to have it guessed, but I am Arnold, I am Reuben, I stand confessed—or 7/14 of confessed—as Eieiaio; when I was eight or nine my dreams were of some discovery that should prove me to be a boy and let me lead forlorn hopes; when I was 18 or 19 I wished to set the world to rights much like Mr. James; and could not see my way (any more than Hecter) towards falling in love; at eight or nine and twenty and onwards I had my period of doubt and darkness; the outcry of the widowed wife represents the shadow that fell on me when She was widowed: the sea and sky consoled me a month or so before She let Herself accept some comfort from Her faithful servant; every word of resignation at the end has been wrung from my soul, slowly, painfully, through nine years of struggling endurance. There is no imagination here, but one thing more I see goes to what produces the effect thereof,—a sense of life's analogies, so that one can confess one's own hidden feeling undisguised in a new framework which disguises our part in it. These three elements made up certainly the greater part of Her creations: She had felt more than other people.

(In the Ms on the page beside May 8 is the comment: Assassination of Lord Frederick Cavendish and Mr. Brooke.)

May 8, 1882

The future of Ireland is made more hopeless than ever. All our private affairs go on—and other public ones, such as they are and one is ashamed of every lapse into levity—with those two innocent men lying dead—a sad, cruel end and one dares not hope that the living will let good be bought by the sacrifice. How She would have grieved. I am too sore to try if the case just sent from Mme Bodichon's letters would hold mine. It is not quite what I wanted and that ruffles me; for the last few days I have felt nervously hurried and fluttered, with a succession of varied worries and engagements. Miss Lankester and National Health Society and Mortimer Street, auditing 19th Century Building Society accounts, attending aggrieved manager's meeting and reporting on Industrial for Pall Mall, Shirtmakers' meeting to arrange &c, and a stupid letter

---

[391] Charles J. Robinson, *Academy* (April 29, 1882), 296-297.

from Mrs. Everest, stupid proofs of my article on Morris[392]—which, with reports of Episodes being found incomprehensible land me in doubts again as to whether "Appropriation" will ever be any good—which if it isn't what is the use of me, since I want to give up manifold worries and work at that alone? I wish I were Lord Frederick Cavendish.

June 4, 1882

On Thursday I went with a "bush of seringa" to Highgate. There were a few withered flowers and a little wire "asleep in Jesus." I filled the glass cross with water and sprays and laid the larger bough round. The ivy round his grave is very fresh, growing thick—as she would have liked to see it. It was afternoon and I noted how far the shadow of her obelisk fell. I would note it too on a December afternoon. If I am not buried within reach of the shadow I would choose my epitaph: "Here lies the body of E. J. S. &c, whose heart's desire lives wherever the name and memory of George Eliot is beloved." The scene was pretty: tears came to me again. My Darling. I have lived—to have loved you suffices me.

I felt very weary and miserable after 2 or 3 days of "sociability" in Oxford, but enjoyed the river and river walks by myself much. The Congress did not come to much, but revived my idea of writing to the Co-Operative organ. I had a vision of reconstructing the Firm at the end of its 7 years' apprenticeship—insisting on all the workers saving; also of a placid, studious 3 years at Oxford, with the Bodleian and the river.

June 6, 1882

Have been looking again at the "data of Ethics" á propos of an Academy review; I think as soon as a decent number of the 2nd edition of Natural Law is sold, I should like to write an Introduction claiming Herbert Spencer's as the real foundation of my scheme and see whether they would sell a 3rd edition.

June 11, 1882

My holidays end today: have written an Academy review, been paid for Morris and had an article on co-operation accepted, so shall not be bankrupt again just yet. Eleanor Cross came yesterday: Mary is very ill, Johnny not well—staying at Sevenoaks poor fellow: he bought his short happiness dear. Was glad that they seemed really to have liked "Episodes."

July 23, 1882

It is more significant than any written entries that I am not tempted to write here for weeks together. I am tired—looking forward eagerly to a month's holiday, for the mere sake of rest, which is something new,—not without promise

---

[392] "Mr. Morris's Hopes and Fears for Art," *Fortnightly Review* (June 1882): 771-779.

of a new pleasure. This evening Charles Lewes has been: bringing me a brooch of Hers.—there is room for hair in it. It will be very precious to me. I hardly know whether I shall keep it in a case to look at; or wear it every day, with a sense of recalling vows every morning and night. Johnny Cross is giving up the Chelsea House quite suddenly. All but the books he or Charles wish to keep are to be given to the "Williams Library."[393] Much of the furniture will be scattered. I hardly know whether I might hint that if they ever did find Her writing table *de trop* I would give all my worldly wealth to redeem it.

September 10, 1882

We came back 2 days ago from a month's round in the Bavarian Alps and Salzkammergut. I was interested in the old towns and could not but find some pleasure in lakes and mountains, but on the whole I got little delight and less rest—was mainly glad to be at home again. Missed Mrs. Congreve yesterday by calling on the Crosses—our travels lay mostly in the region of wayside shrines—one to every body who had been drowned or "killed by a cart" within the last 30 or 40 years, or as long as colours stay distinguishable. I thought the commemorative pictures, with their prayer for the charity of a pater noster, touching; and I wished for an emblem that should speak of things divine in a universal language, to take the place of the misleading crucifix.

October 1, 1882

Have been keeping shop for a fortnight; fancy that the School Board has made "business" a little easier. Have announced my intention not to stand; my last doubts disappeared with some days ailment of my mother. The "History of Ownership" will be enough to keep me out of mischief, without the harress of incompatible claims. I keep talking of that magnum opus as a protest that I mean to think about it when at last the convenient season comes,[394] but I have made no way towards it in these last 3 years. I have also not renounced the thought of a book of secular meditations or devotions. "The Voice of the Crucifix" by the way side in the Tyrol suggested possibilities—one more effort to grasp and continue all that is vital in the religion that grasps a soul completely in proportion to either its depth or narrowness: why cannot a wider grasp be as firm? What is the moral of a suffering God? We have seen embodied goodness wrestling with pain, victorious over pain in the power of love. How does this stir our soul, writhing in selfish misery? We love our suffering friend, we share the pain, we shrink from the endurance even of sympathy, yet our friend endures,—has generous tenderness to spare even in the midst of endurance; the mystery of pain subdues us, loving reverence shuts out rebellion. What is our small pain by the side of this? But human pain is here to be lightened by our love, and we are touched to pity even the pain that is borne amiss—that has been justly earned.

---

[393] At London University. See William Baker, *The Libraries of GE and GHL English Literary Studies*, ed. by Samuel L. Macey (University of Victoria, 1981).

[394] An echo of Acts 24:25

The crucifix represents the sins and sorrows of the world; do not let us make a graven image of this symbol and wring our hearts over the vision of the more than mortal anguish of a superhuman sacrifice; let us strive rather to realize how the mass of sin and sorrow for which a god might die is being added to—in our own house, our own street, in town and village, in every country where the foot of man had trod. Christendom has bowed in awe before this infinitude of woe—because Christ died—(to appease this wrath of God at the sins of man born suffering)—let us look the sin and suffering of man in the face and seek in awe and reverence to make atonement upon earth for the sinners and for the suffering. (The crucifix)[395] Our religion will no longer (then represent the object of our worship)[396] be an idolatry of a pain, but we shall not turn from the crucifix as a false or repulsive symbol; it is sanctified by the memories of ages and we should do well to let it speak to us, as it has to those who understood its voice before, not of sin and suffering atoned for long ago, but of the sin within us and the suffering without for which we ourselves are called yearns to make atonement—to the God within us and the men without.

(In the Ms this note is on page opposite the last part of the entry for October 1, which seems to have been written and rewritten with great anxiety.)

> The sorrows of the world are multiplied by sin; let us
> strive to turn from the sins we know of: the sorrows of the
> world are embittered by passionate resentment, let us not
> forget how to love while we endure; the burdens of the
> world's sorrow can be lightened by our labours and our love:
> in the name of the love which has comforted and the labour
> which has served us, in the name of the bitterness we knew
> when love and help forsook us, let us spare no labour that may help,
> no tenderness that may comfort our sorrowing fellows in their
> weariness and pain.

October 15, 1882

The inequality of moral love in different social circles is quite as remarkable as the varying degrees of theological orthodoxy. Religious feeling must be newly heated, fresh and vivid, to have any effect on the habitual intuitions of social right and wrong. Most religion is inherited from as far back as the intuitions.

It is strange how, since I lost Her, my heart has ceased to hunger for the happiness of love returned. I longed madly for *Her* love. Now I am growing more and more prepared to take up life "at a lower level of expectation." I see the wisdom and even to a certain extent feel a prompting to the course of filling up one's days with smaller interests and distractions—to live more for oneself, as if life were its own end. To follow innocent inclinations without too strict

---

[395] "The crucifix" is marked out.

[396] "Then represent the object of our worship" is marked out.

querying "Is it worth while?" This is what She used to preach, but naturally when I wanted one real thing supremely, I cared for nothing else by comparison with that, I hated every thing else that gave itself the airs of a substitute. I have never had my heart's desire. I have only this,—and this is precious to me beyond everything else I can imagine—a love that death and change have been powerless to change or stay, a sweet unchanging image of my own Beloved and within my soul the sweetness of this boundless love of Her. Having this I have nothing else to long for, the day of small things no longer prompts one's hatred or contempt: nothing is gained by making oneself miserable and I propose to give art, letters and scenery a fair chance of only using my spare moments, while I interest myself seriously in "Ownership." It is true that now and again by night the thought rises "How much trouble it would save if one never woke again!" but for years I have not "indulged" in that reflection. It is one to be put aside unless one means seriously to act on it.

November 2, 1882

Have been occupied with the School Board elections and ought—if I were not too lazy to note a few of one's experiences by way of social and political landmark. Three years ago I wrote such experiences to Her—which of itself disinclines one. I certainly ought, before forgetting details, to set down what struck me most,—viz. the illustration of how popular *malentendus*[397] are got up, and how a misunderstanding which might at the outset have been explained away ends in hostilities that can't. One sees how just the same thing can occur (and does) in the larger political world, in regard to questions that have to be decided by more persons than can be thoroughly instructed concerning them. The danger is least where large interests are known, but I incline to think it is an argument, as far as it goes, for non-intervention in matters not involving the interests of the political agents, though it is also an argument for the widest possible general culture.

November 30, 1882

The School Board has been over for a week, but I have not yet had any sense of leisure. Good books are in the house but I have not had time to read. A visit from Mrs. Paterson, correspondence &c about Rhoda's Erratta,[398] after echoes of the election and so on have filled the week and I am ready for a week or two's rest and quiet before taking up the history. Drove this afternoon with Mrs. Sydney Buxton[399] and did not offend her by frankness as to her husband's

---

[397] "misunderstandings"

[398] Rhoda Broughton (1840-1920) published twenty-six novels which were among the best-selling novels of the time. Her writing was often ungrammatical. EJS reviewed one of her novels in the *Academy*, January 24, 1874. See January 5, 1879 and November 30, 1882.

[399] See March 9, 1880, June 23, 1880 and July 23, 1881.

indiscretions or infirmities of temper. I discovered (for his benefit) that one ought not to be too proud to do electioneering on one's own behalf, because if one agrees to stand, one stands no longer for oneself, but for one's cause, to represent the views one feels to need oneself for representation. Went last night to the "Promise of May." Had a letter yesterday from a reader of "Episodes." Miss Williams is very forbearing.

December 24, 1882

Three weeks and more have slipped by, over nothing in particular, but without any sense of leisure. Have been arranging a Co-Operative Constitution for "Hamilton and Co" and hope before the year—i.e.—the week—is out, to have cleared up old letters and papers and all arrears of work for the "shop." Then, should like to stay at home for a week or two, looking over the old Ms, reading "Sacred Books," and writing draft Introduction. Then begin B. M. R. Have been a little edified by Sir A. Alison's autobiography[400]—good temper and industry make the ponderous old Tory quite an object of liking and admiration in Johnsonian phrase, there was a bottom of rightmindedness in him. Also should take a hint from Samuel Wilberforce—his industry. Saw poor Agnes[401] yesterday. The day before went to Highgate with two wreaths. Wondered at my own calm. Ten years since I saw her: 4 years since his death, two years since Hers. Two years more and the time of loss will equal the six years that were so fondly full of pain. I have not looked at Her letters for months—or a year: but Her influence on one's nature, even more than one's life continues and gathers strength. Hence such calm as makes life less unbearable than it has often been before. At Highgate I was calm enough to go into the office and ask the price of such plot of ground as I wish for. A man was there doing business with the clerk—undertakers it seems have a "discount" allowed. Not being an undertaker, I shall have to pay 15 guineas, but there is time enough, for joining Mr. Lewes's grave there is to be a passage paved with flat stones, and this will not begin I think till the cross rows are filled. It is just possible that they will sell in the same way the other passage, so that one may lie at Her feet.

January 8, 1883

If I am no more diffuse than last year, this book will last on to the nineties; it is rather startling to think one is within 17 years of the next century, and yet I might always have known it would come in my time if I live to be 56! The last week's papers have been full of Gambetta;[402] I am rather glad to find

---

[400] Sir Archibald Alison (1792-1867), *Some Account of My Life and Writings*, edited by his daughter-in-law, Lady Alison. (Edinburgh: W. Blackwood and Sons, 1883).

[401] Agnes Jervis Lewes (1822-1902) lived for more than 50 years in the area around Kensington High Street where she and GHL had lived as husband and wife.

[402] Léon Gambetta (1838-1882)

there is nothing worse to be said against *him, as a politician.* He seems to have been one of the able men, who are not dishonest or unprincipled, but able enough to do great things for the cause they believe in, if opportunity serves them, but they are not quite great enough or devoted enough to any ruling principle to *make* opportunities for moulding the course of events their own way. Gambetta has done good service in establishing the Republic, one would admire him more if he had known more clearly what his Republic was going to do when established: he required opponents to play up to him, to "serve" as in tennis, and then he would make a good hit off very difficult balls. No one seems to draw the moral I do, that Providence has its eyes upon Republics as well as empires and a leading statesman cannot afford to be a loose liver. Gambetta would have been alive and flourishing if his private conduct had been as correct, say, as Fawcett's.[403] Should like to have that moral driven home to young even in France. Except in the technical use of the word "morals" there seems to have been no vice in him,—a good natured man, with a certain genius for ruling, but, a character not sufficiently high pitched all round to keep him uniformly at his best when there was not external provocation or solicitation.

January 10, 1883[404]

I have been maundering about the "History of Ownership" for the last 4 years or more; but have done nothing towards it for the last three years. Have now just begun to read through my notes, made in the end of 79, concerning property in Egypt and Assyria. The School Board and "Episodes" have intervened, and the former has set me forcibly free from Mortimer Street, so that if the History is to come off at all, now is its time. I have underlined the date of this beginning, because one must begin from now to judge the pace of one's work.

January 21, 1883

Have not yet begun regular work; have collected and arranged former introductory remarks, but of course the real introduction is the last thing one writes; the "Contents" is the first and most agreeable.

January 25, 1883

Have not done much in a fortnight—have been waiting for the days *too long* then to go to the Museum to look up a little Egyptian language, etymology and description before finally writing out the "Ownership in Egypt."

---

[403] Henry Fawcett (1833-1884), *Economic Position of the English Labourer,* was a radical Professor of Economics at Cambridge and Postmaster General in Gladstone's government (H, VII, 277, n. 7).

[404] underlined twice in MS

February 11, 1883

Have been reading through all Her letters. Took some comfort from knowing that She can never have imagined half the foolish sensitive selfishness which sometimes turned her innocent words into racks and scourges. I was stupidly silent when for my own sake often I had better have spoken, but in the latter years especially I think she was at ease with me without being indifferent and that might pass for a definition of the natural friendship I was wont to long for so despairingly. I was stirred by the letters to have her brooch inscribed— when I begin to wear it, it will be for always; I almost dread it, like a sacrament of which one may be unworthy. Day and night it would speak to me of Her and how could I look at it after or before the selfish idleness of some of these days? I never read that letter with the sentence "My auguries tell me" without a shock, half unbelief and half passionate desire to do not better, but well enough to excuse her humility for the rash prophecy. Yet I fancy afterward She came to expect less from me—and one's idleness hails that as an excuse for lower aspirations. Any way, do I not owe it to Her to do all I can? My Darling—and by God's help, so I will. I have written to a jeweller about my brooch. I say nothing here of things objective, but yesterday week marks a turning point in the family life. I did not think that life had such shocks left for us.

March 13, 1883

Have not thrown off this depression: have been wasting time over H & Co and find my self very stupid about appropriation. I want to be away—in sight of pleasant things and rest: only can't afford it and feel it to be a vanity and idleness to wish. Mr. Green and poor young Toynbee[405] are dead. Am reading Carlyle's letters to Emerson,[406] with a feeling that the poor fellow did his best, and so is not to blame,—to praise rather for just as much good as came of his doing. Have done nothing all the morning. Might say, looking at an entry last April, have done nothing all the year: and to make the history even all that I know can be tried for is a big business. Too big for me I am tempted to fancy, but like poor Carlyle I will do it as I can. Time that used to move so slowly has taken to trotting. I have been more than 3 months off the Board and have not once felt the depression of unemployedness. Next week the day comes when I have meant to begin wearing Her brooch—ten years that day from the time of what I used to think of as my "conversion":—the beginning of it rather, for I am not yet wholly "turned" from evil—as indeed how can one hope to be completely? I have put off this wearing in a kind of cowardice, distrusting my power to be continuously good and industrious afterwards and dreading to add a touch of sacrilege to one's omissions by falling into them in the talisman's despite.

---

[405] Arnold J. Toynbee (1852-1883) was on the Committee for the Women's Protective and Provident League.

[406] Charles Eliot Norton (1827-1908) brought out an edition of Carlyle's letters to Emerson in 1883.

April 1, 1883

I wear it always indoors; not out for fear of accident; and am never unconscious of wearing it.

May 12, 1883

In the last 6 weeks have finished writing out what is still only a first draft of the first section on Egypt, have spent a fortnight at Shottermill—found much pleasure in the tranquil but varied views from endless lovely tracks over the hills, and this week was for 2 days at Lye, among the nailmakers. Saw Mrs. Green on Thursday; am somewhat rested and much ashamed of having spent 4 months in rearranging the forgotten notes. Should be better pleased if China were finished in 3 months—by the 12th of August.

June 14, 1883

Have been somewhat hindered with Mortimer Street, but have got through yule, a good deal of Legge, Richthofen[407] &c and have written some first draft. Dim hopes that I daren't indulge are held out to us of a company (with Co-Operative clause) buying Mortimer Street. Then I should have paid my taxes for life! The ownership can't and shan't be hurried. Richthofen is a model, but between ourselves I am beginning to wonder whether I am a very eminent author! however this time also I will do my best. The Episodes episode fills me with amazement—my mind is a blank now in that direction. I couldn't invent even a landscape.

July 21, 1883

Decidedly I don't think my mind is as good as it used to be: *si jeunesse savait!*[408] I know now what I want to do and must see if taking pains will make up. Except for the calamity mentioned in February, I have been more placidly contented this year than ever within my memory: it seems after outgrowing the troublesomely vehement appetites of youth I am learning now for the first time to find satisfaction in the commonest pleasures of existence. Let us imagine it is the virtue of my brooch. It comes to me that I haven't seen "Johnny" for two years. I am rather glad *not* to see him, but wonder with a rather ironic smile whether if out of the body She could revisit us now whether she would be kind and admit that it wasn't *my* fault! I am in some terror as to what his book will be like—poor fellow.

(In the Ms this published poem was cut out and taped in journal on page opposite August 20.)

---

[407] Baron Ferdinand Paul Wilhelm Richthofen wrote extensively on China; *Ergebnisse eigener Reisen unddar auf gegündeter studien* (5 Bde. Berlin, 1877-1912; *Atlas*, 1885).

[408] "if youth but knew"

Then a man shall work and bethink him, and rejoice
in the deeds of his hand,
Nor yet come home in the even too faint and weary
to stand.

Men in that time a'coming shall work and have no fear
For to-morrow's lack of earning and the hunger-wolf anear.

O strange new wonderful justice! But for whom shall we
gather the gain?
For ourselves and for each of our fellows, and no hand
shall labour in vain.

Then all *mine* and all *thine* shall be *ours*, and no more
shall any man crave
For riches that serve for nothing but to fetter a
friend for a slave.

And what wealth then shall be left us when none shall
gather gold
To buy his friend in the market, and pinch and pipe
the sold?

Nay what save the lovely city, and the little house
on the hill,
And the wastes and the woodland beauty, and the
happy fields we till.

And the homes of ancient stones, the tombs of the
mighty dead;
And the wise men seeking out marvels, and the poet's
teeming head.

And the painter's hand of wonder; and the marvellous
fiddle-bow,
And the banded choirs of music:—all those that do
and know.

For all these shall be ours and all men's, nor shall
any lack a share
Of the toil and the gain of living in the days when
the world grows fair.

"Such," says the singer, "are the days that shall be."
"But what," he asks, "are the deeds of to-day?"

O why and for what are we waiting, while our brothers
droop and die,
And on every wind of the heavens a wasted life goes by?

How long shall they reproach us where crowd on crowd
they dwell,
Poor ghosts of the wicked city, the gold-crushed
hungry hell?

Through squalid life they laboured, in sordid grief
they died.
Those sons of a mighty mother, those props of
England's pride.

They are gone; there is none can undo it nor save
our souls from the curse;
But many a million cometh, and shall they be better
or worse?

It is we must answer and hasten, and open wide the door
For the rich man's hurrying terror, and the slow-foot
hope of the poor.

Yea, the voiceless wrath of the wretched, and their
unlearned discontent,
We must give it voice and wisdom till the waiting-tide
be spent.

Come then, since all things call us, the living and
the dead,
And o'er the weltering tangle a glimmering light
is shed.

Come then, let us cast off fooling, and put by
ease and rest,
For the CAUSE alone is worthy till the good days
bring the best.

Come, join in the only battle wherein no man can fail,
Where whoso fadeth and dieth, yet his deed shall still
prevail.

Ah! come, cast *off* all fooling, for this, at least,
we know:
That the Dawn and the Day is coming, and forth the
Banners go.

August 20, 1883

It is 6 years less a day since I quoted with feeling Byron's "Through life's dull road so dim and dirty, I have dragged to three and thirty." Let youths to come take comfort from my verdict—it seems less dim and the turf on the downs was elastic as I did 20 odd miles by Arundel to Worthing. Since then I have passed some melancholy hours; have been alone at home; re-read some "Middlemarch" at night and recalled the memory of old foolish misery. Was thrilled through and through again as always by that book which is still to me the one in which Her whole very self speaks plainest. These memories will never be more sad to me than now: there is nothing unbearable: Ich habe genoßen desirdischen Glückes.[409]—If Mortimer Street is off my hands I ought to have a vol ready to open the next decade, but I do not build on any great success for the History of Ownership—my happiness does not depend on that—She would not have loved me the more for being able to write a book worthy of Her name—only for having in my self the desire after all such worthiness. It would be intolerable to me to think that the life of one who loved Her wholly should be a palpable failure. But, besides the quantity of objective achievement, the artistic completeness of each individual life depends much, as Herbert Spencer would say, on the completeness of the adjustment between external and internal relations. For instance there is a pathetic flaw in the life of a born mother who dies unmarried: for me the flaw would have been to live in a phase of society that made marriage a thing of course, spoiling my life and perhaps hindering my love. One can love one's mother and one's Lady—not one's Lady and any other lord.—Then again a life as solitary as mine would be a failure to one like Her who *needed* that consciousness of a wide response to the outflowing of Her own nature but I never felt the need of any love but Hers and my love for Her and the memory of Her sweet kindness is enough to fill with bloom and fragrance all the days of the years of my life.

September 23, 1883

The good Morris[410] always stirs my conscience to aspirations that make me think of Her. I am now bent on freeing myself from Mortimer Street—for

---

[409] "I have tasted the fulness of bliss below" or "I have enjoyed earthly happiness," Schiller: *Gedichte*. Des Mädchens Klage; also Die Piccolomini, III, 7.—(Thekla.)

[410] William Morris (1834-1896) was one of the founders of the Socialist League in 1884 and was one of the most vocal literary supporters of socialism. He was member of the Democratic Federation, the first editor of *Commonweal* (1885), and a delegate to the Interational Socialist Congress at Paris, 1889. On May 25, 1886, Morris wrote to his daughter Jenny that the "meetings went off well on Sunday. Miss Simcox was not bad!" (Kelvin Norman, *The Collected Letters of William Morris*, 2 vols., Princeton University Press, 1984, II, 552). EJS had lectured on "Sober Socialism" before the Hammersmith Branch of the Socialist League on May 23 (*Commonweal*, May 22, 1886, 64).

which I have done all it is in me to do, ending with an appeal to others to do more. Have just been reading again some of her letters—very sweet they are. My interest in books—of a kind—has come back and I shall not be afraid of *ennui*[411] if I get all my time for "Ownership."

November 11, 1883

A fortnight yesterday, the 27th went over alone to Paris for the International Workmens Conference, the determining motive being that She had wished me to go to Lyons in 76. There is no one now to whom I have to write all my story as I should have done to Her, yet I ought not to let it escape me, so that it is as if to Her that I write. My own Darling! She would have followed the story with pleasure. Arriving about 6, after tea I tried to find my way to the office of the reception Committee, 49 Rue de Clèry, but lost my bearings after the first start and came round and round bewilderedly till I gave it up. Next morning called at the Hotel du Prince Albert, Rue de Hyacinthe, where the English brethren were staying and took a North country man, Trow and his wife round to the Louvre, seeing the Egyptian things I wanted. We were invited to repair at 4 to a "friendly reception" at a "Taverne Grueber," Boulevard Street Dimis (in Montmartre) and I hesitated a little before making my way in through the crowd outside a third rate *café*, however, (as I have observed before) whatever queer places one finds oneself in; the people of it seem to find one's presence quite natural, and I made my way up unnoticed to the "Circle" au primier. There was a gathering of men in numbers about such as at Radical Club on Sunday evening, they asked if I minded smoke. Was introduced to Joffrin of the Municipal Council, and hastened to ask him about the inspectresses of workshops: was told it wasn't serious; they are paid 2000 francs only, and the better are sinecures given to lady friends of the Councillors who have some "protection" which the others of course haven't. Any woman who began to report and hunt down abuses would be slandered and got rid of. Complimentary speeches were exchanged and I had to let the brethren pay for a glass of iced pomegrante syrup for me! A Mr. Whiteing, correspondent of the Manchester Guardian, attached himself to me and walked back and I profited by his escort to get Zola's[412] "Bonheur des Dames." Monday at 10 Joffrin came to the Hotel to guide the Brethren to the Hotel de Ville, they hadn't all breakfasted and he was afraid of keeping Costa, the Italian, waiting, so I walked off with him, leaving the others to follow. I thought Hamerton had rather over praised the building; our men depreciated the workmanship, Broadhurst said they would have better panelling in a Methodist Chapel at home, and Burnett the Engineer reminded the mason that accuracy in the matter of joints was after all the speciality of the metal workers. They also criticised the scaffolding, the weight of the planks and the unscientific tying,— weights resting on unsupported ends &c. The first meeting of the Conference— (an International *Congress* would have been illegal) was due to begin at 2:30, but

---

[411] "boredom"

[412] Émile Zola (1840-1902), French naturalist

we soon found an hour's grace was the usual thing. The French at once moved Broadhurst into the Chair; he was much frightened and his friends advised him to decline with thanks for fear what the proceedings might be. It was explained that they had a fresh president for each sitting so that it was a matter of pure compliment, and I urged him not to hurt their feelings by refusing, so he was appointed with Allemane[413] for an auxiliary. The proceedings were a little tame to me, as the Englishman did most of the speaking, however we sent a fraternal greeting to all the world and met again in the evening at 5:30 to begin the real business. Dr. Brousse[414] opened and after some expression of English vs. French views on International labour laws a committee was appointed to draft a resolution embodying the points of agreement. Next day I made an abortive attempt to get into the Chamber for the Tonguin Interpellation and returned at past 4 to find the conference not yet resumed and the Committee still at war about the terms of the resolution. When these were at last hurriedly agreed on, the English were not quite satisfied and the French though murmuring with good reason at the unparliamentary changeableness referred the resolution back to the Committee with the addition of the ladies as linguists. It was really a question of patience in translating backwards and forwards and I finally got Burnett's draft done into French and back into literal English to reassure Broadhurst and 'twas finally accepted without further debates next afternoon, though too late for reporting to public meeting that (Monday) evening. This meeting was well attended: I thought the audiences cooler than English; they don't applaud favorite speakers when they come forward and the speakers don't praise each other. There is no "vote of thanks" except *from* "the Chair" to the meeting at its close. The Italian anarchists who came to make a row against Costa were of three types,—interesting to see in the flesh, a pretty young fellow, whom I should have liked to have photographed in character, a perfect little demon, a little fiend of fury; the next who spoke had got his shirt torn open to the waist, and looked the sort of figure for a barricade; the third, an unwashed, unshaved, ill favoured citizen in a blouse, wished to speak after the meeting was dissolved and when I asked him politely what he wanted to say, turned from me with a gesture of the most magnificent and aristocratic scorn! In general the Frenchman seemed to me to take less notice of the women as such, than English Unionists, but also to treat them more entirely as equals. Wednesday afternoon for example la citoyenne[415] Simcox was moved "au bureau,"—and rather enjoyed according *la parole*[416] with

---

[413] Jean Allemane, a French printer, socialist, and journalist, who was sentenced to hard labour for life because of his participation in the Commune in 1871; he became one of the leaders of the workers' party and formed the revolutionary socialist group (McK, 45).

[414] Dr. Paul Brousse (1844-1912), French medical man, was one of the most active members of the International (McK, 45).

[415] "citizen"

[416] "right to speak"

great impartiality to the citzens who handed in their names—mostly very well written. This was to me the most interesting of the meetings as a number of the natives spoke about trade details instead of political commonplaces. The closure was adopted without reluctance though several speakers had not been heard. At the evening meeting, which was not full, Brousse made a sober Parliamentary speech about the foreigners in Paris—the English being money spenders and living in rich quarters, while the Italians, Germans and Belgians mostly live in working class districts. Allemane who was the most warmly received, ventured to tell them that the vice and indifference of workmen themselves was the worst difficulty in their way. He and Joffrin did not gain as speakers by repetition, one seemed to come to the end of their ideas and without a practical campaign to organize they must get tiresome or violent for want of concrete applications to vary the circumstances. On approaching the Salle Lévis I thought at first that a meeting was going on, the chant of a vendor of Revolutionary pamphlets was so continous; I had helped myself from the *étalege*[417] round the hall and was much amused by his "Comptoir chère citoyenne"[418] as I proposed to pay for them. I spoke from notes, saying about what I had meant, but finding even in a foreign tongue that preparation is embarrassing. Thursday morning I went to see Mme Roger, breakfasted and fraternized with her, then assisted at the two sittings which decided the third and most actively "International" of the resolutions in favor of abrogating laws that the Dufaure of 1872 against international associations. Tortellier objected that the English trade Societies were let alone because they did the enemy no harm, an accusation against which Joffrin defended them. The next day went with Drummond, King, and Allemane, the homme de métier[419] over l'Imprimerie Nouvelle,[420] and in the evening had an hour with Davey, the tailor, at the Chambre Syndicale of that ilk; the sweaters' labourers are called *les boeufs*[421]—earn about 4 francs a day. Got to Belleville in time enough, a friendly, rather English sort of audience. A Spanish compositor argued in French of Spain that workmen ought to earn enough to keep their wives without other work than the domestic stocking. Poor Mr. Heatherly made what appears to have figured as the one joke of the conference, passing from the study of languages to International marriages and the great product of civilisation an international child! That evening Whiteing handed me a telegram from his paper asking for impressions of the Congress at 3 francs a column—a first installment

---

[417] "display"

[418] "trading fair dear citizen"

[419] "professional"

[420] "news printing office"

[421] "the oxen"

of which I sent off on Saturday, going also to call on Mr. Hodgson Pratt[422] with whom I left the question of the Inspectresses. He had come to the English hotel with an impassioned Provencal of the name of Lionnet, who was very angry with the Parti Ouvrier for claiming to represent French workmen's Associations: the moniteur des chambre syndicales[423] took a very hostile tone towards the Conference and Mr. Pratt was afraid we had come to the wrong shop, but got reassured by Simonone—whom by the way I was to have seen, but did not. After a good deal of hesitation I determined to go to the "Banquet and Ball" as my only chance of acquainting with any of the women, though 'twas at variance with my normal practice in England. The fact is I had been getting kindled (my beloved One!) at finding myself by the side of men who had suffered imprisonment, exile and risks such as are a thing of the past with us; I felt somewhat ashamed of our cheap and respectable philanthropy and I saw myself in imagination proposing for fraternal commemoration: "the dead, the wounded and the captives of the war for liberty." In truth I did not go so far as this, but when I was set on to speak to the friendly Bellevillois after hearing that the Daily Telegraph had already turned me into a pétroleuse[424] for my former moderate and diplomatic effusion, my tongue was loosened and I spoke not without vivacity—of the release of Louise Michel,[425] the organization of women's labour and the commonwealth of nations, with a little trite eloquence reflected from the warmth of the friendly applause. Adolphe Smith who had been pining for a little Buncombe to make the Englishmen's speeches go off faster was delighted and thought we had at last got the right thing in the right place, but when shortly afterwards a bevy of hard featured elderly women—one with very crazy eyes—came up and proceeded to embrace me on both cheeks, I was basely reminded of Henriette in the Femmes Savantes and wondered for a moment whether I could be Henriette? and Louise Michel Bélise![426] However I resigned myself and felt as if there were certainly something of 1789 in the air, the nice looking, smart, young dress makers were

---

[422] Hodgson Pratt (1824-1907) was active in the industrial co-operative movement and in 1880 helped to found the International Arbitration and Peace Association.

[423] "supervisor of the trade union chamber"

[424] "firebrand"

[425] Louise Michel was a Parisian school teacher, who was deported to New Caledonia for her part in the Commune; after the amnesty of 1880 she returned to Paris, gave anarchist lectures, and was punished again and again for her anarchist acts and speeches. She was also the author of several books (McK, 49, n. 1).

[426] In Molière's Les femmes savantes (1672) Henriette is simple, charming, and unaffected in contrast to the affected Bélise who is a devotee of the new cult of grammar, philosophy, and astronomy.

content to shake hands and I was soon in interesting converse with some of them. I should say that I had sat by Allemane at the dinner—and had a good deal of talk with him, and allowed myself to preach some. He said very naively that as long as people were only stupid and did not know, he was capable of infinite patience and douceur,[427] but he could not stand it when the rights of things had been clearly put before them so that they *must* understand and they still persisted in not admitting what was plain. I submitted that that was a common and miserable complaint and that there were people who would remain honestly in error to their dying day; the thing was to work with people as far and as long as they would work with you even though they would not go all the way: urging him to be as patient with the Union des Chambre Syndicales as with the English delegation. He said one couldn't always be *de bonne humeur*,[428] instancing rather pathetically, the difficulties of getting a living, of keeping clear of the police and then being bothered by stupid and self-seeking talkers. He introduced me to his wife and 3 children the youngest a very fraternal baby of 4 months who clasped my finger confidingly and let itself be kissed by any number of citizens. After this I had some talk with two women one who lost her husband in the Commune—and doesn't dare to say so to the ladies whose dresses she makes. I was sitting with them when an elderly citizen approached and begged me to come and make his daughters' acquaintance—introduced me to wife, aunt, daughters, married and otherwise and son in law. The married daughter was very *empressée*[429] and I am seriously half inclined to regard *her* as our *agente provocatrice*[430] of the police! for somewhat as years ago at Mortimer Street poor Miss Newbery put her arm round my waist and by main force lifted me onto the ground and made me dance a polka with her, so this wretched young woman, by force that I could only have resisted by a real struggle, dragged me into the ring that was circling to the words of the Carmagnole—which, by the way, the dancers knew very imperfectly. I was really not responsible and carried off a resolve not to fraternize too easily with citizens to whom I hadn't been introduced. I intend to see how far it will be possible to help the episode to assume a mythical aspect:—as I can honestly deny having *sung* the profane ditty I hope the rest of it will soon come to pass for an imaginative legend. The unaminous recommendation of unionism and international intercourse between unions, and the absence of any narrow hostility towards "foreign competition" were the most encouraging features and I really had the feeling of assisting at an "historic moment" in the intercourse of peoples. *Mem*: I want to learn a little practical Spanish and Italian conversation before a congress in Turin.

---

[427] "gentleness"

[428] "in a good mood"

[429] "attentive"

[430] "agitator"

(In Ms this note is on the page opposite the entry for November 24.)
I asked Tom about the "underhands" in his trade and he
says they don't belong to the society but 'tis their
fault—adding naively, that they are employed by the
peddlers and so have nothing to do with the masters.

November 24, 1883

I omitted to enter memos of the interesting conversation I had with
Drummond, the compositor and Davy the tailor, on the way back. Latter was
very strong about the folly of Parlimentary Committee in the Juggins business,
and also about the villeisage a deserving little society of "hammermen" had
suffered from the boiler-maker's society. The skilled artizians used to be paid at
the rate of 12/ and the hammermen 8/ for their respective shares in a common
job, and this worked fairly for if the boiler maker played 2 days and slaved for the
rest of the week, his man who slaved too had the same chance as himself of
making up a week's earnings. The boiler makers however insisted on paying the
hammermen day wages, and crushed their society, having got the ear of the
committee appointed to arbitrate at Bristol, where the hammermen were
inadequately represented. Drummond married on 8/ a week, before he was out of
his apprenticeship, because his father was unkind to him, though he was a very
good boy. Cassell's firm is called the "stone-yard" in the trade and they have a
bad custom of paying day wages and expecting the hands to earn about 20%
more (at piece work prices) than they are paid. This custom was at last resisted
by the men and referred to arbitration, but Tom Hughes, the umpire, was easily
led to give it against the men who thought their case had not been fairly stated.
Drummond had an amusing story of how an advertisement warning men against
seeking work on account of a trade dispute acted the other way and brought up a
heap of unemployed. Have been exchanging pretty revolutionary letters with the
dear Morris.

December 23, 1883

Yesterday I went to Highgate—perhaps it is best to go only once a
year. The ivy that was so slow at rooting is now abundant. I wish the like might
be planted round the stone coping of the later grave—since the two may not be
quite alike. I think no one goes but me. As usual I laid my twin wreaths then—
in a thickening crowd, though my two passages are still unappropriated. I came
away dry eyed. The thought of Her is not a memory or a regret: it blends with the
knowledge driven home by that moving preface to poor Green's last book[431]—
The night cometh wherein no man can work.[432] Her old feeling begins to grow
upon me—that life is sacred, because death is near.

---

[431] John Richard Green (1837-1883) was a historian; EJS refers to *Conquest of
England* (London: Macmillan, 1883). See June 9, 1879 and March 13, 1883.

[432] John 9:4

January 27, 1884
On Friday evening, the 25th, we finally signed the document which completes my release from Hamilton and Co. By February I shall thus really be quite free for Ownership and general "causes." It must be confessed I am secretly exceedingly rejoiced. I propose to work steadily each morning at China, to go out most days, or when fine between luncheon and tea, do what idling or light literature I am tempted to (or letters) then and read something relevant to Ownership in the evening—going to bed not later than 11:30 and breakfasting not later than 8:30. With 4 hours writing and 4 hours reading I shall overhaul my materials and I hope not lose grip of the subject. On the whole think it better to go ahead with China now and hark back to finish Egypt afterwards.

February 1, 1884
On the 29th went to Stepney to "Poor Men's Politics" on Rack rents. Local Committee appointed on which I serve. Was a little depressed by observing that the audience, with less political information and wide awakeness than I am accustomed to at Radical Club or say, in Southwark and decidedly less enthusiasm for fine moral sentiments, was rather more violent in an unpractical sort of way and applauded with laughter a vehement bill-sticker of the old revolutionary sort who gave me pamphlets of his own composition, one of which proved to be of the Bradlaugh-Besant school. They seemed about at the French workman's level, *minus* the literateness of the best of these.

February 22, 1884
Since then the Committee has met—from 30 to 40 sensible, respectable men—some very poor: a most creditable result of self-election from an open meeting. Mr. Peach moved the constitution of my "Lodger's League." Have also been to Oxford on a quaint errand—to "read a paper" on Women's Work, at an assemblage of town and gown in a room at Balliol and yesterday corrected proofs of the autobiography of a shirtmaker;[433] have also cleared up all letters and papers and Mss, School Board accumulations &c, so am really and truly free for ownership now—have no claims on my time except my mother's occasional days of invalidedness. I intend to try and keep this tenants and lodgers defense league going—and growing, but that is only enough to keep one alive. We have Her last words now: there is one sentence of great weight, which I think would have once grieved me much; but it is true, and where the joy of intercourse is unequal, what more natural than that the love should be so too?—But one has the love-bearing joy and the joy in the love that is borne. She has made the happiness and the contentment of my life. It struck me, just as curious, not as any way vexatious, in looking through my letters that there was a total absence of self-regarding ones— letters that come for my pleasure or wants: they are either the fruit of old ties "which it seems unduteous to break" or purely objective, people who want

---

[433] This refers to the article which EJS published as "Eight Years of Co-Operative Shirtmaking," *Nineteenth Century* 15 (June 1884): 1037-1054.

April 6, 1884

Yesterday afternoon went to Hillside, Highgate, to claim Charles Lewes's promise to show me some of the parts in the notebook which he had not reprinted. The longest I thought he was right not to print, though if I were Mr. Cross I should use it, the latter part especially: it begins with remarks about social "continuity" and then discusses the present and future chances of a "priesthood." C. Lewes thought it too "positivist" but in fact it is a valuable criticism of the pretensions of that hierarchy; it comes to no precise conclusion, the future not to be bound by our guesses, but the ground is kept clear for an ideal of a teaching order which shall not exactly be limited to teaching what the scholars desire to learn though it shall not be suffered to inherit any power to tyrannise. The other piece on "Conformity" I should like to publish almost if not quite *in extenso*. C. Lewes said it was curious, written perhaps to clear her own mind by stating the opposite side to the one she generally took. I thought it expressed the deliberate conclusion of Her reason as against inclination and temperament. It stated the case of a rationalist living in an average country parish, or one even less troubled than the average by dissent, manufacturing neighbors or changing population. The Church stands for a sort of vague embodiment of order and right-reasons rather deeper than can be seen for doing what we ought, and a common law to which Sir John's dealings with the wheelwright are as much subject as the latter's conduct towards the blacksmith. Then She states the case for congregational sympathy and tolerance which desires to avoid offending other consciences, putting the case without difficulty in quite all its strength. Then on the other hand it has to be considered what is the service in which you are invited to take part. Prayers which rest throughout on a false assumption as to the kind of causes at work in the world; sermons which appeal to unreal motives, both stuffed with appeals to imaginary facts. Then as to the effect of our non-conformity—of two things one, either the opinion of orthodoxy is so strong in the locality that our absence from church is more likely to cause practical inconvenience to ourselves than mental distress to our neighbours or the public mind is already unsettled in which case we ought to strive to help it towards the acceptance of new truth rather than probing a moribund belief in error. Therefore she says definitely, do not conform. Two or three sentences on ethics at the beginning might I think have been printed with advantage. He asked if I had not got letters from Her and if I had sent them to Mr. Cross. I said he had not asked me and I was glad he had not. He that I ought to offer them, as Cross does not like to ask—apparently is afraid of being refused, or of being expected to print all that are shown him, instead of using them at his discretion. I said I did not want too many letters given *in extenso*, not enough to challenge criticism of Her as a letter writer. He said that the best letters as such were those written before she took to authorship. The note book was in the same exquisite hand-writing—neatly paged and indexed and he showed me other note books, one with alphabet cut by Her and oriental notes, one with skeleton for a 3 act tragedy to be written some day if they went to Sicily, also notes for the novel just begun which Mr. Cross destroyed. A great deal of reflection and workmanship went to the building up of the naturalness of the course of events in most of Her books. Have some reason to hope that I may have stopped a little house building job in Soho. (Alas! No)

May 4, 1884

I never knew the months go so fast and have so little to show for themselves. Putter for hours almost every day over China and make very little way; much less and I'm afraid certainly no better than when I began Egypt in 79 or the abortive book in 75; however there will not in future be so much waste time in picking up the threads of old reading. Last Monday and the preceeding Sunday week had a new experience in "League" meetings; the latter called at 5 p.m. on Sunday to attract Polish Jews, Moeatta in the chair. The Jewish Chronicle has recently been inserting some sensational articles upon letters by a new factory inspector, and these had brought up the local sweaters *en masse*, few women and two masters about to every one man:—whence a row. At the subsequent meeting for women only there were some mistresses, but the mass present were workers who put the dots on the i's of the men's speeches in a very instructive way. The notorious grievances are long hours,—any time from 6 a.m. to midnight or even later, Thursday being always the longest day and the result of these long days being that half the week is on an average short time, and that even when the day wages are normally 4/ the *week* wages never come near 24/ or even £1. Moreover since several tailors were fired for breaches of the factory act, they began to work from 8 to 8 paying for this legal day only as 3/4 — 3/= instead of 4/=. The idea of 1/2 an hour for tea-time was laughed to scorn, the food is put by them and they bite and drink as they work, and dinner is little better. The girls were a rather, larky, saucy lot;—*not* very poor and not likely to do much in the way of combination. A woman said afterward the Jews would "hold by their own"—and it is possible in a way that a sweater of the chosen people does show more of the inexpensive humanities to her girls than a Christian of the same order.

May, 17, 1884

Have been with Mrs. Paterson to see the secretary of one of the masters' Societies—not a bad fellow who began by assuring us that we were all misinformed and then practically volunteered information to just the same effect. Last Sunday Jung came about "International" talk, I suggested that we should get names and particulars of as many Continental *Trade* Societies as possible and urge the Parliamentary Committee to send to them a circular asking if they adhere to the 3 resolutions of the Conference.—The answers to be had before next Congress at Aberdeen which would then doubtless authorize invitations to foreign unionists to attend the Congress of 85.

June 19, 1884

After finishing in about 110 pps of print, the first draft of the first half of history of China I have put the Ms aside, idled for a week at Weyhill, done a review or two for the Academy and some promiscuous "propagande," have met polyglot tailors at "The Brown Bear" Fishman Street, Whitechapel on Sunday night and remained in conclave with them till the legal hour for closing: have had the problem of open air preaching brought before me, being invited by the Lodgers' League to hold forth on "Whitechapel Work" and as I have not intimated as much to a living soul, I may confess here that I am somewhat exercised in spirit as to whether my respectability does not draw the line on the hither side of stumping on the waste. My doubt is not wholly a base cowardice; I should not mind preaching to a crowd that wanted to hear and could not afford a hall, but I don't like competing with street preachers and the rest for the ears of mere loafers. Wasted a day in preparing a very short speech, not all delivered, for great suffrage meeting at St. James Hall: learnt 2 things from the experiment, that my voice will fill a Hall that size, and that a prepared sentence does not necessarily come to grief. Have ascertained that Broadhurst will do nothing international; and yesterday and today have been visiting Jew tailors' workshops. I got this book out to make notes of what we have been told on both sides. Large masters complain of small masters underselling for work and over bidding for wages. Small masters and men say it is the larger masters who underbid on condition of getting "the quantity." Common complaint that men set up as tailors who don't know the work and "spoil the trade." One man said he used to be busier out of the season than he is now in it. We were assured everywhere that the girls leave work at 8, and *only* work 11 hours, and were told they were paid 5/, 4/ and 3/ a day, but judging from the numbers of shops where they were not at work today, the busiest of the week, one could judge that the number of days' work in the week was not likely to exceed the average a master mentioned— about 3. One man and his wife complained of the people with families who would work underprice rather than feed their children while they were doing nothing; also said the men preferred to spend their time in the numerous gambling houses all round, where they have a speaking tube to send up word if a suspicious stranger is about. Smith tried to get an introduction to these houses with a view to "copy" and asked what games they played, a girl volunteered "brag." The work rooms were either 3rd floor or back yard. "Plumber's Row," which I selected because of the number of shops, consists of 3 roomed cottages with an underground kitchen and a work shop built in the back yard:—rent for this £1 a week and when the rain comes in at the roof the landlord says he has nothing to do but take the rent. The man here welcomed the suggestion of a "strike" against rents. In most cases the masters were civil, though in some a little anxious to be plausible, but one had only to allude to the badness of trade to set them off on quite sincere denunciations of the want of union and public spirit &c among tailors. Of course the shops we visited are those of the higher class of tailors (though one man was doing shop work—a man's pea jacket for 1/9 at which he said himself he had to work 18 hours for he should starve on what he could earn in 12). Some were clean, and in none were the tenants to blame for the unsatisfactory state of the premises.

June 22, 1884

The next day we found rents not quite so high 18/ for a 6 roomed house with the darkest and most delapidated staircase we have come to yet, and 15/ for a much larger and better house with a ramshackle lean to workshop, in Varden

Street not much east of Plumber's Row. We saw a coat, much superior to the 7/9 pea jacket and braided all round for 1/6. This man grew quite sympathetic and confidential, while his girls (of course he swore) all left work at 8, he and his sons worked from 6 to 10; I quoted this to another man who got 9/ to 8/ for not very different coats and he was very scornful and indignant, *he* would never work more than from 8 to 9. I suggested that was a good deal too long. He also boasted of paying a man 7/ a day = 42/ a week and girls 3/ a day. I asked how many days in the week they worked and then he said sometimes 5 (i.e. never 6 so 35/ would be the maximum) sometimes 4, sometimes 3, and a young man added sometimes one! We also went to several shops where they professed to employ no girls now—they couldn't afford it,—girls were too much trouble—you have an order to finish and the girls must leave at 8 whether or no, and they won't come in at 8—it is 1/2 past or 1/4 to 9 and if you stop 6 for being late they won't stand it.

July 13, 1884

We are off in 2 days for Switzerland, where I mean to see if climbing will brighten my wits a little as a preparation for putting on a spurt with "Ownership": when Egypt and China are finished the end of vol 1 will be comparatively in sight. It is nearly 6 years since my last taste of the wildjoy of a fortunate lover—my one visit to Witley. It would not be hard to count the moments of such pleasure which formed the landmarks in the 6 years before, but it is only when happiness seems as if it might be in reach that it is so hard to do without it. If barren of anything that can be called delight, the last 3 years have been more free from pain than any one of the three such periods before.

September 6, 1884

We came back a week ago and I don't find my wits as much improved as I should have liked though I myself was more refreshed than by the Bavarian tour. The itinerary was Paris, where the "parti ouvrier" continued to miss the interview I asked for. Admired the work, but not the monotonous subjects of Meissonier[434]—the street view of a barricade after the fight was gloomily instructive—and one would have thought one specimen of each of his types of subject admirably true and living. But his works like Alma-Tademas'[435] don't gain by being seen together; I think for them to do so an artist must have some variety of meaning and intellectual range. Pleasant afternoon drive in Bois de Boulogne and stroll in through Elyace—Streets still gay with flags and little girls had their hair tied up with tricolor ribbons in honour of the fête on Monday. Through to Lucerne by a fine thunder storm which lighted up the line for moments. Some days rain: read idly Tanchinty novels and walked from Beckenried to Bauen; the rest by water; Swiss soldiers singing prettily on the

---

[434] Jean Louis Ernest Meissonier (1815-1891), a French artist, whose work is frequently compared to that of Alma-Tadema

[435] Sir Lawrence Alma-Tadema (1836-1912), Anglo-Dutch painter

steamer. Stayed at Beckenried and remember a pleasant walk (to Spires) and a sunset row on the lake. Thence to Engelberg, by Joch Pass to Engstlen Alp and back, a place to stay at in July while the alpine roses cover the ground. Back to Lucerne for a Sunday; walk over the bridge at sunset. Then to Hospenthal, from Amstey go to look up the Maderander Thal. Walked up the St. Gotthard, mostly by old road and back in gathering thunder. Then left my mother for a week which included all my real mountaineering—a stroll on the Shoke glacier, ascent of the Galenstock, which was never in the least alarming, though to be roped next to Augustus is naturally not an aid or encouragement: pretty walk over rocks and snow to Grimsel Lake. Morning canter down to Handeck falls and back and over the pass to Rhone glacier where picked up the luggage and came by diligence to Fiesch. Tiring grind up hill to Eggishorn. Next day to Corcordia Hütte (in 4 hours) *iced air* air of the glacier delightful, but *not* a specific for mucous membrane, which therefore one must put up with. (Scenery of the Grimsel very pretty, pretty foregrounds and fine back). Next day up Eggishorn and over Riffel Alp to Bel Alp Inn. Dawdled morning there and afternoon down slowly to Briej. Back next day by diligence paying a visit to the ice grotts and skirting the ice fall on foot ahead of diligence. A day at Hospental making routes and resting. Then drive by Ober Alp to Disentis, lunch on trout and strawberries with milk, stroll to big hotel then to Ilanz: quaint tiny fortified village; old town hall with oriel window worthy of Neuenbürg—all other antiquities of interest had been sold, according to our driver who came from a neighboring village and was very proud of talking Romanish—"the key to every other language." Next day by Versamer Tobel and Bonaduz to Giornice, picturesque convent turned into lunatic asylum at mouth of the valley. Walked some way above the Via Mala. Next day drive to Chur, train to Zurich by very pretty shores of Wollensea. Glimpse in passing of fine valley of the Linth which should have been taken *en route*. Stayed for a week at Zurich, saw Jung's friends, an old Fournierist now town councillor and another and two Socialist newspaper writers—both very harmless fellows but could get us introduction to operative class. The "Social Democrat"[436] which is prosecuted in Germany struck me as milder and perhaps both less of the "agitator's" love than "Justice";[437] a pamphlet about the police gave a ghastly picture of the spy system and the involuntary degradation even of honest men set to beat spies at their own tricks. The German government is certainly dry-nursing a revolution of some kind. Hamburgh is the stronghold of working class democracy. Bebel is a cabinet maker at Leipzig. Assisted at a discussion on capital punishment in Cantonal Council—instructive glimpse at working of Lucania constitution. The taking of *plébiscite*, and that on the "initiation" of the people if a certain number agree, makes the one elected chamber of delegates take rather the place of an upper house which does not necessarily agree with the

---

[436] The *Social Democrat* was the socialist paper edited in Zurich by the German exiles Bebel and Bern Stein.

[437] *Justice* was the weekly paper of the Democratic Federation. It first appeared in January 1884.

constituencies. Pleasant stroll the last evening along the ridge of the Uttibery. Saturday afternoon to Lohaffhausen for falls—hills very pretty, both *au natural* in blue sky and when lighted up. On Sunday round by the chateau and back to centre rock. Wrote letters. Next day to St. Blasien by Albbruck. Next to Freiburg by Fhei Lee. Höllenthal rather spoilt by rain. Next day saw the Cathedral and hill above the town and reached Strasburg by night. Next day to Brussels first looking in at Cathedral where mass was going on. From Holbein and woodcarvings at Freiburg. Spent a day at Brussels idly. In general, idleness and keeping my mother company went together, so that I didn't feel like sacrificing a pleasure or neglecting a duty when not sightseeing or exploring. 47 days for the 3 cost a little over £130. My mother enjoyed herself and has been well since but I feel more and more that her strength mustn't be tried too far and am glad on that ground to be free from outside claims. Must not forget that while at Zurich I reached the mature age of 40! "No-doubts-old." Incline to however doubt whether my history will amount to more than a moderately instructive compilation. Egypt and China between them will about fill a volume and I don't want to print them without Assyria, Mexico and Peru, and the simplest forms of property in unprogressive races—which would make two volumes for the first instalment. Shall be content if I have really done China by the end of this year: for that must be industrious—not waste time over Mudie books—or the lowest order of day-dreaming! I have an idea which may perhaps go into an article—the "social revolution" turned into an "Emancipation Act" to take effect at a date distant enough to let the injured interests prepare themselves for the catastrophe. Say for instance that all 99 year leaseholders should become free hold, and all obligations in perpetuity as to freeholders reconverted into 99 year lien on the industry of the community. Entails and settlements to be swept away at once and no person now living under the age of 21 to be allowed to inherit more than a fixed minimum (with specified exceptions for the weak or helpless). All property lapsing in consequence of this rule to belong to the state, which will vest the administration—e.g. of farms or factories—in the whole of the then working staff.

October 5, 1884

Time is flying with me just now. In last week have drafted some 30 pps (of small Ms) finishing the Hans and have read a little ahead, Chinese authorities to Gang dynasty; have also almost finished letters Erfraistes—and seen Holly Lodge.

November 6, 1884

Have sketched the Gang dynasty and been somewhat hindered with guests and colds. Snatched a lovely autumnal walk of 2 1/2 hours one Saturday, from Oxted to Limpsfield over that and Windmill common into Edenbridge road and back through "Squerries" woods. Asking my way at 4 cross roads I observed to my informant that "they" should put up finger posts, who replied that there were a few now but "there never used to be none in Surrey"—so that their existence apparently was nothing to be proud of. Have done two small Academy reviews. Think I should like to spend next summer in the country by a river, making the written materials more my own. Am uneasy at hearing that Mr. Cross is publishing 3 volumes mostly of journals and letters. How She would have hated it. Did not mention that Mme Bodichon asked me to go down to Scalands, (she had found some more letters) and then telegraphed to put off. Went to see Rosamond, with whom she was staying last month and was affectionately greeted; next day a bad seizure.

December 4, 1884

Get on but slowly—as regards quality and definitiveness; some 100 pps of print read for and written in the 3 months: China episode is getting woefully long; shall have to be content if it is done by Easter instead of Xmas. Am tolerably happy over it, which I'm afraid is a bad sign, as I liked writing both the books that nobody in particular has yet liked to read.

January 3, 1885

Have been idle for the last fortnight or so resolving statistics and papers for the futile "Industrial Remuneration Conference." The year has gone as aforesaid, very quickly, and I am beginning to feel that "Ownership" will miss the 6 or 8 years I muddled away for want of an object before taking to shirtmaking. I wonder if my two volumes can be ready by next autumn twelve monthly,—not at my present rate.

January 14, 1885

Annie dangerously ill—{She said to the nurse "I daresay this night seems strange to you, different from other nights but it doesn't seem strange to me."}

(In the Ms this note is on the page opposite the entry for January 3, 1885.)
On Thursday she went to Clareville for a "Mother's Meeting"
—got wet on the lining and seat—in a stuffy cottage room—in
wet clothes. Felt chilled and shivers and went to bed. Mr. Hutton
was sent for on Friday, but gave no alarm. Will wrote to my
mother that she was poorly, and had been shivering. We
got this Saturday and my mother at once tely replied
"Should she come?" Will asked Annie, who said Julia could
do all she wanted—who let her get out of bed and one day
spilt lemonade over her and changed her things. Monday morning
there was a letter saying she was very ill, would my mother come.
She went at once. Thought her dying and—too late—tried to warm
the room, sent for a nurse and a physician, and for her brother, who
came Tuesday night just in time to see her alive.

January 15, 1885

Died this morning "very peacefully at 2:20." We hardly knew of danger for more than 24 hours which seemed very long though a telegram at 2:30 and letter at 9:00 for me came yesterday; this morning's letter said "no change" and I had not hastened to expect a fatal ending:—felt rather a brute for not being more selfishly anxious—only as it were reasonably concerned for my brother and the sadness of a young life cut short. When the telegram came poor Ada (the cook) burst out crying. I too have reddened my eyes some, but it is hardly the same uncontrollable feeling that has possessed me at deaths that people would have said were no concern of mine. I do not mean the two with whom my own life ended, but such friends as Mr. Hursfield when I was a child, Mr. Priest and Mr. Keysner later, and John Rodgers whom I only knew by himself, not like the others through their wives. Poor Will! I half hope that it is not his nature to mourn as passionately for the dead as he longed for the living.

January 31, 1885

The book[438] came out on Tuesday. Sat up half the night—first reading and then devouring the outline. It has made evenings of intense occupation follow the days much grudged to the "Conference." In many ways it is a relief to me—the blasphemers I think will be at a loss for anything to take hold of and the invention of the arrangement is good. For myself I should have liked more of the letters to other people, not autobiographical but dealing with their questions or circumstances—though naturally the most interesting of these are just what the recipients would not wish to give and he has perhaps done wisely in giving only one sample of the class. I could have spared all the references to myself, especially the last, which seems to me in questionable taste—as it is nothing to the outer world that She was generous enough to recognize my affection as giving me a right to feel personally concerned in what She did. The only thing that could make me glad for it to stand, would be if my name ever seemed to any one to carry with it a vestige of added probability that all She did was right—I am content that my acquiescence should be put down as given without hesitation or delay, such as that of two of the older correspondents.

February 3, 1885

Saw Mrs. Congreve yesterday who shares my feeling of relief. Was interested in the first volume but did not feel that the others added much to her knowledge. They do not add much to mine after reading all Mme Bodichon's letters; and I am not sure that the book will give a very true or complete picture to those who did not know Her at all. Its value to me seems to be that it gives the world as much as it deserves and is not likely to misuse. It was in the early days at Wandsworth that the absence happened of which Mrs. Congreve told me before. Her recollection is very strong of the intense sadness of the Madonna's habitual expression; it was the time of the great success of Adam Bede,[439] but She was unhappy and—"you will hardly be able to believe this"—irritable: it was for Mr. Lewes's sake that she struggled with the melancholy moods the memory of

---

[438] *George Eliot's Life as Related in Her Letters and Journals. Arranged and Edited by Her Husband* (Edinburgh and London: W. Blackwood and Sons, 1885).

[439] *Adam Bede* (1859)

which no doubt inspired her remorseful speeches to the Brays. The fact that She needed in some ways almost as much forbearance as She showed is a point to be remembered on Mr. Lewes's side—he was not a mere recipient. Servants were an infinite trouble to Her then. Mrs. Congreve was sorry to hear Morley spoke of the life as a sad one,—she thought that was not true where there was a constant *crescendo*. There are only two remedies for that sadness—of mind and body—which Her passionate nature knew as much (or more of) as even my coldblooded Ego did. They are—love and work: Her happiness began as She got Her fill of these. My happiness began and ended with the joy of loving Her and I am and shall be content henceforward with the memory of that love and the presence of work enough such as She would have approved of. For Her sake I want to put my whole mind and heart into the "Ownership,"—but I do miss the inspiration of a living love, such as made my two useless books write themselves.

February 5, 1885

The evening papers announce the fall of Khartoum. The tragic thing is such a triumph of heroism having been wasted—for anything but an example of what man may do. For Gordon's[440] sake one was anxious for the rescue, though no good was in prospect for the gallant Arabs—one's conscience is unable to regret a deserved disgrace but the blundering has been horrible—I don't envy Lord Wolseley, for it is impossible that the fatal three days could not have been saved by putting on a little steam at the earlier stages:—they have taken it easily as a promenade and talked of what should be done when they got to Khartoum!—I wonder if the Government will survive the disaster—it isn't logical to blame them for the consequence when the antecedent blundering has been condoned. The force is, I imagine, in great danger, with no base and a triumphant, numerous enemy brave even under difficulties and now of course likely to believe in none and feel few.

February 8, 1885. Sunday

Yesterday afternoon passed a bad hour—which but for Her I should certainly have avoided as was the easier way—with the little clerk of H & Co who at last told me what she had done amiss—as much as I feared, but for her soul's sake I thought it right if possible to get the confession. At one moment I doubted whether I had been uncharitable, but she did not deny having something on her mind and at last with her hand in mine and her head on my shoulder she told me of the least offence, but still something that I had not known. That gave me courage to press her on another point as to which I had not been able to believe her: she said at last she would tell me everything; there were long pauses, I should think it so horridly mean of her, her poor little hand tightened on mine

---

[440] Colonel Charles Gordon (1833-1885) arrived in Khartoum in February 1884, to report on the situation there; after complicating the situation and being killed on January 26, 1885. Sir G. Wolsely (1833-1913) arrived on January 28 and avenged Gordon's death and recovered the Sudan; then following Gladstone's orders, the Sudan was abandoned for a dozen years.

and further confession came; then I felt justified in putting my worst suspicions to the tests,—I wanted her to tell me everything—was it possible that she had sometimes herself used money that was there and not her own? She said it was possible—she was very glad she had told me everything, she had been so miserable, "it looked so different afterward." I had asked her to come to see me in the afternoon and then my mother wanted me much to go with her to the shop in the morning, so I saw the girl for a moment and as she did not come till late I was divided between a brutal feeling of relief that I was going to be spared the interview, regret on her account that she meant to shirk it, and self-reproach because I had not said a word to make sure *of* her coming—which I feared might prove "one of the small leavings undone which make a great difference to other lives." Of course I don't exaggerate what is gained, but at least one has saved the girl (she is 22) from going through life with the memory of a hidden fraud. Now it is time for me myself, after muddling away nearly a couple of months to turn over a new leaf and set to work seriously—especially *Mem*: not to let papers and letters accummulate untidily to the delay of business and the secretion of dust.

February 12, 1885
The girl came again on Sunday rather anxious to minimize her confessions and since then I have been idle and impotent in that direction. Am lazily clearing up arrears of letters &c—William has the offer of Harlaxton near Grantham and I have been looking up Her unsigned reviews in the Westminster. It is curious that even Lewes who had such a ready *flair* for new talent should not have found signs of genius in Her writing like the Cumming article[441] which, like all that followed: it was composed after Her soul had caught fire from the flash of happy passion. I have copied Her ideal of a great and good man's life, and some day before I die perhaps it may be given me to write of Her as She would wish. I am indignant at the stupidity—the hypocritical stupidity of a man like Morley,[442] writing as if Her relation with Mr. Lewes had been something between a blunder and an offence, but I suppose it is in comparative victory that the general press has not said more of the same sort more offensively. There is no doubt that the act was on Her part perfectly deliberate and *conscientious*. She regarded Mr. Lewes as morally free and she Herself was legally as well as morally so. The only valid reason against it was that it would shock people: and She felt it to be right to do what *She* felt to be right though it be sung "of old and young that She should be to blame." She never doubted and never repented Her decision, having weighed the sacrifice before hand and having chosen to make it, because it was at Her own cost alone and Her whole nature was bent to make it for the sake of love and pity—not compassion only which has a less compelling force than love. Now I know Her by heart and I do not love Her blindly. Was

---

[441] "Evangelical Teaching: Dr. Cumming," *Westminster Review*, 44 (October, 1855): 436-462.

[442] John Morley, "The Life of George Eliot." *Macmillan's Magazine* 51 (1855): 241-256. This is a review of Cross. Morley was a frequent visitor at the Priory.

there ought to blame or to regret in what She did? She made the best of Mr. Lewes's life as no other person could; he made the best of Hers as no other living man showed power or will to do. She gave the world an example—which to do it justice it has not altogether failed to understand, of the eternal marriage of love and duty, an object lesson so to speak, in mutual faithfulness and mutual devotion, in love's happiness made subservient to the perfecting of the lover's powers and the application of these powers to the service of their fellows. And if this can be done by one pure heart and will apart from and even at variance with the respectable barriers of law and custom, how much more easily and necessarily may it be sought by every honest couple within the barriers. That is Her lesson for the men and women who are destined to make each other's hell or heaven. To me it was much more. I know now that much of the passion and the tenderness of my love came from my worship of Her character as it was in Her life as it was:—that She should go Her own perfect way unembittered by blame, unmoved by the conciousness of a great sacrifice to either self-pity or self-exaltation, and with a generosity unexhausted by the one great strain, a sweetness made manifold by every temptation resisted, every trial overcome.

February 15, 1885
Rather late in the day have finished sorting and destroying last year's letters. I have such a bad memory that my instinct is to keep all letters as *Memoirs pour servir*[443] if I live to indulge in autobiographical retrospect. Those I have now kept go into 13 rings, those connected with Hamilton and Co; *Re* "housing of the poor"—which includes the struggle with the housefaring vestryman and Mr. Reaney's abortive Committee; Trade Unions and Internationalism; then a mixed packet endorsed "Causes," women sufferage, lectures, Industrial Renumeration Conference &c: School Board matters; (now small) Editors; International; then Mrs. Paterson; Mary; Mrs. Stuart; Miss Williams; sundry friends or acquaintances; *Her* friends, and the "family." A pretty exhaustive picture. It has struck me before how very "objective" all but one of these "interests" are. The internationalism and publishing departments are the only two to which I could look for any personal satisfaction even of the disinterested sort. Yet I am not unhappy now. It seems infinitely probable and natural that one should never be *positively* happy.

February 16, 1885
Went to see Mrs. Congreve again. Looked up with her dates and references to Hennell's book: her private impression had been that the Madonna's radicalism was not suggested by either the Brays or the "Inquiry" and we found this confirmed; not only by what I noticed first that the letter to Miss Lewis intimating a change of view was dated less than a fortnight after her first call on the Brays, to whom she had been apparently only just introduced; but also by a letter in 47 which speaks of her being more impressed by the "Inquiry" then than on her first two readings about 5 years before—which would be 42—i.e. just

---

[443] "aids to remembrance"

after her own change of mind, and there was in this letter no expression of gratitude for special help at that earlier time, such as She would certainly have expressed if the book had proved at all "epoch-making" to Her. Mrs. Congreve once asked Her what began the change and She said *Walter Scott*—he was healthy and historical and it would not fit on to her creed. I think it may be said also about the ease of the transition that Her personal feeling—the impulse of Her whole nature was very irresistible when roused—it was not in Her nature to be a house divided against itself. I at any rate have no reason to suppose it to be natural that people should suffer in their minds from renouncing erroneous opinions.

February 17, 1885
As regards my own affairs, I am in a stupid state of apathy and discouragement. I must be resolute in not letting anything interrupt my China grinding again; I am so slow to get under way again after a pause. But I have also reason for discouragement. If *I* find it hard to read my own Ms through, what hope is there of anyone else caring to do so. It impresses me as a compilation— only at rare intervals do I come to a sentence that I greet as my own. It is very well to have a sort of lifeless skeleton on first outline to be endued afterwards with flesh and blood, but I can't carry the whole draft in my mind at once so as to touch up the parts in reference to the whole. Also I feel none of the irrational inward impulse of production which prompted "Natural Law" and the "Episodes." It is a fine subject but whether that and taking pains can make a book between them is alas! doubtful. I decided however yesterday as to the way in which the pains must be spent. I will first finish the draft, then re-read the whole enough to judge of its divisions, and then revise, re-write and *work-up* each separate section into some approach to literary life. I might have the chance of doing that in the country which will be comparatively wholesome. (Will accepts Harlaxton.)

February 20, 1885
Yesterday by a strange chance saw the record of a pretty tragic passage. Roland Stuart is clerk in a certain San Francisco Bank, and the other day a box was being overhauled into which the documents bearing famous autographs had been hurled together, Tennyson, Browning &c. These Roland saw and seized for his mother several papers. Some share or shares stood in Mr. Lewes's name and bore his signature: then there was the transfer to Her as his executrix—Mary Ann Evans—then a deed of Hers *taking the name of Lewes in addition* and a transfer from M. A. E. to Mary Ann Evans Lewes—an autograph which Mrs. Stuart was able to please herself by imaging unique. Charles Lewes witnessed the first document (I think February 13, 1879) and J. W. Cross the later one in March—there was a pencil memorandum indicating I think that the deed was registered in April. My poor darling! I had worried about that very question of Her having to sign legal documents by a wrong name. I have nearly read the Life through again. I always take it up last thing at night and live as of old in the thought of Her, which possesses me as formerly. I see as it were from outside the pathos there is in the contrast between Her view and mine of what was common

to us in the 8 years—the end of one life, first calm and then with great movements quite apart from me; the beginning, middle and end, the heart and climax of another life, crowded with emotion by which she was hardly touched and very little profited. I mean bit by bit to interpolate my share in those last pages: it occurs to me that when I felt chilled instead of cheered by what was meant for sympathy it was because one only takes pleasure selfishly in sympathy given to our personal feelings—sympathy with sympathetic feelings that, alas! are not quite bone of our own bone and flesh of our flesh, looks not quite untruly like sympathy with other people—not our poor hungry, greedy selves. She would have understood that well enough! Also it is easier for a human and humane person to sympathize with gratifying warmth with outside lives that have other interests of their own, than to make room in their very own life for one whose only personal care in life is love for them. The only way of sympathizing with that love is to return it. It was very good of Her to marry "Johnny"—*quant ámoi*[444]—I have lived and loved and as the years go by the sweetness stays and there comes even to be a little sweetness in the old sensation which some memories have power to recal because no part of my love died with Her: last night after reading from December 72 to 76 I was possessed body and soul by the thought—love and consciousness of Her and just now as I began to write of it with tears "My heart was soir for somebody"—as pray Heaven it may never grow too dead and cold to be till my dust is scattered on Her grave.

February 21, 1885

This afternoon in the midst of the lecture I should have been preparing about China for tonight I have been fitting the last letters and interviews into their place. That little outburst of unresignation "I have done my duty," on the 25th of March was just before the last decisive visit to Weybridge. I am almost glad I chanced to be away in that last month—. I did not see her till April 27—I could not wholly have guessed and without that I might have spoken at cross purposes. For any little comfort my love or vanity can take in it, I find by the dates that after Her marriage on every fresh occasion one of the earliest letters was for me. She wrote *en voyage* to Weybridge and Charles Lewes; the first letters from Milan (May 26) were to her brother and to me—unworthy!

February, 24, 1885

Was pleased with the Toynbee Hall boys. Yesterday saw Mrs. Congreve again: stayed with her a long time; she thought men ought to consider their duty to their friends in marrying; and was exercised about a woman who to secure domestic peace renounced her higher aspirations &c 20 years ago and had sunk consertedly to the lower family level. The family was one that made bad jokes; she began by smiling out of complaisance; "Now she makes them herself!" I quite understand the Madonna's admiration for this gentle, sensitive nature with a clear, firm understanding. There was an amusing, profane Sunday letter from Lewes, meant to enliven Mrs. Geddes when ill, warning her to

---

[444] "as for me" or "as far as I am concerned"

recognize "God in disease," not believe in nurses who gave her too few sweets and too much beef, tea &c. Mrs. Congreve's flight to India was quite heroic, undertaken at 4 days notice for her sister's sake who was ill and without a good nurse. I was asking about Mrs. Burne-Jones, of whom the Madonna had not spoken to her; she saw her once at the Priory (and then was not grateful for her presence) and thought he was the original acquaintance. I spoke as if a little envious of her earlier acquaintance and Mrs. Congreve said "oh but you were more to Her than Mrs. B. J." I—"Surely not, she was very fond of her!" "Yes, She was fond of her but She valued you more—had such a high opinion of your judgment."—I put it down for what it is worth though I fancy I know better—or rather worse. She Herself once used the words "respect and admiration"—which I longed to change for a little irrational liking; but after all the Life and Letters are a little soothing to my hunger—I feel that it was not to be expected or desired that, at 53 She should be able very quickly or easily to "set Her heart" on a new friend, however loving, to the extent of finding Her own happiness to any appreciable extent in the relation—which involves a certain degree of dependence on it. If She had liked and I had not been a fool, She might have come to lean a little on my love; but it was not my fault that I came too late to get all my share of either happiness or good.

3:00 p.m. This morning which was to be my first good day at China has been spent in reading Her letters down to 78—without missing any. I see now that Her anger was not quite all impersonal righteousness—Good God, how I must have loved Her to survive that letter. It is a little sad to think that maybe one of the mere friend's letters which rather perplexed me by coming in 77 would have saved me in 75 from the fit of physical despondency that began with my foolish visit to Rickmansworth. But *then* my poor Darling wanted to receive comfort not to give it and I was rather a brute not to have generously responded then to that sweet letter of 74. But some things are too strong for me—I was born a good for nothing creature that could only wax the more miserable for being hopelessly in love with some one who liked people to be good for something. Tomorrow China shall really and truly begin for Her sweet sake. I think I will make Mrs. Congreve criticise "Eclipse" from Madonna's point of view.

February 25, 1885

There was happily of course less consciousness in Her mind than in mine of all that was morbid in one's miserable moods. One must pay one's taxes to the physical universe and I am quite willing to admit that the physical base of my despondency as of Hers, was very likely to be connected with the shutting down of the normal feminine escape pipe sacred to the memory of Eve's transgressions. I don't savor this rather brutal observation a recommendation that women should marry at any price. I only argue that if they don't, they want the more distractions instead of getting the less. But that is all ancient history now, and I am not now sad for the sake of it beneath the blessed sunshine. I do believe that my love gave Her some pleasure; Her sweetness gave me much joy—it revealed to me what gladness was, and it is a perfectly adequate reason for existing now that I wish to dedicate to Her dear memory "with endless love" a book that should and may be useful. I ought to have twenty years of good work in me wherewith to build Her monument. I wish I had been kinder to my Darling, but still it is folly not to allow myself to believe that my love was real to Her when She spoke of it more than once in words which She had before appropriated to Her most loving husband.

February 27, 1885

It is not easy now to think of anything but the hateful imbecility of the rulers of men. I suppose it is nothing new, it is so we have drifted into crimes and duties beyond our strength but it is peculiarly depressing to find not a single voice in power raised to say what one thinks right. I did not write here about Gordon's mission last year tho' I felt strongly about the folly and from the Government's point of view the unprincipledness of it. We had then just read Gordon's letters from the Sudan, which showed him to be very interesting and indeed admirable person but politically unstable, impulsive and impressionable to a degree utterly fatal in a position where a line of conduct has to be invented, and is not inspired from without or above. He would have been consistent enough with a cause ready made like Garibaldi's;[445] as it is, the blundering of others has saved him from the risk of failure, for he had more genius for generalship than anything else and the singlehanded defense of Khartoum remains a magnificent achievement. When we have done so much evil already irrevocably to both Egyptians and Sudanese—and can by no possibility be held back from doing more—I cannot sympathize with the non-interventionists who would make a platform of doing as little as possible. Why not resolve to atone and so far as may be undo the evil by a sincere and disinterested rush at the scarcely harder problem, to do a real solid good—to the martyred masses.

February 28, 1885

Have re-read Lélia[446]—á propos of Her interest in it long ago. I had forgotten the outline but the impression the book made 20 years ago was vivid enough for me to feel a sort of revival, like that on reading Wilhelm Meister two or three years ago. The difference—i.e. the thing which strikes me now and did not then—is the shade of unreality about doubt and discontent both so much in the air—unconditioned generalities so to speak: but of course discontent with things in general really means the want of content with things in particular, and that is calamity enough to excuse, not to say justify, all the lamentations of youth. In looking up my old comments on Lélia found a draft of my letter to Newman. I think it was really very clever: what a tremendous difference it would have made to me if I had come to know Her then—if She had seen and had the answering of that letter (Government majority of 14.)

---

[445] Giuseppe Garibaldi (1807-1882), Italian general and patriot

[446] A novel by George Sand (1804-1876)

March 1, 1885

Have been very idle and self-indulgent all this week—"indulging" wantonly in the sensation that "My heart is soir for somebody," rehearsing in spirit with equally small shares of profit all that was and all that might have been, instead of concentrating my passionate purpose upon what is and "what may yet be better." I don't condemn myself wholly, I have a right to give days and weeks to the feeling of this last great chapter in my life's romance. But unless I am the "absolute fool and weakling" she once thought it necessary to state She was not—I shall now cease to call the ghosts of dead days and nights from the slumber of the grave.—"Ach Mütter, Mütter, hin ist hin, verloren, ist verloren."[447]—but I will draw life instead of death from the crucible of time, the furnace that has been fed with my love, my pain—self made some and some self—chosen for a worthy price,—and her sweet goodness which turned love and pain into gladness; may I think it is my life, made of all those, that has been thrown into the furnace and the pure ore that should come out should be the disinterested force of living love. The "passion" whereof She wrote once as wanting in my book has now at least nowhere else to go.

March 3, 1885

Charles Lewes came Sunday afternoon. Had not much to say, except (what Harrison says) that She burnt all Her own letters to Mr. Lewes after his death. No one writing on their relation seems to understand Her point of view— that a law was not to be kept always because it formulated the conduct generally desirable, but on the contrary was to be honoured alike by the breach or the observance as dictated by the fundamental moral needs and feelings which found their normal satisfaction within it. Fedalma[448] is not sacrificed to a theory of nationality but to the living need of a living people. The marriage law consecrates constant faithful devotion; when the demand for conjugal devotion arises, the fulfilment of the law cannot lie in a *refusal* of love's devotion, in a mere negation or going without the desired good. No one knows better than I how little food there is for the soul in that kind of fast even when the nature of things makes it unsuitable. When it is unsuitable, let us bear the loss like men and be as little the worse for it as we may, but then sparing those dull of understanding the perplexity of a reminder that *they* must keep the law not "because it is right and lawful," but for the true natural reasons which make it right. All that is written about Her now ought to drive my soul—if it had any good energy of passion in it, to earn the right of pleading with authority for a more intelligent cannon of moral criticism in this matter. It is strange in the face of Her belief that "men were kinder to Her than women" to see men whom she counted friends or something like it, giving voice now to womanish concessions

---

[447] "Oh, Mother, Mother, gone is gone, lost is lost."

[448] Fedalma is GE's Spanish Gypsy.

to the mere Mrs. Grundy line of thought.[449] As Mr. Cadwallader says: "We now think so poorly of each other that we can't call a woman exactly wise who gives up—even *a* fortune for a man."[450]

March 8, 1885

Have relieved my feelings by writing to Miss Hennell about the chronology of the first theological *Aufklärung*[451] and to F. Harrison partly to protest against his claiming Her authority for a Positivist conception of "women's sphere" with a remark by the way on the moral question.

March 17, 1885

Useful information in reply from Miss Hennell; useless sentiments from F. H. On Saturday (14th) went Six Mile Bottom—the Hall's place—sacred ground—very pretty house and grounds with belts of firs behind which the sun set: happy united family—Druces,[452] Eleanor Cross and "Johnny" were there besides Sidgwicks, Sedley Taylor[453] and a young professor Foxwell. Talk and Stories: the good Hall was converted to Anarchism by Sidgwick's account of Godwin's "Political Justice."[454] I delivered my message to Mr. Cross, in part, about the chronological inaccuracy, but he like, Charles, did not much trouble about it; it vexes me rather to have two men with so little understanding of Her *mind* endowed with authority to say how much shall be known of its workings. It was good news to me that Roger is to do an etching of the photograph. I asked if Mrs. Druce was not like the elder sister who was thought like Her; Eleanor was surprised at my asking but said Madonna exclaimed when She saw Anna first at the likeness to Her own sister Chrissy. The resemblance I saw was in the mouth when she smiled and showed large, long regular teeth. I talked a great deal—some foolishly.

---

[449] Mrs. Grundy was a character referred to in *Speed the Plough*, a play by Thomas Morton (1764-1838). Her judgments represent her as a ridiculously strict upholder of social conventions.

[450] In *Middlemarch*

[451] "Enlightenment"

[452] Albert Druce was married to Anna Cross; he "gave GE away" at her wedding.

[453] Sedley Taylor (1834-1920) (H, VI, 413; VIII, 73)

[454] William Godwin (1756-1836), radical philosopher and author of *An Enquiry Concerning Political Justice* (London: G. G. J. and J. Robinson, 1793). Henry Sidgwick (1838-1900) was known for his *The Methods of Ethics* (London: Macmillan, 1874), an examination of Mill's utilitarian theories in light of Kant's philosophy.

220

March 26, 1885

My mother is now at Weyhill and there is absolutely nothing to hinder my working hard and fast.—An unpardonable sin against my divinity if I don't, but when I am once started I must shun like the gates of hell any interruption that makes the beginning again so slow and unwelcome.

March 27, 1885

There is no one who loved Her so well for whom She cared so little— but no one can know as I do how little that proves against Her tenderness and generosity—I who know how utterly remote from every normally constituted disposition the idea of myself as a thing to be loved would seem, if it were even so absurd as to present itself. It does not distress me now as it used to do, even though I have better means of knowing how true it is. I find a certain pleasure in the latent consciousness that there is a sensation about my heart which will live as long as I do as if a clean, short sword had just passed through me, once and again, carving a mystic cross which aches like a bodily wound on the bodily organ, associated I know not why with the soul's affection.

March 28, 1885

Tempted again to write (this time to the "Guardian") and reason with well meant misunderstanding of Her ethical position. It is best to forbear and reserve oneself.

April 8, 1885

Have been gathering myself together slowly on the subject of the Ming dynasty. 'Tis the last but one and even the last isn't quite infinite.

April 19, 1885

Will's wife has been dead 3 months. I wonder if they have seemed long to him. They have gone very *trivially* with me; and now that my mother looks forward, not quite reluctantly, to being with him for more than half her time, I feel rather an impostor for having shaken myself clear (honestly on her account) of such outside work as the shop and the Board. After the first bother of moving and settling at Harlaxton the result of course will be to leave me still more free for "Ownership."

May 10, 1885

But meanwhile I find it impossible to do more than bits of scrappy reading and I have given up the idea of doing any work to speak of for the next month—instead perhaps I shall snatch a few day's play—enjoyment of green woods—and I am not without hope of driving to Lincolnshire through Warwickshire (so as to see Miss Lewis and Mrs. Bray and her sister). Have not written out any part of the Ming dynasty and have yet to read up all foreign authorities prior to the Mantchus; when that is done should be ready to revise all the rest before writing the last section on contemporary China.

June 12, 1885

Have been at Weyhill most of the interval; spent one day last week in Savernake Forest, walking to Marlborough Town from the station and thence to The Forest and back to Savernake station; glorious leafy solitudes and the play of sun and shade among the beech trunks that it is an inexhaustible pleasure to re-discover. Last Monday, the 8th after despairing of the family consent I got off peaceably with John and the dog cart[455] at 6 p.m. Newbury a little before 9, slept at White Hart; rain and drizzle most of the way, but was all right with mackintosh. After Penton there were miles without signs of human life; even the old turnpike houses unoccupied, and this was the rule along the greater part of the 150 miles of high road through this over populated country. Sometimes the solitude was broken by wayside inns but not always that. Left Newbury at 7, but on feeling for my watch at the first milestone discovered that I had left it under my pillow, so half an hour was wasted in returning for it; rain lasted for an hour or two, then greyness. Stopped to give the horse half an hour's rest at East or Market Ilsley, a cozy little village with many inns for market folk and sheep pens down the village street. Walked up the hill ahead of which the top is still open down with thicket of may and gorse flowering together. Reached Oxford from Abingdon by the road pointed out as shortest, which enters by St. Aldates. At the Clawdon asked for a dressing room and hot water; though there was no sun my face was scorched to a flaming red and burnt as in Switzerland. Walked round to Dr. Legge[456] who was just dismissing a student. Had luncheon with him and a daughter, but did not find that he had any view about Wang-ngan-shi nor could he tell me off hand the dynasty of Yang-chi whose will is given in the Mém. conc. les Chinois. He spoke of the difficulty of getting his pupils to compose in Chinese i.e. and think in the characters—wanted to find a passage in Hume[457] against translation into Latin. Said Giles[458] was fairly accurate and asked if one or two pieces (the Old Drunkard's ardour and another) were given in his German;

---

[455] A dog cart is so named because of a box which accommodates a dog underneath the seat with vents on the sides and an opening on the end. This journey provides the details for "Rural Roads," *Macmillan's Magazine* (September, 1885): 371-382.

[456] James Legge (1815-1897) was author of *The Chinese Classics* (London: Trübner, 1861-1871), *The Life and Works of Mencius* (London: Trübner, 1875), and many other works. He delivered the Inaugural Lecture on the Constituting of A Chinese Chair in the University of Oxford, 1876.

[457] David Hume (1711-1776), Scottish moral and political philosopher

[458] Herbert Allen Giles (1845-1935), translated *Chuang Tu* (London: Bernard Quaritch, 1889) and many related works and prepared *A Catalogue of the Wade Collection of Chinese and Manchu Books of the Library of the University of Cambridge* (Cambridge, 1898).

spoke of "balance" and "harmony" peculiar to best Chinese composition. The self taught Manchester linguist he told me of before is in trouble having got a Chinese Scholarship but is ploughed for smalls[459] in Greek and Latin. Pleasant drive from Oxford to Banbury, halting for an hour at a country inn halfway where I had tea and a novel—1830 dedicated to newly confessed "Author of Waverley"[460] in a little parlour facing the fir trees of a cross road. The sun was setting behind Banbury as we got in, the horse very fairly fresh after its 50 miles. Off at 7:30 having first sent a telegram to Coventry to say I hoped to arrive about 5. Found the road uninhabited for miles but 13 miles from Banbury found the little village of Ladbroke a halting place worth waiting for; walked round it, up to the church which is reached by 3 or 4 paths crossing a fair meadow, sat on walls or gates and did not find the halt long; reached Leamington 12:30 and Harriet Bradly showed me the way at once to Miss Lewis. A nice little fair old lady, with one eye gone, which they say was an ugly squint in youth. She was governess at the Nuneaton school and had evidently been the superior person of that period: the virtuous cultivated young lady whom Mrs. Evans held up as a model for imitation to her aspiring little daughter. Miss Lewis used to visit at Griff— remembered going to see Polly and Chrissy in bed with measles, was "like an elder sister" to them. Spoke of the child so very loveable, but unhappy, given to great bursts of weeping; finding it impossible to care for childish games and occupations:—it is of course significant that as a mere child, the governess should have been her friend rather than any schoolfellow. Poor little Miss Lewis as a "good churchwoman" of a sober sort thinks the fall into infidelity was due to the over excitement, fostered by the Methodist Franklins and the Aunt leading to a reaction. I asked when the correspondence really ceased, and she thought not long before Mr. Evans's death, though after the change of views it dropped into a matter of friendly notes; she still visited—which is how the Brays knew her as "the squinting Miss Lewis"—in spite of the dissuasion of clerical employers— she refused to give up her old pupil and the hope of influencing her for good! Her account of the breach was that Marian wrote to her that "a friend" had suggested to her (Marian) that Miss Lewis's friendship was not disinterested. The old lady said she replied that she was much surprised that Marian could entertain such a thought and that if she could Miss Lewis would not trouble her with another letter. This was a true reminiscence—i.e. what Miss Lewis has long believed to be true, she spoke with a hurt tone—that whatever faults she had, that of thinking too much of her own interests was not one, her only grief now being that she is alone, with no one but herself to care for. Of course she viewed with some jealousy the new and evidently more valued relationship with the Brays; she said that when Marian asked to have her letters back she said she would lend them her, but must have them returned; then Marian did not return them and told

---

[459] "rejected as a candidate"

[460] Sir Walter Scott (1771-1832) wrote the Waverly novels anonymously; the series, which brought him fame; the first was *Waverly* (1814) and the last was *Redgauntlet* (Edinburgh: Archibald Constable, 1824).

Miss Lewis (according to the latter) that Mr. Bray said they were the property of the writer or to that effect. I asked when the acquaintance was renewed and she thought at about the time when mine began: one knew it must have been before the letter to Mme Bodichon in July 74. It was pretty of the old lady that she would not give up this first letter in which Miss Lewis apparently spoke of old days with her wonted generous gratitude—would only let Mr. Cross have a copy of it for himself, and not use it at all for publication. She also volunteered the information that she was then poorly off and that ever after a letter came once or twice a year with a cheque enclosed. She had had a slight paralytic stroke lately and had been watching the clock for me all the morning so I did not stay long and in fact without thinking things over had nothing fresh to say to her; I am a bad hand at asking for information as it did not occur to me till afterwards that if one were not afraid of being indiscreet I might have asked her to show me the letter she would not have published. She spoke of Polly having the run of the Newdigate library and of herself as having the commission to lay out £20 for her in books, the beginning of her library—perhaps *á propos* of the move to Foleshill or how? About 6 reached Coventry having given an hour to Kenilworth on John's account. Found Mrs. Bray and Miss Hennell at tea. Miss Hennell knew nothing about the cause of the breach with Miss Lewis, thought it was gradual, incompatibility of opinions &c—it had long been a tax; thought that the quarrel was by word of mouth, that Miss Lewis had been finding fault, governess fashion, with what was imprudent or unusual in Marian's manners and that Marian always resented this and that it was some verbal *tu quoique*[461] leading to a misunderstanding—as if perhaps Miss Lewis had reproached her with seeming to take too much "interest" in somebody—of the opposite sex—: whereto she angrily—it might as well be said that *you* have an interest or are interested in your friendship for me. I don't attach much weight to this hypothetical explanation. Miss Hennell went on to complain that Mme Bodichon had soon cultivated her acquaintance, she guessed because of her (Mme Bodichon's) dislike to "visiting her friends"—a dislike which I have heard Barbara ascribe to Marian; and I seeing the two old friends in succession can well understand that the Brays never understood Miss Lewis's place and the regard continued her for oldsake's sake, and their want of sympathy, while Marian was in full sympathy with them, would rather put Miss Lewis in the background, while at the same time the habit began which undoubtedly grew with time of avoiding chills and checks by taking each friendship as it came by itself and not trying to work it in along with others. It was a part of the reserve—I might almost say the cowardice which must grow on a sensitive nature after it has risked more rebuffs than it can bear—to let each friend take and make its own place apart, while she cared from outside for the friend's life, but did not make a life of her own the open centre for the lives of those who loved her. It is easy to guess from the softened experience of Maggie and Dorothea what was the sort of over ready expansiveness for which an old governess might scold. Poor little Miss Hennell apparently always disapproved of Marian for depending too much on the arm of man and Miss

---

[461] "you although"

Lewis—spoke of her walking about with Charles Bray "like lovers." According to Sara she did not discuss theology "questions" with him any more than her; the main lines were taken for granted; they talked and quarrelled about marriage and such like! When one of them Miss Lewis spoke of her as having read books unsuitable for a girl, I said that when one thought of a household like Mr. Evans's in a village 50 years ago one might be sure that any girl who thought about what she heard would have nothing to learn from books of the world's wickedness. This sort of realism is without any false shame—there is no wrong in knowing what is—so I thought it an absurd suggestion that her Methodism or phase of Evangelical devotion had to do with some desire to purify her mind from the knowledge of evil. She gave them no warning of her intention as regarded Mr. Lewes. She knew they would not like it and it would have been only painful: they thought it was only a few months during which they did not write though the date shows it to be a year since the letter of 55 was an answer to Mrs. Bray's first. They did not believe it would last; Charles Bray was not surprised—had of course seen signs when in London. They thought the first letters must have been to him, and Mrs. Bray sought anxiously though in vain for one to him which gave more fully than that published the grounds on which she acted. For 7 years Lewes and his wife had been practically separated and Mrs. Bray said expressing what I had known *á priori* that she insisted on the question being asked on both sides—was there any possibility of bringing about a reunion and Mrs. Lewes—the *de facto* Mrs. *Hunt* said no, never—and she should be very glad if he could marry Miss Evans; at first she signed herself so still, then came to Marian alone, till (I know not at what date) the Lewes was added. Mr. Cross has the phrenological cast about which Mrs. Bray was very anxious and he has also still the letters to Miss Lewis at which I was disappointed—as I would rather have asked her than him to let me see them. Mrs. Bray was turning over old letters of hers to Charles and herself; there was one when she had gone to Dr. Brabant after his daughter's marriage; apparently it was a very ugly family—she wrote of them as being all "almost as ugly as I am"—the sweet darling. Mrs. Bray was very vehement against Mrs. Lynn Linton's article[462]—the two had met at their house and they had rather admired Miss Lynn, but there was never the slightest intimacy between her and the Madonna; only some jealousy of the latter on her part;—they remembered her exclaiming—that woman is always in my way!—*á propos* of her small essays in enlightened literary enterprise here and there where I suppose she found the Madonna doing more brilliantly what she intended. The gentle old lady was quite fiery—it was wicked to hint such things—there was nothing to be known, nothing to hide and nothing to tell and Mrs. Linton had no means of knowing whether there was or not! In the absence of the letters I could learn nothing more definite about the transition in 1841. They acquiesced but without clear recollections when I asked if she was already

---

[462] Eliza Lynn Linton (1822-1898), novelist and journalist was wife of William James Linton, a life-long agnostic. She married William James Linton in 1858. She warned against too much education for women and attacks the "new woman" for unfeminine aggressiveness.

in the period of disagreement with her father about church going when they knew her first. Miss Hennell spoke of her mind being in a "chaotic" state and reiterated what I do accept, that she welcomed Hennell's book as giving the rationale of what she was already prepared to believe and reject. The Madonna once said that I reminded her of Sara (at which I was moderately flattered from what I knew of her "works") but I see now part of the resemblance—in temperament at least though after all the difference is greater than *la resemblance* as in George Sand's couplet. Sara has always regretted and a little condemned that side of my darling's nature: by the light of which *I* have tried hard to condemn my own—that side which made the friendship of men more to her than that of women—and which led her to believe—erroneously as regarded her men friends that men were kinder to her than women. I think Mrs. Cash's reminiscences might be definite enough to throw light on the period about November '41.

July 15, 1885

Unpacked at Harlaxton, came up here on the 2nd—nearly a fortnight ago, which has flown, though (or because) I have been quite alone with China. The jessamine is coming out—associated with the old summer reveries and longings. I think of her constantly with just the same kind of love as used to pour itself out in endless letters, but the undercurrent of personal pain and bitterness has ceased to exist. Life is not unendurable to me because half of the one supreme felicity has been out of reach. Much of the *Wille zum Sterben*[463] of all youth is made of repressed or unoccupied *Wille zum Leben*,[464] but there are many mansions in the "House of Life." I have worked off some of the steam that used to choke me, but when I contrast the dull quiet, the mild industry and new freedom from vexation which pleases me now with the savage misery I have endured under objectively identical conditions, I feel that work alone could not make all the difference and I am sorry for the young bears whose troubles have come and have not yet gone. It is a pity that one can't have two lives so as to judge for oneself which is best. It seems to me that it must be better for the young bears to get their honey combs (chancing the bees) instead of sucking their own paws till they have learnt to put up with a den and rations in the menagerie of a civilized world, Yet I, a tame beast now, who have given up climbing trees, and have lost my appetite for sweets, feel for a moment just tempted to wonder whether the honey combs were worth the hunting and the stings. It is an intellectual doubt that forced itself in, for what can one be more than content? but I don't *wish* to think the grapes are sour and apart from every other consideration I hold it to be desirable that if possible youth and nature should have their way, that, so far as possible a way should be cleared to let them go—because the years are so much longer when we are young; three months, then, hold so much more consciousness of pain than a whole year now can hold of anything, that it is

---

[463] "will to die"

[464] "will to live"

brutal to be indifferent—when the young bear tugs at his chain—because, with luck, he won't be always young!

September 27, 1885

Have been idle and too lazy even to spare a word of greeting to 41. Unwell also in a tiresome way—psoriasis of the palms which the family agree is deriving from hereditary gout and is thus their real opinion; I have felt my brains rather limp all the year, so it is a consolation to imagine a depressed level of vitality as perhaps responsible; but it is rather absurd the way in which my machine breaks down at the extremities. It would also be rather unfortunate for a person of socialistic proclivities to have to confess to the possession of "an itching palm." I am obliged to put this mild "goak" down here, as Mrs. Anderson is not yet back with her daughter from Australia and I could hardly bestow it upon the laity or upon any other doctor.

November 8, 1885

Went yesterday with Mrs. Paterson, whom I thought very ill, to Mrs. Anderson: "She is dying," was the verdict[465] though there is a gleam of hope till proper treatment has been tried and failed. Mrs. Anderson does not expect it to succeed; thinks she will not live 6 months—or three. My business is to get her at least to try. Mrs. Anderson is very good—offers to attend her constantly as is needed if she takes lodging near enough, since she will not entertain the idea of a hospital.

December 13, 1885

Shall have to give up 85 as hopelessly unproductive. Have just finished up the Ms of the Ming, but find it only too possible when it is dark and I am lazy or seedy to find the days too short for more than household affairs, letters, the newspapers, outdoor exercise and miscellaneous literature in the evening. This won't do. A paper for the Fabian Society[466] and a lecture for Socialists have been edged in, but very little real work, and perhaps I ought in candor to put down the woeful doubt which has presented itself to my inconveniently candid mind. Tell it not in Gath,[467] but it *has* occurred to me to wonder whether perhaps the female brain comes to the end of its tether in early middle age;—as the young of barbarous races do at early manhood. There is this analogy in favor of the gloomy view, and I fear only an example—that of my

---

[465] Emma Smith Paterson died at age 38 in 1886 while reading proofs of the *Women's Union Journal* (Norbert C. Soldon, *Women in British Trade Unions: 1874-1976*. [Dublin: Gill and Macmillan, 1878], 25).

[466] The Socialist group began in 1884; George Bernard Shaw (1856-1950) was one of the major supporters. Their motto was educate, agitate, and organize.

[467] 2 Sam. 1:20

Dear one—to quote against it. Hitherto I have never seen or felt reason to doubt that my brain—"what there is of it" as She says *á propos* of Sir James Chettam[468]—was of entirely masculine quality, but I am perhaps a little less confidently prepared than of old to back its staying power. The moral of this doubt is of course nothing unfavorable to the capacities of my sex. I am only warned yet regarding myself as a typical She.

January 17, 1886

Only open this book on a solitary Sunday evening to insure that the year shall not go too far without a word of recognition. Family claims have prevented my usual yearly visit to Highgate. William has been ill and I am always anxious about the effect of fresh anxiety or trouble on my mother's health; it would be hard if we were to lose her on his account—who has become, one may guess, the least necessary to her of the three. I am still limp and idle; League business now serving as an excuse for the lack of other work, which I physically could go on with in spite of flights up and down to Harlaxton. I think I will refuse all invitations to lecture. I don't like it well enough to practice and cultivate skill to do it well and 'tis hardly profitable to do anything as middlingly as I do this. Have said nothing about Mrs. Cash's pretty—and very true Appendix;[469] am waiting for a quiet space to write to her; and with a miser like dread of coming to the end of my store I have not yet got the new 3rd volume. I don't forgive Mr. Cross for leaving the reference to Lord Acton in the preface to the new edition.[470]

May 17, 1886

Returned to Harlaxton for a fortnight—just after the above. Then here; Will ordered abroad, so to Rome with Augustus. I meanwhile busy about Pimlico factory women; a deputation of them here one Tuesday evening to tea and talk (for the substance of which see W. U. J.)[471] was curiously associated with a sudden sick-headache; the next Thursday after a long afternoon Committee and delayed dinner, same phenomenon recurred, with a slight development of "shingles" next morning. Mrs. Anderson advised quinine "nervous exhaustion,"

---

[468] Sir James Chettam is a character in *Middlemarch*.

[469] The Appendix to Volume One is a statement by Mrs. John Cash of Coventry "in regard to the important subject of Miss Evans' change of religious belief in 1841-42 and for her further general recollections of the Coventry period of GE's life."

[470] JWC refers to Lord Acton in the Preface as "a friend always most kindly ready to assist me with valuable counsel and with cordial generous sympathy."

[471] *Women's Union Journal* was the monthly paper of the Women's Protective and Provident League, founded by Emma Paterson in 1874.

but either that remedy or a common cause a week or two later led to a mild cold (aggravated by 20 minutes in the garden on a damp, cold day) turning into spasmodic asthma—a fit which the doctors insisted on taking seriously, though I did not feel bad myself. Came up to London with difficulty and went to bed again here, wriggling through the League business and Pimilco controversy without material hindrance. Asthma followed by "psoriasis gultata" about elbows and ankles which disappears in two or three weeks to be succeeded by affection of the calf of the legs; and that, on next visit to Harlaxton by slight exzema about the back of the hand and fingers. Harrogate recommended; also assiduous Turkish baths. These small matters and the need for being always with my mother to prevent her bothering about the boys or feeling too forlorn have helped to excuse me for doing nothing—but light reading in these months. After Harrogate may get some quiet months and try again at the opus. But unless William gets stronger and succeeds in managing parish and curates with less fatigue to his mother, my influence will go into the scale in favor of his giving up his living and coming to live with us where ever suits her—not him. I see it is just ten years since this book was first written in. It is a longtime ago; and I am as different now from then as then from the she of ten years before—which is saying a great deal. Curious that a man like Carlyle should change so little in 60 or 70 years. Have just been looking at Masson's criticisms on Froude's presentation which are mostly fair enough. All that is written in this book is a part of me, but the objective ego looks and is from most points of view very much the same whether one's private soliloquies tell of uncontrollable agony or effortless calm. The curious thing about Carlyle is not that his Journals tell of the Abysmal darkness but that they never tell of any thing else. His objective self very likely changed as little as his Journalizings, which is a reason for abridging the personal element in the biography; a sample of the groanings within in each decade would show that he never ceased to groan—a fact which the veracities require us to know; but however inveterate a groaner he may have been, it must be an injustice to represent him as having spent—say 5/7 of his life in the process, as is done when that proportion of the memoir is spent in printing groans. Even the groans of a cheerful person who journalizes for more than 60 years might someday be constructed so as to fill half a dozen volumes. Carlyle did groan long and bitterly, but we are not obliged to believe that he groaned incessantly—tho' that is the impression Froude's treatment naturally conveys. Deo graties,[472] my groaning days seem over for the present and if I were industrious enough to journalize it would be with Pepysian objectivity[473]—about labour in Belgium and the states and as "alternative policy" to Mr. Gladstone's Irish bills.[474]

---

[472] "Thank God"

[473] Samuel Pepys (1633-1703), *Diary 1660-1669* (London: F. Warne, [1825]).

[474] W. E. Gladstone (1809-1898)

June 14, 1886. Harrogate.

Ten days of the waters don't seem to have done much for my small ailments which the local doctor regards as rather "anomalous." Feel rather annoyed with myself for not being able to contribute effectively to the problem of the election, but a non-election has less *locus standi*[475] than even when candidates and constituencies are all at sixes and sevens. Literally no one seems to be taking the line that seems to me clearly right for radicals. Gladstone's bill was stuffed with "guarantees" to pacify the middle class, and if carried by a coalition of Irish, radicals and docile liberals (of whom the two first would regard it as an instalment) the land bill, saddling "the English people" with more debt on the interest of landlords, would infallibly be carried afterwards, probably with aggravation by a coalition of docile liberals and conservative landlord's friends. I don't care a hang about "Imperial Unity" and wonder at Chamberlain's taking up so anti-popular a "cry," but I object to Gladstone's bills as not radical enough: it is logical to trust the Irish altogether if you trust them at all, and I should go with Davitt[476] in maintaining that the bills don't go far enough. If I were in the House I should either have voted against it on that ground, or have voted for it when it was doomed to defeat upon a clear statement that I should vote against any equally incomplete measure when in the domain of "practical politics." In the constituencies meanwhile I should vote only for those who opposed the bill as incomplete or who supported it with the intention of completing it before it passed. Failing such a candidate I should abstain, the result of which would be to let in the Whigs or Conservatives, but also to let the radical vote consolidate in opposition. If I were obliged to offer an "alternative policy" it would be the creation of a Statutory Parliament, the first business of which should be to pass a bill regulating the connection between the two countries; this bill when passed, should be brought by the Irish representatives to Westminster, to pass if it could, if at first defeated, one could go to the country with more enthusiasm for it than for Mr. Gladstone's elastic "principle." The bill would probably be reasonable in substance and given adequate protection to Ulster by minor "Home Rule" concessions to the provinces, because it should be known that a majority at Westminster would be on the side of the English minority. If—to put an improbable case—the bill were egregiously absurd, the Irish would have damaged their own cause at the least expense to other people, and there would be some rational ground for curtailing their political liberties.

November 7, 1886

Ten days ago going to call on Mrs. Congreve I had the good luck to find Mrs. John Cash[477] with her; a bright eyed, silver haired version of the pretty

---

[475] "to take a stand"

[476] Michael Davitt was a member of the Irish Republican and Fenian Brotherhoods, dedicated to the overthrow of British rule in Ireland.

[477] Mary Sibree Cash was the daughter of a minister who lived at Foleshill when GE was a young woman.

fair girl to whom she taught German and for whose straight-forward character she had much regard. She talked a good deal, more out of her own head than about the Madonna; said it was curious that she remembered more of Mrs. Bray's particular sayings than of hers, though the society of both was an unspeakable delight to a dissenting minister's daughter used to narrow views at home, (though her own mother was originally a churchwoman). Marian's revulsion from Evangelicalism they thought was partly the result of disgust at the low moral standard of "Christians," but it was also suggested that it was hardly fair to compare the standard of Coventry trades folk with that of country gentlemen and beneficed clergy—as Mrs. Cash *mére* was inclined to do. Mrs. Cash spoke strongly as to the absurdity of supposing her views to have changed with the suddenness the first edition of the memoir implies, or that she needed any one to put doubts into her head; and she confirmed Miss Hennell's account of the service rendered by the brother's book:—after she had given up all her old convictions, and felt at sea for want of them, it reconciled her to her own and the world's past by making the discarded faith appear historically intelligible if not theologically true. She thought that it ought to be more generally understood that in marrying Mr. Lewes she was doing what she had long before maintained to be right and lawful in other cases. Apparently there was some well known case of a non-conformist minister, separated from his wife with whom a certain Miss—— ——went to live; and when the ladies of the congregation sent a deputation to remonstrate, she calmly justified herself and Mrs. Lewes (or rather then Miss Evans) justified her. They said that she felt strongly about the hardship to the man, when practically divorced and of course from the higher ground of an equal moral standard, it is impossible to say that under such circumstances a man *may* associate with a "light woman" and may *not* form a true union with a true and loyal wife. At the same time, these speculative views of the "rights" of men or women to a divorce under certain circumstances, had unquestionably fallen much into the background when I knew her and she was much more anxious to insist upon the duty of satisfying every claim to which one's own action had given rise than upon any personal right. But on the main issue her opinion had not changed: her own conduct had been more than justified by the event and all that experience could suggest to her in the way of doubt as to how far her example should be counted as a precedent would be in connection with her knowledge of the rare qualities demanded on both sides to avoid the risk of what, as she said of it once, might have made a hell for her:—no sense of duty would have made it possible to her to continue to give a wife's devotion to one who proved unworthy, but this is not saying that she was capable—like George Sand[478]—of passions ending in disenchantment. It is inconceivable that such a woman could love—as she could and did love—any one unworthy of her, or that any one blessed with her love should fail to feel that love the crowning joy of life and

---

[478] George Sand (1804-1876) was a French woman novelist whose many passionate love affairs and life of bohemianism led her to confess that her emotions were always stronger than the arguments of reason.

seek to pay for it with growing worthiness. Mrs. Cash quoted her nephew F. Evans[479] as saying it would be a life-long regret not to have known her.

January 31, 1887

Dined with the Congreves on the 19th. Not much speech of Her and it seems not to occur to me to write of much else here. Mrs. Congreve had noticed independently the likeness in Mrs. Druce. In the last 6 months have done no good between this and Harlaxton—my mother here or I there and intervening weeks too short for anything but waiting. I rebel and offer to leave London so as to have but one house on my mind and my mother in it. For her sake did parochial festivities at Xmas—am decidedly growing old. Mrs. Paterson lived little more than a twelve month after Mrs. Anderson's verdict. The shock to me came then; her temper and character were suffering from the struggle with the world and illness together and for her sake it was as well. We are to see if it is possible to build her a worthy monument. It is nearly a month since I came up here—have done no China and have felt continuously busy—sometimes even over done—so easy is it as one grows old to fill the days without any affairs of one's own—though in fact I have given two—last Thursday and today—to the inspection of houses—at Marks Cross near Tunbridge Wells and Harmondsworth in West Drayton—the last a picturesque Queen Anne house which may tempt Augustus.

April 15, 1887

Interval muddled away; my mother here; house-hunting continued at intervals; have learnt something of geography of home counties. Necessity for change increasingly apparent. China has been stationary for nearly two years.

July 13, 1887

Ditto ditto—Hope rather despairingly to be settled in pretty country place by Michaelmas. A high school head mistress proposes to take Douro Place, which reminds me disagreeably of the objective failure a combination of circumstances have induced me to make of my existence, with at least a measurable material loss.

September 12, 1887

(In the Ms Woodleigh Mayfield is on the page opposite.)

Came hither on August 30, my mother following next day; so far as well as could have been hoped and better than was expected. Place very lovely, house comfortable and when all in order will be rather luxurious; when settled here shall hope to avoid all that makes the process of aging painful. If so shall be quite happy myself with the scenery and book.

---

[479] Reverend Frederick Rawlins Evans, son of GE's brother Isaac

September 28, 1887

Do not open to recant these cheerful auguries, though I feel a little unreasonable nervousness lest something should misbefal my mother just in the last 3 or 4 weeks which have to pass before she comes here "for good." The changing lights and shades of the day and the distances are inexhaustibly pretty: and I can't believe but what my wretched little ailments will disappear when we are at peace here. I can—at last get on with Ownership—or admit that I shall never do so anymore. Nothing meanwhile will amuse me better than to employ labours enough to get this pretty place made as pretty in detail as it is now in outline.

October 17, 1887

Heard a few days back that a man, not so much older than Augustus— or at least not outrageously his senior had just married the daughter of their old college head, who was regarded by fellows as well as undergraduates as an old maid when I might have been called a young one. It was an open question whether he did it from good nature, to bring her back to her old home, she being lonely else, or as moved by a thousand reasons per annum which had accrued along with the loneliness. This bit of college gossip somehow started me on reminiscences which I think I may venture at this time of day to set down without danger of having to swallow hereafter any of the sauce in which they dress themselves now. Such confidences—if they ever get published encourage others and I confess I should like to hear a few more frank autobiographical details as to women's intimate natural feeling about men than the sex has yet indulged in. Historically, psychologically, intellectually—and it may be admitted from pure carnal curiosity too I should like to know how many women there are who have honestly no story to tell, how many have some other story than the one which alone is supposed to count and how many of those who think it worth while to dissect themselves are in a position to tell all they know of the result. To begin with: "I say it and I think to be believed"—there is nothing at all in my memory or consciousness (in *this* chapter) which it makes me the least uncomfortable to remember or which I feel the least reluctance to communicate—in befitting time and place. When a small child (under 12) I remember being rebuked for a not infrequent remark that I "liked boys best" and it was a mild domestic joke to enquire after the "three" boys. My brothers, it may be observed were rather imperfectly boyish and I was certainly in things physical more of a "muff" than many girls now a days who are not called tomboys. The base of the above preference was a want of sympathy with girls' games and talk—I did not care for dolls or dress or any sort of needlework—and I think a quite simple natural predisposition to "like" any nice looking boy of the not uncommon type of fair, frank faced friendliness—freckles and reddish hair not being at all objected to. If I remember right such a boy had to be 3 or 4 years older than myself, for I was anything but flattered when a "little boy"—a year or so my junior—took upon himself to send me a Valentine after we had met at one of my rare "parties." As it happened none of the families we visited with constantly had some of this description, so any potentialities of friendship in this direction remained undeveloped; if I had been pressed to analyse the ground of my inclination towards either of the boys—I could mention 3 or 4—that I am thinking of, as far as I can guess I should have described them as likely to be jolly to play with—cleverer at games than my brothers or myself and less obedient to instructions about what not to do than girls. At exactly the same period I was annoyed and affronted, in a child's inarticulate way, at any thing approaching to chaff about any supposed admiration of me as a girl by any boy, as a boy. I was passionately and spoonily fond of my mother, and easily attached myself to older girls or women, if, as at school intimacy was achieved in spite of my shyness. My affection was of a demonstrative, "fondling" sort, not at all deeply sentimental, as I am helped to realize by one curious reminiscence. At school I belonged emphatically to George Sand's class of *diables* and was generally at feud with the authorities—the French governess of the period being generally an exception for one thing because "discipline" was not so much in her department and for another—I now surmise—because we found each other more conversable and companionable than the general run of school girls and third rate English assistants. I didn't always kiss the people I was on friendly terms with, but there was one big, plain Mademoiselle Legrand about whom I used to hang or romp caressingly at times and I still have a lively recollection of the amazement that possessed me when the mistress of the school once asked me if I was really fond of Mademoiselle—as I gave myself the appearance of being by such conduct. I had never asked myself the question and on reflection now I am aware that my liking was of the most childishly superficial kind, as it was no particular grief to me when she left. What amazed me was the suggestion that it was possible to kiss *de parti pris*:[480] the idea was too remote and inconceivable for me to be hurt or offended and I think even at the time I was a little amused at my instructress having made such a bad shot.—for which never the less, she was not so much to blame, for she had discovered, what I am sorry to say was the fact, that I was not an entirely veracious child. There is a degree of shyness which runs into secretiveness and that again into untruthfulness—sometimes quite irrational—a sort of "ask me no questions and I'll tell you no lies," feeling or rather instinct, which makes a child conceal things indifferent and doubly inclined to conceal any thing likely to be criticised—not by any means so much from fear of blame as dislike of comment. I was quite capable of telling my French friend a lie (tho' I don't remember having done so) but I either could not, would nor should ever have imagined the possibility of doing such a thing as bestowing a pet name or a caress for any other reason than that I felt so disposed. I don't blame the schoolmistress because it is certainly odd that—for instance I should have had too little fear of blame or desire for approbation to prevent my being outrageously defiant and disobedient—over the small matters that used to be made so much too much of in small girls' schools—and yet at the same time should have been capable—if asked what book I had been reading, of saying one rather than another when I had an equal right to read both and there was no particular merit or demerit about the act—except the demerits of inveracity which the instinct of secretiveness quite gratuitously induced me to incur.

---

[480] "with detachment"

At the very time when I didn't know that I didn't care really very much for the French governess I kissed, I found out that I *had* cared much more than I knew for the old family doctor who used to call me "Poppet" and wound my dignity by complimentary remarks about my calves. He died when I was at school; my mother nursed him and he sent a message to "Missy"—that was another name "she little knows how I loved her." I was 12 at the time and at no interval in the 30 years and more that have passed since have I been able to recal this without tears coming into my eyes. It was misery to me to hear people talk about him—as my mother would about his illness—and as I *couldn't* help crying; I used to go and hide and hated again to feel that people exchanged significant looks—though I neither knew nor cared what they meant—it was just an intrusion into the privacy of one's soul that they should notice at all—anything that I didn't choose to have noticed. But it would no more have occurred to me to pretend not to care for Mr. Hursfield than to pretend to care for anyone I didn't more or less irrationally "like."

If we advance a stage, from 12 to 16, it occurs to me that I never felt towards young men anything approaching that sort of inclination I have confessed towards the boys. At a German school party I remember declining to dance with the poor unsure students but talking to professors and being offered their arm to supper—which I gauchely declined as giving me undue precedence: but I had no embarrassment about accepting the loan of *Wahrheit und Dichtung*[481] from a professor I would not waltz with. A year or two later we had some boys staying with us for a month to escape measles, one of them a dark-haired, rosy, grey eyed young rascal of 13 or 14, of whom I was rather fond, so much so that when he was going away I felt half-inclined to kiss him and half-thought he would not mind—in which I was not "deceived by my own vanity," as I was reproached a minute later for not having done so, as he wanted! Alas! there are more regrettable omissions than that due to the same cause—shyness and what I have called secretiveness reduced from active inveracity to a sort of habit of non-committal, which I repent now as a real insincerity—the opposite of the one to which I pled truly not guilty years before.

An intimate friend once described to me the emotions of delight and awe with which at about sixteen, it first dawned upon her that she might be an object of interest to an interesting young man; she is still unmarried and has felt dawnings of interest in several men young or otherwise which have not led to ulterior consequences. For myself I must confess that I have never known any man show the smallest inclination to take a particular interest of this kind in me: and I must also confess that I never met any man whom I in the slightest degree wished to take such an interest. I never came nearer than on the one occasion quoted above to including any man and myself in the most imaginative proposition with a matrimonial term. To say that I never was in love with a mortal man is to say too little; I never wished to be nor contemplated the possibility of being—except in the abstract under the pressure of Mrs. Lewes's real and supposed preferences and that very reluctantly and against the grain.

---

[481] John Wolfgang von Goethe (1749-1832)

Not that I had or have any prejudice against marriage—on the contrary, given a man who is adorably lovable and marriage is the natural climax of celestial bliss. I only objected to the view that, for the sake of marriage in the abstract I should be expected to espouse concretely any particular person of my acquaintance. Many of them no doubt only needed the love imagined to be made adorable, but "if they were not so to me"—I did not see that this was my fault. I remember having towards two rather different heroes—Garibaldi[482] that is and John Stuart Mill[483]—perhaps the same sort of *tendre*[484] as that professed by Charlotte Brontë for the Duke of Wellington[485] and I can imagine myself to have been predisposed to fall femininely in love if I had met in the flesh with any man who would have excited my admiration "in that sort of way;" and if the hero had been so hard up as to idealize reciprocally, I should have surrendered at discretion like so many of my betters. As it happened the woman I knew was sweeter and wiser, better and greater than any man of my acquaintance, but I did not fall in love with her person but with her qualities, nay: this is not quite exact. I did fall in love with her person, so as to care infinitely more for her—qualities and all—than I could care for any human qualities otherwise embodied, and therefore I think the same qualities in a man would have produced the same effect on me, notwithstanding any slackness there may be on my part to become sensible to the personal charm of men—I admit however that such irrational liking as I have described myself feeling for women and boys, might in many cases start an intimacy that should open the way to admiration and end in love. It just occurs to me to mention that I like and know girls really more and better than boys, but in their case I think I expect them to do the unreasoning beginning; that is, I am both seriously and superficially fond of them provided they begin by being superficially fond of me.

I have never wished to be married in the abstract and I would decidedly much rather not be married to any concrete Dick or Tom. But I have also no practical doubt that the melancholia which darkened many years of my life was due to what I may call the emotional inanition of spinsterhood and I quite recognize that for some people marriage may be the best, and for some the only alternative or remedy. But for most it is not the only and for some few not even the best; and for all those to whom it is not the only alternative it is an immense

---

[482] Giuseppe Garibaldi (1807-1882), picaresque Italian military leader and intrepid fighter

[483] John Stuart Mill (1806-1873) was a philosopher and author of *A System of Logic* (London: J. W. Parker, 1843), *On Liberty* (London: J. W. Parker, 1859), *Utilitarianism* (London: Parker, Son and Bourn, 1863), *On the Subjection of Women* (London: Longmans, 1869), and other works.

[484] "tenderness"

[485] Lord Arthur Wellesley Wellington (1769-1852) was an Irish soldier and statesman.

mistake not to cultivate all the rest, at all events *en attendant*.[486] In some people literary or scientific pursuits might be sufficient. I didn't find them so, for one thing because I don't really enjoy anything except generalizations out of my own head, while my mind is barrenly unproductive unless the rest of me is animated by some outside stimulus. I was happy in writing the book which grew up under the prompting of my passion for Her. But work done to order was as dull as idleness; I was alone at it, the world not helping me and that was just what was the matter with the rest of my existence. For anyone in the same state I should prescribe active not sedentary work and the luck which sent me on the School Board just when I must have been otherwise most desolate was one of the very few—if not the only good turn I owe to the chapter of accidents. Some people may think it a curious cure, but the fact is that the administrative details of the work were an amusement as well as an occupation to me, and it is amusement that we all want when we are young—and adoring each other isn't by any means the only one available. Every thing else pales in comparison with real worship, if the occasion for that comes to us, but it is like taking the consecrated bread for breakfast to depend on love for one's amusement though if we have that we may need no other. Time I expect would only aggravate one's melancholy if one had done nothing else to cure it, but three things together have availed in my own bad case and I am now proof even against the dangers of idleness and solitude: Love, occupation and time have done their part in turn, and without undervaluing other people's lives, I don't, honestly, wish to change mine for theirs.

I have thought my experience in this matter worth recording, for the benefit of young folks, not of my own sex exclusively. There is more common human nature in *both* boys and girls than anything else; my own nature any way I have a million reasons in prose and verse to know to be eminently human, and not the less because so far as humanity differentiates into sex, my temperament leans towards the masculine. Full grown young men and women suffer—sometimes bitterly and intensely from weary or restless discontent and dissatisfaction, which they explain to themselves in a thousand queer ways—John Stuart Mill's being by no means singularly queer: mine at its worst was compounded of the two states approximately described in the "Episodes" called "A Rainbow" and "Eclipse." Whatever one supposes to be the reason, the real reason is that we have more or less conscious desires and capacities for more and different enjoyment than life happens to afford us just then. I think it is on the whole a progress that the devil appears to modern St. Anthonys in the form of despair at the exhaustibility of musical forms rather than in cruder, more penetrable disguises. The fact that he does thus disguise himself among the better sort is I take it decidedly a reason against taking a purely materialistic view of the difficulty and getting the family doctor to prescribe marriage or a liaison—in acute cases—according to the sex of the patient. The melancholy is a mental affection, whatever its remotest origin and it takes its colour from the habitual furniture of one's mental chamber. In no case is this so perfect and complete as to need only the installation of a domestic idol, and everything that would be

---

[486] "while waiting"

good and needful to make a perfect life for a favoured lover is also—and all the more, good and needful to those who are not yet in that blessed position. They are not yet, and if they never should be, they will yet be better off possessed of all the rest of life's good necessaries than one who has begun with luck in love and thought, too fondly, "love is enough." For love is after all only a means of grace; it doesn't of itself carry with it all things necessary to salvation: and the duty of temperance, which means leaving room for all the rest of life's due interests, is all the harder when its practice is in a manner voluntary. On the other hand, real love is so much better than anything else and may make every thing else so perfectly good that I should be sorry for any one who is capable of feeling it to put up with less—as a man does, if he marries upon a mere superficial liking merely to escape privation. This is to escape a finite evil by surrendering a possibility of infinite good: and for some it may be wise to conclude such a bargain. I only want to help every one to know what they are doing, and to aim at the best result within their powers. As to the girls, I speak, strange to say, more diffidently: I fancy only our matrons know how much misery in marriage there is among women, so much that there is even perhaps a half cynical tendency among them to think it must be so and to acquiesce, hoping the victims may find compensation in their children, a calculation, if there is any thing in heredity, the less likely to be realized where the father's character makes compensation most desirable. Without entering upon the trite ground of what women have to gain by wider interests and more varied avocations, it may suffice to show that women are not constitutionally inconsolable for the calamity of not finding a marriageable hero, if we remember what a disproportionate number of the women with plenty of money of their own remain single. If women have money enough to provide themselves with other amusements, they do not take a husband unless they care for him, and when the other amusements are plentiful and partaken of with humanly wise discretion the melancholy of youth is outgrown naturally. Heretofore as a rule only rich women have had as much amusement as the average educated man who isn't rich. As I reflect that of these two classes the men probably make a larger percentage of positive blunders in their relations with the other sex, I conclude that women as a class already fill up what voids they feel in their affections by the miscellaneous interests of family and friendship so that if material interests and variety are provided in addition, they rest farely well content. And since men have already the material interests and occupations in plenty, to secure for them the same calm of provisional content, they should probably be advised to depend more upon the pleasures of ordinary affection, loving and liking friends and relations and cultivating the consciousness of such feeling, without thinking it necessary to be "in love" with a woman, unless the time comes when they can't help being in love with the one woman they can love all over for life. Just in due exercise of the bodily powers checks the visited growth of physical appetites so due exercise of the mental powers, in disinterested thought, emotion and will, restrains the disproportionate absorption of the mind itself in the cravings and moanings of disguised desire.

To summarize my prescription for all young sufferers from the malady of Weltschmerz[487]—and I am the last person in the world to underrate their severity—: I should say: Do more work; get enough play; know more people intimately; like more people well; in fact, know and like so many more than you could possibly marry that you would not begin to think about marrying any of them unless there turns out to be something quite different from all the rest in that one liking as to reveal itself—the true god of love. Of course this advice won't help the melancholy unless we all try to multiply opportunities for wholesome work, play and friendly intercourse; one doesn't cure a disease by saying what waters the patient should drink, only in so far as it is a symptom of the disease to esteem itself incurable, something may be gained by a mere enumeration of remedies proved and recommended by a former sufferer.

Though I agree with Mill in thinking it a fault in English life that intimacy and friendship for the sake of it are not sufficiently cultivated, I cannot say that I owe much of my deliverance to such relations, as indeed I have not been tempted to desire such for myself except in relation to Her. I still find it difficult to get on with people unless I am brought forcibly in contact with them. My mind is a blank if I have to talk to anyone and more especially to men, about nothing in particular; I always liked the conversation of men of business, started on a subject of their own and remember with interest after 25 years one such with an uncle, director of the Bank of England, of whom I was usually shyly afraid; but this account of his experience of the changes in the conditions of business during his lifetime interested me at once; as a rule the men I have known best have been introduced to me as their wives' husbands, my brother's pupils, or my own colleagues on the School Board or "Societies." I was on pleasantly fraternal terms with the best members and officials of the former body, and without going so far as to affirm that I still "liked boys best," it is a fact that I more often found myself working with the men than women. I eschewed both cookery and needlework and my favorite Committee was the Sites and Buildings Subcommittee of the Works and General Purposes. Had I stayed on the Board and the parties remained unchanged, I should probably have been proposed to succeed Lyulph Stanley on the Statistical Committee, and tho' I'm not sure that a majority of men would have cared to give such a post of honour to a woman, they would have given it to me as readily as to any (in fact *entrê nous* more readily). I did not however get very far towards intimacy in private life even with the few who were on the natural social level for such a result, and it is perhaps characteristic that the one occasion upon which I was made a confidante of (as to the religious difficulties of a non-conformist minister) was due to the prompting of another woman, who told *me* that he would be glad to talk and *him* that I should be glad to hear; whereupon we spent 2 or 3 hours in walking round Kensington Gardens (a walk that I remember the more because an unaccustomed attack of vertigo made it difficult to me to keep my legs at starting), with the result that he proposed to retain his cure as long as the congregation was content with such teaching as he was conscientiously free to bestow on it. I note this

---

[487] "pain over the world"

because I am not otherwise able to endorse Miss Cobbe's accusation against men of always wanting to talk about themselves, from my own experience, while yet I do not wish to explain their reserve, if unusually developed towards me, by any incapacity on my part to bestow lawful sympathy. The fact that I found it easier to talk "Academy" shop to poor Appleton than social platitudes to other people probably gave rise to the *canard*[488] exaggerating my intimacy with him. I have little doubt that in general my manners are more reserved than my feelings and when I come to think of it I am aware that I rather take for granted that the ice of customary conventions is to be broken—whenever any body else pleases though there is no reason why I should not take my share in beginning that disruptive process. The fact that I don't feel a craving to talk about my *self* to others ought not to be a disqualification for receiving their talk; but I fancy the communicative temperament, even though chastened into discreet silence is the one naturally found sympathetic.

Before leaving the interesting—and cognate—subjects of kisses and the School Board, I should be ungrateful not to mention one of the former to which I was indebted for my official duties. I had gone to see a school of high reputation in Southwark and happened to reach it the day after the Government inspection, when the elder infants had just been promoted to the boys' and girls' departments and their places filled en bloc by the respectable babies whose parents only waited for vacancies to enrol them. The small new comers were just being taught to walk in procession and I stopped one little three year older, a white and pink, blue eyed, flaxen curled pet, just like the babies brought in for dessert in well-appointed households. I knelt down by the little she Bouddha and asked her name—which the mistress at least was able to hear and then I asked her to give me a kiss and was delighted to receive one, quite real, soft, warm and affectionate, telling more conclusively than the smart frock and curls of a family life with all its gentlest elements full grown. In the course of my democratic wanderings, I have found, with less unqualified satisfaction that small children, frequently with imperfectly clean faces, confidently expect to have them kissed by their mothers' friends; and I heard lately of a baby being kissed till it was black in the face—with dirt not convulsions—by an affectionate upper standard of Board schoolgirls; but this baby bestowed its clean caress in a leisurely, gentle, clinging fashion proving conclusively that it had been taught to "kiss and love" not merely to endure rough hugs. As a rule I think kisses are wasted upon babies, the animals being unresponsive as a class, and even these charming appearances of affection, which one gets now and then, being probably imitative, like the precocious dramatic power which these same 3 year olders sometimes put into their little "action songs." It seems therefore that nice boys, only very nice babies and the women one likes are the classes of beings which my unassisted nature would have recognized as naturally to be kissed. Lover's kisses of course never grow old, otherwise I confess I have always had rather a feeling of incongruity about the kissing of full grown men and women, as for instance between brothers

---

[488] "falsehood"

and sisters-in-law or such elderly philanderers as Anthony Trollope[489] somewhere describes, with sympathetic feeling. My sympathies go quite with the young man—in any class of life—who finds temptation almost or quite irresistible when some fair maiden who wants mind is there, yet I am rather shocked when we hear in these days of girls in one's own class letting themselves be kissed, and therewith an end, but not by one pair of lips only. I am not laying down principles, only describing my own natural prejudices—which made me also long earnestly to unfrock a well known elderly clergyman who tried to kiss the plain, elderly manageress of a co-operative work shop when they had offered to sew a button on his glove. If anyone is offended at my prudishness they may have their revenge upon me, for if the whole tale of my kissing were to be told, it would include a good many given to a man 20 years older than myself and no relation after the flesh. There was something very innocently boyish about Mr. Lewes and it did not seem to me unnatural that he should expect to be kissed or petted a little when he was ill, but when he was well, in the palace of Truth I think, I should have betrayed an impression that he was rather too hairy for the purpose. But since he thought it appropriate to our relationship as brother worshipers at one dear shrine, I had nothing against it; indeed I remember an impulse, counted among those that I have restrained, to put an arm round both their necks as they stood close together and kiss first one and then the other as a parent does two happy children. The fact is there are as many kinds of good kisses as there are of dear loves; friendly, filial or fraternal; a mother's, a lover's and those appropriate to any composite relation in law or love, provided always that two things separately lawful are not contaminated by an unavowed admixture, as when something amorous sneaks into the relation between two persons who are not lovers or who stand to each other in some other relation incompatible with that.

Here ends a chapter which is rather long considering how little there is in it.

March 18, 1888

It was after Whitsuntide this year that we came up to Lancaster Gate and old Merriman said "no disease of the kidney, but grave functional disorder." He then gave her Rubyiat water instead of cascara, which kept her pretty well.

January 4, 1889

Last month I observed with surprise that I had written nothing here all the year, and meant to supply the deficiency with memoranda about the International Workman's Congress in London.

April 27, 1889

As to said Congress, I reported daily to the Manchester Guardian, handing in a column or so of stuff between 5 and 8 p.m. for telegraphing. Noted

---

[489] Anthony Trollope (1815-1882) wrote novels which deal with life and love in a cathedral city with a background of ecclesiastical politics.

that telegrams came out more free from printer's errors than uncorrected Ms. Paid my expenses and bought winter garments with the proceeds. Saw Eccarius,[490] looking very feeble, since dead. Had small room (42 Great Russell Street) 12/6 a week, and had a party of miners to breakfast one morning, and in an evening when the Metallurgists wished to meet and had no where to go, was pleased again to receive them. The function at Toynbee Hall was interesting, tho' I was very much struck by the *gaucherie*[491] of the Oxonians, who seemed utterly unable to talk to any one without having been "introduced." One boy who was singular in being able to talk French sat by Tortellier (the Anarchist) and did talk to him, but when I asked Tortellier to ask him how he liked Anseele's[492] speech he only blushed and made no answer! I am so incorrigibly impractical that I listened to the speeches in complete serenity, never dreaming to be called on myself—as I was of course for the women of East London. Brought in a few sentences that I had thought of for the Congress on the theme I have often set forth without much convincing anyone—that the masses may really learn that selfishness does not pay—for them—and therefore cultivate the social virtues as the easiest—not to say the only way in which they, all together, can have good times. In English here also it fell rather flat, but the spokesman of the French delegation thanked me and said it was "trés pesé et trés profond."[493] On the Saturday night after the Congress I went with Tortellier and another delegate and the big fellow who was turned out as a "patron," to a tea-fight got up by the Socialist League in honour of Mrs. Parsons, widow of one of the men—I think one must call it, judicially murdered—at Chicago; there and at a meeting of the same set on the following Monday I got the reports of the speeches and the trial by which it seemed that all but a German or two were perfectly innocent of everything except such agitation as I and all the rest do securely. Two men are still in prison, Fielding and Neck, for the most innocent and disinterested trade unionism. Kropotkin[494] and his wife, Cunninghame Graham[495] and Morris[496]

---

[490] J. G. Eccarius was a naturalized German and follower of Karl Marx; he and Marx were associated with the International Working Men's Association from its beginning in 1864. Marx assumed the leadership and Eccarius was secretary (McK, 41, n. 3).

[491] "awkwardness"

[492] Edouard Anseele (1856-1928) was co-founder of the Belgian Socialist Party and leader of the Belgian Workmen's Association (McK, 53).

[493] "very weighty and very profound"

[494] Prince P. A. Kropotkin (1842-1921) was a Russian geographer, author, and revolutionary. In 1872 he became a member of the International Workingmen's Association at Geneva, then an anarchist. He was expelled from Switzerland and imprisoned by the French Government; he settled in London in 1886 (McK, 52).

were at the tea fight and I went to the station with the two former, who was pretty ready in his exposition of anarchism: even reason does not *command*, at rule, it suggests and inspires. The Parliamentary Committee behaved all through like the lower order of Britisher; the average delegate found the translating rather slow, while the better class were interested and vowed they must learn French. After the Congress I did a little letter writing between English and other Societies, but as the practical intercourse is still undeveloped, the mere exchange of information doesn't inspire much enthusiasm. At Toynbee Hall the Dutch interpreter proposed to translate the Chairman's (Mr. Barnett's) speech to his flock and I was disgusted to find how little I could guess at the meaning. Coming back Anseele, who was talking equally tantalizing Flemish gave me a Ghent paper the Tockomst, and after returning home I had a try at that with the Dutch dictionary A. had got for his Theological Commentaries. I found the language manageable and had the inspiration of getting a Dutch or Belgian governess for a "holiday engagement." Succeeded better than might have been expected, with an intelligent "Remonstrant" who lent me as many books as I could read in the month, corrected letters to Dutch and Flemish Socialists and gave half the sense and—or at least all the objections and all the language in a dialogue on Socialism which I wrote as an exercise. Have been taking in the Dutch Socialist paper since as a reading book. As compared with German and English the differences are mainly a matter of spelling, but the language seems to be a degree more natural than either of the others: it has purged itself of Gallicisms to an admirable extent. The English Congress voted for the holding of a Paris Congress in 89 to be got up by our friends of the *Parti Ouvrière* and I have been much exercised for the last month upon this subject. The Parlimentary Committee declined to take my part in the Congress, even to the extent of transmitting invitations to the Societies. There upon the Socialist Trade Unionist called a T. U. Protest Committee on 18th March seeing the report of which in "Justice" I felt moved to suggest that they should not only protest, but set up a provisional organisation for international correspondence, which was done April 1. But while England was thus being reconciled with the Continental Socialists, the latter were falling out among themselves. Apparently the Germans have not forgiven the Londoners for not inviting them to the 88 Congress and they and the French Marxists, the party of Guarde and Lafargue, were united in grudging to the French Possibilists the management of the 89 Congress. Consequently they between them persuaded the Dutch and Belgians, that the proposed "order of the Day" of the National Committee of the Parti Ouvrier (or Possibilists) covered all sorts of dark designs about the exclusion of Marxist organisations and at a Conference at the Hague on

---

[495] R. B. Cunninghame Graham, author and socialist, was a Labour M.P. from 1886 to 1892. He was imprisoned during 1887 as a result of the Trafalgar Square riots; he and Hardie organized the Scottish Labour Party (McK, 52).

[496] William Morris joined the Social Democratic Federation in 1883. On its disruption in 1884 he became head of the seceders who organized themselves as the Socialist League (McK, 52).

February 28 Lafargue, Bebel and Liebknecht, Croll and Mincerhins, and Morris, Anseele and another Belgian, in the absence of any Possibilists, who complain that they only had a week's notice of the meeting, and no answer to their questions preliminary to attending it—drew up some "demands" which the Possibilists were for the most part already prepared to accept, tho' they don't seem to have said so in conciliatory terms. Curiously enough, Bowers and Mann, who were the friends of the French at the last Congress, are more or less inspired by the Marxists, their Bernstein,[497] my old Zurich acquaintance, and they wished before English Trade Unionists went further, to ask for information from the Hague people as to those difficulties. So I wrote to Croll, Bernstein and Anseele on one side and Gély on the other on behalf of a very sensible little Correspondence Committee we had got the "Protestants" to appoint. Anseele was on the war path, curt, illegible and I thought less conciliatory than if he had been more literate; Bernstein was civil and not obviously ill-meaning; Gély was in Spain, and Croll waited for his council to meet. Meanwhile Adolphe Smith had written in alarm from Paris thinking we were going over to the Marxists as against his clients, so altogether, there was a pretty imitation of diplomatic *embroillments*.[498] The Correspondence Committee tho' mainly Socialist in composition had all the British Trade Unionist feelings and apart from unions, they were all disposed to support the orthodox French mandatories of the London Congress and after their first meeting (April 8) I wrote again to Anseele and Gély, and to Bebel and Christensen. By the 15th I had heard from Bebel and there was a discussion in the main Committee showing just the same British feeling somebody observed: "I don't think much of those Germans." However as we were too poor to send an ambassador to the Flemish Congress at Joluinsut, not to mention that our only linguist, the cabinet maker Parsell, had just gone to a "new shop" and dares not be away Easter Tuesday—I was instructed to write the English views to the French delegate who was going and the Belgian secretary of the Congress, which I did next day, also by A. Smith's wish sending a copy to the Belgian paper "Le Peuple." Letters from Croll and Lavy for Gély reached me next day and since then I have also heard from Christensen, the Dane. Most of the letters always contrive to answer just wide of one another; so that tho' with good will all might be agreed, it is easy to see how without it, the squabbling may go on for ever in spite of there being no real issue in dispute. The nominal issue is whether the Congress or the Nationalities are to verify the credentials of delegates and whether the order of the day is to be fixed before the Congress meets by putting together the subjects asked for by all the nations, or to be left open for indefinite enlargement or alteration after the meeting. From conversation with A. Smith I gather that the National Committee *don't* much wish to conciliate the Marxists, who, they think, would only try to "upset the

---

[497] Eduard Bernstein (1850-1932) was a bank clerk who became a member of the German Social Democratic Party in 1872. He was forced to leave Germany in 1878; he lived in Switzerland until he moved to London in 1888 (McK, 53).

[498] "confusions"

Congress" if they attended it, at the same time they are committed not to exclude them if they apply for admission in the name of genuine societies with any stated number of members. The Marxists are well organised for Bernstein had news at once of Gély's mission to Spain, but I daresay it is true that they are mainly middle-class politicians—perhaps some enthusiasts, some intriguers,—were pullers of different degrees of honesty, the professional politicians to speak of internationalism, living rather in the world of Socialist newspapers than of real working class organisation. This would account for their having more money in proportion than men, and so being able as Smith declares to put embarrassed workmen in their debt. He accuses Champion of aligning himself with Maltman Barry, who is notoriously venal and was accused of trying to sell the old international, and is still suspected of selling Socialist discord to the Tories. Champion is said (still by Smith) to have given Burns £50, and Engels through Bernstein is supposed to influence Mann. On the other hand, before all this Burns had talked in much disgust about the S.D.F.[499] intrigues, suspicion, and so on, instancing Champion as a man who had been hunted out of the body by Hyndman's slander and jealousy, which fasten on every one who threatens his chieftanship—and obviously implying that his own turn was beginning to come. I heard all this on April 1, when, instead of walking the streets as an experimental experience between the meeting and the first down train, as I had meant to do, I went back with Burns to his diggings, and—after rather shocking his wife by my advent—spent the night on their sofa in the kitchen, leaving between 4 and 5 in time to see the workmen's trains at Clapham junction, with heavy eyed men, some of whom most likely had been up till midnight, like me, trying to set the world to rights. The Belgian Congress decided to send representatives to Paris, so the disunion is not likely to spread and I had today a letter from French Boiler-makers' Society which gave an opportunity of "drawing" a member of the Parliamentary Committee as to the attitude of his society to the Congress. This is some hindrance to the opus,—of which Augustus takes a very unfavorable view. Have just put together a Phoenician chapter, and practically finished Egypt.

(In the Ms this note is on the page opposite the entry for September 28.)
> There are no account book entries between the end of June and
> beginning of October. The time after my return from Paris
> till September—i.e. two months before Michaelmas being
> taken up with house-hunting expeditions preparatory to the
> move to Ellesborough. She and I drove from Rickmansworth
> (when I saw the little socialist colony on the way to a
> house) to Chesham and Ellesborough, returning through
> Amersham, settling at last in haste to take the
> Ellesborough house for a year on trial when Gray agreed to
> take Woodleigh from Michaelmas.

---

[499] Social Democratic Federation

September 28, 1889

The above was written on a Saturday evening, when my mother had gone off to Harlaxton in consequence of a telegram saying William had had an attack of haemonlege. This has happened so often that I was not alarmed, except for the fatigue to my mother. The attack however was very different from any former ones and he died within a week, early on the morning of May 4. Augustus went down on the Monday and I next day, then there seemed some amendment and I came back here for a day, stopping each time in an somnambulistic sort of way to help on the internationalists. Mercifully my mother was well in health and the illness did not last long enough for the fatigue to do more than in a way deaden the shock, but it was very pathetic to me to see her—at that age for the first time in her life touched by a real *heart* sorrow, her hands working nervously and the simple *grief* coming back again and again, while she made no attempt to pretend to find any real solace in visions of another world. There was, happily, nothing that she could fix upon to regret or reproach herself with in any possible way, every thing was done and it could not possibly have been helped: she was tempted to regret not having sat up with him the whole of the last night, but that was all that she could be even tempted to wish different; now after 4 months and more she is as well as could be expected or hoped. We are leaving Woodleigh and I write this the night before. Appropriation of course has been put on the side again. I thought the Paris Congress such an exceptional occasion that it would be wrong to miss doing one's share to keep the nations together, so I went over for 10 days in July, though loth to leave my mother then for so long. Before going I had written to a good many Trade Unionists, trying in one way or another to stir them up to "adhere" in spite of the P. C. and the German miners' strikes having just excited attention, I wrote specially to the men of that trade at home and also to Bernstein for Germany, Defuet and Anseele for Belgium and the French miners' delegate and the Parti Ouvrier in France, saying to each "it had been suggested" that the miners should profit by the Paris Congress to hold an international Conference, to arrange for future concert and correspondence, so that movements like those in Germany and Belgium should be timed so as to receive the support of other countries &c. I did *not* say to all my correspondents that the suggestion proceeded from me, though I made it with a heavy sense of responsibility knowing that if ever the Miners' International became a reality, there would be martyrs to the cause, and I most likely not the first, as would be equitable. The response was more ready than I ventured to hope for and at Paris a score of miners from 4 countries did meet and discourse, and resolved to invite England to take the lead in a more complete and longer Congress, which proposal will be considered at Birmingham this October. So far the ball is rolling; I have also through Bernstein got at the Editor of a German Miners' paper, from whose letters I gather that it will be very difficult indeed under present circumstances to have direct intercourse with German Trade Societies, they have so much to fear from the suspicion of Socialism and perhaps even from the rivalry of Socialists with "corporating" propaganda that one doesn't know which of their countrymen they trust and not trusting all their own countrymen, it will be a wonder if they trust any foreigners. The Congress itself went off very well, the only drawback being the irreconcilability—of a purely personal kind, of the two French Socialist factions, how far the Germans share the feuds on their own account I must confess I was unable to find out. I allowed myself this time to shirk all the private hospitalities of the parti ouvrier, tho' I went to the so called ball at the Palais d'Industrie and to the Hotel de Ville. Hyndman and his wife stayed at the same hotel on Adolphe Smith's recommendation and I went about a little with them—ending up after the Congress with *sirop*[500] at some café in the small hours, which I suppose was rather scandalous. Felt that the problem as to "women's rights" would be rather difficult in Paris where private sitting rooms are dear and the Boulevards pleasant, so that it is a hardship if the *feme sole*[501] can't hire a chair and newspaper for an hour at the same cheap rate as a man. Hyndman is extraordinarily conceited, naively and transparently so; but he behaved well enough through the Congress and was perfectly civil to me. They are altogether "middle-class." I did not see my friend Tortellier, the anarchists bestowing most of their attentions on the Marxists. I took a good deal of trouble in drawing up a report of the Congress in the normal Trade Society style, and by that and other means succeeded in earning something so different from gratitude from Broadhurst that he thought it worthwhile to try quite unparliamentary devices to prevent my attending the Dundee Congress. As it happened nothing that I cared about fared the worse in consequence, though of course it would have been better if I could have explained a little about the different circumstances of English and Continental Societies. I thought Broadhurst's case was too bad for him to have got even a momentary success, but finding I was mistaken, I am less sure now than before that he was only preparing for a future defeat. I am ashamed to say that personally it would be rather a relief to me then not to be dispensed by no fault of my own from taking further part in the trade union movement, because all work that brings one closely and continuously in relation with one's fellow creatures brings one into disagreeable contact with some of the less creditable specimens among them, and I am as morbidly sensitive to annoyance from that cause as I am abnormally indifferent to other persons' opinion about myself. I am quite certain that my want of vanity and of the self-consciousness which comes from the vain desire to please goes far on the other side of the virtuous mean of self-respecting modesty and passes into inhuman insensibility. I don't *care* as much as I ought how people think and feel about me and find it almost impossible to understand how for example Hyndman, or still more Burns, can want to stop in the midst of what they are doing to protest that it is they—and no one else—who does it.

December 20, 1889. 69 Porchester Terrace.

But—to continue—I don't care to identify myself so completely with any "movement" or any set of colleagues as to be obliged to stick to it when—as generally happens after a few years—the element of personal squabbling and

---

[500] "cordial"

[501] "woman alone"

jealousy comes in. Of course I am only speaking of machinery, not principles, but unluckily there is machinery in all practical politics. I am not content to be a theoretical politician—but I can't stand the machinery after it gets too big to be worked exclusively by purists. Something of this sort will do for an explanation of why I was content to retire from H & Co and the School Board, tho' it isn't much á propos now, as instead of retiring from the Women's Unions I am just now endeavoring to nurse the Women's Trades Council into larger life, so that the Unions may be independent of the quarrels and jealousies of their outside friends. Of this more after January 15 next year. The Miners did resolve unanimously to invite an International Miners' Congress to meet next year and I was asked to give Crawford the addresses of Secretaries &c in foreign parts. On the strength of the Congress resolution and this invitation I wrote again to Ebert (editor of the Saxon Miners' paper) asking for Secretaries' addresses which he sent, tho' Bernstein—to whom I had also written, thought he would not and warned me not to address him any more but Strung. I am rather afraid Crawford is going to mistake the Parliamentary Committee and discourage his constituents' zeal for internationalism as he has done nothing since October, however it may be only that he is busy—as I tell our friends—with native *revindications*.[502] For the rest, I prevailed on my mother to furnish these rooms with odds and ends from Woodleigh so that I might be able to come up to town when I wanted without expense. I aim now at combining a few days at the museum with an evening or so of trade unionism. Butler's Cross fortunately suits my mother as far as appears—and me also better than Sussex as there are extremely pretty quite solitary short walks near, as well as a good variety of pleasant drives. Since we have been settled I am really beginning to try to finish the first 2 vols of the book and if nothing unforeseen occurs I really ought to be get it ready for next autumn. My mother finds some consolation in getting poor Will's books[503] out, and for her sake I have to worry over the proofs of notes on the "Revelation"—which is a little incongruous. She and I made the Index in the summer to the Greek Testament Grammar and she works at the Revelation proofs for hours at a stretch more industriously than Augustus can—which is another sign of improved health. I have still to write Modern China and to read for and write the Babylonish section. Have just been looking up the Etruscans. I daresay I haven't written the book so as to convey the impression that has been made on my own mind—and if so authorship is even less my forte than practical politics—but if I haven't 'tis this time no one's fault but my own: the subject is a good one and unless (as would serve me right) some one takes the wind out of my sails in the next 9 months, the moment is fortunate for the subject—and as a rule I am if possible even less fortunate than capable—because the relationships which my book illustrates are not yet generally known or positively proved tho' far enough on the way to it for such corroboration to count for a good deal. Still my hopes

---

[502] "making demands and taking them back"

[503] *The Language of the New Testament* (London: Hodder and Stoughton, 1889) and *Revelation of St. John the Divine* (Cambridge University, 1891).

and expectations are comfortably fixed at zero. It amuses me to write, but I really am not quite sure but what that may be the most desperate sign of all. I own it probable that Miss Hennell for instance writes—or wrote—for her own satisfaction with a fine disdain for the reader's feelings. I still have a vain belief that I read my own Mss critically, but I have so much esteem for myself as a critic as to be discouraged because I don't see my way to an entirely favorable criticism.

I should observe with regard to the curious absence of entries here in 1888 that there was no good reason for it. My mother was not well for the first 6 months and some of my time went in housekeeping and puttering about after her, but 'twas mostly idleness that hindered me, and 'twas not till autumn that I really began to work a little at Egypt again. I am coming up to town again on the 13th January and want between this and then to have written out a draft of modern China to be revised with references there. When Egypt and China are finished, I should not mind trying a publisher because I could read and write up Babylonia while the reader was wading through the other two only I must have the final peroration done before inviting judgment.

(In the Ms this note is on the page opposite the beginning of the entry for March 2.)

1890 January 7. We drive through Checkers Court. 13th. I seem to go to London. February 2. Jasmine and wall-flower, laurustinus and polyanthus bouquet. 3rd. Round Whiteleafhill and Hampden, doubtless with her. 5th. We to Wendover. 18th. To Miss Bridges and Wendover (Rowleys). Then in town for a few days and writing about Joluinsut Congress. March 10. Green goes over the house i.e. we decide to stay. April 15. To Porchester Terrace, with her. 20th. "Burt to lunch"—whom she liked. 22nd. She goes to Weyhill. 25th. "Back after surgical aid"— the maid cutting her arm badly with glass. May 7. She goes to Hillside (with Margaret) returning 13th. I stay in town; home 28th and 29th to Oxford where stay till June 7. The 11th we go back to Oxford, I more or less asthmatic. The 18th she has down "book and chair," 20th home. 25th. I to London for 2 days alone. July 15th. "Lornely Row and Hampden," another time "Pervial Court and Duitor." Long drives for calls; but the August seaside excursion was made because she was not quite feeling up to the mark.

March 2, 1890

This year have written over 200 pps of new Ms and have only about 1 more chapter to write before attacking a publisher; may be able to improve the book a little in proof, but it certainly has suffered from being written in fragments at long intervals and tho' parts seem to me fairly good, I think it lags between whiles. Miners' Congress is proposed for Whitemede this year in Belgium.

April 5, 1890

Wrote on the 31st to Longman and by return received promise to consider: "much interested on my account but in such a work all depends upon the execution"—too true! I am really curious to know how it will strike a dispassionate reader. Augustus tried it and gave it up—partly I suspect as a matter of eyesight and partly no doubt because our minds are uncongenial. There is a lot of information in it, of which a good deal is interesting, a little theorizing, some of which is original, but, as observed above, it lags in places and it is not certain that the points which I have gone into most thoroughly are those most interesting to the general reader. It would certainly have been better if I could have had it to revise in proof instead of Ms. People print such dull and empty books that I shouldn't be surprised if L. agrees to print this, but I can't screw up the smallest fragment of a sincere expectation that when printed it would seem more than the pallid succès d'estime of the writer's former works. I have still the Babylonian section to write.

December 4, 1890

Have just opened on a rather pathetic entry of nearly 10 years ago. When that sort of pain has become entirely a thing of the past, there is nothing painful in the memory of it, I suppose because one's natural sympathy is with the self that remembers—now—not the self that suffered then. Any way one cannot wish—now—that one had suffered and known less. This autumn read poor Marie Bashkirtseff's journal[504] with much interest and a good deal of sympathy, not diminished by the fact that her case is a strong argument in favor of what I said a while back. Brought up to think of lovers, frocks and husbands, this is a miserable mix, an Ouida[505] in the nursery, in love with the Duke of Hamilton's turnout. But she had a real desire to learn and would have been perfectly happy taking a brilliant University degree, and as soon as she got into the studio life, she began to grow happy and to forget herself in work. Evidently family distractions threw her back for a while but she had begun to work seriously the year before she died. She had plenty of cleverness and it was really pathetic that she should have found it so hard to find any use for it all, and indeed hardly have been able to imagine that a woman's wits could be good for anything except to make a position in "Society." Give her Philippe Fawcett's chances and she would have been happy enough—with no worse trials than the chance of a "Breslaw." As to the book: Longman declined curtly—type written with no reasons. I wrote to Murray who declined civilly having other big books on hand, so would not look at Ms. Have been hindered through spring and summer, as

---

[504] Mariya Konstantinovna Bashkirtseff (1860-1884), *Journal*, 2 vols., trans. Matilde Blind (London, 1890; Virago, 1985). She was a Russian artist.

[505] "Ouida" was the pseudonym of Marie Louise de la Ramée (1839-1908); it was a childish mispronunciation of Louise. She was a popular novelist and wrote animal stories, essays, and tales for children. Her financial success allowed her to live out the fantasies otherwise denied by her lack of beauty and social status.

usual, with family movements and distractions—house-altering, servants going and my mother not well, which took us to Lomersch and Dover for 3 weeks; so I have only just begun Babylonia, having found things to add to the miscellaneous chapter. When the Ms is really done at last shall offer it to Macmillan. The Miners' Congress was a success, and resulted in the Trades Congress at Liverpool resoluting in favor of the Belgian International which last year was successfully snubbed by the P C so in my little duel with Broadhurst, the nations and I win. When one is contending for any small public end, one has a lively sense of its importance; when one is not—an equally lively sense of the little difference that even victory makes to the many dwellers in the wide world. If it were not that faith without works is apt to die, I would like to keep the faith and have a holiday from work.

(In the Ms this note is on the page opposite the entry for December 4.)
August 29 She and I went to Oxford, slept at the Randolph (with a swelled face from a tooth wh. has given no trouble since); the next day to Taunton, where I walked about the town while she rested; then to Blue Anchor Inn, where didn't stay and on to Minehead via Dunster where tea and walk. 25th We drive to Porlock and back. 28th drive to Dulverton whence sail to Dawlish. September 1 drive to Teignmouth, September 5th to London, Lancaster Gate where she saw Dr. Ogilorie and is photographed (still in deep mourning). September 29th "moving fence" (either then, or in October—I think then—she stayed at Lancaster Gate). October 5th I go to Porchester Terrace to 18th. October 21st to 28th she was at Porchester Terrace (I think) again and went to see Sir Alfred Garrod whom she used to quote as diagnosing "a low type of rheumatism." We go home the 29th—22nd "Margaret leaves" (perhaps she was not up quite so long).

December 2 till the 6th and again on 10th. I seem to have gone up to Porchester Terrace for British Museum &c. Mrs. Chapman was ill and died as overleaf on Tuesday the 14th. I believe I had been to enquire. Monday and Tuesday telegrams are passing. She came up afterwards—am not quite sure which day, but we certainly went down together on the 23rd. My entry on the 19th was I think before she came. On the 24th she sent a cheque (5 francs each) to Mrs. Pratt[506] and Mrs. MacClymont. The former in special sympathy about the will.

November 14th same year Robin was bought: 5 off i.e. 4 years old still with his colt's teeth; he was born in the spring of 86.

---

[506] Susanna Pratt, see December 19, 1890.

December 19, 1890. 69 Porchester Terrace.

It has been an unusually exciting autumn; the newspapers so full of so many "sensations" that it would have been impossible for any one in the sleepiest rural outback to have found life "slow." Stanley's rearguard,[507] Koch's safe cure,[508] the Barings in liquidation[509] and Mr. Parnell in the divorce court,[510] besides such minor matters as wrecks and railway accidents, which like murders are too much alike to interest a critical curiosity. Add General Booth[511] and I think that nearly ends the list. I am rather glad now—though I used to suppose it was want of knowledge or sympathy on my part—that I was never quite able to tell *why* Parnell was the renowned king. It is plain enough now—a sort of General Boulanger business[512]—a little cleverness in getting money to handle, a little skill in keeping people together, and an enormous power of making people believe there was something behind all that he didn't say and that he didn't do. It is an absurd example of the foolishness of newspaper government that he is to be

---

[507] Sir Henry Morton Stanley (1841-1904) landed at the mouth of the Congo and in June 1886, was left with 388 men to march into the forest. Disaster overtook the rear column, but Emin Pasha and Stanley met in April, 1888 on the shores of Lake Albert. After relieving the rearguard, he returned with Emin Pasha overland to Bagamoyuo in December 1889.

[508] Robert Koch (1834-1910) was a German physician and pioneer in the field of bacteriology; in 1890 he produced tuberculin as a lymph-inoculation cure for tuberculosis.

[509] The House of Baring had long been the keystone of English commercial credit; its collapse in 1890 had terrible consequences for banking and for English trade in all parts of the world.

[510] Charles Stewart Parnell (1846-1891) was an Irish politician; his frequent mysterious absences from parliamentary duties were unexplained until he was named as a co-respondent in a divorce case brought by Captain William Henry O'Shea (1840-1905) against Parnell and his wife Katherine. The divorce was granted with costs against Parnell on November 17,1890. The Gladstonian party demanded his retirement from leadership.

[511] Captain William Booth (1829-1912) was a religious leader who founded the Salvation Army; he was made freeman of London and doctor of Oxford after enduring much persecution against his social and regenerative efforts at reform.

[512] The Boulanger episode of 1887 is an example of the impression given by Disraeli's international relations of attempting to create British policy which involved no risk and gave the impression of doing more than had been done. However, the case of Boulanger caused almost as much alarm in London as it did in Berlin.

deposed now, not for flagrant political corruption—giving a seat to a man whom he must have known to be either wilfully blind for a consideration, or an absolute idiot and on either ground unfit for public duties, *not* because he had done his Don Juanary in an ungentlemanly way, not—which would have been the simplest argument, because a politician ought to be honourable all through, and a man of honour who finds it necessary to annex his neighbour's wife must go through with it and take the consequences and not condemn himself to years of lying and his mistress to polygamy. One can imagine cases—the first marriage a tragic mistake and the second perfect in all but being second—in which a politician's public character would not suffer by his being a co-respondent. It is a misfortune any way and some people call it sin but it is not dishonourable to have the courage of a great passion when the man has no tie to break and the woman worse than none. But instead of the man being judged on his merits, we are told only "the non-conformists are shocked and won't vote for home rule"—as if it was a bit of sectarian prejudice such as some devout persons would feel about any breach of the 7th Commandment by the light of the marriage law of the country. And Gladstone, who surely might have, must have been capable of judging the matter by the light of common secular honesty and honour, virtually endorses the view that Parnell is to be sacrificed—in spite of all his merits—as a matter of tactics or electioneering expediency! The trial showed that his merits had been exaggerated and that he had faults outweighing whatever merits he may have had. The cause of home rule is quite independent of his qualities, bad or good, which is fortunate, for if he represented the cause it would be in a bad way now that he tells us that 2-thirds of the representatives he chose for it are dishonest. Did a little gardening in November and have begun "Babylonia" though distracted from it by musing over Greek inscriptions. If I had begun to work seriously at the book 10 years ago or had stuck to it for 3 years on end any where, it might have been tolerable.—I shall have to make haste even to get it out by next autumn. Happily my mother is tolerably well again. Mrs. Chapman[513] died on the 14th at only 85 after only a fortnight's illness. Surprised at both. Her will is not much more inequitable than was to be expected—only omits my uncle Lancelot against whom my aunt Oldham had a grudge, while the latter is residuary legatee and her sons treated like the other sisters. The poor old woman in about 20 years saved £40,000 out of an income of £3,000—truly an example of thrift. She left my mother £1,000 and me £100, which I shall give my self the amusement of spending, on books and—for a variety,—doing what I like without having to "get leave."

---

[513] Mary Elizabeth Chapman was the sister of EJS's mother, Jemima Haslope Simcox, and Emma Oldham. Lancelot Haslope was their brother. Susanna Pratt was another sister. Mrs. Chapman's will was probated January 24, 1891.

(In the Ms this note is on the page opposite beside the entry for March 2.)

The beginning of the year[514] there was a hard frost and long snow (I got snow boots and saw a white ferret on Comb Hill) and the Chequers tableaus (which we declined) were almost inaccessible from post. January 19th Miss Bridges to lunch, next day frost ends. She was drinking Pitkeathly. 23rd We drive into Aylesbury. I spread flower seeds down and laying turf. February 9th There are 2 days of my entering the end of January 3 and 5. We go up to Porchester Terrace, shopping she has "dresses 9.17.8." Bert and Mord were at work in the garden and the new piece from the field being laid out. February 23 we drove to Berkhamsted to choose plants. Nurse Sylvester to stay 2 days later. Winifred was there thinking of moving. March 3 we go up to town mainly to choose a brougham.[515] She goes to Higgin, oculist about the surviving eye— said to be all right. We engage Whybrow[516] on the 16th. She walked from Porchester Terrace to Princess Square Bayswater. 28th She went home. I stay to learn to type and try riding; have something like a turn of influenza and go home April 18th-the 20th my scrawl reappears in account book. Next day MacClymonts came. May 11 she went through London and to Grantham for restored church. We go home the 14th April after long ride from Bedford Park to Richmond. Gertrude comes for Whitsun holidays. Mrs. Phillips and children come to stay. 30th There is no bed. I get beef juice, linseed and champagne she does some sparkey sorts mixed with wine. I ride like a prig. 13th June I call for medicine: 15 Lancelot before starting for Indies. 19th and 26th she drives with us.

March 2, 1891. Ellesborough

Since Xmas I'm afraid it is only my own fault that I haven't done much. Only written a baddish abstract of Babylonian and Assyrian history and just began 50 (Ms) pages of the proper subject. Now was sent to London, just when it would suit me to stay here, because of bath room pipes; so am rather savagely bent on staying there till the draft of book is really finished and specimens type written, without regard for family wants. But I don't think it will be any good. I don't find any satisfaction in reading any of it over myself and when I began giving my mother and Augustus half hour doses of one section

---

[514] 1891

[515] This is a one-horse closed carriage, with two or four wheels, for two or four persons.

[516] Walter Wybrow, formerly of Aspley Guise, is still with EJS when she dies. She left him 8 shares in the Aerated Bread Company.

aloud, they were both so much bored I stopped in pity—and they were silently grateful. If it were only the latter I might think it was the difference of taste in the family which makes A's theological putterings quite as uninteresting to me as my opus is to him: but I retain some confidence in my own critical judgment and nothing consoles me for not admiring myself. Poor Mrs. Chapman's death has set my mother's conscience to work upon the duty of making a will. I am a little amused that both she and Augustus have entirely forgotten that poor Will's elaborate testamentary desposition began by leaving all his worldly wealth to me for life with succession to Augustus and then to I know not what pious uses. I prevailed upon him to substitute for this a simple bequest to his mother absolutely, representing that if he survived her he could make another will and that if not, it was scarcely seemly to give her a limited estate. But the amusing thing is not that they had forgotten this, but that I should have been so unimaginative as to take for granted that they would be as much aware of it as I was. I have repeatedly congratulated myself on having urged it on poor Will, who rather resented the intervention: (I remember saying to him: If it were mine . . . and being answered "But it isn't") because though her sons always wished her to treat their money as hers, she is clearly happier in spending what *is* her own, and the situation is more normal so. She has an income, mostly coming from poor Will's wife's intestacy, of about £370, and A. (with his fellowship) about £470. Some years ago my mother amused herself by making a will desiring all she had—about £800-£500 left her by my uncle Chapman with the recommendation she should leave it to me and £300 the mangled remains of her marriage settlement (of £5000). I was such a goose as to assume that was still in force and when she began on the subject lately, suggested that she should qualify it by a proviso that if Augustus married and so lost his fellowship, he should have Will's land at Harborne, which brings in about £120. It then appeared that I had added more than I knew of to her happiness, since the having money enabled her to leave some to her son and she was only a little exercised as to how much she could leave him while leaving me enough to live on, and the darling never guessed that there was the ghost of an under tone of irony in my suggestion that she should first settle what income she would like her son to have and leave the rest to me. I am amused that the result of 46 years intercourse with as devout a believer in the rights of women and the rights of younger children as myself should have left her in the mood to desire spontaneously that her son should be "worth" just as much as her daughter. She is really quite as fond of me as of him, in proof of which she proposed to leave twice as much to me as to him and the executricity is in me who thinks—tho' this time I can't say—if it were mine, I should divide between my 2 children, so as either a) to make the total income of the two equal or as nearly so as possible or b) to make their property equal apart from personal acquisitions, (like the fellowship). It is characteristic too that A.— who really didn't at all wish poor Will's intention to be altered—remains passive in the way most advantageous to his pecuniary interests, not from any calculation to that effect, but from an amiable desire to acquiesce in what my mother and I wish! To be perfectly honest, I don't wish at all to give him £120 a year more to keep up a small "establishment" with, instead of having a couple of hundred a year myself to spare for deserving "causes." I can't imagine myself spending more than £3 a week upon my own existence so that it is from that point of view only that I have anything to lose: my feeling that I should spend money better than A. was just so strong that I did not really encourage my mother in anything except leaving £100 to a MacClymont and Phillips boy, but her feeling was so pronounced that she didn't need encouragement, and I ask myself now doubtfully which is really most natural, to wish—when wishing equally well to two people—to wish the same gift to each or to wish that the two should *have* the same gifts whence solace derived.[517]

July 5, 1891
     As usual have wasted something like 4/5 of my time this spring, what with slight recurring unwellnesses of my mother, goings and comings to town, visits from MacClymont family and Mrs. Phillips with 2 babies, my own slackness to take up interrupted work, and pure sheer idleness—I have not quite finished off the draft of the whole book and have still to revise it all and cut out about 1/3 of 1000 pages to reduce it to a manageable scale. The abridgement will improve the matter immensely, but it is a good deal harder than what I have been doing until now—viz. sandwiching in little additions. Then Miners had another big Congress at Paris, when I was *en train*[518] with Babylonian weights and measures. Was too idle—and unpractical—to telephone a greeting as I wished. Some of the wasted time this spring has—for a variety—been wasted on amusing myself. Pourquoi non?[519] I believe I thought it necessary to mix a little concern for my health among the motives—that is, I thought that I and my mind might grow old a little slower if the circulation were a little quickened—but having begun to spend money upon that plea, I admit now that I shall only ride because I like it. Now I come to think of it, I believe a few pony rides were the only thorough, unmixed pleasures of my youth, or rather childhood, (as boating was of my early—man-hood): then—in youth and childhood I would have taken kindly to congenial pleasures had the fates given them me—: The gods—or the psychologists—only know why, failing felicific fates—for about a quarter of a century I took for granted that things in general were *not* made for my amusement, nor I to be amused. Now, at 46, when other people might think such a mental attitude perhaps appropriate, I note, wish a little sober, disinterested amusement—why not I as well as another if I can find *de quoi*?[520] After all the

---

[517] The will of Jemima Haslope Simcox was probated February 2, 1898. She left to EJS the property at Harborne, Staffordship, and investments to yield £200 a year and to Augustus the property at St. Mary's Row, Birmingham. The Phillips boy is Will's godson Alfred.

[518] "busy"

[519] "why not?"

[520] will "to endure"

play is of a very sober, thrifty kind. A young strong horse bought last winter, gets no work in the many weeks when weather, nerves or *vis inertiae*[521] keep my mother from driving out, so I thought if I could ride him, I might find the exercise as beneficial as Carlyle did. But 'twas an immense enterprise—a habit and breeches—a saddle and bridle—a horse to practice upon and somebody to pick up the pieces if there were any! it seemed quite too much to grapple with merely on the off chance of being amused. Yet I persevered—good Mrs. Congreve of all people in the world sustaining me with encouragement at the outset. I tried to combine patronage of the sex, but a well meaning horsewoman and consort-miss,[522] who was to have done mentor got frightened, because I lost my spectacles before I had found my seat in a random trot among streets. 'Twas not so unreasonable because of course a mortal in a habit on a side-saddle would be comparatively helpless if a duffer were in danger of coming to grief and she wasn't bound to know that I wasn't likely to come off though I had never had 4 reins in my hand before. This warned me that I couldn't experiment alone in London streets so I submitted to the humiliation of entering a riding school! and I am bound to say it took me the best part of an hour to recover the power I had vainly imagined came by nature and was inalienable—of "rising in the stirrup." After that at intervals I rode thrice in London, twice round Regents Park and once round Hyde and—for once—enjoyed that, though I couldn't imagine any one who cared for riding caring for such a scrap of a round. I had lighted upon a tutor who took his vocation seriously so got candid criticism and really useful hints: then rode from Bedford Park to Richmond, and on the grass in the Park, with a less scrupulous Professor, who won my distrust by compliments; yet I believed him in the particular—viz. that I had ridden further in 2 1/2 hours than his young ladies generally in 3—that they normally got tired of trotting sooner than I did: (I had in fact gone on a little longer than I cared to) and it certainly was strange that neither then nor ever was I conscious of the slightest stiffness in any member whatever after riding. I attribute this partly to the improvements in saddles and "togs," partly also to the absence of stays. I had the mare I rode to Richmond down here for 5 weeks, but only scored 20 rides in the time an average of 4 a week, including one experimental canter on Robin under the hill and 3 rides on him, he having had absolutely no "breaking" for the side-saddle as such. Since then I have ridden him 4 times (twice each week) alone and am in two minds as to whether it is safe for such a duffer to ride an unbroken horse, (however quiet), or not. If there were a riding school in Oxford where I could have some jumping, I should not be afraid of trying to cure his roughness. As compared with the mare who was well broken and well-bred, his 12 miles are about equivalent in time and exercise to her 16. I guess I had better stick to 10 or 12 miles in a 2 hour ride till we both do that dependably well and take longer explorations in the cool of the autumn. Mrs. Chapman's legacy pays for all this play—also for a type writer with which I propose to abridge my Ms for the publisher's reader.

---

[521] "lack of inertia"

[522] "companion"

July 26, 1891
Have done 3 more rides since, and now got a turn of asthma. China wants more re-writing than abridging. I have cut a good deal and on coming back to the Ms as a whole I find it less impossible than on former re-readings to get a grip of what ought to be the skeleton. I alter so much in abridging that a virtually fresh copy is wanted, and I can't get a type writer. I want to keep on polishing off 10 pps of revised vol 1 a day—while reconstructing vol 2! Poor little Defuet sends me a "Peuple" with report of International Executive Committee of Miners' Meeting at Cologne and paragraph expressing Belgian Miners' gratitude to me for putting them in relations in 1888 with the Britons. I confess I have difficulty in believing that so big a child has grown in 3 years from so small a germ as my amateur diplomacy.

Xmas 1893 — Guise House Aspley Guise

December 26, 1893
—A gap indeed. Before I come to the last year and days that I meant to write at length, I must just bridge the interval from July 91. In November 91 she was taken ill—mostly asthma for I remember a bed being made up for her on the sofa in the oriel room and sleeping there with her and by constant stoking keeping the room warm through cold nights. November 23 had nurse Augustine Marshall down from Mrs. Anderson, who stayed till January 11. [I seem to have done a great deal of typing besides, as she liked the nurse and had long toilettes with her.] About Xmas or sooner she felt very ill; we talked of sending for Mrs. Anderson and she did see Woollerton's old partner or predecessor, whose nurse Grinsy now says was counted a loser. There did not seem much wrong except great prostration and January 11, 1892 we parted with nurse Marshall (a clergyman's daughter with a sister married near Weyhill) and started for the Grosvenor and the next morning for St. Raphael. She was carried on board at Dover (from the 11 o'clock train) and then to a through Coupe'lit carriage[523] with three places; we had a spirit lamp, strong beef tea and a whole chicken or pheasant pounded and ready made Cocon ribs for warming, which we lived upon without needing to alight. We were just able to keep her warm with dressing gowns, duvets and foot warmers, but the night was bitterly cold, with deep snow on the ground at Lyon. In the morning as always sun and blue sky came about Avignon and from Marseille it was warm—She was not over done getting in 2:20 Thursday; I went out to reconnoiter and caught a cold from leaving off too much at once. On Saturday drove to Valescure where a nice 2 bedded semi-sitting room did us well from 16th to 26th. The Bullock Halls are neighbours. On the 26th drove to Cannes which she liked much. 30th to Grasse which she liked not quite so well, tho' the chaplain, Douglas was an old acquaintance. February 4 one long walk, guidebook calls 28 miles, the 6th rail to Menton for Cap Martin. 7th "Lift out of order"; she goes twice up 115 stairs. Had dismissed useless maid at Cannes, and did all her valeting. 16th Cuirerz; walk straight to our old chalet,

---

[523] This is a carriage with sleeping accommodations.

below La Terram and Villa Freeman. Find and bring Madame Luim from Vallon Obscur and hepatica from—much cultivated—Vallon des fleurs. 18th to Nice by hotel omnibus and rather foolishly walked from shop to shop, tiring her too much. On the 26th back to Valescure. March 6th "snow and rain." David Grieve. Home of Luveret on a Valescure boulevard. March 11 to Hyères by new coast railway. 19th had Dr. Biden for a sore throat which kept her 2 days in bed and yielded to Friars Balsam and Juniper inhalations. One day she has diarrhea, but there are constant notes of drives and walking in the garden on warm days and down stairs rooms as well as the drawing room were pleasant. Mrs. Annie Edwards and other 2nd hand acquaintances in Hotel. Country bright with peach blossoms. I have notes of many walks myself, but I don't think I ever left her longer than she liked. She got pattern for light crochet shawls which it amused her to make from Miss Tugran. April 4 "Cloudless warm day," drive to Chartreuse de Nombreux—between 30 to 40 miles out and back, lunching on stone bench outside convent. 8th got nettle rash (told to take tonic afterwards but didn't). 12th drive to Toulon, ending 3 months. Sleep Marseille and Dijon for Good Friday. Paris Saturday 16. 21st to Louvre where she got her cloth mantle, given away last winter. Very cold and she was laid up with violent cold rather than asthma. Dr. Herbert recommended via Beauvais. We came through, May 3, Paris to Victoria, though intending to stop Calais or Dover. Then home. May 10 I write "Is quite 'spry.'" Then sore throatish. 21st "Is in garden quite convalescent." Hot summer, get on with book. MacClymonts come for Whitsuntide holiday, I for a day or two in town, Miners' Congress. I notice she drove out but seldom. June to stay. July 1 first dogcart drive out on back seat. Then nearly 77. Home Friday to rest for a bit; ride before breakfast, Ms for 3 hours and type till lunch. Shirtmakers for Bank Holiday. (A good many rides and Misses Aimes). Visit from Steadman. August 23. She seems to have gone up to London and back in the day—9:30 to 5. I wrote some letters *re* miners in Labour Tribune. September. She is in town with me for a few days. Mary Hamilton for a night. I try different publishers and we play some with the garden; order bulbs from Holland.

1893

Two months, January to March no entry. March 11 she made the new path by drawing room window. I note early flowering of all spring things and 4 weeks of almost continuous sunshine. In April Sophy the housemaid succeeded by Jame, so I suppose Fanny was already cook—viz. Markham. April 14 a wasp seen. 18th MacClymonts come. I think all this time she must have been really pretty well as I note May 3: "M's throat bad." This must be the time when she had Agnes Housey from Harlaxton as we stay with the Davenport Hills on the 9th to 15th and I take Rosamond to the Haymarket ("A Woman of No Importance").[524] Wild roses out May 17. May 20 drive Beacon End to see house. No entry for 2 months but day's reading at Oxford. Autumn berries &c

---

[524] Oscar Wilde (1854-1900), *A Woman of No Importance* (London: J. Lane, 1894).

colouring in July. July 21. "To London with Ms." July 31 We drive to Oxford. Her fall and bruised arm. August the Steadmans come. I take the girls on river. Great heat. August 18 temperature 83° indoors = Garden of Eden. Shirtmakers again for Bank holiday. August 28 to Mary at Albert Gate and Dahomey and Bernard Shaw's play Amazons.[525] September 26 agree with Swan Sonnenschein. October 2 Up at Borers. October 5 To Sir Andrew Clark's Pioneer Club in Cork Street. Index and references. Proofs begin October 22. November 7 Sir Andrew's death. Fine autumn. [age irregularity]. She reads all my proofs. Deep snow. Up at Cork Street November 27-December 2. Mention a good deal of migraine and apparently *not* her devotion in ordering dinner as well as reading proofs and revises.

(In the Ms this note is on the page opposite the entry for 1893.)
In her account book I find January 17 Woollerton £1..15.6—
[Note at the top of the Ms page: He died this year (98)]
meaning practically no doctor after the winter on the Riviera.
Poor Monte's euthanasia in January. January 28 Charlie
(alias Sandy) 6 or 9 months old. March 22 "2 loads
stones"—for rockery between old and new kitchengarden.
April 8 Cox and men tipped for big flint. Most weeks
have daily entries of small household expenses, but May
2, 3 and 4 there are none. [Apparently she came up to town
with me April 11 to 17 or 20th. I start apparently May 2.]
She continues entries almost daily. June 8 Cocoa nut fiber
to conceal the chaulky white of borders. July 21—she seems
to have gone home same afternoon after a little shopping while
I stayed at the club to read. More exactly for the Monday
after the flower show: this August 10—the "Women's fair" in
account book—Steadmans on 11th. Return over Sholden.
September 8 Greenhouse put up this autumn. Bulbs from
Holland in November.

1894
Miss Bridges stays a week in January. "The hardest frost I remember." Very few entries—evidently proofs and India, frequent migraines. Mrs. G. Anderson. Beginning of May start for Walen Lakes with Maude, Augustus following after Ascension day. Sleep at Lord-Warwick instead of London.

---

[525] George Bernard Shaw (1856-1950) had written five unsuccessful novels before his first play *Widowers' Houses* was produced in 1982. Shaw mentions the Amazons in the Preface to *Saint Joan* (1923): "In reactionary Russia in our own century a woman soldier organized an effective regiment of Amazons, which disappeared only because it was Aldershottian enough to be against the Revolution." In the Preface to *Widowers' Houses* Shaw states his opinion that the exemption of women from the military was founded not on any natural inaptitude of women but because they are needed for reproduction.

Lunch at Calais. Then through to Lucerne. Stop at Locarno, Stresa, Como, Cadenabbia, Lugano, Göschenen, Armstey and Basle—I up Maderander Thal, Paris, then home June 14. Rockery made last year and now planted. Begin "Love is A Must!" Pioneer, Miss Paget. Mrs. Stuart. Marlborough Mission entertained July 11. (Accident) Mrs. Congreve down (feeling very ill). Stay at Mrs. Eldridge's. August 7. Miss Paget to stay and Miss Anotrutten Thompson for a day. Library catalogued. August 27 Mrs. Tysen to stay. September 12 over to Ermine for day. September 24. M. in bed with rheumatism. County Council lectures. Ossington Street taken. Stay at Ford's Hotel to October 12. Her sealskin altered and—I *think* tan bonnet bought. Mr. Grantham takes locus tenere.[526] 16 November. Parish Meeting to discuss act "adjourned to public house for real debate." She, is much upset later by discovery of domestic tragedy—Jame's hurried departure. Fanny and new parlour dismissed and we come to Ossington Street for a break of 6 weeks.

(In the Ms this note is on the page opposite the last part of the entry for 1894.)
> June 15. Her accounts begin again.
> September 25. Accounts resumed next day.
> October 31. Hutchison to lecture. Ashleys to
> supper. Maud leaves November 8. The reason
> of Jame's leaving not known till afterwards.
> Then a month's notice given to the others. Fanny
> leaves January 14. So it was nearly a month before we knew.

1895. Home February 28.

1895

Home end of February. All pipes frozen and my asthma getting very bad—day at Museum (February 22) returning in black fog. Three weeks in March I very bad, to Elma and Kenilworth. May 4 M. up to meet me in Ossington Street. June 22 Mrs. Nettleshop and daughter. Saturday to home. 29th Dr. Vernon Lee and Marie Belloc.[527] (Lighest weight July is under 6 stones). She is a little bored with vehement chatter. September 12 We go to Seaford: enjoyed drives and my sketches. October 2 To Ossington Street. October 4 She is ill. We go home on the 15th and on the 18th she resumes her account book entries but in the interval she had a sharp attack of diarrhea and I paid 1 1/2 go to Miss Luckes (London Hospital) for a nurse and 4/ to Dr. Balten—which I suppose means 8 days of the doctor and 7 of the nurse—no doubt Saturday 5th to 12th. I remember sending to MacClymonts and wiring wildly all about. I remember both Dr. Balten and the nurse being sceptical over her age—79—and wondering at her prompt recovery.

---

[526] "position or post"

[527] Marie Belloc (1868-1947) was the daughter of Bessie Rayner Parkes Belloc and sister of Hilaire Belloc. She married Frederick Lowndes and knew most of the celebrities of her time. She wrote 45 novels.

November 18 she pays for chrysanthemums I had chosen from Acquarium show on the 4th. 28th pays 18/ for a ladder. Wyatt[528] had come October 15 and as I was up in Ossington Street soon after, she had to do with her mostly at first. I had had a bit of inflammation of the lung at Seaford and kept hovering between 6 stones 3 and 6 stones 8, so that the family agreed to spend a bit of a quaint little windfall of some £350 on sending me to Egypt—of which we had thought rather desperately about February the year before. She decided that she would get thro' the winter, more safely and comfortably in Ossington Street with friends and doctors in reach than in the cold lone country, and she came up with Wyatt and Powell, and new maid who gave warning almost immediately to go and marry an Engineer at the Cape, on the 6th leaving in the morning of that day, Friday, made them witness her will, which she had written "all by herself with nobody to help her" and so omitted to date, owing to the little flutter of the journey. She was to have Mary Baron for house—parlourmaid, Wyatt for cook and Margaret—married to her butler, for maid. There are scribbled entries of mine in her account book December 20 and 21. Her writing on the 23rd (Monday) is beautifully firm and clear. I would not let her get up to breakfast or come with me to the station—and we did our best not to cry—helping each other not to break-down. The story of that winter is so full in our letters, I need say no more of that.

(In the Ms this note is beside the entry for 1895 and is to be inserted at this point.)

> The mild winter and the handiness of bath chairs, together
> with little objects for a cab drive with Margaret enabled her to
> be out 44 times in about 15 weeks—or 30 days in a chair and
> 14 in a cab—just on 3 times a week which was much above her
> normal average. And she was at church 12 Sundays. March 9
> after days of agony she went to a dentist and was cured the
> following Monday 16th.

I came from Paris Sunday, April 19 to Victoria, slept at the Grosvenor and got home 10:52 Monday. On that day in her account book—with a triumphant slant I find "E weighed 7 1/2 stones." I had brought back a tooth *in extranies*[529] and on the 23rd I find she went up and down with me—she going to a chiropodist in Regent Street while I to Hanover Square near by. We got some velvet—for which I can't remember the use—at Liberty's. Ruth a "stop gap" parlourmaid from Oxford left, to her regret April 27. April 29 to May 1 I go to look at house from Touby Hall. For the next few days there are no entries; from the payment to a China shop &c. 16th I guess that she drove into Aylesbury May

---

[528] Elizabeth Wyatt and M. Williams Powell witnessed the writing of the will of Jemima Haslop Simcox in December 6, 1895. EJS left Elizabeth Wyatt 8 shares in the Aerated Bread Company. She signed the death certificate when EJS died.

[529] "in the last extremity"

15, and the periodic box goes up and down once a week. May 21 the Bosworth Smiths came down, with the brother Noel. A. and I met them at Wendover, we drove through Holton before lunch, while Augustus takes them for a walk in the afternoon. Her way of putting down the offertory at church is x x 1/—or whatever it may be. Whitsunday—May 24—I put down abruptly 2 books as read. Whit Tuesday there is an entry "Fare J. H.—6/1" which I can't understand. Augustus is going about a good deal after houses. May 31 I put down "asthma pretty bad by night." She must have been poorly I think as there are then 3 days with only one entry. June 9 a rather inefficient maid "Grace" leaves and Jessie Hookway comes:—the "fare" of course is Jessie Hookway who came to be seen. Neat looking but with rather negroid features, and a ghastly story of her late mistress, who did not ring at the normal time so Jessie went in and came away without seeing that she had fallen on the floor insensible—where she found her later. The 18th she and I went over to look at an old house A. had seen, Begbroke, near Oxford. June 22 I find "Fares 11/6" and my note "To London to give up Ossington Street, where we seem to have stayed till the 29th or 30th. July 1 I go to Lyme—to see another house "asthma pretty bad." Slept the first night at Lyme, drove to Fernhill *en route* for Charmouth, where sleep Thursday, see the house again and drive down to reach house next day, Thursday 23rd July she goes with me to Lyme, sleeping at Salisbury, where I "crawl to Cathedral after tea." Next morning we go to Charmouth and in the afternoon to Fernhill. 26th we send for local doctor for my asthma, who disrecommended the locality. Monday we return to Salisbury. Tuesday morning drive round the town and I on home 4:52. [It is, I think, in this July that she wrote the codicil to her will which Jessie Hookway and Laura Newman witnessed.[530] Perhaps the difference was meant to pay doctors' bills.] August 3 she has a note of number of eggs—215— in stand. On the 14th I walk along the grass path under Comb Hill without benefit and on 22nd note "relapse begins." 25th. "the twins"—alias Misses Brodrick and Morton down for the day. Miss Morton had sent me her Egyptian photos to see, when we were at Lyme:—a real pleasure to her. 31st drive to Aylesbury and Wendover, where get a parcel of books. Note books read next two days. September 3 Augustus goes up to see about "St. Ann's Villa"—little house to be sold cheap. She is at church on the 5th—has been 15 times at Ellesborough, 27 Sundays in 8 months, only missing about 7 Sundays. Whybrow used to come in for orders after breakfast, "the carriage at 1/4 to 11"—being the formula. I used to sit in the oriel room and run down, as soon as I heard the carriage wheels to meet her at the door: often instead of going indoors she would take a turn round the garden first. September 28 to October 3 marked " " October 15 "asthma very bad last night and this morning." Monday, 19th we go up to London to lodgings for me to see Dr. Douglas Powell. I remember crawling up the Baker Street steps holding on to the rail and pausing to gasp. Douglas Powell's perscription acts immediately in relief, so see him again the sooner, i.e. 24th and go to Bournemouth on Monday, 26th. Stay at Boscombe

---

[530] The date given in the will for the codicil is June 23, 1896. Mrs. Simcox raised the yearly income she left EJS from £170 to £200.

Chenies hotel till Tuesday, when take rooms for a week at the Wilgberries. Sunday November 1 I walk down to the "Invalids walk" and drive back. Go about househunting. She approves "Chesterford." We go home November 3 and November 7 I write "no morning cough." I saw to the packing of books, house linens and her things as far as possible, but as R. D. P. had been peremptory in telling me not to leave Bournemouth at all, as I said I must, and as I had a vile tooth born swelled face, I left 2 days before her, November 10, stopping in town to see a dentist. This was Tuesday and I continued sorry for my jaws for the next week. Thursday she and Augustus came down with the servants. She was a little over done, with the last days and the journey. I wanted her to bring Whybrow with her and carriage, to which she demurred a good deal on the score of expense, but was persuaded to consent and I was rather reckless in my assurances that the year income would not be any the more exceeded for the complete move. My tooth kept pretty bad and on Monday 16th I went to a local dentist. She I think was resting meanwhile tho' I remember on Friday, 20th we went for a drive on the Poole road and back through Branksome; because I was made late for my dentist appointment—it was a fine evening and the carriage dropped me, then took her home and fetched me later. The tooth being no better, I went up to town next day and agreed to return on Monday, which I did, with a black fog, after which asthma returned. I have down Tuesday, 24th "a wet day"—the beginning of the end, for we drove into the town—stopping at a basket shop to get a brush and such like—as I remember and her accounts date. It was to going out in the damp that she attributed the attack of bronchitis that followed. On Friday and Saturday there are entries, the last of all a payment for the tea gown I had, with difficulty, persuaded her to buy for the winter, which Ada Filley—a rather half-witted girl we picked up in London in October—afterwards made or began for her. We had down an easy chair for her from Whiteley's (and Ossington Street) and a spare table and her bath shawl—all I am glad to think at my strong persuasion. The next day, the 29th she did not come downstairs nor on the Monday. December 1 I sent to Isabella Lea to ask the best near doctor, who named Musprat, one of those whom R. D. P. had named. He came, was very serious and telephoned for a nurse. The next day she was rather better (I wrote about myself to R. D. P.): the next "not so well, extreme drowsiness, doctor calls twice." That was Thursday; Saturday was "better." Sunday, December 6—an anniversary now—"not so well"—my asthma bad again. Then no entry for 2 days. (On the 5th account book tells of champagne—we got 1/2 a bottle in trade from an hotel). The 5th was Saturday when I have "better." Sunday when I wrote the champagne was got "not as well." I add "my asthma bad again." It must have been one of those days, when she could not lie down, that Musprat proposed and helped to carry the sitting room sofa upstairs for her to pass the night on. Wednesday the 9th "upstairs sitting room arranged"—i.e. all the bow window in my bedroom was cleared and easy chair, table &c brought in so that she could have change without going downstairs. On Saturday 12th she was downstairs and Dr. Musprat called as he was to be away next day; Sunday she was downstairs and next day, Monday Dr. Musprat proposed not to call again till Thursday. Tuesday 15th "Try an hour's biking"—partly to amuse her. I went up and down the road in front a few times with a black boy, and found it rather easier that I expected. Next day paid a call, next Dr. Musprat as proposed and next day but one, Saturday 19th he took leave, the nurse was paid off on the 15th (Tuesday). All this time however I had been rather anxious at her constant drowsiness—falling asleep in the straight backed cane chair so as to sit "hunched up,"—even while playing bezique[531] or Halma[532] she would half doze and wake with effort. She sat all day in the little drawing room and had her meals brought her there, but sometimes walked upstairs to bed quite easily. I doubt whether Musprat paid sufficient attention to the state of the kidneys as indicated by drowsiness. That Friday or Saturday or both I was out, driving down town shopping or paying bills and on Monday, choosing Xmas present for Wyatt and again, according to account book, Tuesday. Wednesday an entry "gates" 1/= means a drive thro' Talbot Woods with Mrs. Patmore (daughter-in-law of the poet),[533] whom I took for drives on Musprat's introduction and asked for I think the second week, when she was better and I wanted the inducement of a "convalescent to take for drives." Friday afternoon (Christmas Day) Nathen Bodington called—whom she saw in the afternoon.

(In the Ms this chart is at the top of the page opposite.)

Sunday December	27	3	10	17	24th
Monday	28	4	11	18	25
Tuesday	29	5	12	+19	26
Wednesday	30	6	13	20	27
Thursday	31	7	14	21	28
Friday	1	+ 8	15	22	29
Saturday	2	9	16	23	30

There was a short spell of frost, with slippery roads and Whybrow remembers her driving once and meeting Dr. Musprat walking because of the state of the roads, so I think she must have been out one day between the 19th and 26th though I have no note of it. On the 27th Sunday she went to church—communion service—at St. Stithians was rather nervous, had too far to walk and was not the better. On Christmas day morning she had a shock—of which she made little at the time. Getting out of bed alone between 6 and 7 or just after 7, she fell somehow and found herself on the floor, not hurt, but not able to get up or reach the bell. At last she did the latter and then—by ill luck, Ada, the maid who always came at once was downstairs—called by the other servants to look at their Xmas presents &c. Monday she was not so well, faint, and Musprat was sent for again. 28th. Perhaps I drove with the message as I got her Pearson's Magazine,

[531] a card game

[532] a game played on a checkerboard of 256 squares by two or four persons; also called hoppity

[533] Coventry Patmore (Kersey Dighton) (1823-1896) was associated with the Pre-Raphaelite Brotherhood.

for the sake of a story of Kipling's,[534] [She was not well enough to be read to: she dozed a great deal, and even as the days passed I could hardly tell one from the other. I sat with her all day—except the hour now and then when I went out, and the papers of food and stimulant must have belonged to the first fortnight of the illness before the nurse was recalled. Dr. Robert Thompson—like Musprat—thought the case very grave.] at the station and got my (maximum) weight at the chemist. Next day my asthma was worse again and I went on Thursday, 31st, for a drive alone, trying to rest and quiet myself; so again for an hour January 1. She was well enough then to wish me to write to Mrs. Phillips. Went for a short walk Sunday morning. Musprat had urged our leasing Spencer Road and on the 4th there are memoranda about Torwood, but she was very ill and on the 5th Dr. Robert Thomson was called in consultation. I destroyed last autumn the pages I had torn off her brown pad of "notes" with record of food and stimulants taken every two hours: I think the orders were not less than 2 ounces brandy and 2 whisky every 24 hours. A fresh nurse was engaged the same day, [January 1, I bought a dressing gown for her to put on if soiled.] Ada having hitherto attended at night and I by day. The frost Whybrow spoke of began on the 18th. On the 19th she was downstairs on the library sofa in the afternoon. Next day I look at houses (asthma worse). January 22nd and 23rd she was not so well, I look at Torwood again. The 24th, Sunday, she wants to get away from Bournemouth and I inquire—about Wellington College hotel—I have asked to take her abroad. Musprat thinks the risk of moving too great. The next ten days are blank—house hunting went on, she was little better and I remember one morning vainly trying to break through A's carelessness and feeling as if I would like to kill him for it! My Convalescents got no more drives and I only went out for errands, on—January 13—1 dozen 1/4 bottles of champagne. February 1 she drives to Torwood, which she never much liked, the first 11 days then were wet or grey. 12th she "very poorly, better for drive"—though she felt ill soon with the motion and we turned back after a little. The next morning we went only a little way, starting at a walk. On Sunday we went a longer drive, Talbot village and Park: "M. faint." On the 15th Dr. Musprat proposes not to come till 18th. I remember more drives with her than I noted at the time—through the golf-links Branksome Park, and little rounds and more than once driving slowly up and down its East cliff. On Thursday, 18th she went to 12 o'clock celebration at St. Peter's, seeing Bertha from Dorchester and Dr. Musprat in the afternoon. On the 22nd I note "M. drives out" and some bother about telegrams. The nurse stayed till the 26th, as she was not allowed to be left at night. It was one of her trials being asked to take food then and disturbed in her sleep for the sake of what she did not wish for but might have been faint for want of. Ada left on Monday and I got a nurse for that night. Bertha came on the 26th and for the intervening two nights Ada had slept in her room. On Monday we see the last of Dr. Musprat; on Tuesday March 2 proceed to lodgings in Manchester Street, leaving A. to give up the house. Details of 12 days in London are in my pocketbook. Her asthma being no better

---

[534] Rudyard Kipling (1865-1936), "Captain's Courageous. A Story of the Grand Banks," *Pearson's Magazine* no. 12, December, 1896-no. 16, April, 1897.

in town Sir R. D. Powell said on the 11th she might as well go home, as we did therefore on Saturday 13th. He said to me that there was no special cause for anxiety, only that at her age one could not never say—To her, when she gave her age, oh that was only *annus dormire*,[535] which didn't count. Dr. Branmouth, especially after the second attack she used to say she should not get better, should not live to get home. When I spoke of moving to Douglas Powell, he said Don't—probably anticipating the event—which however leaves us nothing to regret. On the 19th she went for a drive, being carried upstairs after it. On the 29th I drove over to look at the house. April 5 drive to Wendover with her, calling on Andersons and Mrs. Crobly afterwards, whence conjunctivitis. She reads most of a story "Pinchbeck Goddess"[536] aloud to me. [I went to Douglas Powell.] Easter Sunday she drove up the hill and was carried into church for Communion service. [Soon after our return, we had Jowett's "Life,"[537] which she read through with interest and at her usual pace being the first to come to the conversion of Wolhain—which naturally touched and pleased her much. It was nearly the only book of that bulk she read in the year.]

August 28, 1895

The above was written at intervals in the early part of the year. After which I began to read through her letters to me and William—with some of his to her:—also one (from the Elms) from him to me, most sentences beginning "My Mother says"—with annotations from her—"William's letter seems to be made up of his mother's sayings" and in another phrase "Paddy." I am glad—or at least not sorry—to know that in all my youthful foolishness and fractiousness I never ceased to be fond of her—as fond as possible, and to know it and to let her know it. Her letters from Eton were admirable—after that we were scarcely apart for a day till I went to Oakley Street. Augustus has not kept any of her early letters. I find from hers to William that it was in the Nice winter he began to tell cock and bull stories about letters to ladies—written—a vice which was still more disgustingly indulged when she was ill at Bude. I finished the letters down to 89—when those to William end—There was my letter to her—saying rather more than I could say to my self. Then I came up to Chenies Street Chambers where I have been dull and idle. Went down for a Sunday to meet the Midgilleys and found in one of her later letters that she wanted just this for me in town. Have just read Romanes's Life and Letters[538] which she read and wrote to me about

---

[535] "an inactive year"

[536] Alice Macdonald Fleming, *A Pinchbeck Goddess* (London: W. Heineman, 1897). "Pinchbeck" implies being counterfeit or a sham.

[537] Evelyn Abbot (1843-1901) *Life and Letters of Benjamin Jowett*, 2 vols. (London: J. Murray, 1897).

[538] *The Life and Letters of George John Romanes, ed. by his Wife*, (London: Longmans, Green, 1896).

while she was at Ossington Street and I in Egypt. She borrowed his signature "ever the same" and quoted *his* quotation (to his wife) "of the distinguished man who lived apart from his wife because he so much enjoyed her letters."

As to G. J. R.'s questions (p. 189) concerning death[539] — I should answer:

1)   with personal indifference but disinterested wish to "put things straight" first.

2)   0

3)   A reasonable certainty that there is none.

4)   Am not an emotional person but so far as my moral convictions are "touched with emotion" I am probably rather more anxious to apply them to life and conduct than when merely "syllogising" but I would not venture to say belief either way has *much* practical instance *versus* original sin.

5)   Of a physically timid order, but not imaginatively nervous.

6)   Strong, nervous, self-reliant, despondent, the latter mostly in youth.

7)   Intellectual.   Abstract.   Aims—with unequal success—at giving practical effect to theoretical beliefs. Practically tender, theoretically heroic. No.

---

[539]   (1) Do you regard the prospect of your own death (A) with indifference, (B) with dislike, (C) with dread, or (D) with inexpressible horror?

(2) If you entertain any fear of death at all, is the cause of it (A) prospect of bodily suffering only, (B) dread of the unknown, (C) idea of loneliness and separation from friends, or (D) in addition to all or any of these, a peculiar horror of an indescribable kind?

(3) Is the state of your belief with regard to a future life that of (A) virtual conviction that there is a future life, (B) suspended judgment inclining towards such belief, (C) suspended judgment inclining against such belief, or (D) virtual conviction that there is no such life?

(4) Is your religious belief, if any, (A) of a vivid order, or (B) without much practical influence on your life and conduct?

(5) Is your temperament naturally of (A) a courageous or (B) of a timid order as regards the prospect of bodily pain or mental distress?

(6) More generally, do you regard your own disposition as (A) strong, determined, and self-reliant; (B) nervous, shrinking, and despondent; or (C) medium in this respect?

(7) Should you say that in your character the intellectual or the emotional predominates? Does your intellect incline to abstract or concrete ways of thought? Is it theoretical, practical, or both? Are your emotions of the tender or heroic order, or both? Are your tastes in any way artistic, and, if so, in what way, and with what strength?

(8) What is your age or occupation? Can you trace any change in your feelings with regard to death as having taken place during the course of your life?

(9) If ever you have been in danger of death what were the circumstances, and what your feelings?

(10) Remarks.

8)   Yes. Am much less in love with death than 20 or 30 years ago—this applies perhaps mainly for last 7 years—say when nearer 50 than 40.

9)   When knocked down by a dray and had ribs nearly broken, my first thought was certainly for my spectacles and the 2nd to get inconspicuously out of the way. When the carriage was upset and my mother's leg broken, and my foot caught between the shaft and the struggling horse, I did *not*—my mind moves very slowly—think of my mother, or of anything, except how to get my foot out. These were not, in fact, dangerous accidents—to me, but I couldn't tell this so conclude that my mind would work too slowly to take alarm in a mortal danger. When I was found to weigh 6 stones (2/3 of the normal), my reason admitted that it was time to reconsider our formulae that "asthma isn't a killing complaint" but my natural impulse was to make a joke of what I arrogantly flattered myself was a record light weight. Besides I couldn't imagine myself really dying and leaving my mother—tho' thoughts of Mrs. Clifford's tragedy would cross my mind. Reason however prevailed with me to the extent of going to Egypt.

Under Romanes's final head of Remarks—I might give the epitaph I composed for an autobiographical heroine in my nonage "Je suis morte sans regretter la vie que j'ai passée sans espoir. Toi qui me plains, réfléchis que les plaintesque t'arracheront, tes espérances trompées, tes pertes déplorables, ne troubleront plus mon sommeil."[540]—while for something like the last 20 years I have preferred this from Goethe

"Schwarzer schatten ist über dem Staube/Der Geliebten Gefährte/Ich machte mich zum Staube/Aber der Schatten ging über mich hin."[541]

October 30, 1895

To continue after Easter Sunday: My second eye became affected and on April 23 my mother entered accounts. The eyes were better next day, and the 28th (Wednesday) my mother went round the garden in the birch chair, I walking with her. May 1 Augustus went over to Aspley Guise. [I remember that it was a shorter journey than any in Surrey.]   On the 3rd she was not so well. "Woollerton uneasy" is my note: yet the next day—Tuesday May 4, we drove to Princes Risborough to see Beatrice, (a parlourmaid) at the station. Wednesday: "not so well." I sent for Woollerton—who was very grave (the swelling of the legs was new to him). Still she came into the oriel room most days: on the 7th Mrs. Ashley and Miss Bridges called and she saw them there alone, while I entertained their visitor—a friend of Emily Wright's. Next day, Saturday, she came down to luncheon: tried a little Halma between dinner and bed, but it tired

---

[540] "I have died without regretting the life I have spent without hope. You who pity me, consider that the laments that your dashed hopes have wrenched from you, your regrettable losses will no longer trouble my dreams."

[541] "A black shadow about the road is the companion of lovers, I turned myself to dust, but the shadow went over me." Goethe, *West-östlicher Divan, Goethes Werke*, Weimar, VI, 286. Haight says that EJS wrote this opposite the dedication of *Natural Law* to GE (H, IX, 203, n. 1). See November 9, 1877.

her. Slept nearly all next day (Sunday). Woollerton "feels the gravity"—I think it was then he warned Augustus. 10th my asthma worse. I have no note for 10 days, but she was not in bed for quite a week. Bertha was a very good nurse—but not very accurate in narrative. I think A. went to Aspley (or London) again on the 13th. She was in the oriel room on the 19th when I noted the sizes of our carpets—measuring the oriel room one. May 20 I have down "Jubilee treats £1," besides which she gave a decorated tea canister to all the parishioners over 70. Mr. Woollerton reported parish rebellion against the naive proposal of the Rector: (to have the feeds some other day as *he* was going to London to see the procession!). Friday 28th she wrote to Augustus, (at Oxford for Ascension day) and I note that she is better—"volunteers the consideration of a visit to Aspley." June 1 I see in account book "Debenham 10.9 1/2"—Suede gloves—2 of which pairs were for her. Vichy water sent pretty frequently from Aylesbury. June 4 "Bedding sent"—I pulled her in the chair. Saturday 5th I came over here and back, liking the place better than in March. She came to meet me in Aylesbury, but I note "drowsy advance." 10th I go into Aylesbury on errands and one day in the week we drove round Hampden Common and Lacey Green without her being over tired. Sunday 13th (all fine warm days) we had tea under the beech. Next day to Aylesbury in the morning, going upstairs afterwards. Next day 15th send for Woollerton, who tells her to stay in bed "to ease the action of the heart": she does not feel ill; plays Halma before going to bed. Next day "drowsy," uneasy Woollerton viz. thinks "some albumen." 17th Woollerton tries piperazine, no solid food. 19th we have gazagun charged with citric acid and potash. We are both upstairs (after she is out of bed) till the 26th. She was carried (in the chair got in 92) from the bedroom to oriel room. I think she came down to luncheon Sunday 27th. 28th A. to London. She and I breakfasted downstairs at 9:30 and just afterwards I missed her, and she was across the lawn, at the seat by the arborvitae and the hedge. We drove round Halton afterwards "In the open carriage closed"—which she found it difficult to "get into." After tea walks and chaired round garden, carried upstairs. 29th Drove out in the morning and again in the afternoon to meet A. in Aylesbury. It was settled to take this house. Next day "not quite so well." July 1 drives after tea through the Park. 2nd July to Aylesbury about the carriage step. 3rd "not quite so well." On Sunday upstairs all day. 5th up early but not so well, Alice Raleigh called when she was in the drawing room. 9th Woollerton sent for again: she is to stay in bed again. 12th I take the electric bell to Aylesbury to be re-charged: Note asthma, which had been mending "showing signs of return 'anxiety.'" 14th "nap from 6 to 8." 15th "Drowsy" all day, up at 6. Woollerton late, thinks "no worse." This lease signed. 16th carried into oriel room. 17th I to Aspley Guise, interviewing Luisfield. 18th Sunday, she was carried to drawing room. Next day Woollerton prescribed the clothiapine pill, which she thought disagreed: She was in bed for the next 4 days, only up on the sofa for a little while on Friday, 23rd. We were feeding her with sweetbreads, turtle soup, and Brand's essence, also Woollerton's explosive gazagun powders. Saturday 24th July she was in the oriel room. Nodine and Phillips from Leighton Buzzard came to view about the move. Our own sloe gin, which she liked as a liquor was exhausted and we bought a much inferior bottle. The 26th "to call on Miss Bridges"—at Wendover—on her behalf: 28th I write the family documents to Kemp and Luisfield. 29th "ultimatum for Grinshave." 30th "M. better" in drawing room 10:30. August 1 Sunday "In the garden for a few minutes." August 4th I was afraid of even warm summer evening air so A. drove to Quinton to fetch puppy. Thursday 5th she drove out to see his sire, boarding at a farm beyond Kemble,—the carriage going across a field—we both hesitated over a smooth haired dog as not the real thing but on the whole she liked the prospect and next day, Saturday: I drove over to fetch the remaining sister for Woollerton. The two playing together—like sooty imps—suggested Soot's name. Same day Mrs. Webb was thrown from a cart. Next day I was asthmatic and had bed put up in oriel room. Monday 9th—Write Luisfield about estimate. Continued seedy all the week and on Saturday was in bed, temperature 101. She was staying in the oriel room and well enough to walk along the passage to see me—as she did at least twice a day, in spite of my protests. All the summer I was apt to have coughing fits putting me in a tremendous perspiration in the hot weather. Tuesday 17th was up in the afternoon and next day in the morning but was left very feeble. Friday 20th I went up to town to choose papers at Woollam and see Sir R. D. P. before he left town:—who rang the bell and asked if there was any beef tea in the house—so likely when he was going out of town that afternoon! and on finding I was going back by rail and had sandwiches with me, took me into a little room where he brought me brandy and water ("old cognac") with his own lean mighty hands. I put this down because my mother was intimately delighted with his humanity to her dilapidated kitten. The bones of my back were tired in the train returning, and in a drizzle I took a cab from High Street Marleborne to Wimpole Street! I have a memorandum of what I had to tell him about her. He said we had a good doctor (Lucas), for Aspley Guise. 25th I came over to Aspley with Emily, staying at the post office and inspecting the Ossington Street furniture from Whiteleys. [Poor Mrs. Piet was scrubbing the house.] My mother thought herself better and told Woollerton (August 26) she was going to leave off all remedies. She wrote to me—a letter in a painfully shaky hand—which some how or other, strange to say, I have not been able to find. Home next day. Saturday 28th she is "better" drives to the manor and Miss Bridges—where she got out to call. 30th Monday. To London with Augustus, zoo &c. It must have been on Monday 23rd that we drove over to Hampden to see the Shetlands. Sir R. D. P. recommended a chair for my mother and Woollerton told us of the boat load of Shetlands Lady Buckinghamshire had imported. We drove over grass to an enclosure into which the remainder were driven. It was one of my feeble jokes that she would only drive out to see dogs and horses. September 1 A. went to Aspley and next day to Radcliffe. We drove to Wendover, meeting Mrs. Godwin and leaving cards on Charles and Albert Smiths. 3rd on the way to Chequers met the Rector and Lady Sutton so could not call so left a card on Hampden, Mrs. Murray and Ralieghs. 6th she drove with A. to Wendover Station. I went next day p.p.c.[542] to the Joques. 8th We drove together to leave cards at Chequers and kind Mrs. Astley and Rector which did for the manor. 9th I did Wendover farewells, Watson and Miss Bridges. Friday

---

[542] "to take leave"

10th went up to town for dentist (3.3.0) and brought Miss Bridges out to tea as I returned—this tired her a little. Monday, 13th we drove to Grensdyke; she did not get out but Mrs. Forrest came out to speak. The next two days I must have been packing clothes and papers and September 16, Thursday to Saturday I go over to Aspley with house—and—parlourmaids to get some things straight: we take over endless boxes and luggage. I had the drawing room garden door rehung and the drawing room hearth tile arranged; Monday, 20th the two maids go to stay, and I drive over to leave the carriage returning Tuesday—walking— then a heroic exertion—to Woburn Sands station (in about 3/4 of an hour!) Wednesday, 22nd, we pay off Beatrice, drop Bertha at Aylesbury station and drive to Aspley. We had meant for her to sleep at Woburn, telegraphing for rooms, but they had none without stairs or otherwise suitable, so we drove on here, stopping the bus with Bertha on the road—all which she bore calmly: noticed the drawing room door as she came in; did not mind the utter confusion, but stayed in bed next day to rest and be out of the mess. Snorter came with one of the vans and grazed lying down on the lawn in sight of her window. Saturday 25th Augustus and Wyatt came; latter nearly collapsed when the kitchen chimney smoked on Sunday. Tuesday A. went back to give up key. Whybrow drove over with his family, arriving late. Trolleys with plants came as it began to rain. The end of this week the dining room was made usable and chairs and rugs were put out in the drawing room. Friday I drove A. over to Leighton Buzzard to hunt Overhurst Park Saturday night, October 2, she complained of a tooth, and Sunday it got bad. Before leaving Ellesborough I had tried to get Mrs. Bolton Lasingdron to take it out without fatigue. I quieted it for the time with some dentist's stuff, and ought to have sent for Lucas. I did not dare to risk her having pain as in 96, and persuaded her to let me telegraph for an appointment next day and to Bletchley for carrying chairs. She did achieve the journey there and back—and had the tooth out, only resting for 5 minutes after; I was to blame again in not telegraphing for a brougham, as she had difficulty in getting into the cab—fell into it. She was not apparently the worse, but thought she missed the "phiz" while the gazagun was delayed *en route*—had Bertha to sleep in her room for the first few nights and then we had an electric bell fixed to ring both upstairs and down at once: and as Bertha always came at once and never minded being called, she was quite safe. On the 5th the bookcases were unpacked and set up: a carpet sewer was had in and on October 8th the drawing room was "done." She liked the room, the fireplace and all the house, "had never lived in such a handsome one"; thought I had done everything very cleverly, wondered it all came in so well, but changed cabinet and book case for the better in drawing room, which she liked and admired when done. Saturday the library carpet was put down and the back settlements tidied. She was a good deal in bed, as I left her to receive visitors. Monday I went up to town for dentist, mats, poker, maids &c. The 15th when Major and Mrs. Downes called she was only just up and in her crimson dressing gown. 18th "an hour in garden." She had been for a short drive one day before (to Woburn Park Lodge and back, over the water). The last pictures &c were not hung till the 20th and all the little flutter of that sort of thing naturally tired her a little. She rejoiced much in the bedroom and drawing room on same level. She found her room rather small at first, but got reconciled to it after a time. October 21 Mrs. MacClymont came. She slept badly that night and was poorly—indifferent and depressed—all the time Mrs. MacClymont was here. I drove and walked in the wood with her. The 27th the last revival began—the characteristic sign being that she looked through muslin blinds and curtains for her son's bedroom. 28th "Better" we drove through the park and back by Ridgmont. Next day, Friday, she went to church. In the afternoon Augustus lost himself: I would not let her wait dinner long, but for the last hour she was very troubled and uneasy. He came in at 8:30 having driven most of the way back. I was very much afraid it would throw her back, but it did not: of course I spent all the time in inventing things that could have hindered him, but as he had called in starting at Woburn for money, she was afraid of his having been robbed. Next morning she was carried upstairs to see the library, and then drove before lunch to Woodside and Aspley Heath—especially to see the woodland paths along which Snorter was to take her chair. She sometimes came into the dining room for meals—and said it was only laziness when she did not. Twice she dressed and came before we had quite finished breakfast. Once we brought Snorter in at the back door to the dining room for her to see and pat him.

November   [several people called]

A. went to Oxford November 1. His hymn for All Saints day was printed in the Guardian soon after: she concurred in my criticism of two verses, but of course liked it on the whole much. Tuesday We drove round Wavendon and Salford in the morning. After lunch she was lying down and asleep so I had the Dymonds shown into dining room. She wrote to A. quite easily—without the tremor that distressed me in her last from Ellesborough. She also wrote to Miss Bridges, Mrs. Raliegh and Mrs. Tibbs. November 3 She was disappointed at not having a letter from A.—"but does not worry"—I wrote. She saw Miss Stevens who called in the afternoon and talked about Challis and his sister. Whybrow brought some fine fowls to show her in case we could manage to put up a fowlhouse anywhere. November 4 We spent the morning upstairs: the room and the day were cold and I shivered a good deal: she was not the worse: liked A's bedroom and the bathroom where she wanted the hooks moved. Next day she wrote again to A.—expecting him to come back on Saturday—which he did not do. Her writing was not quite itself, but the hand was not jerking. She wanted Augustus to look up the 2nd edition of Jowett,[543] to see what use had been made of our letters. I had been getting seedy for some days and on Sunday 7th was in bed with some "temperature." She did not get up till lunch, and went to sleep afterwards while waiting for Whybrow to help carry her upstairs—which was done about 4, and she had tea and spent most of the evening in my room—which we had all agreed was "too—too." Of course she had her own chair up. The next day I was still in bed. She came up earlier and had tea with me. Thought Augustus could not have come as he did not appear (staying down to tea)

---

[543] Benjamin Jowett, Master of Balliol College, His Life and Works with Reminiscences and Memorials by Pupils and Friends (London: J. Murray, 1893).

however went down to dinner. That evening we exchanged the notes I have. The week was damp and foggy, so there was no going out, even to Chrysanthemum show. 13th Saturday I drove out to pay return calls and á propos of her wish at Ellesborough "that somebody would sometimes open a book" told her that Miss Carter Smith had been reading Mrs. Earle's Surrey Garden[544] (out of which we got the suggestion of training the wisteria across the corner by front door) and Mrs. Dymond was talking about Jowett's Life and other books. Sunday, November 14th she went to church and round the garden in the chair afterwards. It was very warm and we sat with the garden door open and had no fire till evening. She found the church seats uncomfortable and liked for the bath chair to go into church as at Bournemouth. We laid out the bottom of the garden, making a path round in front of the summerhouse, cutting in the holly hedge and sowing grass in front of the border—a change, which all the old residents noticed. On Monday we drove round Woburn, Milton Bryan, Eversholt and Ridgmont. It was a brilliant day and the autumn tints were extraordinarily bright; the leaves had hardly begun to fall. She liked it all very much and when I used to ask my baby question "Was it kind of me to take her such nice drives" she protested it was all much prettier than Ellesborough, which we were supposed to regret. Next day I went up to see Douglas Powell: when I told him she had not yet seen Dr. Lucas he said—quite right as long as she did not want him. She drove with me to Woburn Sands station and back by the cutting and Woburn Lane. 18th I have down "To Woburn Sands"—I know not what for. 19th We drove along the Ampthill road, which was, as Miss Carter Smith had told me, very pretty. Afternoon I walked down the avenue to the Unwins. Saturday 20th she was in the garden—I think approving outline of path. Monday 22nd was very fine; we drove round little Brickhill and Bow Brickhill. Tuesday was foggy. Whybrow was making the openings into Kemp's Garden. Thursday 25th she was in the garden for half an hour and that day or next Saturday Whybrow got her to come into the yard and look at the stable, where he wanted a manger—just got and put up before her illness. Read bits of "Africana" to her out of geological societies parcel, and also from Mudie Sir Harry Johnston[545] on Idrophanthis[546] and the curious idea of its causing invisibility. 26th we went the short drive round Woburn Sands and Salford. Sunday 28th I stayed in bed till lunch—was rather seedy all the time and on Sunday when A. lived in the drawing room, I could be spared. Next day went over to Bedford to hunt register office—through wh. I engaged Lily—via a pretty, lazy, anaemic girl Fanny. 30th St. Andrews day She went to church and was grateful to Maltby for having the communion service

---

[544] Alice Morse Earle (1851-1911), Old Times Gardens and other works about gardening and about women's lives in colonial times.

[545] Sir Harry Hamilton Johnston (1858-1927) of the London Missionary Society wrote on Africa; Night and Morning in Dark Africa (London: London Missionary Society, [1902]).

[546] "dwarfism," see E. J. Wood, Giants and Dwarfs (London: R. Bentley, 1868).

for her benefit. Directly after, we drove round Lidlington, Jackdow Hill and Ridgmont—the last time. December 1, Wednesday thought yesterday's doings had been rather too much, but did not feel poorly. About this time put case of conscience to her á propos of Africana—a Missionaries' duty to runaway slaves. In the last box from Mudie was a book "Here We Are"[547] with one really comic bit of fooling "the blue eyed fly," which I got her to hear with mild amusement. She did not care for much occupation: Bertha used to rub her feet after dinner and she went to bed early. The only thing that could have made any difference would have been more faithful reports from Bertha as to state of kidneys. She had some difficulty at times in getting into the carriage from jerking of the legs, but she liked the drives and felt better for them. In the garden she had spoken of "next summer"—tea and strawberries in the summer house and spoke of having Miss Paget here. We had Tennyson's Life[548] of which I skimmed a good deal to her. Thursday 2nd and next 2 days I stayed in bed till breakfast and got cold feet in looking after the rockery walls of new opening. Sunday 5th I did not come down till tea. Bertha told me she seemed bright,—walked about the room and to the garden door. I noticed at bed time her legs were much swollen and persuaded her not to get up early that—as I said—I needn't. I came down at 11. She was in bed and they were still bad so I got her to let me send for Mr. Lucas. Monday, December 6th She told him more than once she was "quite well." Of course he said she must stay in bed and to me he intimated that it was serious. I spoke of former attacks of the kind having gone off: whereto he, there was less power of resistance after each. This was afternoon, Lily came over and I brought her in to see my mother in bed. He came next morning and said she must not get up before the end of the week. Next day also the legs were better, but she was not anxious to be up and he said perhaps if all went on well very early next week. I told him of a prescription of Woollerton that at once increased the action of the kidneys: he said of course one could do so, but that might produce other bad effects. She was interested in the Guardian's memoir of Mr. Addenbroke—who would have been 82 in January, and talked of her wedding call and of Mrs. Addenbroke coming down to show her baby (Annie) with great pride and how pretty Mrs. Addenbroke was. I was always with her all day except for meals but that afternoon while she slept a little I went to leave cards at the Maltbys and went about the garden. On Friday, 10th, just after luncheon she said "now I want to say something sensible"—deprecating any protest of mine against her speaking of any thing after her death.—She was not feeling ill or depressed and spoke quite cheerfully, not as a very near future. Soon after we came to Aspley she made me write to Adeline at Bedford—which she had left 3 years ago and I had lately had an answer from Sir Reading—She wished some good to go to Adeline and her husband out of gratitude to my uncles Chapman and Bagnall; also to her brother Lancelot, who had always been kind to her and not kindly used by Mrs.

---

[547] collection of popular songs, *Jim Crack Corn, or, the Blue Tail Fly.*

[548] Hallam Tennyson, *The Life and Works of Alfred, Lord Tennyson* (London: Macmillan, 1897).

C.[549] Also to Mrs. MacClymont's boys and Mrs. Phillips. She wrote a post card to the former when the Balliol scholarships were announced—got by a St Pride and a Fetter boy. She used to get up for half an hour in the evening to have her bed made. She had her usual meals and once or twice the tea table was brought into her room and Augustus came in, but that rather tired her, so I brought hers and mine in from the drawing room. On Saturday I brought Soot in to see her, only for a moment as he was doggy. Mr. Lucas came in the afternoon, was going to Brighton for Sunday, we must send for Mr. Holines if anything was wanted. My mother had already asked him about a beautiful baby she used to meet on her drives. She had Whybrow in to speak to her; and heard the story of a horse and cart run over at a local crossing. I finished Tennyson—whom she did not like the better for the memoir—"did not think much of him." I also showed her a picture or two out of Schweinfurth[550]—the King dancing before his wives—. On Sunday she had an apple for breakfast: I was with her all day. Read tentatively little bits of "Captain Courageous"[551]—an ill omen as it was the first chapter she was too ill to have at Bournemouth. Her speech was sometimes a little laboured, and it was from this day that I felt—what no warnings had ever made me do before—that the end might not be far off. In the evening she thought she saw "a bough of lilac hanging down or a great bunch of violets against the wall" and was not quite satisfied by my pretense it was something in the shadows. Next day Mr. Lucas was late. She told him the story of Williams' ring and the "Italian doctor" about "the turn of the blood" thinking Whybrow's story on Saturday might account for her not being so well. Her mind was always quite clear when fully awake but she said to me once that day "Am I in bed?" He ordered hot strips with turpentine and I sometimes wonder if it would have made any difference if we had done on Tuesday what we did on Thursday. The doctors think not—that the only wonder was that she could live so long with the feeble heart. Tuesday he came in the morning. She generally slept for an hour or more in the afternoon and I drove Snorter for half an hour in the chair—making believe that she would use it soon. When I came in there was a pretty group at the stable door, Robin and the Shetland nuzzling each other and Soot jumping up to kiss both while the kitten arched her back at them from under the wheel barrow. She tried to be interested as I described it, but every thing was a little effort. Yet in the morning when Fanny was leaving, she corrected my calculation of her wages! Happily she had no discomfort as sometimes from constipation, and said of every meal it was "very nice"—roast mutton and pineapple fritter. She still sat up to have her bed made: at 4 in the night she rang for Bertha—we had both scolded her so for

---

[549] See December 19, 1890. EJS left money to Adeline Chapman Bagnall and her husband Henry Bagnall, both cousins.

[550] Georg August Schweinfurth (1836-1925) wrote about travels in Egypt and Africa.

[551] Rudyard Kipling (1865-1936), "Captain's Courageous. A Story of the Grand Banks," *Pearson's Magazine* no. 12, December, 1896-no. 16, April, 1897.

getting up alone. After leaving her at 10 I used to read some old magazine for an hour in bed to force myself not to think. Wednesday morning (15th) I was down early, to give her her breakfast: she thought she had been up alone and fallen—Bertha said it was a fancy but at first I thought there must be some foundation, till she got faintly annoyed (as about the violets) when I asked questions. We had a bed for Bertha put up that day. Mr. Lucas did not come till afternoon and said such translation of possibilities into fact was not uncommon. The swelling of the legs had gone down and he wished her to sit up longer—to let the legs swell to relieve the heart. She asked for Augustus in the afternoon—when he was gone for his usual walk! She was not strong enough to sit up in the evening and grew a little confused. "He thought she might as well die sitting up." She said once or twice he did not think she would get better, but only in a semi-conscious fashion. Her roast chicken and cup pudding for dinner were "very nice"—but the kidneys did not act at all. Thursday morning I told her that the cloth she had embroidered, which was sent to be died old gold, had come back: "Would she like to see it?" She said yes, admired it when spread out, smiled when I said it was rhubarb and sal:polychroite:colour and asked if Augustus had seen it,—this to L's amazement. He came early, telegraphed for a nurse, and said—when I asked—that I had better write to people. I went to get something from the library and could not answer Augustus' question except by saying I was writing. She was now taking only liquids, milk and stimulants. In the afternoon her sleep grew heavy: I shuddered to see her dear hands groping in the dark. The nurse had missed a train and did not come till 7. At 5:30 L. came again: she was nearly unconscious: I should have let her sleep herself away in ignorance. I cannot be too grateful for his skill and energy: he had the bed filled with footwarmers and hot bottles and himself wrung out the scalding strips in which she was swathed. She grew half conscious and moaned to me to save her—she was being burnt: the struggle for life was continued for 2 hours: then the nurse came; he left and just afterwards she—as it were *woke*: mind and speech quite clear—she was "sorry to give everyone so much trouble"—asked for her son and was quite herself, as I sat with her from 8 to 11. Whybrow slept on the library sofa to be ready to go for the doctor if needful. She slept comfortably. I was with her early: she had barley water and milk and more whisky. The hot bottles &c were repeated and I sat by her all day, pulling up the clothes as she grew impatient of this—saying once as I put little shawls at every opening "you do worry me so." She did not seem fully awake always, but she knew that her son had been in and she noticed most things: when I spoke of getting another pillow for her she thought it was for the nurse and said "Doesn't she like her bed," and kept joining in the conversation. In the afternoon she told Mr. Lucas to tell her what he wanted done, or else she might think *we* made mistakes. Each time that day Lucas was surprised at the recovery. In the evening I noticed he felt her pulse repeatedly—he said it varied; sometimes quite strong and then imperceptible. He said that—according to all his experience it was impossible—and he rehearsed what his experience was—for anyone to recover from the state she was in yesterday, but she was so much better than could have been imagined that he could hardly say for certain what was possible. He thought there was no need for Whybrow to wait that night. She got up, wrapped in hot flannel and had her hair "done." And when I bid her good night said: "Then I'll send you a cup of tea in the morning"—which she used to like to do from her early breakfast! She told Bertha to tell me that she had had a good night and to ask after me. (All the week Bertha had come to me with an early bulletin). I came to her just before 8—to give her her breakfast while the nurse and Bertha had theirs. I came in asking how she was, and she answered in her natural voice "How are you?" She drank half a cup of tea, but she was hardly able to swallow my toast. She got out of bed and back once and I left the room while one more attempt at responding was made. I left the room and put out the things just come from the stores—all the little things I had ordered to tempt her appetite—and powders for the gazagun. Then I came back. Nothing was of use. She was still kept warm—into a perspiration—which doubtless spared her conscious distress—only her dear hands were cold, as she let me clasp them. Then she slept, the breathing gradually grew more still: it would have been cruel to try to rouse her again. The nurse fetched Augustus. We had tried to give her milk and brandy before. I think I was with her just one hour, then another in which she hardly spoke—no unutterable last words. At the last there was one almost imperceptible raile, twice or thrice the shoulders heaved together, then stillness. Mr. Lucas came just after. Spent nearly all Sunday with her—the face did not change, there was no deathlike chill on her sweet lips or hands which I kissed. I put poor Will's slate in her hands. I said she did not leave an unpaid bill or an unanswered letter. After she was in bed she got me to draw a cheque of £100 on account for Luisfield—which she thought he must want and not like to ask for. I had the photograph taken on Saturday. 'Twas I suggested Augustus' hymn should be sung—and 'twas I chose the texts for the cross &c[552]—poor Will would have been able to help me. The cross was put up last month there is a tall yew on one side, a forgotten and a nameless grave with an evergreen beyond upon the other and this little plot—which I consider hers—for she was a kindly neighbour— shall be scattered over with crocuses. She had in the last year times of distress and depression and I cannot be too thankful that there was little or none of this even in the last 12 days. Mr. Lucas asked several times if she had any cough— she wondered and I asked why. Am thankful she was spared that too, an incident sometimes of effusion at the back of the lungs. I had begun, as an idle

---

[552] The rose granite cross is about four feet high and its base is formed by three tiered marble rectangles; on the top one is inscribed "To the Most Loving Most Loved Most Longed For Mother"; on the second is "Jemima Haslope Simcox The Beloved Wife of George Price Simcox and daughter of"; and on the third "Lancelot and Harriet Haslope March 26, 1816-December 18, 1897." The grave is outlined with marble strips; a quotation from the Bible is inscibed on each; at the head of the grave: "Out of the strong came forth sweetness" (Judg. 14:14); at the foot: "There is that scattereth and yet increaseth" (Prov. 11:24); on the right side: "Even so, saith the spirit, for they rest from their labours and their works do follow them" (Rev. 14:13); and on the left: "And they that be wise shall shine as the firmament and they that turn many to righteousness as the stars for ever and ever" (Dan. 12:3).

amusement for some evening, to make out a list of flower seeds in the catalogue of the man Mrs. Earle recommended, and we got about half way thro' the alphabet—up to which point I ordered in the spring. The first week she was in bed I had a card from Mary's friend "Patty" who was going to Florence and wished to be recalled to Miss Paget's memory. I mention this because she made me read her my letters to both—it being one of her amusements always to do so—so that perhaps if I tried to be amusing, it was as much for her sake in the correspondence. After this nothing is worth recording. I think she said once that the servants' sitting room would make an excellent parish room, so I quote her in suggesting my present experiment of lending it as a reading room for young men.—This is thought wonderfully good and generous:—they little know that nothing is of the slightest use or value to me now—so that to give it costs me nothing. The year is nearly over and the grief is no less constant and near. One reads of people shocked at themselves for ceasing for a moment to grieve. I try *not* to give my self up to the one thought, but day after day—walking in the streets, reading alone, as well as speaking of her to any one—my eyes fill with tears behind the spectacles.—You hear where people have been in love over 50 years—the time for a golden wedding, if they part, both are older than I, old enough to feel that it is not for long—or if they *feel* much more then it *is* not for long. With me, unluckily,—as it was with her after poor Will's death—one's health mends when one's *anxiety* for the precious life is at an end. I am better now than for the last 4 years—Well enough to get to work, which will be my best anodyne. But I am widowed when not far past the prime of a modern life.

January 29, 1900. 10 Lansdowne Road

As the December days came near in 98 I had a foolish craving to go somewhere quite new by my self and chose Buxton as the nearest. But it was cold and I had to come back with asthma and influenza which nearly killed all last year. I had begun to do a little work in the summer, but Douglas Powell would not let me go as I wanted to Auvergne in August and I took rooms at Chenies Street instead, to little profit, except for house hunting. I saw this house in January, took it in March from bids: and moved in at Michaelmas. In June I seemed getting well—full weight and a 19th century article[553] written at normal pace. Then the mustony asthma turned into exspthalmos and is there still, with "flocculi" to help it. But I am otherwise mending, and reading early Victorian Memoirs with some purpose—towards my notion of a literary history of the period. If I can keep eyes and the rest of me fit for moderate work, I shall manage well enough and not go much to seek after causes and people. Have read a good deal of sorts the last few weeks and can take hold a little, though I postpone the big book for the moment. Anon the two might go on together; 4 hours writing in the morning for the first; afternoon out on fine days only; writing or typing of notes after tea and reading for one or other purpose in the evening. This year with doctors and miniature I can't afford to go abroad and have been so much in bed that there's no need now. But I shall take a good 5 weeks July-August, in

---

[553] "The Native Australian Family." *Nineteenth Century* 46 (July 1899): 51-64.

Switzerland for choice and next year go south too in January-February. There will be no other break if I keep well, except a chance week end and if so be, Commencement at Oxford for the MacClymont girls, and in that case one must get through a good deal in the year. Ainsi soit-il.[554] When I was in bed I cried remembering how I had written to her from Egypt after 3 months away, that I was getting disgracefully mammy sick. I have a vision of her portrait—in pen and ink—somewhere in that book. Ainsi soit-il—if it might be like. I rank her above my other love in perfection for all human relations. She did not reason about right doing. Why do it? "It wants doing, it has to be done, how can any body do any thing else?" Would perhaps reflect her thought if she had been compelled to transcribe the unconscious process. This is written large to spare my precious eyes from stooping. The few pages that remain will serve to report if any work gets done in the few years that remain.[555]

---

[554] "in this way" or "so be it"

[555] According to her death certificate EJS died on September 15, 1901, at the age of 57, of pneumonia, pleuritis, and tachycardia exhaustion. Her occupation is listed as "Gentlewoman of independent means." Her obituary appeared in the *Times*, September 18, 1901. Her ashes are buried with her mother in the graveyard at Aspley Guise.

[These three letters from Annie L. C. Gill to Gerald Bullett are inserted at the end of the Ms.]

55 Jackson Avenue
Roundhay
Leeds 8

24 January 1951
Dear Mr. Bulett

      After hearing your broadcast on George Elliott in Woman's Hour in the BBC Programme I wonder if you would be interested in a Diary entitled "Autobiography of a Shirtmaker" which came into my possession about 20 years ago. Altho' no name is attached to the book it dates from 1876 and is evidently written by someone I think called Edith—who was on intimate terms with George Eliot and Mr. Lewis. Later after her marriage to Mr. Cross. If this interests you I'll be pleased to forward the book to let you read it.

I am
Yours faithfully
ALC Gill (Mrs)

55 Jackson Avenue
Roundhay
Leeds 8

February 3, 1951

Dear Mr. Bullett,

      Enclosed is the Diary I wrote of. If you find it of any interest please keep it. I should however be interested to know who wrote it and what connection the author had with George Elliott.

Yours sincerely,
ALC Gill

55 Jackson Avenue
Roundhay
Leeds 8

Dear Mr. Bullett,

    I was pleased to receive your letter with your comments about "The Shirtmaker." I had formed a like opinion from overlooking the Diary with the aid of a magnifying glass. I was surprised to find that George Elliott and Lewes were at one time so poor.

    The Diary came into my possession after the death of my son while an undergraduate at Oxford. It was amongst his books and whether he picked it up secondhand, or had it lent I do not know. I am pleased that you have it.

Yours sincerely,
Annie L C Gill

[This note on a torn slip of paper was also inserted at the end of the Ms; it appears to be in Edith Simcox's handwriting.]

There has been much talk about George Eliot's "example" which is not to be deprecated so long as it is remembered that in speaking of the example of a woman of this value we can only mean example for good. Exemplary indeed in her long connection with George Henry Lewes were the qualities on which beneficant intimacy rests.
Partial Portraits
p. 117 Henry James's saying attributed to Coleridge
the main desires for the woman remains for the desire of the man.

INDEX

K

L

M